The NEW
ENCYCLOPEDIA
of
FISHING

The NEW
ENCYCLOPEDIA
of
FISHING

A DORLING KINDERSLEY BOOK

LONDON, NEW YORK, MUNICH,
MELBOURNE, DELHI

A PENGUIN COMPANY

Devised, designed, and
edited for Dorling Kindersley
by Bookbourne Limited,
The Old Farmhouse,
Newton, Sleaford,
Lincs NG34 0DT
Editor: Ian Wood
Art Editor: Steve Leaning
Designer: Stuart John
Fish Species Illustrator:
Colin Newman

This edition revised in 2001 for
Dorling Kindersley Limited by
Design Revolution Limited,
Queens Park Villa,
30 West Drive,
Brighton BN2 0QW
Editor: Julie Whitaker
Art Editor: Andrew Easton

Managing Editors:
Krystyna Mayer, Sharon Lucas
Senior Managing Art Editor:
Derek Coombes
Production Controllers:
Antony Heller, Louise Daly

Contributors: John Bailey,
Peter Gathercole, Trevor Housby,
Dennis Moss, Bruce Vaughan,
Phill Williams

First published in Great
Britain in 1994 by
Dorling Kindersley Limited,
80 Strand,
London WC2R 0RL

A CIP catalogue record for
this book is available
from the British Library

ISBN 0 7513 3973 3

Typeset by Ace Filmsetting
Limited, Somerset
Reproduced by
Colourscan, Singapore
Printed and bound
in Hong Kong by Toppan

See our complete catalogue at
www.dk.com

CONTENTS

FOREWORD

JOHN BAILEY
The author of nearly 30 books on fishing, angling tutor, and television presenter, John Bailey has brought his deep knowledge and years of experience to the task of revising this edition of *The Encyclopedia of Fishing*. Having fished rivers, lakes, and coasts in North America, Europe, Russia, Mongolia, India, Nepal, Australia, and New Zealand, John is uniquely qualified to bring this best-selling and authoritative volume fully up to date.

For the best part of a decade, Dorling Kindersley's *The Encyclopedia of Fishing* has been one of the best-selling books on the sport throughout the world – and for good reason. It was largely put together by anglers of the stature of the late and great Trevor Housby, by Peter Gathercole, Phill Williams, Dennis Moss, and Bruce Vaughan, and with this vast store of knowledge to draw upon, the book could hardly go wrong. For thousands of anglers, the *Encyclopedia* has proved to be the most invaluable of handbooks. Beginners have drunk in a lifetime of information, laid out so attractively, explained so comprehensively. Experienced anglers, too, have benefited whenever they have faced new water types, new species, new methods, or any one of a host of new challenges the sport throws up. There has never been an angler who knows it all, and there never will be, but at least with this treasury of angling lore, the basic keys to unlocking any situation worldwide can be found.

Everything in the modern age moves at pell-mell speed. Angling is like every other sport in that it rockets forwards each year, and it is hugely to this book's credit that the majority remains absolutely current. There are, however, places, especially in the areas of tackle, where time and tide have inevitably moved on, and this new edition ensures that the reader in the 21st century has a book that is absolutely up to date with the fast-paced state of the art.

When Trevor Housby first described the *Encyclopedia*, he saw it as, "A hundred angling books rolled into one. Essential reading for any angler, it is a book that will spend little time on the shelf." Given the book's staggering success, Trevor could hardly have been proved more correct. For me, it has been a privilege to update this extraordinary work and to follow in the footsteps of those giants who worked on it originally. For every detail that it has been necessary to change, a hundred facts have remained as sensible and worthy as they ever were. Truly, it doesn't matter what stage you are at in your angling career, this is the guide for you.

JOHN BAILEY

INTRODUCTION

You often hear the phrase, "He, or she, is a good angler." But what does that mean? What, in truth, makes the good angler? A knowledge of the basics is absolutely vital. Upon that, the fisher who really wants to succeed adds layer upon layer of experience. Watercraft is essential. The really good angler learns to use his or her eyes and ears, to keep alert, to keep a mind open to anything that might occur at the waterside. The angler becomes, in a benign way, the predator – hungry for success at times, but also capable of relaxing and letting the spirit of the water take over. The good angler has the confidence to try new approaches, even if they seem ridiculously bizarre. This good angler will, in the fullness of time, develop a kind of sixth sense, an inner voice, whispering just when, where, and how the fishes of dreams can be caught. Of course, this book can't give you all these gifts, but all the basics are on offer, the surest directions to point you towards a lifetime of fishing success.

A WORLD OF YOUR OWN
Perhaps the greatest gifts that angling offers are a chance to relax in the beauty of nature and an excuse to focus wholly on an absorbing and bewitching pastime.

TACKLE

Tackle comes before everything – you just can't do anything without it. It's got to be good quality and, above all, well-maintained and carefully put together so that it doesn't let you down in the heat of the battle. Many of us have lost big fish, and it's a gut-wrenching experience; don't let a bad knot or a blunt hook let you down at one of the great moments of your life. Perhaps the most important aspect of choosing tackle is understanding exactly what is right for the job. This book explains precisely what you need for every possible angling situation. It is important that you make the right choice and stick by it.

TOOLS FOR THE JOB
Good quality equipment will give you confidence and is a pleasure to use.

BAITS

There never will be the perfect bait, the one that will never fail. And thank goodness for that, for what fun would there be in fishing once the uncertainty was taken away? But there are good baits – some that have established themselves over time and others that suddenly burst onto the scene. Nature gives us her own baits, such as worms, minnows, or big, black slugs. Baits can come from the kitchen – for example, bread, cheese, or sweetcorn. There are also manufactured baits full of colourings, scents, and stimulators. Spinners, spoons, and plugs are made from wood, plastic, and metal. Imitation flies are made from even more complex lists of materials. It's all rather like alchemy. Bait devising, lure making, fly tying – these are subjects that have dominated the thinking of anglers for over 2,000 years.

WORKS OF ART
The design and technical skills that go into lures like these make them collectable in their own right.

ARTIFICIAL FLIES

Let's concentrate on what is arguably the most delicate of baits – the artificial fly. Indeed, many of those who tie flies never fish them and aren't even anglers, but they find the greatest satisfaction in creating jewels of imitative perfection. And who can blame them? The tying of flies is an art form: using hair, bristle, wool, fur, tinsel, and a whole host of other materials, the fly tier creates a replica to mimic, and perhaps even crown, natural creation. The search for the ultimate fly has been at the core of anglers' dreams for centuries, and though perfection will never be achieved, fly tying geniuses have come fairly close.

Fly fishing was once the preserve of the rich, but today the growth of transport, the extension of holidays, and, above all, the proliferation of well-stocked reservoirs and commercial fisheries mean that fly fishing is for everyone. *The New Encyclopedia of Fishing* will explain the natural menu that the crafted flies are designed to imitate and how to tie them for yourself. It will also explain how to use your fly box to lure salmon, trout, bass, and even the game fish of salt water.

TACKLE BOX JEWELS
Feather and thread creations like these are now being used to fool a far wider range of fish than just trout, salmon, and grayling.

FISH SPECIES

The waters of the world throb with thousands of fish species, and it's a good bet that many still remain to be discovered. *The New Encyclopedia* looks at some 250 of the fish that are central to the sport of angling. You will learn to recognize them from the stunningly accurate illustrations. Details of their geographical spread, size, habit, diet, and characteristics are all given concisely and accurately. There are also tips on what tackle, methods, and baits to use when fishing for a particular species. Above all, though, this section is your boarding pass to a world beyond compare – the world of water. Look carefully at these drawings and appreciate the subtleties of what you observe. See how nature has created the perfect shape, colouring, or fin pattern. Look at the delicacy of the scales, the shading around the gills, and the way the fins wave like the most exotic of fans. Fisher folk are privileged to witness beauty beyond anything "landlubbers" can even guess at.

A SOURCE OF ENDLESS WONDER
The angler who lands a fish like this can only gaze in awe at its beauty.

ANGLING TECHNIQUES

The footballer, cricketer, or baseball or tennis player all like to win the game, but that's not the main reason for participating. Think of the joy of making the right stroke, timing the perfect kick, and relishing all the skills of each different sport. And so it is with fishing. Of course, the ultimate goal is to catch a fish, but there is a huge amount of satisfaction to be enjoyed along the way. The techniques described here are indeed the way to put a fish on the bank, but they are also physical activities to be enjoyed in their own right. As you learn to trot a float, for example, you'll begin to see how your rod works with the line and the float and the pull of the water. As your fly casting improves, you'll relish the rhythm of the rod and the shape of the line cutting through the air. There's a physical pleasure in making a long cast from a moonlit beach, or making your pole cut like a wand through a strong breeze.

The *Encyclopedia* describes just about every technique you will ever need throughout your fishing life, but it is up to you to go out and make chosen methods work for you. You will develop them, improve them, and make them your own. This in itself brings almost as much satisfaction as actually feeling a fish wriggle on the hook.

STEPPING INTO
ANOTHER WORLD
*Wading in a fast-moving
stream can give a sense of
entering and sharing the
fish's own environment.*

THE WATERS

The *Encyclopedia* looks in depth at the different waters that the various fish species inhabit. There is a good reason for this: you will never come across an experienced angler who doesn't believe watercraft to be his most important weapon. The more you understand the habits of fish and the properties of the waters they live in, the better angler you are bound to become. In fact, all good anglers are accomplished aquatic naturalists. Currents, tidal flows, bankside vegetation, submerged weed, plateaux, ledges, drop-offs, aquatic insects – the whole world of water is waiting to be explored. Learn to think of fish as the most delicate and responsive of barometers, supremely sensitive to any variations in air temperature or weather changes. There's no doubt that they can detect minute fluctuations in barometric pressure, and they are highly sensitive to the phases of the moon.

INFORMATION CAN
BE THE KEY
*Luck alone is often not
enough. Knowing where
the fish are likely to be
and what they are eating
makes all the difference.*

There is very little that goes on in the world of water that is haphazard, that doesn't have a meaning. For example, if you are beside a winter lake and you see a pair of grebes diving repeatedly in the same area, what does this mean? In all probability, you will find a died-back weed bed that is sheltering a shoal of small fish. Small fish attract grebes, but they also attract the predators that feed on them, such as pike, zander, perch, and bass. The experienced predator fisher knows this and moves in....

Let *The New Encyclopedia of Fishing* inspire you to visit some waters without your fishing tackle, with just your polarizing glasses and a pair of binoculars, and perhaps a notepad and pen. Take the time to sit, watch, and learn. You'll gain valuable information that will undoubtedly be put to good use the next time you have your tackle to hand.

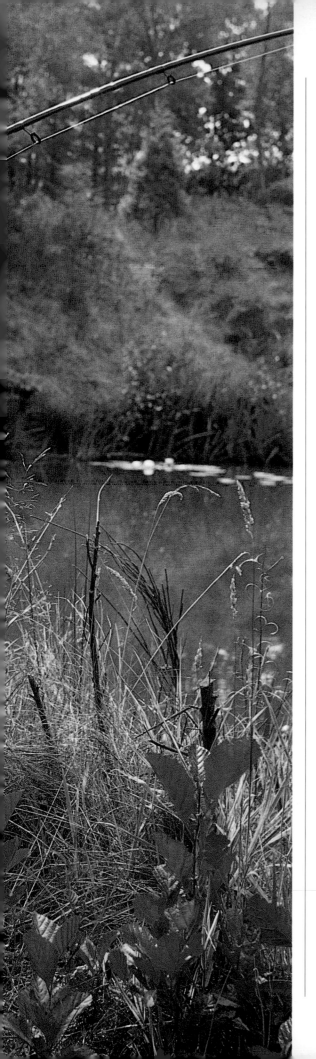

TACKLE

Tens of thousands of years ago, when they first set their eyes on fish, our hunter-gatherer forebears began to devise ways of catching them. Early fishing tackle was crude – a rock aimed at the skull of a salmon skulking in low water, perhaps. Then spears, harpoons, arrows, nets, dams, and, at last, some 14 or 15,000 years ago, the first rudimentary fish hooks made from bone. Rods and reels emerged in China and Macedonia more than 2,000 years ago, but they were a far cry from the efficiency and delicacy of our angling gear today.

Times have changed and few, if any, of us actually need to catch our fish to survive in the modern age. We fish for fun, as sport, and this is where tackle takes on a new complexity. Not only must fishing tackle do a supreme job, but it must look good and feel fantastic, too. Fishing tackle today is designed to be a joy to use in every respect. New materials and superlative engineering both mean that anglers in the 21st century have tackle choices that our ancestors wouldn't even recognize. But with such a bewildering range of alternatives on the market, how should these choices be made?

CHOICE OF TACKLE
Good-quality, well-balanced tackle is a pleasure to use and will improve your chances of landing a good catch.

BASIC TACKLE

Your first trip to a tackle shop will inevitably be a bewildering experience. There is simply so much choice on offer that even the expert angler often finds it difficult to make a right decision. No doubt you will be looking for advice from the tackle dealer, and there are three key questions that you will need to consider: what kinds of water are you likely to be fishing; what species of fish do they hold; and what methods do you plan to use to catch them? That way you can at least narrow down the options. A couple of tips: if the tackle dealer isn't welcoming and generous with advice, then simply move on to another shop. Secondly, don't wildly exceed your budget, but do make sure that the tackle that you buy is competent and reliable. There's nothing that saps the enthusiasm more quickly than gear that is inefficient and clumsy. Finally, although mail order might often appear cheaper, until you are more experienced and know exactly what you want, it's probably wisest to buy from a shop to which you can return if you're having problems or making mistakes.

SALTWATER FISHING

The world of saltwater fishing is immensely complex, and if you're going to be a sea angler, you've got to think hard about what areas are open to you before committing yourself to any major tackle purchases. The characterstics of the coast vary widely, from sandy beaches to sheltered harbours, and from salt flats to plunging cliffs. Will you be fishing from the shore, long casting for cod or whiting, or using a spinning rod to chase wrasse, bass, or mackerel close in to the beach or around rocky headlands? Offshore waters, too, differ greatly from place to place. Maybe boat fishing is for you, but will it be on warm, shallow waters catching flat fish or colourful reef-dwelling species, or will you be deep-water fishing, perking for big cod, or baitfishing for gigantic conger eels around a submerged wreck?

Shark fishing is a growing sport in many parts of the world, and it doesn't require very expensive gear. Then, of course, there is the exotic side of things – the world of big game fishing that takes you to the tropical seas where you can hunt for tuna or marlin. So, you see, there's no such thing as the all-round sea fishing kit, but as your enthusiasm and experience build up, you'll come to know exactly what you need to buy for each particular kind of fishing.

BASIC SEA FISHING TACKLE

Bead

Plastic lure

Pirk lure

Weights

Hooks

Metal lure

Swivels

Plastic lures

Wire trace

Float

Boom

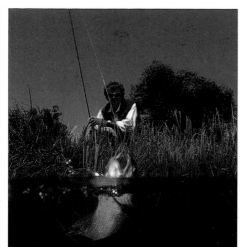

ON THE FLY
Despite a somewhat elitist reputation, fly fishing really is for everyone, and a basic set-up need not be costly. As well as game fish, such as trout and salmon, many species of coarse fish can be fished for in this way, including pike, zander, and other predators.

HI-TECH ANGLING
A rig like this one has only one species in view – carp, and big ones at that! Many carp anglers are fanatical specialists, and recent years have seen a boom in tackle devoted to this one species, but as a beginner you can fish for them perfectly well with a simple leger set-up.

FRESHWATER FISHING

Basically, freshwater fishing breaks down into three main areas depending on the means you use to persuade the fish to take your hook. Bait fishing is exactly as it sounds, and an edible bait is used for most non-predatory fish, such as carp or barbel. Of course, you can use baits for predators, too – baits including small freshwater fish or, very commonly, sea fish such as mackerel, herring, or smelts.

The second type of freshwater fishing is lure fishing, almost always for the big predators. Lures are man-made creations of metal, wood, or plastic that imitate a small prey fish. These can either be metal spoons or spinners or plugs that can work on the surface, in mid-water or bouncing along the bottom. The lure world is expanding quickly: there are thousands of lures now on the market, each doing its own specific job. It's fascinating and it's fun, and there is no better way to catch a pike or a zander.

Thirdly, we have fly fishing, perhaps the purest art form in all the sport. The concept is to tie an artificial fly out of fur, feather, tinsel, or whatever, to imitate the natural. The major species caught on fly are salmon, trout, and grayling, but in recent years flies have been tied to attract pike, perch, and zander, as well as all manner of saltwater fish.

BASIC FRESHWATER FISHING TACKLE

Forceps
Weight
Hooks
Weights and split shot
Floats
Surface lure
Spoon
Plastic lure
Polarizing sunglasses
Artificial flies
Plug
Swimfeeder

THE ROD

A good fishing rod is a beautiful tool – light, well-balanced, responsive, and almost like an extension of the angler's arm. Simply to hold and cast with it are pleasures in themselves. Rods have been made from a vast array of materials in the past. Woods such as hazel, ash, hickory, and greenheart have been used. Tubular steel and aluminium have had their time. Rods of split bamboo cane and either solid or hollow glass both enjoyed periods of ascendancy. In the late 20th century, space-age materials, including boron and Kevlar, came and went, to be replaced by the current wonder material of the day – carbon fibre. Yes, rods are glorious creations, but it's important to retain a perspective. When I was in India some years ago, I met a renowned Indian ghilly, a man named Bhola, who told me how his mother once landed an Indian mahseer of 50 kilograms (112 lb) on a hand line!

ROD COMPONENTS

BUTT SECTION

Ferrule whipping

Male ferrule (spigot)

TIP SECTION

Butt ring

Rod blank

Tip ring

Intermediate ring

ROD CONSTRUCTION

The rod of the 21st century is exquisitely designed and made out of the most modern materials. The blank will almost certainly be constructed from carbon fibre, but there are different qualities of carbon fibre. Super high modulus carbon is the best and most expensive, producing lighter blanks that are rigid and have a fast, crisp action. As a general rule, the cheaper the rod, the more resin will remain in the carbon fibre and the heavier and less delicate will be the action. Rod designers can sandwich different carbon fibres together to achieve different action, so the range of carbon fibre is immense. All designers have different targets and they mix and match different cloths of carbon to achieve their overall aim. Strength and durability can be increased by entwining a woven, graphite overlap that is wound round and round the blank like a spiral towards the tip.

Because carbon fibre is so extraordinarily light, rods in general have become longer. For example, 3.5-m (12-ft) float fishing rods were once popular, but now 4 m (13 ft) is the shortest generally made, and many rods are 4.25 or even 4.5 m (14 or 15 ft) long. This extra length gives greater control and better line pick up. It's the same with feeder rods, which were once 3 or 3.3 m (10 or 11 ft) in length. They are now a standard 3.5 or 4 m (12 or 13 ft), which gives them more leverage for better casting.

Line guides, or rings, are also dictated by price. The very best guides today are made of titanium, and these are unbelievably light and strong. Super oxide guides are an excellent alternative and are somewhat cheaper.

Most reel seats now have a screw-down fitting that locks the reel to the blank. This is particularly useful when the angler is playing a big fish and the rod really begins to move under the pressure.

Handles can be made of duplon, but cork still seems to be the favourite. There are different grades of cork and the very best you'll find has the fewest craters and needs hardly any filling to produce a smooth finish.

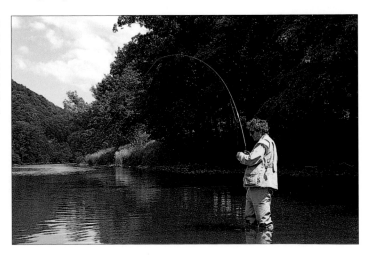

TAKING THE STRAIN
Perhaps the greatest improvement in rod design, and a direct consequence of the development of new materials, is the lightness of long, strong rods. This means that the angler can work a stretch of water – spinning or trotting – without having to feel the strain of aching arms that an older rod would cause.

TIP-ACTION

MIDDLE-TO-TIP-ACTION

THROUGH-ACTION

ROD ACTIONS
The action of a rod is the way in which it bends. Tip-action rods are designed for fast striking and long-distance casting, middle-to-tip-action rods for use where the ability to play big fish is more important. Through-action rods bend from tip to butt, which is useful for playing big fish at close range.

GLOSSARY OF TERMS
AFTM scale A method of classifying fly lines according to their weight and other characteristics, devised by the American Fishing Tackle Manufacturers Association (AFTMA). Fly rods are classified by the AFTM number of the line they are designed to cast (the higher the AFTM number, the heavier the line).
Blank The basic rod minus its fittings such as rings, reel, seat, and ferrules.
Butt The handle section of the rod.
Line class Boat rods are classified by the breaking strain of the line with which they should be used, for example a 14-kg (30-lb) class rod with 14-kg (30-lb) line.
Reel seat Device for fixing reel to rod.
Taper The change in the diameter and wall thickness of the rod from butt to tip. The taper of a rod has a direct effect on its action.
Test curve This gives an indication of the power a rod possesses. It is the amount of force that is needed to pull the tip end of the rod around until it is at a right angle to the butt end.
Winch fitting Another term for reel seat.

Reel seat   Handle   Butt cap or button

Intermediate ring   Ring whipping   Female ferrule

CHOOSING A ROD

Firstly, pick your budget and stick to it. It's all too easy to be seduced into higher and higher price brackets, and in the case of rods, the sky is the limit. However, it always pays to buy the best that you can afford. Be quite sure where, and for what, you intend to use your rod. Rods today are designed with specific jobs in mind, so it could be that the attractive-looking rod that catches your eye is quite the wrong tool for the purpose you have in mind.

Look at the quality of build. Is the finish flawless? Factors such as the colour, whipping, and varnish might all seem mere cosmetic touches, but if they are done well they can act as a general pointer to the standard of the rod. Look for any extra features, too: for example, if you are choosing a carp rod, then built-in line clips can be a great bonus. Does that feeder rod come with a selection of quiver tips?

Always try the rod with a reel in position and make sure the whole outfit feels comfortable and well-balanced. Finally, always choose a rod from a well-known, reputable company. That way, if you do have any problems with the rod, you will find that you have a sympathetic ear if you ever encounter faults or difficulties, and hopefully any problems can be resolved to your satisfaction.

CARING FOR YOUR ROD

Always wipe your rod down after a fishing session. Make sure, too, that the line guides are free from dirt and grit – it's all too easy for them to become caked in mud and forgotten about. Make sure that the cloth you use is damp and soft, to avoid scratching the varnish. Clean off your cork handle and, if the cork is wet, let it dry naturally before putting it back in the bag – otherwise it will grow mould. By and large, carbon fibre rods do look after themselves, but if you follow these quick, easy guidelines that take a maximum of five minutes after a fishing session, you will find that the life of your rod is prolonged immensely. One last tip: do make sure that your fishing tackle is adequately insured, especially if you have an expensive rod and reel. Good tackle is a prime target for thieves, and you'll be surprised how quickly the cost of what you've collected begins to mount up.

THE RIGHT ROD FOR THE JOB
Few of us are ever likely to find a gigantic sturgeon on the end of our line, but if that's your goal, the rod exists to tackle the task. Consider carefully the kind of fishing you intend to do, and choose a rod that is well suited. If you take up another branch of the sport, you may well need an additional rod.

SPINNING RODS

Spinning rods are great for tackling narrow, clear rivers where fish are wary and hanging close to their rocky lies. Designed to cast artificial lures of all shapes and sizes, most spinning rods are between 1.5 and 2.7 m (5 and 9 ft) in length. Being quite short, they also tend to be light, which is an advantage as they are in the hand for hours at a time. A short rod also produces casts of pinpoint accuracy. The action of the rod, too, is all-important. Powerful butt and middle sections are vital, both to set the hooks into the bony jaws of a predator and also to give plenty of power during the fight. The tip of the rod, however, needs to have a great deal of action in it, both to direct the lure and also to tell the angler what's going on under the surface. For example, a sensitive tip will wobble and pulsate, showing the angler that his lure is working properly and is not weeded up. Also, not all predators take with a bang and they will sometimes almost imperceptibly sip the lure in.

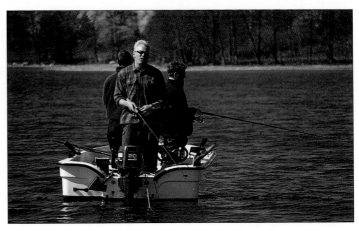

CASTING FROM A SMALL BOAT
Short rods are of great benefit in boats where space is tight, especially when two, three, or even four anglers are casting in tandem. Even when using the correct rods, do take great care on your backcast and always check that you lure is well away from your partner's head or body before casting.

SHIMANO TECHNIUM

Handle
The slim cork handle offers perfect control and total comfort all day long.

SPORTFISH AVANTA

The keep ring
Just nick one of your lure's hook points through the keep ring and it will be safe and secure as you move from one swim to the next. This is far kinder on the rod than putting hooks in the cork handle. If you do this, the handle will eventually disintegrate.

SHIMANO TECHNIUM
This 2.7-m (9-ft) rod is typical of the modern generation of spinning rods. It is made from an ultra-slim carbon blank that serves two purposes. Firstly, there is plenty of power down in the middle and the butt section for controlling a big, lively fish. Secondly, the tip is very slender and delicate, which means that casting is pinpoint and that bites are registered immediately. Another good point is that the tip throbs to the motion of the lure. If it stops moving, then you can guarantee that your lure is weeded or snagged in some way.

SALMON ON THE LINE
Spinning rods are great for tackling narrow, clear rivers where fish are scarce and hanging close to their rocky lies. It's in these situations that the casting accuracy of the short rod can provide pinpoint presentation over and over again. Small rivers can, however, throw up big fish, so choose a rod with enough backbone to hold a hard fighting specimen out of the snags.

SPORTFISH AVANTA
Made by the Sportfish company, this Avanta spinning rod is a deceptive beast indeed. Although it looks, feels, and handles like a very delicate tool, it's still got a huge reserve of hidden power, which makes it ideal for pursuing really big fish – from Mongolian taimen through to big salmon or even Egyptian Nile perch.

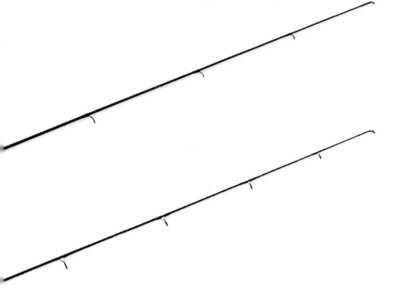

DAM BLACK PANTHER
This DAM rod is a tremendous middle-range product capable of handling almost anything the lure angler might throw at it. Perch, pike, bass, zander – even sea trout – are all well within its range. It's a light rod, but that doesn't mean to say that power has been sacrificed. At 2.2 m (7½ ft), it gives nice tight control when it comes to playing the fish and also when casting.

DAM BLACK PANTHER

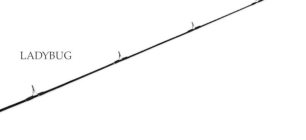

LADYBUG

LADYBUG
This is a wand of a rod, beautiful to fish with day long. It is based on an American blank, but made up by the Irish Rod Company. Even though it's only 1.8 m (6 ft) long, it still has the guts to cast medium-sized lures with no stress or strain. The great thing about having a rod so short is that the angler's contact with the lure is absolutely precise and immediate. The rod really does become an extension of the angler's arm. Casting with a very short rod can also be extremely accurate, something an angler needs when pursuing bass or pike in weedy, snaggy conditions. The trigger grip shows that this rod is to be used with a baitcaster reel mounted on top of the rod.

Trigger grip
Notice the rod's trigger grip. This allows the angler to hold the rod securely, but without undue effort, throughout the day. It also provides that extra little bit of control when a difficult angled cast is being made.

LEGER RODS

A leger rod presents a bait hard on the bottom, held there either by a weight or a swim feeder. There are three broad types of leger rod available. Firstly, there is the quiver tip rod. This has a slender tip to provide extreme bite sensitivity. A typical quiver tip rod will be 3–4.25 m (10–14 ft) in length, with plenty of power at the butt to deal with heavier fish. The second type of leger rod is a variation on the traditional Avon-type rod, used to present a bait to medium-sized fish on either still or running waters. Traditionally, such a rod will be 3–3.6 m (10–12 ft) long, capable of casting fair-sized baits such as slugs or big pieces of breadflake, and with the power to handle fish in the 2–9 kg (5–20 lb) bracket. At the extreme end of the range, there is the specialist leger rod designed to catch very large fish, such as carp, pike, or catfish, sometimes at extreme range. This rod will generally be 3.4–4 m (11–13 ft) in length, with power in reserve for casting and striking at great distances and playing big fish back, even over potentially fatal gravel bars.

READY FOR ACTION

Specialist rods for the big-fish angler are often too heavy to be held for long periods and are designed to be put in rests until the fish bites. The all-round rod has the power to cast quite long distances, but it is sensitive enough not to break the line on a big specimen fighting hard close to the bank.

SHIMANO MULTI-
RANGE FEEDER

SHIMANO ANTARES
SPECIALIST QUIVER

The bottom ring
This good-sized ring allows heavier lines to pass through easily on the cast without building up friction and slowing down the line.

SHIMANO
SPECIMEN

Reel seat
The secure screw-down reel seat is essential when casting long distances and playing big fish. The handgrip at the bottom of the rod allows secure handling when screwing up for the longest of casts.

Hand grip

SHIMANO MULTI-RANGE FEEDER

Carbon fibre construction has meant that rods are now a lot lighter than they've ever been. This gives rod designers the scope to make a longer rod, and this one comes in at 3.6 or 4.25 m (12 or 14 ft) in length – that extra half a metre (2 ft) being provided by an optional extra bottom section. A long rod like this allows for long, easy casting. You can also keep more line off the surface of the water – particularly useful when fishing a strong current. Striking is also more immediate and positive than with a shorter rod.

SHIMANO ANTARES SPECIALIST QUIVER

This is the modern version of the old Avon-type rod of the mid 20th century. It can be used for good-sized river fish, medium-sized carp, or even catfish. The action of a rod like this is called "progressive", meaning that it offers a steady build-up of power down towards the butt section. This allows you to fish delicately, but when the battle's really started, you can pile on the power. The rod also comes with an optional quiver tip.

Isotope holders
Luminous isotopes are a godsend for the nocturnal angler.

White quiver tip
This makes the rod perfect for fishing at dusk, and even through the night, when the white stands out very well against the dark sky.

SHIMANO SPECIMEN

This 3.6-metre (12-ft) rod is typical of the excellent carp rods that are now available for a surprisingly low cost. Even though the price is modest, this rod is well-designed and well up to the demanding job that carp gear has to face. It provides the length and power for long casting, and with a test curve of 1.2 kg (2¾ lb), there's plenty of power there for bullying big fish over gravel bars and away from snags.

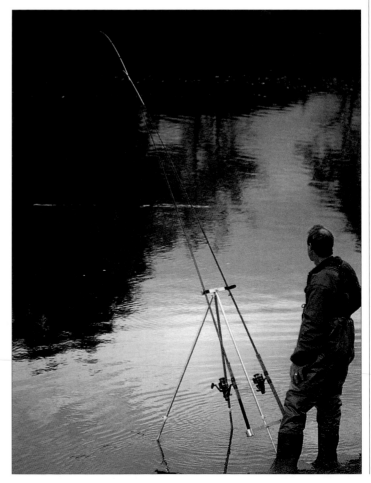

THE HIGHLY VISIBLE QUIVER TIP

Space-age, lightweight materials have resulted in quiver tip rods becoming ever longer. The standard today has a length of 3.6–4 m (12–13 ft) – great for casting, striking, and controlling a hard fighting fish. However, the tip is that much further from the angler's eye, and must be clearly visible. White is the angler's first choice of colour, as it shows up boldly against a dark background. Many rods come with a selection of tips. One of the most important distinctions is between carbon and fibreglass. Under normal conditions, most anglers prefer glass quiver tips as they are softer and register delicate bites more obviously. However, in a wind, carbon takes over. It is stiffer, and less affected by the gusts, so false bites are reduced.

19

FLOAT RODS

A really good float rod is a true test of the rod-maker's art, as it has to be both long and light – qualities that don't always sit easily together. A float rod is nearly always 4 or 4.2 m (13 or 14 ft) long, those extra centimetres designed to give additional control when it comes to working a float, either on still or running water. The float rod must be as light and as well-balanced as possible, since it is held all day long, especially for river work where the need for control is continuous. Float rods fall into two basic categories. Firstly, there is the match rod, generally designed to be as light, as responsive, and as quickly actioned as possible. This type of rod is designed primarily for catching smaller fish at a high rate. It is generally used in conjunction with a very light line, so the whole action has to be forgiving to avoid line breakage. In recent times, more specialized float rods have been heavily in demand. Anglers have wanted rods with greater power than the average match tool to let them trot bigger rivers for barbel or chub. Even more significant has been the rise in commercial carp fisheries around Europe. Here, the fish average 1.8–4.5 kg (4–10 lb), and to land fish of this size successfully and swiftly, the float rod has to have the extra muscle.

SHIMANO SUPER
ULTEGRA MATCH
This is typical of the modern range of carbon match rods – a delight to use with any type of float. The blank is ultra slim, and this provides lightning-fast tip speed, as well as immaculate control in the heaviest of winds. The rod has power but also the delicacy to cope with the ultra light hook lengths that are often necessary on match waters, especially in the winter when the waters are low and clear.

Rod rings
Note the rod rings on this match rod: by standing well away from the blank, they keep light lines free running, even when the rod is wet in heavy rains. Casting and striking are therefore unimpaired.

SHIMANO SUPER
ULTEGRA MATCH

The screw handle
Reel seats on modern rods are increasingly of the screw-down variety, so that the reel sits snugly and safely throughout the longest of sessions. A secure reel footing means that there is less chance of a disaster occurring during a long fight with a big fish.

SHIMANO ANTARES SPECIALIST FLOAT

This particular rod is 4 m (13 ft) in length but still feels very light and balanced, with a crisp action and plenty of power, when playing a big fish. A rod like this is the perfect tool for long-trotting on big, deep rivers for barbel and chub, as well as for float fishing for tench on gravel pits and estate lakes, or for perch and roach on smaller rivers. It can also be taken to the commercial carp fisheries, where it is capable of landing carp well into double figures. A supremely adaptable rod for any angler wanting to catch serious fish on a float.

SHIMANO ANTARES
SPECIALIST FLOAT

SHIMANO CARP CRUNCHER
SPECIMEN MATCH

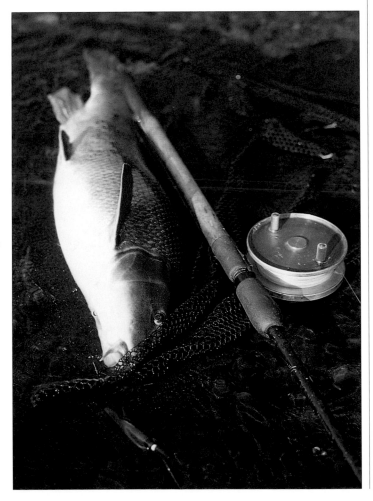

SHIMANO CARP CRUNCHER SPECIMEN MATCH

Recent changes in angling have seen the rapid advance of commercial fisheries where carp are the main target species. These are generally fished between 1.4 and 4.5 kg (3 and 10 lb) in weight, and when they are present in great numbers they make the ideal match target. As a result, rods have begun to appear on the market designed specifically for this booming niche market. What is required is a rod that is light to hold, delicate to use, but still has the power to land several big fish during the course of a three or four hour match. This particular rod is ideal for float fishing – still an excellent way of fishing carp at this type of venue.

UP TO THE TASK

A float rod works perfectly with a centre pin reel for river work, whilst, on still water, a fixed spool reel gives greater casting flexibility. In either case, a screw reel fitting on the handle gives a constantly reliable grip during repeated casting and retrieval. As this picture proves, the ideal float rod must have reserves of power to deal with a big fish in snaggy situations.

FLY RODS 1

Fly rods designed to catch smaller game fish, such as trout and grayling, can be absolutely exquisite. The most delicate are the "zero-weight" rods – these work with gossamer-like lines – that can land a tiny artificial fly, such as a midge pattern or buzzer, with the barest ripple on the water's surface. More common and more adaptable are the mid-range rods, used with lines of between a five- and a seven-weight rating. The important thing is to choose a rod and line that suit the job in hand. Begin with a flexible kit that can cope with most conditions and only add more specialized gear as you become more experienced.

LANDING A FIGHTER
The fly rod is a magician's mix of power and delicacy. It will be light enough to wield all day long, but it still has the power to master a wild fighting fish such as this fresh-run arctic char. A secure reel fitting is essential because of the constant stress of casting.

SAGE 2.4 M (8 FT) 0-WT FLY ROD
Average fly lines are weighted between five and eight, whilst heavy fly lines are nine and upwards. Lines weighted two and three are like gossamer, so you can imagine what this Sage 0-wt rod is like. The ultimate presentation rod, it is highly specialist with a soft through action and is often used by float tubing anglers. The float tube gets you very close to feeding fish, and the 0-wt allows you to put down a line with barely a whisper. It is also used for very calm conditions on crystal clear waters where the fish are highly educated and wary of anything landing on the water above them. It's important that you use the right line with a delicate rod like this – Sage designed the rod to go with their Quiet Taper line.

Snake ring
The snake ring is still the traditional intermediate line guide on any fly rod. Minimum resistance is afforded, which is very important when using an outfit as delicate as this one.

Reel seat
This beautifully finished reel seat has a screw fitting to keep the reel perfectly secure during long periods of casting. Note also the high-grade cork.

Keeper ring
This neat keeper ring is ideal for holding the fly when you're moving from one lie to the next. It is tempting simply to stick the fly into the cork handle, but do refrain from doing this. Cork is a strong material but it will nevertheless break down under this kind of treatment.

THE LIGHT KIT

A light fly rod is so responsive that it becomes almost like an extra limb, truly a part of the angler. However, to get the best from a light rod, it should always be teamed with the correct weight of fly line so that the rod works to peak efficiency. A light kit is perfect for species such as this beautiful grayling.

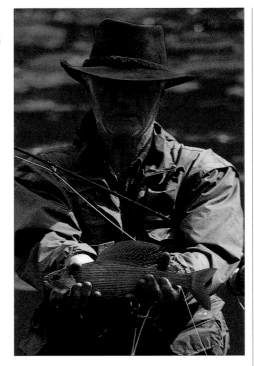

SAGE 2.4 M (8 FT)
0-WEIGHT FLY ROD

SHIMANO SUPER ULTEGRA FLY

This great all-round fly rod is rated for seven- and eight-weight lines, making it the perfect tool for fishing gravel pits or reservoirs, even in breezy conditions. There's a lot of power packed into a rod like this, so it's also ideal for big rainbows on small still waters. A good feature of this rod is that it comes in four pieces, so it breaks down to less than 0.75 m (2½ ft) in length, making it the ideal travel rod.

Big end ring

The large ring at the rod tip allows for quick and easy casting. The line can whip through it without touching the sides of the guide and so avoid building up troublesome friction.

SHIMANO SUPER
ULTEGRA FLY

THOMAS AND
THOMAS 3 M (10 FT)

THOMAS AND THOMAS 3 M (10 FT)

This rod is designed to work in conjunction with a comparatively light five-weight line. The length of the rod makes it perfect for several specialized pieces of work, such as the Czech nymphing technique that is now sweeping rivers throughout Europe. At 3 m (10 ft), the rod gives the angler a whole new control over his team of nymphs as he works them through the water in front of him. The rod is also excellent for fishing dry flies, for example, from a boat. Casting is delicate but powerful, and the number five line lands like a dream on calm, still water. Overall, the action is crisp and accurate.

MID-RANGE, MID-STREAM

A mid-range rod, designed for a line weight rating of between five and seven, is a good all-round choice if you are likely to find yourself on waters of any size. This rod will have the power you need to bring a fish to the landing net even in a fairly fast-moving stream.

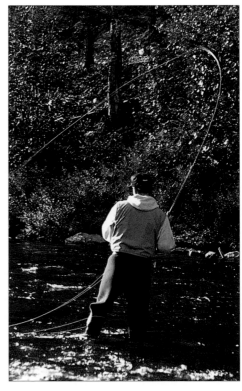

FLY RODS 2

At the heavier end of the market, fly rods become longer and capable of casting heavier lines into stronger waters for larger fish. Salmon, sea trout, and steelhead are the common targets. Heavy does not mean clumsy: modern materials and superb engineering once again combine to ensure that casting is a delight and the tackle is still light enough to wield all day long. The art of fly fishing is spreading to species once considered only approachable with either bait or lure. Perhaps the most remarkable development over the past years has been the advance in saltwater fly fishing. Bonefish, permit, barracuda, and even tuna are now targeted by the fly fisherman, and the tackle makers have had to react accordingly.

LANDING A MONSTER
This photograph proves that there is no task beyond the abilities of a heavy-duty fly rod. This 110-kg (250-lb) beluga sturgeon was taken from the Caspian Sea on gear designed for heavy salmon fishing. The battle lasted for over two hours and was fought over five kilometres (three miles) of water.

Cutting down on flash
Note that although the lower part of the blank and the line guide whippings are securely varnished, the lengths between are left matt. This is to cut down on "flash" – reflections from the sun in bright conditions as the rod is being wielded back and forth. There are times when flash can startle a big fish in shallow, clear water and put it off the feed altogether.

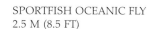

SPORTFISH OCEANIC FLY
2.5 M (8.5 FT)

IN THE BIG LEAGUE
It takes a fairly serious kind of fly rod to tame a steelhead of this size, and a good deal of power to cast across a wide river. Nothing short of a specialist rod will do.

Gimbal fitting
The gimbal fitting at the bottom of the rod fits securely into a butt pad so that the angler has extra leverage when it comes to lifting a big fish up through deep water.

SPORTFISH 4.5 M (15 FT) SPEY

The principal of the Spey rod is that it can be used with a double-handed action, enabling the angler to cast the fly a considerable distance. The length and strength of the rod are designed for playing large salmon. This Sportfish-designed rod is based on a Sage action, but is a good deal cheaper – though with little sacrifice in quality, making it the ideal beginner's rod for tackling large waters and large fish.

SPORTFISH 4.5 M (15 FT) SPEY

SPORTFISH OCEANIC FLY 2.5 M (8.5 FT)

This really is a tremendously powerful bill fish rod, the sort of tool that can handle virtually anything that swims in the sea, or in freshwater come to that. It's a really stiff rod, and can whack out the heaviest of lines. Mind you, it's not really designed to do a lot of casting. Most commonly, with a rod like this, you'd flick your big, heavy fly over the side of the boat, let out line, and then begin to do some trolling. The power is really immense, and it's hard to appreciate it until the rod hoops round as you encounter some of the biggest fish that swim anywhere in the world. An amazing rod, and one that will never let you down.

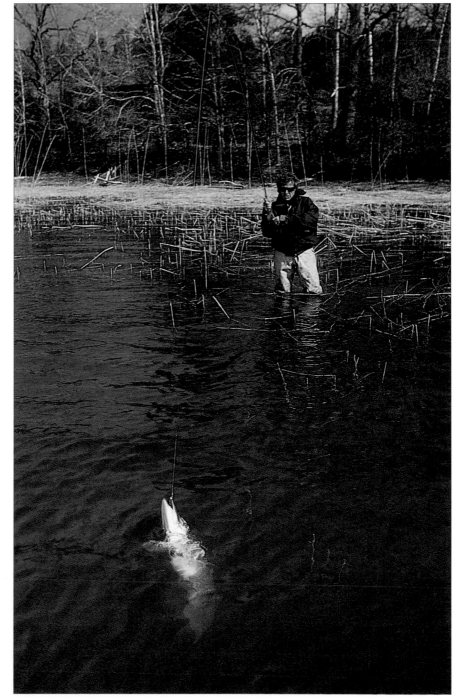

PREDATOR ON THE FLY

Fly fishing is moving into new realms with the new century, and anglers are becoming more daring and inventive. Using a fly for big predators such as the pike is now standard practice in the United States and over large parts of Europe. Never forget that a wire trace is necessary to withstand the sharp cutting teeth of both pike and zander.

POLES & WHIPS

A pole is probably the most expensive item any angler will buy, so it's important to make sure that the right one is chosen. Before a purchase, decide exactly what the pole is needed for. Do you want a light pole that you can fish at 13 metres (40 feet) on the canal or do you only need a strong 9-m (30-ft) pole for big fish on a small river perhaps? Or maybe you need a whip, a miniature version of the pole often used to build up a big catch of small fish, such as bleak or panfish. The weight of the pole and how it feels in the hand is important. All manufacturers list the weight of their poles, but this is only a rough guide to quality. The balance of that weight is much more important than the weight itself, and the only way to check that out is to handle the pole at full length and compare it with others in the same price, length, and weight bracket that you have set yourself. The actual pole and how it works on the bank has also got to be considered: if the pole does not feel right after ten minutes at a tackle dealers, it is going to feel awful after a couple of hours on the bank.

LONG DISTANCE FISHING
Today's poles are designed to deal with a wide range of jobs. They are traditionally the favourite tool for snatching tiny fish from hard waters, but with the advent of commercial fisheries especially, many designs can cope with larger carp or tench. At either end of the scale, a pole offers perfect bait presentation and control over a hooked fish.

SHIMANO CARP
CRUNCHER POLE

TOP BUNG
At the top end of the pole, the end of the core elastic is attached to a bung like this one to prevent the elastic from pulling back through the pole. The line and rig are attached to the other end of the bung, allowing the whole set-up to be changed as conditions demand, putting on a larger float and hook, for example.

BUTT BUNG AND BUNG EXTRACTOR
At the butt end of the pole, the central elastic, which takes the shock of a fish on the line, is attached to a large bung. A long, thin diamond-eye threader is used to thread the elastic through the pole before attaching the top bung.

DANGER WARNING

Carbon fibre is an excellent conductor of electricity, so NEVER use a carbon pole or rod anywhere near overhead power lines, or during a thunderstorm. And remember, your pole or rod does not need to touch a live line for you to get a potentially fatal electric shock: electricity can arc through the air to it if it comes near a line, especially in humid or wet weather.

SHIMANO CARP CRUNCHER POLE

This amazing piece of equipment is designed specifically for the new carp fisheries that are springing up around the country. These are traditionally stocked with fish in the 2- to 5-kg (3- to 10-lb) range – sometimes bigger – and these are fish that really put a huge amount of pressure on the pole. There's real power here, and the carbon resins can flex when subjected to the bending and twisting forces of a big, angry carp. The pole has many advantages over a traditional rod when it comes to this style of fishing. First and foremost, float control is much more precise – something often very important, as the carp begin to wise-up after a few matches. This pole, however, is very adaptable and can be used in most situations, especially when bigger than average fish are being sought. It's a good pole, for example, for tench or bream on stillwaters, and why not try it for chub and barbel on the rivers? Although the sections of this pole are stored inside each other, this is a take-apart, rather than telescopic, pole – the sections push together for added strength and stiffness.

Hollow tip

The tip demonstrates the whole principle of the pole – the elastic passes through the centre of the rod and out through the tip, and the line and rig are attached to this.

POLE ELASTIC

The strength of the pole elastic is chosen to match the intended fish – you can imagine what a giant carp would do to the kind of elastic intended for tiny roach! A number code is used to indicate the power of the elastic.

THE ART OF LANDING A FISH

Once a fish is on the hook, how do you bring it to the bank if your rod is 13 m (40 ft) in length? The answer is that you dismantle, or unship, the rod. Special rod rests with rollers allow the sections of rod to be slid back as they are drawn in.

ALMOST THERE

Some poles are telescopic, but others must be unshipped by removing sections from the butt end until the fish can be brought to the net. Small fish can be swung ashore without unshipping if the line is the same length as the extended pole.

BOAT RODS

Boat fishing is a really strenuous, gut-busting style of fishing – especially if you're pursuing very big fish over real depth in bad weather. A boat rod, therefore, needs to be tough, well-made, and able to stand up to real punishment. You've got to look for a compromise, though, between power and flexibility, as all power and no give kills the action. Also, without some flexibility in the rod, there's the danger that you're going to snap up on a big fish when it dives unexpectedly, even when you're using very strong line. A growing option in sea fishing is the uptide rod, which has a longer casting butt and a long, soft tip to cast the weight and play the fish with real sensitivity.

PUNISHING CONDITIONS
A boat rod takes a good deal of mistreatment – not only the strain of fighting big fish in big seas, but also the ravages of sand and salt, and the chance of being knocked around in the boat, so choose a well-made rod.

SHIMANO SOLSTACE UPTIDE
Uptide rods are a joy to use and take boat fishing into a different domain. Always make sure, however, that you're using the right rod for the weight to be cast: you shouldn't over or underload a rod, or it won't work to its full efficiency. Look for good quality rings, a screw reel seat, comfortable handles, and a strong spigot so that the rod won't crack up under pressure. Be aware that uptide rods also double up for very heavy freshwater work – big catfish and mahseer, for example, are frequently targeted with uptide rods.

SHIMANO SOLSTACE
UPTIDE

SHIMANO ANTARES
BOAT UK

PENN INTERNATIONAL
A real beast of a rod – the type of tool designed to take out the biggest fish in the very heaviest of seas. This is the rod that you'll need for skate fishing, perhaps off the Scottish islands, or even when hunting a giant porbeagle.

Rod tip
The yellow tip is very important as it helps the angler see the most delicate bite. Even in the sea, the rod doesn't always crash round, and the uptider will be watching the tip of his rod with complete concentration, waiting for the first flick to herald a taking fish.

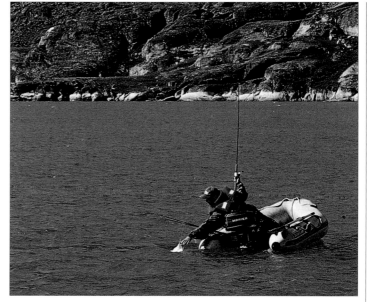

SHIMANO ANTARES BOAT UK
In a boat rod, look for hardwearing rings, a durable handle, and, in very heavy rods, the ability to pack it into a butt pad. Boat rods are typically short rods, 1.8–2.1 m (6–7 ft) in length. This is partly to give plenty of room on the boat, but also to provide tremendous leverage when fighting a conger or giant skate.

GOING IT ALONE
Today's sea angler will often get afloat in his own boat, especially in the safer confines of an estuary or fjord. A lighter boat rod allows for flexible casting, good bite indication, and great fun when playing any size of fish. Never neglect that lifejacket though, however calm the day might seem.

The whipping
A good boat rod is built for action. The rod will take a lot of buffeting, especially in heavy seas, and everything needs to be well-finished and secure. Heavy whippings like these ensure that the rod ring will not drop off under the most extreme pressure.

PENN
INTERNATIONAL

Tip line guide
To withstand the enormous pressure of strong, heavily-loaded line when working a fish up from the bottom, the end ring is a large roller.

PUMPING UP
Almost always used with a multiplier reel, a boat rod is usually held with the rod rings on the top. The rings are designed to keep the line clear of the rod itself.

Butt line guide
The first line guide on this extremely heavy-duty rod is a double roller, through which the line passes.

SHORE RODS

In all probability, shore rods are the most complex example of sea rod design. There are so many tapers, lengths, and materials to choose from that blank design has become a very complex business indeed. A complicating factor is that every shore caster will have his or her own requirements, so there is no such thing as an optimum action, length, or power rating. Anglers are human beings, so of course they differ in casting style, in stature, and in strength. Indeed, many shore anglers will have their own rod made up personally for them, much like a bespoke suit. Most of us, though, buy off the peg, going into the tackle shop and choosing something that fits the bill. To simplify this process, it is important to have a good idea of what you want. Try going down to a popular beach and looking at the rods that fellow anglers are using. If you ask nicely, chances are that they will let you have a cast or two and you can build up your own opinions of what's on offer. Don't rush into a purchase – this is one area of fishing where it is essential to get the right tool from the start.

FISHING FROM THE BEACH
Beach casting is hugely popular all around the world, but there are scores of species that can be targeted so it's important to use the right rod for any particular range of fish. For example, you won't get away with a light shore rod if you're pursuing huge cod in a winter storm. Look carefully at the rod butt: attach a reel and make sure that the whole thing feels balanced in your hands.

Rod rings
All the rod rings are tested severely when the cast is either made or retrieved. Strong rings are therefore essential on any good shore rod.

SHIMANO ANTARES BASS 110

SHIMANO ANTARES
SPECIALIST SURF

A COMMITTED APPROACH
Fishing from the rocks can involve some serious climbing, but always be aware of the risks, which can include being swept from the rocks or trapped by the rising tide.

Light-reflective tip
A lot of beach fishing is done at night when many species move very close into the beach to feed. The foreshore angler will probably be using torches and/or Tilley lamps – a white tip stands out much more starkly against the night sky in their light.

SHIMANO ANTARES BASS 110
Beach casting rods come in a wide range of weights and lengths for the varying conditions and different target fish. As beach rods go, this is a relatively light version, with a length of 3.35 m (11 ft), and an ideal rod for bass fishing.

SHIMANO ANTARES SPECIALIST SURF
Another member of the Antares family, Shimano's Specialist Surf is 30 cm (1 ft) longer than the Antares Bass 110 and is recommended for rockier conditions. Other rods in the range are designed for even heavier work.

ON THE ROCKS
Fishing from rocks can be extremely rewarding, as many different species come in to feed on the wealth of plant and animal life close inshore. The rod for the job needs the power to keep fish out of snags and possibly to raise them some distance from the water.

31

THE REEL

The reel is primarily a line reservoir that enables the angler to fish at a greater range than is possible with a line fixed to the rod tip, which was the only method available to the earliest anglers. The reel has evolved into several different forms, with two distinct types of spool: the revolving spool and the fixed spool. The oldest and simplest form of revolving spool reel is the centre-pin, in which the line is carried on a simple flanged spool that revolves on a steel axle; this reel was once close to extinction but is now showing signs of a comeback. Fly reels and multipliers (including baitcasters) are more complex forms of revolving spool reel. In a fixed-spool reel, the spool does not revolve, and the line is retrieved and wound onto it by a rotating arm, called the bale arm.

THE SPINNER'S CHOICE
The fixed-spool reel is at its best when fishing a light bait, like this spinner, that has to be flipped with both distance and accuracy. Do be aware of the problem of line twist when using a spinner that revolves in the water: a swivel connecting the main line to the hook length generally solves this problem.

REEL CONSTRUCTION

Like the rod, and perhaps to an even greater extent, the reel has been carried along on the wave of technological development. The use of new materials, such as titanium and aluminium alloys, has brought added strength and at the same time has reduced the weight of the reels. The research and development that major companies have invested has led to ever greater refinements of the fixed-spool and the multiplier reel, and even the fly reel – which resembles most closely the centre-pin reel of old – now embodies a wealth of technical advances. Improved balance, gearing, and bearings make the modern reel a pleasure to use. All of this, of course, makes the beginner's choice even more difficult, and the range of extra features now available mean that you really will need some good advice from the tackle dealer.

GLOSSARY OF TERMS

Anti-reverse A mechanism that prevents the spools of multipliers and fixed-spool reels from turning backwards.
Bale arm The arm on a fixed-spool reel that picks up the line and guides it onto the spool.
Check or ratchet A device that varies the tension at which line is pulled from a fly reel.
Drag/slipping clutch A mechanism on multipliers and fixed-spool reels that allows hooked fish to take line from the spool at a preset tension.

Foot The part of the reel that attaches to the rod handle.
Gear ratio The number of times the spool or bale arm of a reel rotates for each turn of the handle.
Level wind Fitted on multipliers to spread line evenly across the spool.
Line guard Found on centre-pin and fly reels, this prevents line from tangling around the drum or handle.
Rotor The turning part of a fixed-spool reel, which revolves around the spool.

FLY REEL

Once fly reels were heavy, with slow retrieves and poor drag systems. In reality, they were little more than reservoirs holding the fly line and keeping it out of tangles. Modern demands, however, have produced a generation of reels that provide much, much more. With the introduction of carbon fibre, fly rods have become ever more wand-like, and it has therefore become important to decrease the weight of fly reels as well. Most reels nowadays are produced from the very best of bar-stock aluminium, generally of aerospace quality. Lighter materials have allowed reels to become somewhat larger and this, allied with better gearing, means that speeds of retrieve are increasing all the time. This allows an angler to play a fish straight off the fly reel, reducing the coils of fly line around the feet just waiting to produce a snag. Drag systems have also improved and, although giving the requisite amount of power, they've become much smoother. Some are designed around pin bearings that grip to the centre shaft of the reel; others use compressed cork – as the drag is tightened, the natural cork gets compressed onto the front plate of the reel and slows it down, like disk braking on a motorcar. All these developments are absolutely essential now the fly reel is being put to ever greater tests, on a Norwegian salmon river, on a North American steelhead river, or on the Bahaman bonefish flats. Durability, reliability, lightness, and efficiency are all vital, but aesthetics are becoming increasingly important as anglers want to fish with reels that not only feel superb but also look individual and inspiring.

FIXED-SPOOL REEL

The fixed-spool reel is the most common model the world over, especially in freshwater, where it is used for everything apart from fly fishing. It even has its uses in the saltwater world for lighter species when very heavy line isn't required. The basic principle behind the fixed-spool reel is that the spool does not revolve to recover line: the line is wound around it by a rotating bail arm. The spool is able to rotate under tension from a slipping clutch to give line to a running fish. The fixed-spool reel has many advantages – casting is supremely easy, line retrieve is very quick, and modern clutches are extremely delicate. Outside the very biggest challenges that fishing can set, the fixed-spool reel will generally be the one for the job.

CLOSED-FACE REEL

This is a fixed-spool reel with an enclosed front face. The line passes through a hole in the centre of the face and is wound onto the spool by a pickup pin. This is a very efficient light line reel, especially for float fishing at comparatively close range. The enclosed spool gives good line control when fishing in windy weather. However, the closed face spool is seen less and less on the match fishing circuit, where it was originally so popular. The main reason for this is that its precise, delicate, close-in job can be done more efficiently with the modern range of lightweight poles.

MULTIPLIER REEL

The multiplier is really a geared version of the traditional centre-pin reel, and it's the one that anglers go for if they're pursuing big fish in really difficult conditions. Multipliers offer huge line capacities, which makes them ideal for long casting or for situations when a fish is likely to run many metres of line off the spool. They are also immensely rugged, built to withstand the most tackle-testing of battles with anything from marlin in the tropical seas to mahseer on the rivers of southern Asia. Most have a free spool facility, allowing the spool to rotate without resistance for casting. There will be a mechanical or magnetic brake, a drag system, and often a level wind mechanism for even line lay upon the spool. This is the reel for the angler with big fish on his or her mind.

BAITCASTING REEL

Baitcasters are small multiplier reels that are designed to be easy to use and comfortable to operate. They are generally fitted with a level wind mechanism and very delicate, adjustable drag systems. These properties make them ideal for the lure fisherman who wishes to cast small plugs and spoons with complete accuracy for hours on end into the most difficult of snags. Very frequently, the predator hooked will be a feisty fighter – a pike, a bass, or even a barracuda in a mangrove swamp. The baitcaster is just the reel to take the heat out of the toughest fight.

FIXED-SPOOL REELS 1

The modern fixed-spool reel is both supremely efficient in operation and an absolute joy to use. Modern technology has created a tool that is light years away from the first fixed-spool reels that appeared around a century ago. However, reels have not gone state-of-the-art merely for the sake of it: the performance of the modern reel is simply sensational. The balance, the lightness, and the smoothness, both of the retrieve and of the clutch, have transformed the fishing experience. The modern fixed-spool reel needs to be light so it can marry well with the new generation of carbon fibre rods. The best fixed-spools are made of aluminium – incredibly light but also very strong. Perfect line lay on the spool is now standard, spreading the line evenly up and down the spool, and the use of the floating spool drive shaft has improved both the efficiency and the longevity of all reels. Fixed-spool reels can now cast further than ever, and with greater ease. The retrieve is faster and smoother than ever before, and when a big fish wants to take line, the clutch operates like silk, avoiding line breaks and lost fish.

TOUCH LEGERING
The fixed-spool reel is the perfect tool for the touch legering technique, where a bite is felt for rather than seen. The line is held tight to the bait by the fingers of the reeling hand, and a strike is made as soon as a bite is felt. This can be anything from the tiniest of nibbles to a full blown tug.

SHIMANO SAHARA GTE 2500
This is a great reel for a wide variety of uses where heavy line is not needed. The spool will take 130 m (140 yd) of 3.6-kg (8-lb) line, which makes this the perfect tool for legering on rivers. It can be used with swimfeeders, and also for light spinning. As the reel is so light, it can also be used comfortably for float fishing when the rod is constantly in the hand. The three ball bearings, roller bearing, floating drive shaft, and positive bail arm action all make this medium capacity reel a joy to use.

Spool
The size of the spool determines how much line will fit comfortably on the reel.

Bail arm
The bail arm is flicked back to allow line to flow off the spool when casting, and should flip back into position easily when the reel handle is wound forwards.

Double handle
Many reels have a symmetrical, balanced handle, which gives a smoother wind, and makes the retrieve much easier, especially when fishing at long distance.

Fighting drag
While playing a fish, you can quickly make adjustments to the drag by moving this lever left or right.

SHIMANO SAHARA
GTE 2500

Drag control
Turning this knob controls the ease with which the spool turns and allows line to be taken by a fish.

SHIMANO STRADIC X GTM 3000

The aluminium body of this respected, all-round reel makes it extremely light and perfect for use in conjunction with a modern carbon fibre rod. The responsive drag system can be tightened or loosened with just a flick of the winding hand. Four ball bearings and a roller bearing ensure a smooth wind, and the double handle balances the whole reel perfectly. This range of reels suits the lighter end of the coarse market, and this particular model is ideal for light to medium leger and feeder work, float fishing, and even light spinning.

Low friction
The spool has a stainless steel lip, which creates very little friction when the line flies over it, making long casting much easier.

SHIMANO STRADIC X GTM 3000

Low capacity spool
For smooth casting, the line must almost fill the spool, so that it flows smoothly over the lip. This very shallow spool is perfect for the moderate lengths of light line that are necessary in match fishing.

SHIMANO SUPER MATCH HS 3000

Match fishing is one of the most demanding disciplines for any fixed-spool, as the reel is in constant use. The rotating body on this one is mounted on a floating shaft to cut down on friction, and a roller bearing reduces the effort of retrieving. The bail arm is reinforced, so there's no fear of it breaking down under the stresses and strains of a gruelling five-hour match. This particular reel comes in two versions with different gear ratios – 7:1 for high speed retrieve, and 5.1:1 to give more power in a fight with a big fish. The shallow spool indicates that this is not a reel for long-distance fishing.

SHIMANO SUPER MATCH HS 3000

FIXED-SPOOL REELS 2

Modern fixed-spool reels are very sophisticated, with a huge number of features. Bail arm rollers are subject to great pressure as they convert the line through 90°, and they need to withstand the fierce, uncompromising tension of modern nylon and braid lines. Drag systems can be placed either in front of the reel on the spool, or mounted on the stern. Some big fish reels today offer a "bait running" facility – a lever located on the rear of the reel allows it to be set so that line is released in controlled free spool, and when a big fish tears off with your bait, line is released freely. This mechanism prevents over-runs, and is an essential feature for anglers fishing with modern, self-hooking rigs. Some reels are also equipped with double handles, which give greater balance.

A COMFORTABLE HOLD
It is important to hold the rod and reel as comfortably as possible, especially when casting for long periods. Clasp the stem of the reel between the index and middle fingers to give a firm grip and perfect balance. Tuck the reel butt along the forearm, and under the armpit if necessary.

SHIMANO BIG BAITRUNNER LONG CAST
As waters have become more heavily fished, and carp in particular have become more wary, the general trend is to fish further from the bankside. Indeed, rods and reels are designed to cast leads and baits way over 90 m (100 yd). To achieve this sort of distance, a true bonding between rod and reel has to be achieved. The spool of the Long Cast holds a huge amount of line – 550 m (600 yd) of 5.4 kg (12 lb) breaking strain. It's also aluminium, so the lip cuts down on friction as line flies across it. This is the perfect reel for fishing huge gravel pits and, especially, the massive reservoirs found in central and southern Europe, the sort of places where carp grow to 23 kg (50 lb) plus. Complete reliability ensures that the reel won't break down when you're far from home.

SHIMANO BIG BAITRUNNER
LONG CAST

Front drag
There's a big debate in specialist fishing circles whether a rear or spool drag system is the best. The general consensus is beginning to plump for a rear drag for smaller species and a spool system for the very biggest fish. The Long Cast is above all a big fish reel, and it has the drag at the front.

SHIMANO BIOMASTER GT 7000
*The features on this reel make it ideal for big water,
long range work when large fish are to be expected.
The spool is wide and deep to hold vast lengths of
strong line. The handle is big and strong, which offers
a really firm grip when winding in a specimen at a
distance. The body and reel stem are strong and rigid
to prevent any chance of buckling under pressure. The
slipping clutch mechanism is especially sensitive,
which means you can clamp down if necessary, but
slacken off the pressure when the fish comes clear.*

Long handle
*The length of the handle crank and the
large hand grip itself provide good
leverage when the pressure is on.*

SHIMANO BIOMASTER GT 7000

SHIMANO NEXUS
BAITRUNNER 8000 GTE
*For well over a decade, baitrunners
have absolutely swept the board when
it comes to the upper end of specialist
fishing, especially for carp. The baitrunner feature allows the spool to run
free when a run occurs, and self-
hooking is achieved. All the angler
needs do is pick up the rod, wind down,
and the reel automatically kicks back
into a retrieve mode. The Nexus, one
of the new generation of baitrunners,
offers a graphite and aluminium-
hybridized body, giving superb power
with very little weight. The gearing is
designed to permit a huge amount of
power with each crank of the reel,
making it ideal in hit-and-hold
situations where a big fish is thrashing
near a potentially terminal snag. The
baitrunners offer a perfect solution to
virtually all big fish angling, whether
it's straightforward legering, feeder
fishing, or dead baiting.*

Baitrunner lever
*Simply click the baitrunner option on
and the spool rotates completely freely.
A turn of the handle and the baitrunner option clicks off and immediate
contact with the fish is achieved. This
is a system that has revolutionized
fixed lead fishing.*

SHIMANO NEXUS
BAITRUNNER 8000 GTE

37

CLOSED-FACE AND CENTRE-PIN REELS

The closed-face reel still has a job to do when an angler wants to fish with very fine lines for close-in, light float work, especially on a windy day when tangles around a typical open-faced reel can occur. One-handed casting is also possible with a closed-face reel, and line control is immaculate. However, the closed-face reel is not generally as fast on the retrieve, nor as good for long casting, nor is it up to the job of hunting big fish.

STALKING THE QUARRY
Both centre-pins and closed-face reels are designed for tight-in situations where the angler can easily spook the fish. Keep low to the skyline, wear drab clothing, and make your movements slow and deliberate. Keep your footsteps light and use natural bankside cover, such as trees and reed beds.

CLOSED-FACE REELS

The closed-face reel is a specialized variation of the fixed-spool reel. The front of the reel is shrouded by a casing through which the line emerges, and line retrieval is by means of a pin that guides the line onto the spool. Pressing a spring-loaded button retracts the pin, leaving the line free for casting. This design eliminates the common problem associated with fine lines, which is that they have a tendency to blow about on windy days, constantly tangling around the reel spool, rotor, or bale arm with potentially disastrous results for the angler. Closed-faced reels are at their very best when fitted with light lines, and are used for light spinning and for match fishing.

ABU GARCIA GOLD MAX
Designed for competition fishing at the highest level, this closed-face model contains no drag system. Instead, big fish are played by backwinding the handle. The extra-wide spool and dual-geared oscillation system produce a criss-cross line lay on the retrieve, eliminating the possibility of coils of line bedding into gaps between the coils beneath them, a traditional problem with closed-face reels, and one that inhibits smooth casting and float control.

Spool casing
The line enters the reel through a small hole in the front of the removable casing that encloses the spool. The casing prevents light line from being blown around and tangling.

ABU GARCIA GOLD MAX

CENTRE-PINS

After a period in the wilderness, the centre-pin is very much a feature of the 21st-century angling scene, especially on rivers where it is unbeatable for trotting a float in moving water. Modern centre-pins spin so easily that the strength of the current is easily sufficient to pull line off the spool as the float meanders its way down the swim. Contact between angler and float is immediate and precise. Once the strike is made, the angler can begin to retrieve line without having to click over the bail arm of a fixed-spool reel. This added second of instant control can often prove vital. Also, for pure aesthetics, there is little to beat playing a good fish on the centre-pin. The sensation is immediate and direct and in no way diluted by highly sophisticated gearing. The centre-pin is a specialized reel, but in its own arena it reigns supreme.

YOUNG'S BOB JAMES 10-CM (4-IN) CENTRE-PIN

The modern generation of centre-pins has taken the angling world by storm and none is better designed than this one, bearing the name of the famous English angler, Bob James. This is a wonderful centre-pin, very strong but exceedingly light and engineered to run under the slightest pressure. Don't put too much line onto the spool or you will find that it beds in and really smooth release is inhibited. The rim of the reel is exposed so that you can bat it with the palm of your hand for a very quick line retrieve. You can also place your hand against the drum to act as a sensitive drag system when a big fish is running.

YOUNG'S BOB JAMES 10-CM (4-IN) CENTRE-PIN

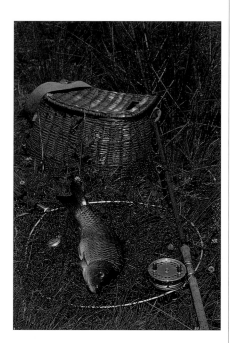

TIMELESS TRADITION

This could be a scene from a hundred years ago, but the task of the centre-pin is changeless. This carp was taken close in from a small lake, and the reel made casting and playing a delight.

The drum

Note the width of the drum. A good wide drum allows the line to be spread thinly and evenly, minimizing the problem of bedding in. Observe also the perforations. Strength is not affected but extreme lightness is achieved.

BAITCASTING REELS

Baitcasting reels are really only small multipliers, and they are very much the tool of the lure angler. Most modern baitcasters are cut from one-piece aluminium bar-stock and are incredibly strong and light. They retrieve very quickly, perfect for the lure angler who wants to give his surface plug a quick spurt. Modern brake systems mean that over runs when casting are now generally a thing of the past. Drag systems are traditionally very precise on baitcasters, and can be loosened or tightened with lightning speed. They also have the ability to work efficiently with both nylon line and braid, an important advantage for any lure angler. Many modern baitcasters also feature a quick-release thumb bar, which disengages the spool and makes for very rapid casting – vital for the lure fisherman who sees a quickly-moving predator.

THE PREDATOR BECOMES THE PREY
The baitcaster is perfect in conjunction with any of the modern jig designs that are the downfall of many a freshwater predator – pike, perch, zander, or bass in particular. Casting with one of these reels is precise, and they offer total control and contact throughout the erratic retrieve that is needed to give life to the lure.

SHIMANO CALCUTTA 251
The Calcutta 251 looks gorgeous, feels beautiful, and in action it is hardly beatable. This is one of the most sought-after small multipliers in the world, absolutely perfect for the lure angler wanting lightness, ease of operation, and extreme reliability. An anti-overrun system and level wind give superb, tangle-free spooling of both mono and, increasingly, braid. The star drag system is easily operated, even during the heat of the battle. The Calcutta 251, in conjunction with a light spinning rod, is perfect for any species from perch or bass right up to pike and even salmon.

Star drag
Readily to hand while playing a fish, the star drag allows the angler to change the pressure needed for a fighting fish to pull line from the spool, giving excellent control.

Level wind
As line is retrieved, the level wind mechanism moves left and right across the reel, laying the line evenly across the spool and ensuring that casting is smooth.

SHIMANO CALCUTTA 251

SHIMANO CORSAIR 400 & 401

SHIMANO CORSAIR 400 & 401
Available in both right-handed and left-handed versions, the Corsair is designed for freshwater plug and lure fishing, and the wide spool gives a good line capacity for trolling from a boat or long-range casting. Like most good modern baitcasters, the Corsair has a level wind mechanism and a quick release thumb bar.

Line guide
At the front of the reel, a circular line guide feeds the line evenly onto the spool.

SHIMANO CURADO 201B
This smooth, sleek, aerodynamic reel is blissfully light, making it the ideal partner for the lightest of spinning rods. It's ideally used with small plugs, spinners, and, especially, rubber jigs. Its fast retrieve means that a bait can be cranked in furiously if a big predator is in pursuit. The Variable Brake System means that overruns are kept to a minimum and the tension can be cranked up if the reel is used for trolling. All in all, a most adaptable, lightweight reel, ideal for the precision and stresses of modern small lure fishing.

SHIMANO CURADO 201B

FLY REELS 1

As you don't need great line storage when you are looking for grayling or small- to medium-sized trout, a small-spooled reel is ideal and it offers you the advantage of lightness. Look for reels that offer a high line recovery rate, so that you can keep up with a fish that's running quickly towards you. Test the reel for a neat, precise drag system that gives line predictably under pressure. Look for an exposed spool rim, as this will allow you to retrieve line with the palm of your hand for extreme speed. Test that drag system again. Does the spool start to spin immediately under very slight pressure and rotate with a minimum of resistance? When a fish takes suddenly, this can help avoid a breakage with the very light tippets so often in use today.

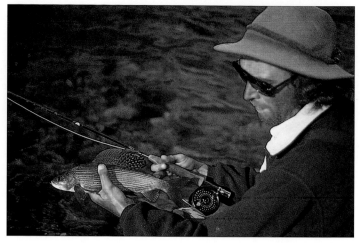

RIGHT-HANDED CASTING
Many manufacturers set their fly reels up for right hand wind at the factory. This is fine if you want to cast with your left hand, but if you are right-handed it makes sense to swap the reel around so that you can wind the reel with your less sensitive fingers.

ARI HART INTERNATIONAL MACH ONE
This is a delightful little trout reel, designed for smaller waters and a 4-weight line. However, with its comparatively large spool, it will store line and pay it off without kinking. The reel also features an excellent drag system, which is very important when you're using light tippets. Indeed, as catch and release becomes more and more popular in the streams and rivers of the world, the fish are bound to become more cautious. Lighter tippets are one way of overcoming a fish's suspicion, but the drag on the modern reel has to be up to the job of cushioning frail lines against a sudden lunge.

ARI HART INTERNATIONAL MACH ONE

Tension knob
Note the large tension knob on the back of the reel. This makes for instant control. The drag can be increased or decreased within a second, often saving a breakage or, alternatively, keeping a running fish out of a snag.

SAGE 3100 LIGHT TROUT REEL

This is a great little reel, one of the most thoughtfully designed on the market. The 3000 series as a whole offers incredibly light reels, with a high line recovery rate and a totally sealed graphite disk drag system to keep water, dirt, and grime out. The reels also offer a click drag with a numbering system so that you can relocate the original setting in a second. There is an exposed rim for palming back line and the large arbor means there is no problem with kinking. In short, this is the ideal reel for precision trout fishing on low, clear rivers.

SAGE 3100 LIGHT TROUT REEL

Open framework
A rear view shows the architecture of this precision-made reel. It is made as light as possible whilst maintaining its rigidity and strength.

LOOP EVOTEC LW 6 NINE

This is a truly modern, up-to-date reel. It has got a pin-bearing drag, which gives low inertia at the start of a run, protecting light tippets from a sudden shock and resulting breakage. This reel is designed for a nine-weight fly line and 140 m (150 yd) of 13.6-kg (30-lb) backing. This makes it the ideal reel for heavy reservoir work, sea trout, and even saltwater fishing. It's a beautiful, yet gutsy performer that can be delicate or powerful as the situation demands.

GETTING OUT INTO THE ACTION

Wading gives an angler total freedom of the river. Unapproachable lies can be fished, and you can get well away from any trees and bushes that may be troublesome on the backcast. Never wade too deep, however, especially in a fast current. Wading sticks, secure grip soles, and buoyancy aids are all sensible precautions.

LOOP EVOTEC
LW 6 NINE

43

FLY REELS 2

When you're thinking about a fly reel for big sea trout; large, fresh run steelhead; Atlantic or Pacific salmon; or even the bigger sea fish species, then you've simply got to go for a reel that gives a high capacity spool. Lines need to be in excess of 10-weight, perhaps considerably above, and you'll need at least 200 metres (650 feet) of backing. A good drag system is essential on any fishing reel, but it's never more important than now, when you've hooked a fleeing steelhead or you're trying to hold a king salmon at the tail of its pool. The reel should also be immensely strong, providing rigidity under pressure. The better quality reels are made out of bar-stock aluminium of the highest quality, which provides both lightness and unbeatable strength.

A SALMON REEL IN ACTION
Traditional gear in a traditional setting – this Scottish ghillie and his dog guide a lady angler through the battle with a fresh-run summer salmon. The long rod makes for easy casting and the large arbor reel allows quick line retrieval.

ARI HART SALMON REEL

ARI HART SALMON REEL
This is a superb salmon reel, with a very large arbor, or line capacity. In fact, it can take a 9- or 10-weight line, and anything up to 180 m (200 yd) of 13.5-kg (30-lb) backing, making it ideal for heavy Norwegian or Russian work. A feature of the reel is its oversized dial drag. This means the drag system is very easy to get to and operate. It's also very accurate, and just a few centimetres turn can make a huge amount of difference – vital when a big fish is running fast and needs to be checked. This really is the reel for those intrepid anglers seeking out big Scandinavian fish, American Pacific salmon, or even Mongolian taimen.

Drag system
The drag system is important on the salmon reel, and on this model you can increase or decrease drag by winding the finger-hold back plate forwards or backwards.

ABEL SUPER 8 SALTWATER REEL

This is arguably the best saltwater reel on the market today, and it's perfect for bone fishing on the flats. One of the main reasons why this particular reel has built up such a dedicated following is its faultless drag system, which is super smooth and works again and again. Anyone who has hooked a running bonefish knows exactly how important this feature is. You have to let a bonefish go on its first run, and frequently that run will be 45 m (150 ft) or even 90 m (300 ft) in length. If your reel catches for any reason whatsoever, then the line goes tight and breaks – something that can happen in a second. The Abel is also extremely resistant to saltwater.

Space-age engineering
Lightness is a real consideration when it comes to the fly reel, and the Abel series are vented using a "rounded-oblong" design. The machining is intense and the parts are trimmed to the bone, yet strength and reliability are maintained.

ABEL SUPER 8 SALTWATER REEL

BILLY PATE BLUEFIN

This giant reel has been designed almost exclusively for the biggest fish that swim in saltwater. Its line capacity is outstanding, and it's made to fit perfectly with the oceanic fly rod. The reel itself probably won't be doing a great deal of casting, as most of this style of fishing is done on the drift or the troll. However, once a big fish is hooked, the reel really comes into its own. The drag system is magnificent, with renowned durability, however long and heavy the fight. There is also an anti-reverse feature, so that the angler can screw everything down tight and really lay on the pressure.

BILLY PATE BLUEFIN

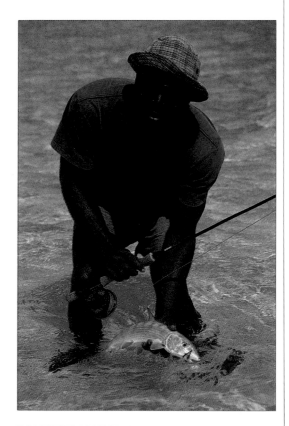

BONEFISH ON THE FLATS
Bonefish are the greyhounds of the tropical seas. Though rarely above 3.5 kg (8 lb) in weight, they are all muscle and can swim in excess of 30 kph (20 mph). The fly line and 100 metres (325 feet) of backing can disappear in seconds.

BOAT REELS

Boat fishing is one of the toughest forms of angling and can really take the guts out of a reel. Often, a reel will be expected to winch up a heavy fish from huge depths, frequently in a big swell. A multiplier reel, therefore, must be strong and well-engineered, with an adequate spool capacity. The gearing is critical, and should be precise and robust, with a smooth and reliable drag mechanism, or you run the risk of line breakage when playing a large, free-running fish. Learn how to use your reel instinctively before going out on the high seas. Work out how to cast and, most importantly, how the drag systems work. Remember that if you do hook a big fish, it's essential to have the tension set properly so that you can reel in, but can also give out line if the fish heads for home.

READY FOR ANYTHING
Make sure you know exactly how all the functions of your reel work before setting out to fish. In a situation like this, when a large cod dives for safety, it's vital you release the tension on the reel and give line immediately to avoid a breakage.

SHIMANO CALCUTTA 700
The Calcutta 700 is one of the most perfect uptide reels available today. Uptiding frequently involves casting – a job that the Calcutta does perfectly. However, if you want to fish under the boat, then nothing could be simpler. The Calcutta offers serious line capacity, making it ideal for taking abroad where big fish can strip line off the spool in the twinkling of an eye.

SHIMANO CALCUTTA 700

PUTTING YOUR GEAR TO THE TEST
The rod is thrust into the butt pad and the angler braces himself for a gruelling fight. It is at times like this that the reliability and engineering of your reel are put to the test. Knowing that your equipment is up to the job is a real confidence booster at such moments.

SHIMANO CALCUTTA 400

Star drag

SHIMANO CALCUTTA 400

An intermediate model between the Calcutta 251 and its big brother, the Calcutta 700, the 400 is superb for light boat work. It won't winch in a huge fish on ultra-thick line, but it's absolutely perfect for smaller species, such as bass. It is also a highly adaptable reel, as it can also be used from the shore – a fine reel for bass fishing in the surf.

SHIMANO CHARTER SPECIAL

The Charter Special is a proven workhorse, the sort of big multiplier that boat anglers around the world appreciate. It offers a level wind system, particularly useful when actively working a bait towards the surface. The centrifugal braking system also eliminates tangles when casting.

SHIMANO CHARTER SPECIAL

Lever drag

SHIMANO TLD TWO SPEED

In the 21st century, anglers are travelling more and more for their fishing, seemingly never content with the challenges in their own backyard. This is where the TLD Two Speed comes to prominence. This reel offers you the option of switching from a high- to a low-speed retrieve, as and when fishing situations dictate. If you are fishing for a mammoth halibut off the coast of Greenland, therefore, you'd click onto the low speed as you try to pump the great fish up from 150 or 180 m (500 or 600 ft) down. If, however, you are fishing for a greyhound tuna, then you'd turn to high speed in an effort to keep pace with the incredible velocity of the fish through the shallow, warm seas.

SHIMANO TLD TWO SPEED

SHORE REELS

Shore reels, just like shore rods, have great demands put on them and are really expected to fulfil a number of functions. Shore fishing is a complex beast – you might be fishing off a pier, or on a shingle bank, wading through the surf, or flicking a bait out from rocks. The scope is enormous and you have to bear this in mind when choosing your equipment. In theory, the multiplier reel is the most robust of reels and capable of casting the greatest distance. If you want to cast to the horizon, then a multiplier is almost inevitably the tool for you. A big, fixed-spool reel, however, is much more suitable for lighter work. If you are going to be a true shore fisherman, you'll need both multipliers and fixed-spool reels and learn to use both with competence. Also, take great care of your tackle. It is easy to get sand and grit into the workings. These are expensive bits of kit. Look after them.

POWER CASTING
For really long casts from the beach, a multiplier has to be the answer. Ensure it is well maintained, and always keep sand and grit out of the precision workings or the spool will not rotate freely. The abrasion can also do permanent damage.

ABU AMBASSADEUR 7000
The Ambassadeur range has been respected around the world for a great many years. The reels are totally reliable and have magnificent precision engineering. The 7000 revolutionized casting and distance fishing, and the design has remained unchanged for well over two decades. It is ideal for medium-range shore casting, with lines of around the 6.8- to 13.6-kg (15- to 30-lb) mark. If heavier lines or extreme distances are necessary, then the 9000, the 7000's big brother, is an available option. The 9000 enjoys the same great casting ability as the 7000, but is also combined with a two speed retrieve. The low speed allows you to play a heavy fish in deep water, whereas the high speed enables a quick retrieve if you are playing a fast-moving species or trying to skip back a lure over snags.

Balanced handle
A counter-weight on the reel handle helps to keep everything in balance during the retrieve.

ABU AMBASSADEUR 7000

Star drag
Ready to hand, and with a very smooth action, the star drag allows the tension on the spool to be continuously varied while playing a fish.

Level wind
The stainless steel level wind on this model is particularly well made.

SHIMANO AERLEX GT 8000

SHIMANO AERLEX GT 8000

This is an absolutely great reel for all heavy duty work when long casting is considered likely. It has a really large spool, capable of taking well over 300 m (330 ft) of 7.7-kg (17-lb) line. Moreover, the line lay is particularly effective, and this ensures trouble-free distance casting. The large, single crank handle and 3.8:1 gearing also makes long-range retrieval fast and effortless – a real consideration if fishing way out from the beach. In short, this is the ideal reel for lighter beach work – and very heavy freshwater duties as well. Use it also on a gravel pit for very long-range carp or pike.

SHIMANO ULTEGRA XT

This model is as ideally suited to the shore fisherman as it is to the freshwater angler after mammoth carp, pike, or catfish. The front drag system works well with big fish in rough seas, and the big, deep spool on the 14000 model allows it to be filled with 400 m (440 yd) of 7.3-kg (16-lb) line. The handle is large, and ideal for cranking a big fish back over a long distance. The bail arm is specially strengthened. This is a tremendous reel for all big fish work.

SHIMANO ULTEGRA XT

ROD-TIP ACTION
Fixed-spool reels have an important job to do when fishing in close to rocks and cliffs. Extra-long casting is not needed, and the fixed-spool reel is particularly forgiving to the light lines needed for bass, mullet, or wrasse.

LINES, CRIMPS, BEADS, & SWIVELS

Although they are small and seem insignificant, leader (or trace) lines, crimps, beads, swivels, and the like are as important as rods and reels because, along with hooks and lures, they constitute the tackle that fish come directly into contact with. Unless they perform correctly and reliably, perfect bait presentation (without which the bait, no matter how good, loses some of its appeal to fish) will be difficult, as will the successful playing and landing of a hooked fish. Similar considerations apply to the reel line, whether it be monofilament, braided fibre (such as braided Dacron), or wire. An outfit can only be as strong and reliable as its weakest link, which is often the line. Look after it and change it regularly, and always use line that is of correct type and breaking strain (the load or weight that a line can take before it breaks) for its intended application.

MONOFILAMENT

For bait and lure fishing, monofilament nylon (mono) far outsells every other line material combined, and it is also used as backing for fly lines, which are usually made of coated Dacron (see page 52). It is cheap, reliable, the only line that can be distance cast, and a virtual must for freshwater fishing. However, there are disadvantages to consider. Different brands stretch to varying degrees. This can be helpful in cushioning violent movement from big fish, but it also cushions the bite and strike in deep water. Other drawbacks of mono are that it is weakened by knotting, its breaking strain is reduced when it is wet, and exposure to the ultraviolet light in sunlight will weaken it. In general, mono line should be changed at least once per year.

9.1 kg (20 lb) MONO

9.1 kg (20 lb) MONO

BRAIDED LINE

Modern braid has advanced massively over the past decade, and is now used exclusively by many anglers. It has great strength for its diameter, and has very little memory, which means it doesn't come off the reel in springy coils, making it perfect for long, accurate casting. Also, as braid has very little stretch, it's very responsive and you can actually "feel" what a fish is doing at the hook end. On the downside, its lack of give can lead to a break if a fish makes an unexpected run. You've also got to be careful with your knots, as braid can pull easily. If you're bait fishing with braid as a hook length, it can rise with a loop off the bottom, so you may need some weight close to the hook to keep the braid on the bottom.

8.2 kg (18 lb) BRAID

11.3 kg (25 lb) BRAID

WIRE LINE

Wire line comes in three forms: single-stranded stainless steel, braided or twisted multi-strand steel, and single-strand Monel (an alloy based on copper and nickel). It is an excellent choice for sea fishing in deep water where tides run particularly hard, because it does not stretch and has a high breaking strain for its diameter. This means instant bite detection at any depth, positive striking, and the ability to hold bottom with a fraction of the additional weight that is required by other lines. Its drawbacks are that it requires a narrow, deep-spooled multiplier reel without a level wind, a rod with roller guides (at least a roller tip), and a monofilament weak link at the end. It cannot be cast, hooks can be ripped out easily because it has no cushioning stretchiness, and care must be taken to avoid cut hands.

13.6 kg (30 lb)

22.7 kg (50 lb)

13.6 kg (30 lb)

18.1 kg (40 lb)

18.1 kg (40 lb)

LEADER LINE

When fishing in freshwater for pike and other species with sharp teeth and strong jaws, a strong leader (trace) between the reel line and the hook or lure is essential. Freshwater leaders should be uncoated braided wire or, for deadbait trolling, single-strand wire. In saltwater, plain mono is adequate for small to medium-sized fish without teeth, but for large fish, or those with sharp teeth, use longliner's nylon or wire. Generally speaking, plain monos from 18.1 kg (40 lb) upwards make the best leaders for boat fishing; anything lighter tends to present the bait poorly. Use nylon of 68 kg (150 lb) for heavy wreck and reef fishing, and at least 91 kg (200 lb) nylon for giant tuna and billfish.

79 kg (175 lb)
STAINLESS STEEL

27.2 kg (60 lb)
MONO

CRIMPS & BEADS

Wire line and heavy-guage mono are joined to other lines and to swivels by means of crimps, which are small metal sleeves. For example, to fix a swivel to a wire line, a crimp is slipped over the end of the line, which is then looped through the eye of the swivel and back into the crimp. Then the crimp is squeezed tight with crimping pliers. Beads are used to protect knots from sliding booms and to act as buffers ahead of fixed stops.

CRIMPS

BEADS

COIL CRIMP (right)
Coil crimp is springy, spiral stainless steel wire. Short lengths of it can be wound onto the line to replace stop knots and plastic stoppers that are superglued into position for fixing droppers and booms in place. They can be repositioned quickly or removed for reuse.

COIL CRIMP

SWIVELS

Every terminal rig, no matter how simple, should ideally contain at least one swivel to prevent twists in the line, and using a swivel is the perfect way to attach a leader or a dropper to the reel line. Even the best brands are cheap, so go for the quality names such as Berkley, Mustad, Drennan, and Sampo; unbranded imitations are generally unreliable and can refuse to turn under stress.

BARREL SWIVELS
Barrel swivels are the best choice for general-purpose work. Their design almost guarantees long-term reliability.

BALL-BEARING SWIVELS
These offer superb, freely rotating twist correction, which is essential for all trolling work.

THREE-WAY SWIVELS
These were once popular for linking in droppers, but standoff booms terminating in barrel swivels are now generally preferred.

CONGER HOOK SWIVEL
This is not to be trusted. The hook has a habit of coming out of the swivel head, which can also prove too weak for a big fish.

LINK SWIVELS

LINK SWIVELS
A link swivel is a swivel with a quick-release link to which the terminal tackle is attached. Several types of link are available, but they all allow easy changing of terminal tackle, either to unhook fish while continuing fishing, or to replace a kinked or damaged leader.

SAMPO SWIVELS

BIG-GAME SWIVEL
Reliable, heavy-duty ball bearing swivels, such as those made by Sampo and Berkley, are essential for the prolonged, tackle-testing battles with exceptionally large fish that are typical of big-game fishing.

51

FLY LINES & LEADERS

Most artificial flies are small and weigh next to nothing, and the casting weight needed to carry them out onto the water is provided by the fly line. The fly is joined to the fly line via a braided or solid leader, and the fly line in turn is attached to a length of braided or solid backing line. The backing provides a reserve of line for playing big, fast-running fish, and, by partly filling the reel spool, it ensures that the fly line coils are of large circumference. These big coils are less likely than small ones to tangle as they are pulled off the reel. Fly lines are made from materials such as braided nylon, braided Dacron, and PVC, and coated with a variety of polymers such as polyurethane and PTFE.

LINE COLOUR
Most floating lines are pale in colour, but sinking lines are usually produced in darker hues.

THE AFTM SYSTEM

Formulated by the American Fishing Tackle Manufacturers Association (AFTMA), this system uses a code of letters and numbers to describe the characteristics of a fly line. The first letters of the code indicate the line's profile or shape, the number that follows indicates its weight, and the last letter (or two letters) signifies its density. The number assigned to a fly line *(see right)* depends on the weight, in grains, of the first 9.1 m (30 ft) of the line, excluding any level tip. AFTM numbers are also assigned to fly rods, and the number of the line should match that of the rod with which it is used.

AFTM LINE WEIGHT NUMBERS

AFTM number	Weight in grains	Weight range
1	60	54–66
2	80	74–86
3	100	94–106
4	120	114–126
5	140	134–146
6	160	152–168
7	185	177–193
8	210	202–218
9	240	230–250
10	280	270–290
11	330	318–342
12	380	368–392
13	430	418–442
14	480	468–492

AFTM FLY LINE PROFILES

ANATOMY OF A FLY LINE (DOUBLE TAPER)

Tip ← Front taper → Coating — Belly (Body) — Core — Rear taper → Tip

The fly line profiles, or tapers, in common use today are the double taper, the weight forward, and the shooting head or shooting taper. The level line, which is the same diameter throughout its length, is difficult to cast and is now seldom used. Double-taper lines are designed to present flies gently at close to medium distance and are easy to cast. Weight-forward lines are intended for medium to long-distance casting, and once the tip and belly of the line have been cast, the thin running line shoots easily through the rod rings. A well-designed weight-forward line will present a fly just as delicately as a double taper. Shooting heads consist of short lengths of fly line, backed by fine braided or flat solid monofilament which produces little resistance when pulled through the rod rings, and are used for casting prodigious distances on big stillwaters.

DOUBLE TAPER
2 ft — 10 ft — 66 ft — 10 ft — 2 ft
90 ft

WEIGHT FORWARD
2 ft — 10 ft — 20 ft — 3 ft — 55 ft
90 ft

SHOOTING TAPER
2 ft — 10 ft — 18 ft
33 ft
Mono shooting line is attached to loop

AFTM FLY LINE SYMBOLS

In the AFTM system of fly line classification, the letters preceding the weight number (DT, WF, or SH – or sometimes L, for level line) indicate the taper of the line. The letter or letters that come after the weight number (such as F, ND, I, S, FS, and VFS) signify the density, or function, of the line, that is, whether the line floats, sinks, or has an intermediate or neutral density and thus sinks very slowly.

For example, a fly line described as DT9F is one that has a double taper, is of weight number 9, and floats, while a number 7 line with a weight-forward taper and a neutral density is described as WF7ND.

FLY LINE SYMBOLS	
DT	Double taper
WF	Weight forward
SH	Shooting head
F	Floating
ND	Neutral density
I	Intermediate
S	Sinking
FS	Fast sinking
VFS	Very fast sinking

LINE DENSITIES

Fly lines are made in a variety of densities, and the density of a line determines whether it will float or sink. Those with the lowest densities are floating lines, and those with the highest are the very fast sinkers. However, the descriptions given to individual lines are not always a reliable guide to their performance, and one manufacturer's fast-sinking line might sink at the same rate as another's very fast sinker.

To give a more accurate indication of how their sinking fly lines perform, many manufacturers publish their sinking rates. These are given in centimetres per second or inches per second, or as the depth to which the line will sink after a specified period of time. The only problem with this is that different parts of a line may sink at different speeds, and sinking rates may be influenced by many factors. For example, water temperature and wind speed (with attendant undertow) both affect the rate at which a line will sink.

AIRFLO DI LINE SINKING RATES

Depth attained after 30 seconds

334	260	212	167	137	123	84	60

DI–2
DI–3
DI–4
DI–5
DI–6
DI–7
DI–8
DI–9

SINKING RATES (above)
This is an example of a manufacturer's sinking rate data, in this case for Airflo's DI range. The depths are stated in inches.

LEADERS

The leader is the length of nylon that connects the fly line to the fly. To ensure a good turnover during casting, it should taper from the fly line down, with the butt section (that closest to the fly line) being at least a third of the fly line's thickness. When surface fishing, use a long leader to put a good distance between the thick, coloured fly line and the fly. This distance is usually not so important when you are using sinking lines.

Braided leaders
These leaders are made of nylon braid that tapers continuously throughout its length and is very supple. They are produced in a range of floating and sinking versions, and because of their excellent turnover they are a great aid to good fly presentation. With some braided leaders, the butt end fits over the tip of the fly line and is held in place by a piece of silicone tubing, while others are joined to the fly line by loops. The fly is attached to a braided leader by a short length of mono called a tippet.

Monofilament leaders
Commercially made mono leaders consist either of a continuous, tapering length of nylon, or of lengths of progressively smaller diameters and lower breaking strains knotted together. The knotless leaders are stronger and less likely to pick up weed than the knotted versions, but they do have the drawback that each time the fly is changed, the tip of the leader becomes thicker. Eventually, the entire leader has to be changed or a finer tip section attached.

ROMAN MOSER
BRAIDED LEADERS

LEADER DENSITIES
The high-density braided leaders now available allow unleaded or very small flies to be fished at depth without the need for a sinking fly line.

AIRFLO
BRAIDED LEADERS

HOOKS 1

Hooks are essential if unglamorous items of tackle. Although their functions are simple, their design is often complex and subtle, and there are innumerable patterns, sizes, and finishes on the market. These have evolved in response to the requirements of the different styles and methods of fishing, the varied sizes, mouth shapes, teeth, and lips of fish, and the baits needed to tempt them. As a result, it is essential to match your choice to your intended method of fishing and the species you intend to catch when buying your hooks. In this respect, as with any other tackle purchase, the advice of a reputable dealer will prove invaluable.

HOOK CHOICE
Always use a hook large enough to cope with the fish you intend to catch.

HOOK TYPES

There are three basic types of hook, the single, the double, and the treble. The range of hooks is enormous, but without doubt the most popular type is the single in its many guises, from the small spade-end hooks used by match fishermen to the large stainless steel hooks used by big-game anglers. Double hooks are used chiefly for fly fishing, but some, such as the Whichway, are used for pike fishing. With its three points, the treble hook offers great hooking potential and is used mainly for spinning baits (plugs and spoons), pike rigs, and salmon flies (either long-shank trebles or tube flies).

SINGLE HOOK   DOUBLE HOOK   TREBLE HOOK

PARTS OF A HOOK

The component parts of a typical hook are the eye, shank, bend, point, barb, throat, and gape (or gap). Hooks are made of high-carbon steel, usually with a corrosion-resistant finish, or of stainless steel.

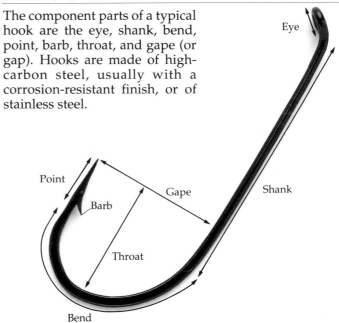

Eye

Point

Barb

Gape

Shank

Throat

Bend

HOOK SIZES

Hook sizes are denoted by numbers, but the number allocated to a particular size of hook may vary from one manufacturer to another. The smallest hook size is the 30, and, as an approximate guide, hooks from size 30 up to size 1 are used for freshwater fishing, and hooks 1/0 up to 16/0 for saltwater fishing. Japanese hooks tend to be a size smaller than European hooks, and importers compensate for this by moving the hooks down one size, so a Japanese size 6 becomes a size 8.

EUROPEAN SIZE 8
Forged heavy wire, round bend

JAPANESE SIZE 6
Medium wire, round bend

JAPANESE SIZE 6
Medium wire, sproat bend

WIRE GAUGES

The diameter, or gauge, of the wire from which a hook is made depends on the hook's pattern and size, but manufacturers now offer a choice of gauges for each pattern and size of hook. Fine-wire hooks are used for light-line fishing and dry flies, and medium-wire hooks for general fishing and most wet flies. Heavy wires are used for very strong hooks for big-game fishing, freshwater fishing for large fish, and heavy flies such as salmon flies and wet flies that are required to sink rapidly through the water.

HEAVY GAUGE

MEDIUM GAUGE

FINE GAUGE

HOOK EYES

Hook eyes come in many different shapes and sizes, and some hooks have spade ends instead of eyes. Flattened shanks were once very popular for hooks tied to nylon, but the labour-intensive whipping and varnishing required is no longer commercially viable when competing with whipped spade-end hooks. Similarly, tapered ring eyes are more expensive to produce than straight-wire ring eyes and are falling out of favour with manufacturers. Straight eyes are very popular with freshwater and sea anglers for bait fishing, and the angle-eyed hooks are popular with fly anglers. When buying a hook, always check that the end of the wire used for forming the eye butts up against the shank; any hook with a gap at the eye should be discarded. A spade-end hook should have no sharp edges at the front of the spade that could cut the nylon when it is pulled tight.

RING EYE
This is a round eye formed from straight wire, and is the most popular type of eye.

TAPERED EYE
The wire is tapered where it meets the shank, giving a neat, unobtrusive eye.

SPADE END
The spade end is formed by flattening the end of the wire.

LOOPED EYE
This very strong eye is used on traditional single salmon hooks.

NEEDLE EYE
The needle eye is used on treble hooks, especially those for tube flies.

SWIVEL EYE
This is used on strong hooks for big game and large sea fish.

Angled eyes
Eyes are formed either straight (in line with the hook) or angled towards or away from the point. The eye of an up-eyed hook is angled away from the point for good clearance between the shank and the point. The down-eyed hook has its eye angled towards the point to give better penetration on the strike.

UP-EYED   STRAIGHT-EYED   DOWN-EYED

GUT EYES
Gut eyes, now obsolete, were formed from gut whipped to the shank before a fly was tied.

HOOK SHANKS

Hooks designed for bait fishing vary less in shape and in shank length than hooks designed for fly fishing, which have to cater for the huge number of different sizes and patterns of fly. Hooks with short or standard-length shanks are used for freshwater bait fishing, but saltwater hooks tend to have long shanks, to accommodate the larger baits used and to protect leaders from the teeth of many species of sea fish. Many large hooks, especially saltwater patterns, have forged shanks and bends. Forging involves hammering the wire of the hook, after it has been shaped, to give it a flattened cross-section. This makes the hook much stronger than one of the same size with an unforged, round cross-section.

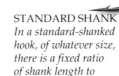

STANDARD SHANK
In a standard-shanked hook, of whatever size, there is a fixed ratio of shank length to gape width.

LONG SHANK
A 2X long-shanked hook has a shank the same length as that of a standard hook two sizes larger.

SHORT SHANK
A 2X short-shanked hook has a shank the same length as that of a standard hook two sizes smaller.

HOOK CROSS-SECTIONS

ROUND WIRE   FORGED WIRE

CURVED SHANK
This shank gives a natural shape to the body of a fly, and is ideal for sedge pupa, midge, and grub patterns.

SLICED SHANK
The slices (barbs) cut into the shank help to hold soft saltwater baits firmly in place on the hook.

HOOKS 2

HOOK BENDS

The shape of the bend is an important distinguishing factor between one hook pattern and another, and as with other features of hooks, such as shank length and eye, a large number of different forms have evolved over the years. The shape of a bend is largely dictated by the intended use of the hook, but in general, a smoothly rounded bend is stronger than one that is sharply angled, while angled bends allow the hook point to penetrate deeper. Some bends are at their best when used for a particular style or method of fishing, but others are more versatile. The Sproat, for example, is an ideal bend for traditional flies, emergers, and dry flies, while the round bend is suitable not only for freshwater and saltwater bait fishing but also for fly hooks.

CRYSTAL BEND
The crystal is a popular bend for freshwater bait fishing, particularly in small sizes.

ROUND BEND
Round bends are used with offset points for bait angling, straight points for fly fishing.

SPROAT
The Sproat is a good fly hook bend. The front angle is not as sharp as that of the crystal.

ABERDEEN
This is a round-bend, fine-wire sea hook with a long shank. It is a good bait hook.

LIMERICK
The Limerick is widely used for freshwater and saltwater hooks and for salmon hooks.

KENDAL ROUND
This is a slightly less rounded, more angular version of the ordinary round bend.

SHRIMP BEND
This long bend is designed for humpbacked flies such as shrimp and bug patterns.

TIEMCO
This has a slightly curved shank and a straight point, and is ideal for emerger and dry-fly patterns.

O'SHAUGNESSY
The O'Shaughnessy is a classic and very strong bend for heavy sea fish, including big-game species.

SPECIMEN BEND
A modern bend, used with an offset point, for freshwater and saltwater bait fishing.

HOOK SHAPES

The overall shape of a hook is its style of bend, point, shank, and eye. Freshwater bait hooks tend to have offset points with short or standard straight shanks, and are either eyed or spade end. The "weedless" hook has a spring-loaded wire guard that shields the point to prevent it snagging in weed. For saltwater bait fishing, the hooks are eyed and usually have longer shanks than those used for freshwater work. The very popular O'Shaughnessy, Kirby, and Aberdeen patterns are good examples of saltwater bait hooks. The majority of fly anglers use up-eyed or down-eyed hooks with straight points, straight shanks of various lengths, and a variety of bends.

KEVIN MADDOCKS CARP HOOK **SWIMMING NYMPH** **KEEL HOOK**

SALMON SINGLE **TERRESTRIAL HOOK** **ABERDEEN**

PIGGYBACK **BEAKED CARP** **STREAMER HOOK**

HOOK POINTS

Hook points vary with the different patterns and from manufacturer to manufacturer; cut hollow and superior points, for example, are typical of the Mustad range of hooks. Most hooks have cut or knife-edge points because these are easier to mass-produce than ground points. The outer edge of the hollow point is straight, while the inner line between the point and the tip of the barb is curved. With the superior point this arrangement is reversed and the outer edge is slightly curved while the inner edge is straight. A Dublin point, found on many salmon hooks, has features of both, and the point curves away from the shank. Some of the best and strongest points, however, are the ground and chemically sharpened needle points with fine-cut barbs that are produced in Japan.

BARBLESS
A point without a barb allows easy unhooking so is ideal for catch-and-release fishing.

HOLLOW POINT
This cut point is used on many of the wide range of hooks produced by Mustad of Norway.

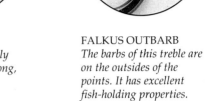

DUBLIN
This point originated in Dublin and is used on salmon "irons" and game fishing hooks.

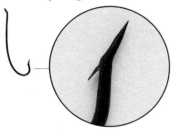

ARROWPOINT
The arrowpoint does not penetrate as easily as a standard barbless point, but it is claimed to hold fish better.

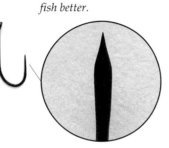

BEAKED
This ground, chemically sharpened point is strong, and penetrates well, because its barb is not deeply cut.

FALKUS OUTBARB
The barbs of this treble are on the outsides of the points. It has excellent fish-holding properties.

OFFSET POINTS

Hook points not only vary in shape but also are either straight or offset. To determine whether a point is straight or offset, check the alignment of the point to the shank. If the point is straight, it will be in line with the shank. An offset point will point either to the left, which is known as kirbed, or to the right, which is reversed. Straight points are ideal for fly fishing, but offset points are better for bait fishing. The most popular offset is the reversed, because most anglers are right-handed: for them, it is easier to bait a hook with a reversed point than one with a kirbed point, because the point is angled upwards when the hook is held in the right hand.

OFFSET LEFT/ KIRBED

OFFSET/RIGHT REVERSED

HOOK FAULTS

UNFORMED EYES

POOR BRAZING

OVERCUT BARB

OVERLONG POINT

Common hook faults include unformed eyes, poor brazing, overcut barbs, poor temper, and overlong points. Most will be obvious, but poor temper may be difficult to detect. Carefully hook the point behind your thumbnail and pull the hook to open the bend. An under-tempered hook will bend out easily and not spring back when released; an overtempered hook will snap.

HOOK FINISHES

Hooks come in a variety of coloured and corrosion-resistant finishes for different styles of fishing. The traditional black japanned finish is still used on some patterns, particularly salmon hooks, but the most unobtrusive colour is bronze, and most hooks are now coated with a bronze finish. Some salt-water hooks are made of stainless steel, which is left uncoated because it is almost totally resistant to the corrosive properties of seawater. Other saltwater hooks are sometimes coloured silver so that they attract fish to the bait.

JAPANNED

NIFLOR

GOLD

COLOURED

BRONZED

SILVERED

FRESHWATER WEIGHTS

The great many sizes and designs of weight are used to perform a variety of functions, from cocking a float to anchoring a legered bait. In the past, almost all weights were made of lead, but in many countries the use of lead weights has been banned or restricted for environmental reasons. In the United Kingdom, for example, all leger weights weighing up to 28 g (1 oz) and split shot between sizes 6 and SSG (swan shot) must be made of non-toxic materials, so leger weights in the affected sizes are usually steel, zinc, or brass, and split shot is made of tungsten or heavy alloys.

CORK-BASED PLUMMET

CLIP-ON PLUMMET

PLUMMETS
These are used in float fishing to find the depth of the swim. With a cork-based plummet, the line is threaded through an eye and the hook embedded in a cork strip at the base; a clip-on plummet has spring-loaded jaws that clamp over the hook.

SSG (SWAN SHOT)

AA

BB

No. 1

No. 4

No. 8

No. 10

No. 12

SPLIT SHOT
Split shot are versatile weights, being used in float fishing to lock eyed floats in position, to cock floats, and to add weight to rigs. In legering, shot are used to lock larger weights in position and to weight light rigs. They are available in a range of sizes from swan shot (SSG) – so called because this size was used in shotgun cartridges when swans were the shooters' quarry – down to "dust" shot (sizes from 8 down to 12). As a rule of thumb, two split shot of any one size are roughly equal in weight to one shot of the size above (see page 222). Always use a finger and thumb, never your teeth, to close shot over the line. Never slide them along the line when altering their position: this causes abrasion and frictional heat that can damage and weaken the line. Open them up with a thumbnail and then reposition them.

TUBE SHOT
These thin, flexible tubes, made of polymer and tungsten, are less likely to snag than shot, and are a good alternative when seed baits are being used: fish often nibble at the shot instead of the bait. They are cut to length with scissors, threaded on the line, and locked in place with tiny shot.

LEADED WIRE
Like tube shot, leaded wire is a good alternative to split shot when float fishing with seed baits. To cock the float, the wire can be twisted directly around its base, or wound around a matchstick then threaded onto the line beneath the float and held in place by a small shot.

PUTTY WEIGHT
This heavy, puttylike material was an early alternative to lead shot, but its use declined when satisfactory non-lead shot was developed. It is now used mainly by carp anglers as a casting weight and to balance the weight of baits for improved presentation.

DRILLED BULLETS
A drilled bullet is used to present a moving bait. It will roll freely through a fast-flowing swim, pulling the bait towards fish holding station in the flow.

HILLMAN
This is used in spinning to take the lure down farther in deep or swift-flowing water, and to help reduce line twist. This weight should be clipped to the eye of the swivel to which the main line tied.

OLIVETTES
These tiny, streamlined weights originated in France, and are used in pole fishing. The smallest, the size 4/0, weighs just 0.081 g (0.003 oz); the largest, the size 12, weighs 3 g (0.106 oz).

BARREL
The barrel weight is designed to roll slowly along the bed of a river to present a moving bait. The line is threaded through the weight's hollow body.

COFFIN WEIGHTS
The coffin weight was designed for presenting static baits in running water. Its flattened shape and sharp edges ensure that it sits tight on the bottom, digging itself into gravel or silt. The line is threaded into a hole drilled down the centre of the weight.

DISC WEIGHTS
These flattened, almost-circular weights will keep baits static in fast-flowing swims. Being flat, a disc weight offers little resistance to the current flowing over it when it is lying on the riverbed, while its large surface area gives it a good grip on the bottom. It is attached to the rig by a swivel, which minimizes the risk of tangling during casting.

SPHERICAL BOMB
This is often used on bolt rigs. It should be attached by a short link of weak line, so that if a hooked fish runs into a snag such as thick weed, the weight will break off. Without the weak link, the reel line may break first, leaving the fish tethered to the snag and condemned to a lingering death.

ARLESEY BOMBS
These were devised by Richard Walker in the 1950s, for catching big fish at long range in deep water. The streamlined shape makes them easy to cast long distances, and their swivel attachments reduce the risk of tangling. Today, they are probably the most widely used of all leger weights, and are as suitable for quivertipping on a river as they are for fishing at long range for perch or carp. They are available in sizes ranging from 3.5 g (1/8 oz) to 113 g (4 oz), and some incorporate a screw-in swivel that allows the size of weight being used on a rig to be changed rapidly.

BOTTLE WEIGHTS
This clever design allows the weight on the line to be changed quickly. A piece of silicone rubber tubing is attached to the line by a snaplock swivel, and a bottle-shaped weight is inserted into its lower end. The weight can be changed simply by pulling it out of the silicone tubing and replacing it with one that is the same size but either lighter or heavier.

WYE
Like the Hillman weight, the Wye is used in spinning to add weight to a lure and to overcome the problem of line twist produced by a revolving lure. Many anglers prefer it to the spiral weight, also used in spinning, which has a tendency to fall off the line. Its shape is not as aerodynamic as that of the spiral, but it casts well enough.

SPIRAL WEIGHT
This is used on spinning rigs to add weight and prevent line twists. It is attached to the reel line above the swivel that joins the line to the lure or leader. The line is wrapped tightly around the body of the weight (in the spiral channel) and through the spirals of wire at each end. The aerodynamic shape of the weight gives good casting distance.

FLAT-BOTTOMED WEIGHT
This type of weight is used mainly in carp fishing. Its flattened shape helps it to rise quickly from the bed and plane through the water when retrieved, and makes it less prone to snagging.

TROLLING WEIGHT
(right)
Trolling weights can weigh up to 1.36 kg (3 lb), and are used to get the bait down quickly in deep water. They are simply lowered into the water, so a streamlined shape is not necessary.

BUZZ BOMB *(right)*
The buzz bomb is a variation of the Arlesey bomb incorporating fins that reduce wobble during flight. It can be cast with consistent accuracy over distances of about 90 m (100 yds) or more.

SALTWATER WEIGHTS & BOOMS

Sea angling often involves coping with strong tidal currents, deep waters, and long casting distances. To avoid problems, make sure you have enough weight on the line to get the bait down and hold it in position, and use standoff booms to prevent traces (leaders) from tangling. In addition, you can minimize the risk of damage to baits during long-distance casting by using devices such as impact shields and bait clips.

WEIGHTS

In general, a weight or sinker is anything an angler cares to put on the end of a line to take it to the bottom. For example, shore anglers fishing heavy ground, where there is a high risk of snagging, often use cheap, expendable sinkers such as old sparkplugs instead of purpose-made weights. It is, however, usually best to use a weight that has been designed for use in the prevailing conditions and for the type of fishing intended.

EXTENDED-NOSE BREAKAWAY

STANDARD BREAKAWAY

BREAKAWAY ADAPTER

LONG-TAILED BREAKAWAY
(with clip-on lifter)

BREAKAWAY SINKERS
The wires of a breakaway sinker dig into the seabed to anchor the bait. They are clipped against the sinker body, and on the retrieve they spring free and trail behind for a snagless return. The extended-nose and long-tailed versions give good grip at short range or in deep water, making them suitable for uptide fishing; the plastic breakaway adapter can be used in tandem with a standard breakaway for increased grip.

BOOMS

Nylon traces tend to tangle, and baits dropped from a boat often spiral as they fall, wrapping their traces around the main line. Mounting the traces on carefully spaced booms will reduce these problems. Droppers (short traces) suspended from booms spaced above the weight are good for shore fishing when large numbers of small fish are sought, because they present multiple baits in the best possible way.

BREAKAWAY BOOMS *(right)*
These booms, attached to the line by beads, are used as flying collar booms and as dropper booms. When bottom drifting, however, they can get choked with sand, which can stop them sliding.

UPTIDE BOOM

DOWNTIDE BOOM

COX & RAWLE BOOMS *(above)*
These sliding booms are used to carry sinkers on flowing traces. They can also be used to attach traces to the main line when bottom fishing with live sandeels, and when fishing imitation sandeels on flying collar rigs.

STANDOFF BOOM

STANDOFF BOOM
(attached with boom bead)

RELAY CLIP
This is attached to the rig to help hold the bait in place and to prevent it breaking apart during casting.

COX & RAWLE STANDOFF BOOMS *(left)*
These are excellent standoff pivoting booms, some requiring beads and stoppers to position them on the line, others with built-in locking fixtures. They are useful for shore angling, and for boat work when small fish are expected.

BREAKAWAY QUICK-FIX

BREAKAWAY PIVOT BOOM

BOOM BEADS

PIVOT BEAD

ROUND BOMB
This is ideal for slow downrigger trolling. It can also be used for bottom fishing, but it tends to roll.

WYE
The streamlined shape of this lure-fishing weight makes it ideal for distance-casting spinners and rubber eels and for getting them down deep.

TORPEDO
Because of its flat sides, this beach sinker is less likely to roll in the current than rounded weights.

PIERCED BALL
This is used for weighting slider float tackle and for helping get large deadbaits down when freelining.

WEIGHT LIFTER
On a fast retrieve with the rod held high, this plastic vane rises in the water. This helps to lift the sinker clear of heavy snags close to your feet.

SPIRAL WEIGHT
This is designed for use with cast or trolled lures. Because the line is simply wrapped around it, its position can be altered quickly and easily. It can also be used to sink slowly trolled livebaits.

UPTIDE WEIGHT
(left)
This weight is favoured by uptiders because its long nose wires give exceptional grip in fierce currents. The wires dig into the bed to anchor the bait, but pull out easily when a fish picks it up, and they spring readily out of snags.

BOMB
The bomb is the best shape for beating snags and tide, and good for working a constantly moving bait from the beach.

SLIDING LINK
Attaching a flowing trace to the main line by a sliding link (or a sliding boom) allows it to move without taking the sinker with it, which could cause a fish to drop the bait.

BELL WEIGHT
This can be used from an anchored boat, but is not the best shape for drift fishing.

WATCH WEIGHT
This is a useful grip sinker for short-range beach work and drift fishing over banks.

PLASTIC BOOM

IMPACT SHIELD
This is similar to the bait clip but offers even more protection to the bait. As well as holding the bait securely during casting, it shields it from impact damage when it hits the water.

PLASTIC BOOMS
These are plastic versions of the French boom. Some types have three or four "teeth", around which the line is wrapped to hold them in place, others have eyelets, through which the line is threaded, and are locked in place with swivels or beads.

PLASTIC BOOM

SHAKESPEARE SEA BOOM

SHAKESPEARE SEA BOOM
This boom is excellent for a flying collar pollack rig, or for presenting live sandeels on the bottom for turbot and bass. Because it curves upward, it cannot become blocked by sand and prevented from sliding when fished on the drift.

FRENCH BOOM
The wire French boom has been superseded to some extent by the plastic varieties, but because it is stronger for direct trace tying it is still widely used by wreck anglers for flying collar rigs.

FRENCH BOOM

61

FLOATS

Floats are extremely sensitive and versatile bite indicators, and much more pleasing to watch than a rod tip. Although they are available in a staggeringly wide variety of materials, shapes, sizes, and colours, all floats have been designed to perform specific tasks.

BALSAS
These floats, made entirely of balsa wood, are superior to stick floats in windy conditions and fast-flowing swims. Fish them close in and attach them top and bottom to the line. They tend to lift out of the water if held back too hard, due to the inherent buoyancy of the balsa wood.

LOAFERS
Made either from hollow plastic or balsa, loafers are very buoyant and designed to fish swift, turbulent waters. They should be attached top and bottom.

POLYWAGS

SWINGERS

POLYWAGS AND SWINGERS
These are ideal for stillwater use where ripples, rather than waves, are being created on the surface by the wind. Both patterns are fished bottom-end only, and a short distance beyond the rod tip.

DRIFTBEATERS
The ideal floats for stillwater fishing in strong winds, when there are big waves on the water. They are fished bottom-end only.

CRYSTAL
AVONS

WIRE
AVONS

AVONS
These floats, attached top and bottom, can present baits in quite turbulent streams and be fished at longer range than stick floats.

BIG
STICK

STICK

STABLE
STICK

WIRE
STICK

STICKS
A stick float is at its best in smoothly flowing swims, attached top and bottom and fished close in. The upper part of the float is made of balsa.

ONIONS
These floats are designed for use in stillwaters, in all but the strongest of winds, and in swims at fairly close range (up to several rod lengths).

BLUES

GREYS

DARTS

BLUES, GREYS, AND DARTS
These are fished bottom-end only and are at their best on stillwaters and canals.

GIANTS

CANAL

INSERT

BODIED

CRYSTALS
Crystals are made of clear plastic, and designed for use in clear, shallow water where wary fish might regard the arrival in the swim of a solid-coloured float as highly suspicious and a sign of danger. They are equally effective on still and slow-flowing waters.

PEACOCKS
Quills taken from the tail feathers of peacocks make superb floats. The quills are long and straight, very light, and completely waterproof. Floats made from the thicker ends of quills are buoyant in turbulent water and easily visible at a distance, while those produced from the thinner ends will be more sensitive to delicate bites.

WAGGLERS
All wagglers are attached to the line bottom-end only, and are designed for use on stillwaters and slow- to medium-paced rivers. They are made from a variety of materials including peacock quill, sarcandas reed, plastic, and balsa.

LOADED
These floats have weighted bases. Their increased weight means that they can be cast greater distances and do not need shotted lines.

ZOOMERS
The zoomer was developed by match anglers for catching wary fish in shallow swims at long distances. It consists of a cane stem with a big balsa body and a brass stem insert at the base. It should be attached top and bottom, and is at its best in light winds on wide rivers and stillwaters.

NIGHT FLOATS
These floats are used for night fishing. They are fitted with Betalights, which are transparent tubes filled with a luminous gas. They will glow for 20 to 30 years.

POLE FLOATS
Floats for pole fishing tend to be small, often with thin bristle tops, to show up the most delicate of bites.

PIKE FLOATS
Most pike floats are built for slider fishing, being either hollow or fitted with eyes. Some, equipped with a dartlike vane above the tip, are designed to catch the wind and take the bait long distances from the bank, to predatory fish lying beyond casting range.

BITE INDICATORS & ROD RESTS

Bite indicators are used primarily in legering, where there is no float to indicate that a fish has taken the bait. Bites can be indicated simply by movement of the rod tip, but often this is not sensitive enough and some other form of indication is needed. This can be a swingtip, springtip, or quivertip fitted to the rod tip, or a device such as a bobbin or electronic alarm that indicates any movement of the line. Rod rests are used when it is not necessary to hold the rod all of the time, for instance when bites are expected to be infrequent, and when two rods are in use at the same time.

DROP-OFF ARM *(left)*
This was developed for pike fishing. The end with the indicator ball clips to the line and the hinged end is attached to the rear rod rest. When a bite occurs, the line pulls free and the end with the ball drops down.

BOBBINS *(right)*
A bobbin is attached to the line between the reel and the butt ring. If a fish takes the bait and moves away, the bobbin climbs towards the rod; if the fish moves towards the bank, the bobbin drops towards the ground.

BELL *(right)*
A bell clipped to the rod tip gives an audible indication of a bite. The use of bells has declined greatly, but they are occasionally used by freshwater anglers and more commonly by sea anglers fishing from beaches and piers.

ELECTRONIC ALARM *(left)*
An electronic bite alarm sounds an audible warning when a fish takes the bait. The line is passed over a sensitive antenna, or a flanged wheel, which triggers the alarm when the line is pulled by a taking fish. The type shown here is designed to be screwed to a bankstick in place of a front rod rest.

SWINGTIP, SPRINGTIP, AND QUIVERTIP *(right)*
These screw into the threaded tip rings found on most leger rods. The swingtip hangs at an angle and indicates bites by lifting or dropping back. The springtip is similar, but has a sprung base. This holds it in line with the rod but acts like a hinge when a bite occurs, allowing the tip to swing down. A quivertip simply acts as a very sensitive extension of the rod tip.

SPRINGTIP

SWINGTIP

QUIVERTIP

MONKEY CLIMBER *(right)*
This is a bobbin that slides freely up and down a shaft pushed into the bank. It is used in the same way as an ordinary bobbin, but is much less likely to give false indications in windy conditions. When a strike is made, the line pulls out of the bobbin clip.

BANKSTICK (below)
This is a spiked metal rod with a threaded top to take a screw-on rod rest head or electronic bite alarm. Most are 60 to 90 cm (2 to 3 ft) long, but telescopic models that extend to 1.2 m (4 ft) are also available.

T-BAR (left)
T-bars double the rod-holding capacity of a pair of banksticks. Instead of screwing a rod rest head onto each bankstick, a T-bar is screwed on and a rod rest is fitted to each end of it.

ROD REST HEADS
Rod rests consist of rest heads screwed onto banksticks, and are normally used in pairs, one supporting the rod ahead of the reel, and the other supporting the rod butt. The rest heads are available in a variety of shapes and sizes to suit different angling styles.

SANDSPIKE (left)
Sandspikes, or monopods, are used by beach anglers to hold their rods upright during the often lengthy intervals between bites. They hold either one or two rods, and have sharp points that can be driven deep into the sand to provide stability.

TRIPOD (right)
Tripod rod rests, especially those with adjustable telescopic legs, are very stable. They are available with single or double rest heads, and are widely used by shore anglers fishing from shingle beaches and harbour walls.

POLE REST (above)
This type can be used either as a front rest or a rear rest. It has a V-shaped section to support the pole when it is used as a front rest, and an inverted V-section to prevent the butt from rising when it is used as the rear rest.

LANDING TACKLE

Every angler has a duty to play, land, unhook, and probably return his catch as gently and carefully as possible. Don't bully a fish during the battle, but equally importantly don't let it fight to the point of total exhaustion. Once it is in the net, hold the fish actually in the water while the hook is slipped free with a pair of forceps. A quick photograph can then be taken just above the waterline before the fish is supported in the water to recover. Barbless hooks are less harmful to the fish, and your landing net should be large enough for the job in hand. Don't weigh a fish until it is absolutely necessary, and remember that every second out of the water causes the fish stress. If the catch is to be eaten, then dispatch it immediately, even before the hook is removed, to avoid prolonging its discomfort.

CAPTURED FOR POSTERITY
If at all possible, always hold the fish in this manner for a trophy shot. Notice how it is held fractionally above the waterline. This means if it struggles free it will not harm itself by falling onto a hard bank. Also, continual immersion in water keeps the fish unstressed and healthy.

TRIANGULAR SPECIMEN NET
This type of net has two rigid arms of solid glass fibre, mounted on a nylon spreader block and connected at their tips by a nylon cord. The nylon net mesh is deep, soft, and knotless, and can accommodate large fish, such as specimen-sized carp, pike, and catfish.

TRIANGULAR PAN NET
This small, shallow net is designed for match fishing and general freshwater angling for small to medium-sized fish. The frame folds up for easy stowing.

FLY ANGLER'S NET
This compact net is popular with anglers who fly fish by wading, or from float tubes, as both methods allow the fish to be brought close to hand. It has a wooden frame and soft, knotless mesh.

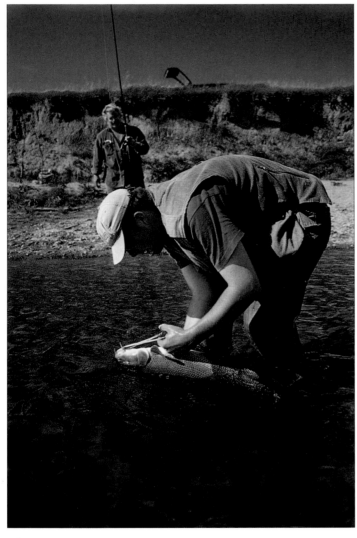

KEPT IN THE WATER
Notice how this angler is supporting the fish in the water over the landing net while unhooking it. This is especially important in hot conditions, when oxygen levels are low and recuperation periods are longer. When bringing a fish to the net, always keep the net still and lead the fish in towards it. Chasing a fighting fish with the landing net scares it into renewed runs and can lead to breakages.

CAREFUL HANDLING
This proud angler is holding his catch expertly. The head is in the water so the gills can still operate. Also his hands support the fish well away from the stomach area where all the delicate organs are located. Hold your fish like this, with its head facing upstream, until you feel it start to flex its muscles, and then allow it to swim away into the current.

FORCEPS
A pair of surgical forceps is an essential unhooking tool for any angler fishing anywhere. They give a really secure hold on the hook shank so that the point can be slipped free easily and quickly.

67

TACKLE BOXES

Tackle boxes fall into two broad categories: the small type, in which you can carry a selection of lures, flies, floats, or other small items when you are actually fishing, and the large, capacious type, in which you can store all your small tackle when it is not in use. Many anglers use improvised tackle boxes, adapted from containers ranging from cigar boxes to toolboxes, but in general there is no substitute for a purpose-made storage system. Wooden tackle boxes look nice, but are heavy and need to be cared for, so most anglers choose plastic or aluminium boxes, which are light, strong, and water resistant.

SEAT BOXES

These are large tackle boxes that double as seats. They are used mainly by freshwater anglers who fish with float or leger tackle and spend long periods fishing one swim. Most have two sections, one large and deep for storing bulky items such as groundbait, and one with drawers that take small items such as floats, sinkers, rigs, and hooks.

SHAKESPEARE/SNOWBEE SPECIMEN TACKLE BOX *(right)*
This is a good example of the cantilever type of tackle box, which offers good storage capacity, gives easy access to the contents when opened out, and is compact when closed. It is made in two-tone green plastic, and has three trays with movable dividers so that the compartment sizes can be adjusted to suit individual requirements. It is also available in one-, two-, and six-tray versions.

FOX BOX *(below)*
This plastic fly box will hold up to 66 dry flies, and its rubberized lining will not retain moisture, which could rust their hooks. The clips are designed to hold the flies securely without crushing their delicate hackles.

WOODEN FLOAT BOX *(below)*
Made of varnished hardwood, this simple, three-tray float box has foam strip inserts, in which you can cut slits to hold the ends of the floats.

RICHARD WHEATLEY FLY BOX MODEL 4607F *(right)*
The lid of this tough aluminium fly box is lined with closed-cell plastic foam, into which wet flies and nymphs can be hooked, and its base contains 16 dry-fly compartments with individual, spring-loaded plastic lids.

RICHARD WHEATLEY TUBE-FLY BOX *(right)*
Tube flies require special boxes for proper storage. Some tube-fly boxes have a row of needles over which the flies are slipped, but this one has bullet-shaped indentations to hold up to 28 of them. The loose treble hooks can be stuck into the foam lining.

FLY-TYING MATERIALS CASE (below)
This type of box is used by fly fishers who tie flies at the waterside to match the insects that the fish are feeding on. The model shown here has a hardwood block, which clips to the side to provide a base for a fly vice, and materials can be stored in both the base and the lid.

SHAKESPEARE/SNOWBEE LURE BOX (right)
The upright dividers in this box have slots in their top edges to take the hooks of plugs, spinners, and spoons. Hanging lures by their hooks prevents tangling, and the divider positions are adjustable to cope with lures of different sizes.

FLAMBEAU TOP FORCE MODEL 7680 (left)
This briefcase-size tackle/lure box has a hinged top lid, and a fixed tackle tray with a sliding drawer in the base. In addition, the front face of the lid is hinged to permit access to the drawer without opening the whole lid.

PLANO 757 (above)
The Plano 757 is one of the largest tackle chests on the market, and is best used as a base from which to load smaller tackle boxes for use at the waterside. It is ideal for long fishing trips when you need a lot of gear: leave it in the car, or in your hotel room, tent, or cabin. If you are boat fishing, take it on the boat with you.

FOOTWEAR

Good footwear is an essential part of any angler's equipment. Whichever type you choose, it should give a secure grip on slippery surfaces, and be both comfortable and suitable for the prevailing conditions. For example, lightweight boots are excellent during the warm summer months, but in cold winter weather you need boots with thick, insulated soles to keep your feet warm. Similarly, waders with lightweight uppers that can be folded down, transforming them into boots for walking to and from the water, are ideal for summer use. But when wading for salmon or trout in the springtime, when the water can be extremely cold, you need thick, thermally insulated waders.

TYPES OF SOLE

Felt soles
Felt soles provide the best grip of all on wet, slippery surfaces, and have the advantage of being quiet, so you can wade without scaring fish.

Studded soles
These are excellent for walking across wet grass or mud banks, but are noisy and do not give as much grip as felt soles do on slippery underwater stones.

Rubber soles
Rubber soles are usually cheaper than felt or studded soles. They give reasonably good grip on grass or mud but are less effective on rocks.

AIR-GRIP KNEE BOOTS (left)
These fully waterproof, knee-length boots are 43 cm (17 in) high and made of nylon-lined rubber. The cushioned soles provide insulation and comfort, and the top straps can be tightened for a snug fit to stop stones, leaves, and other debris from getting in.

EDINGTON WELLY-WADERS (left)
These boots have thin, lightweight wader uppers that can be folded down to below the knee when not required. They can thus be used both as waders and as boots for walking along the bank. The wader uppers should be kept away from snags such as thorns and barbed wire.

SKEE-TEX INSULATED KNEE BOOTS (above)
Insulated knee boots such as these are widely used by winter anglers who choose to sit on the bank and fish in one swim all day. The thick, insulated soles prevent cold from creeping up into the boot and chilling the feet, and because the insulation is so good, a pair of ordinary socks is sufficient to keep feet warm.

ORVIS GREEN MOUNTAIN THIGH BOOTS (above)
These rubber thigh boots have non-slip felt soles, and wader uppers made of lightweight, laminated PVC. In warm weather, the uppers can be folded down and held in clips to allow air to circulate around the legs.

ORVIS LIGHTWEIGHT BOOT-FOOT CHEST WADERS (below)

These waders, made of nylon with all the seams sealed, weigh only 340 g (12 oz) and can be rolled up very small to tuck into the corner of a tackle bag until needed. They are ideal for use in warm weather, and highly resistant to punctures and abrasion.

ORVIS GRAVEL GUARDS (above)

Gravel guards are fixed around the tops of ordinary boots, in effect making them higher, and prevent stones from getting inside. Stones inside boots are uncomfortable, and if they are not removed they may cut into the soles.

ORVIS LIGHTWEIGHT WADING SHOES (below)

The moulded, one-piece heel and sole design of these shoes, and their felt covering, provide excellent stability when wading on slippery riverbeds. In addition, foam-padded insoles, hard toes, and padded ankle collars give good protection on rough ground.

ORVIS GRIP STABIL-ICERS FITTED TO BOOT

ORVIS GUIDEWEIGHT STOCKING-FOOT CHEST WADERS (above)

Being made of nylon and thick neoprene foam, these waders provide comfort and warmth even in icy waters, such as those endured by early-spring salmon anglers. They feature reinforced knees, a handwarmer pocket, and quick-release buckles, and all the seams are sealed. Unlike boot-foot waders, which are a combination of boots and waders, stocking-foot waders do not have tough soles and must be worn with wading shoes.

ORVIS GRIP STABIL-ICERS (above)

These are fitted to the soles of boots, boot-foot waders, or wading shoes to give extra grip when walking on ice or slopes of wet grass or mud. They are also reasonably effective on slippery rocks.

71

Vests & Jackets

The great advantage of fishing vests is that an array of small but essential items of tackle can be carried in their multiple pockets. This makes them very useful in any form of angling where mobility is important, including fly fishing, lure fishing, and stalking freshwater fish such as carp. Most vests are short, so that they do not trail on the water during wading, but longer-length designs are also available for anglers who usually fish from the bank. These keep the lower back area covered, and so in cool weather they are more comfortable to wear than short vests.

Jackets made of traditional materials, such as waxed cotton, are still available, but most are made of lightweight, waterproof, synthetic fabrics (see page 74). These jackets "breathe" to prevent condensation building up inside them, need no reproofing, are fully washable, and can be rolled up and tucked away in a corner of a tackle bag, to be forgotten until the rain comes. Some have detachable linings, and can be used comfortably all year round.

WYCHWOOD FOUR SEASONS (right)
This multi-pocketed vest is designed for use in cool weather. It is made of a polyester/cotton mix with a fleecy lining, and is cut long to ensure that the small of the back is protected from draughts in cold winds. Its features include a rugged two-way zip that can be opened from the bottom to prevent constriction when sitting in a boat, pockets in a variety of sizes, a scissors retainer, and two landing net rings.

ORVIS SUPER TAC-L-PAK (below)
This vest is virtually a wearable tackle bag, with no less than 35 pockets to carry almost everything an angler might need, from a pair of scissors to a set of lightweight waterproofs. Made of a tough polyester/cotton mix, it features a yoke collar for good weight distribution, wide-cut shoulders, and oversize armholes, and it is cut short for deep wading.

STEADE-FAST BAIT SMOCK (above)
Designed for match fishing, the Steade-fast bait smock is light and supple for ample freedom of movement, and has adjustable, quick-release side fastenings for easy fitting and removal. There are two bait pockets, the larger sporting a rain flap to ensure that its contents remain dry in bad weather, three other pockets designed to carry a range of terminal tackle and rigs, and a loop to hold a catapult handle.

SHAKESPEARE SAFETY VEST (below)
This light, comfortable fly-fishing vest doubles as a buoyancy aid should a mishap occur while boat fishing or walking the bank. It can be inflated instantly by pulling a toggle to activate a replaceable carbon dioxide cartridge, and can also be inflated by mouth. It has numerous pockets, a D-ring for scissors, and a loop to carry a landing net.

MUSTO HIGHLANDS JACKET *(right)*
The Highlands jacket has a waterproof Gore-Tex liner between its polyester/cotton outer shell and its inner lining, and can be cleaned in a domestic washing machine. It has a two-way zip for comfort when sitting down, plenty of generously cut pockets, and a built-in waterproof flap to sit on. A hood and a zip-in waistcoat are available as extras.

HARDY WAXED WADING JACKET *(below)*
Designed primarily for use with chest waders, this waist-length jacket has generously cut sleeves for easy casting and features two breast pockets and internal pockets. It is made of waxed Egyptian cotton, with a smart tartan lining, and is fully waterproof, but like all waxed clothing it eventually needs reproofing to prevent water from seeping through it.

NOMAD ⅝ RANGER *(above)*
This five-eighths-length jacket has a stretch cord and toggles at the waist, so that its weight is carried on the hips rather than the shoulders, and its sleeves are generously cut to give unrestricted movement when casting. It is machine-washable and has plenty of pockets, a permanently attached hood, two handwarmer pockets, a double storm flap, and a two-slider main zip.

WATERPROOFS

In the past, the big drawback of most waterproof clothing was that perspiration would condense inside it, making it uncomfortable to wear. The fabrics tended to be heavy, were often difficult to clean, and required regular reproofing, often with waxes that would leave marks on car seats. These problems have been eliminated by the use of new fabrics and proofing processes, and modern waterproofs are comfortable to wear and easy to care for. The use of "breathable" fabrics, which have microscopic pores that prevent water getting in but allow water vapour to escape, has solved the condensation problem, and clothing made from these fabrics is light, washable, needs no reproofing, and does not stain car seats.

ORVIS EASY-ON-AND-OFF OVERTROUSERS (below)
These lightweight, waterproof overtrousers can be rolled up and tucked away in a pocket or bag until needed, and the zips at the bottoms of the legs allow you to put them on or take them off without removing your shoes. Made of nylon waterproofed with polyurethane, they are ideal for bank fishing on showery days and for boat fishing in choppy water. They are also thornproof, so they will protect your trousers if you are pushing through high bankside vegetation when stalking fish.

WYCHWOOD ONE-PIECE
THERMAL SUIT (above)
This light, fully waterproof, one-piece suit has a heat-retaining thermal lining, and is also breathable to prevent condensation. It has a high, protective collar and a zip-on hood, and is ideal for static fishing in cold weather.

WYCHWOOD THERMAL BIB & BRACE (*below*)
In the cooler months of the year, a cold draught in the small of the back can be most uncomfortable and spoil a day's fishing. A bib and brace eliminates this problem, and when teamed with a jacket is more versatile than a one-piece suit. The Wychwood Thermal Bib & Brace is made of a lightweight, thermally lined polyester/cotton mix that has been made fully waterproof and breathable. It has ample pocket space and its two side zips make it easy to put on and take off.

MAINSTREAM SURVIVAL FLOTATION SUIT (*above*)
This is an insulated and waterproof, but not breathable, one-piece suit designed for use at sea. As well as providing protection from spray and the weather, it acts as a buoyancy aid should the wearer be unfortunate enough to fall in (but is not an alternative to a lifejacket). It is produced in a bright red material for maximum visibility. Velcro straps at the ends of the sleeves and legs allow wrists and ankles to be kept snug, and a simple hood, permanently attached, folds up and tucks inside the collar.

HATS, GLOVES, & SUNGLASSES

A suitable hat will keep your head dry in wet weather, cool in summer, and (probably most importantly) warm in winter: in cold weather, you can lose 30 per cent or more of your body heat through your head if it is not covered.

A pair of warm gloves or mittens, preferably waterproof, should always be a part of your outfit in inclement winter weather. Having cold and aching fingers can be very uncomfortable, and makes it difficult to set up your tackle and to use it properly. Gloves are also useful when handling sharp-toothed or sharp-spined fish.

Polarized sunglasses cut out reflected glare from the surface, which helps you to spot fish more easily in clear water. They can also protect your eyes from badly cast hooks – whether your own or someone else's – especially when fly fishing.

SHAKESPEARE OPTI-SHIELDS
The frames of these polarized sunglasses are shaped to provide top shade, and the tinted side panels offer extra protection from miscast flies.

ASSET NIGHT VISION GLASSES
These glasses give enhanced contrast in poor light conditions, which makes them a useful form of eye protection when fly fishing at dusk.

ASSET HALF-EYE MAGNIFIERS
Available in a range of magnification strengths, these are useful when you are performing intricate tasks such as tying on flies at the waterside.

ORVIS NEOPRENE GLOVES
Neoprene is an excellent glove material, providing both warmth and resistance to water. These neoprene gloves are nylon lined, to make them easy to take off and pull on, and have adjustable Velcro closures at the wrist to ensure a snug fit.

GUL NEOPRENE GLOVES
These gloves are designed to keep hands warm and dry in the foulest of weather. They are also supple and flexible, allowing the freedom of movement that is essential when, for example, you are tying knots or unhooking lively fish.

DAIWA SHOWERPROOF SPLIT-PALM MITTENS
The split-palm design of these fully lined mittens permits the end sections to be folded back to expose the fingers. This is useful when setting up tackle and when sensitive control is required, for instance during casting.

DAIWA THERMAL FINGERLESS MITTS
Fingerless mitts keep hands warm but leave fingers free for fiddly tasks such as controlling the line as it leaves the reel, and making up or adjusting terminal rigs. These Daiwa mitts have elasticated wrists for a snug, draught-free fit.

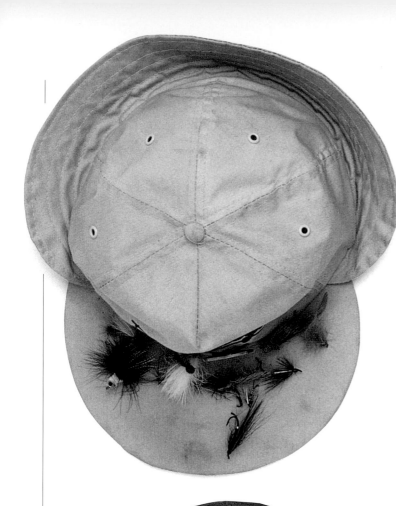

UP-DOWNER *(left)*
This lightweight hat is similar in style to those that were worn by the French Foreign Legion in North Africa, having a large visor to shade the eyes and a back-flap to cover the nape of the neck. It gives excellent sun protection in hot weather, and has become popular with American fishing guides.

SHAKESPEARE SUN VISOR
The Shakespeare sun visor has a tinted plastic peak and a lined, elasticated headband that acts as a sweatband on hot days. A sun visor leaves the top of the head exposed to any cooling breeze that might blow, but a cap is preferable in very hot weather because it shields the head from the sun.

DAIWA BASEBALL CAP *(above)*
This nylon cap is available in either a full cloth style or a half-mesh version that provides better ventilation for the back of the head. A large peak shields the face from the sun, and an adjustable, press-studded strap at the back ensures that the cap will fit all head sizes.

DEERSTALKER
The deerstalker is a traditional type of tweed hat, made either with a rigid rim all the way around or peaked front and back. The peaked versions usually have side flaps to cover the ears for warmth or to keep biting midges at bay.

ACCESSORIES

In addition to basic gear such as rods, reels, lines, and hooks, there are a number of items of tackle, broadly categorized as accessories, that every well-equipped angler should have. These include equipment for unhooking fish, weighing them, and dispatching and cleaning those retained for eating. Additional accessories, not described here but worth considering, include padded unhooking mats, a pair of binoculars for watching for signs of fish activity, and a compass. The last should be considered essential by any angler who wishes to explore some remote hill lake or a stream far from the beaten track, and cannot afford the luxury of a GPS (Global Positioning System) receiver.

HARDY PIN-ON RETRACTOR (below)
This contains a spring-loaded spool of cord carrying a snaplock swivel. Items such as scissors can be clipped to the swivel, where they hang out of the way until needed.

SHAKESPEARE KNOT-TYING TOOL (left)
This is useful if you do not have nimble fingers, and when cold weather makes knot-tying difficult.

HARDY POCKET THERMOMETER (right)
A thermometer helps you to find the areas of a water that are likely to be holding fish, such as cool spots in hot weather and warm ones in cold weather. Tie it to a line, lower or cast it into the water, and leave it there for a few minutes to get an accurate reading.

LUCKY TOOLS ANGLING PLIERS
Heavy-duty angling pliers such as these are essential when you are using wire line or traces. They have long handles for good leverage, their strong jaws make crimping easy, and their wirecutter blades are capable of cutting heavy wire line.

DAIWA HEADLAMP LIGHT (right)
Anglers who fish at night, such as beach anglers, find lights of this type very useful because they are worn strapped to the forehead, leaving the hands free to handle the tackle. The model shown here is powered by a battery pack that clips to your belt.

DAIWA FLEXI-LIGHT (right)
A lamp is a very useful implement to have to hand when fishing on into darkness, and this clip-on model incorporates a flexible stem that allows the light to be directed onto a specific point.

DAIWA SEA KING FILLET KNIFE (left)
Fish that are to be retained for the table should be gutted with a sharp filleting knife, such as this one, as soon after capture as possible.

HARDY ARTERY FORCEPS (above)
These are an excellent tool for removing hooks of about size 10 upwards, especially from sharp-toothed fish such as pike. The finer wire of smaller hooks is easily bent by forceps, and these hooks are best removed with a disgorger.

HARDY SCISSOR PLIERS (left)
This versatile tool has many uses, such as pinching on split shot, debarbing hooks for barbless fishing, and (using the cutting blades) cutting through monofilament and light wire.

HARDY HOOK SHARPENER (left)
Hook sharpeners can improve the points of mechanically sharpened hooks, but chemically etched points to not need further sharpening.

NICAN ENTERPRISES UNI-LOADA (left)
The onerous task of loading line onto a reel is made easier if you use a line spool holder such as this. This tool is adjustable so that line spools can be aligned correctly for loading either fixed-spool or multiplier reels, and it can cope with all but the largest bulk line spools.

HUFF FISHING FLY ROD BUTT GRIP (left)
This 50 cm (20 in) aluminium spike is designed to hold your fly rod so that it does not get trodden on when you are resting or changing your terminal tackle. The rod butt sits in a cup, and a spring clip at the top of the grip holds the rod upright.

SHAKESPEARE PIKE GAG (right)
A gag is used to hold open the sharp-toothed mouth of a pike or other predatory fish while it is being unhooked. The sprung arms of this model are ball-ended so that they do not damage the mouth of the fish.

HARDY PRIEST (left)
Using a priest is a humane way of dispatching fish that are to be retained for eating. The weighted head should be brought down smartly on the skull of the fish at least twice.

HARDY SPRING BALANCE (below)
Using a spring balance is a convenient method of weighing fish. This balance is calibrated in kilograms and pounds, and has a micrometer adjustment for accurate zeroing.

79

BAIT

USING A SUITABLE BAIT is one of the secrets of successful angling, whether you are fishing for carp on a small pond or marlin on a tropical ocean. But the variety of baits used by today's anglers is huge, and choosing the right one requires a good knowledge not only of the diet and feeding habits of your chosen quarry but also of the range of baits that have proved effective in luring it. Baits can be divided into naturals, artificials, and processed baits, but the essential function of all of them is to fool fish into taking the hook.

Naturals are whole or cut items of the natural diet of the quarry, and are therefore inherently attractive to it. Most can be collected easily and free of charge from the water, its banks, or the shore; some, such as worms and maggots, are available from tackle dealers. Artificials, such as plugs and spinners, either mimic natural food items, such as small fish, or are designed to incite fish to grab them out of aggression, curiosity, or hunger. Their benefits include their ease of use and the fact that they can be used time and time again. Processed baits, such as cheese and bread, although edible, are obviously not part of any wild fish's natural diet. For fish, their attraction lies in their smell and taste, and for anglers, in their convenience and proven effectiveness.

This chapter describes the most effective and widely used baits for both freshwater and saltwater species.

THE RIGHT BAIT
Using a bait that will tempt your quarry into taking the hook is one of the secrets of angling success.

NATURAL BAITS

Most natural baits cost nothing and often have the additional benefit of being part of the diet of the fish you are seeking. For example, earthworms (usually called lobworms or nightcrawlers) will tempt almost every freshwater fish worth catching, while water-based fauna that make good baits include freshwater shrimp and caddis grubs. Never collect more naturals than you think you will need, and always return any that are unused.

MAGGOTS & CASTERS

The type of maggot most often used as bait is the larva of the bluebottle fly, a proven catcher of fish of all species. Maggots are usually sold in their natural white or dyed bronze, although they can be changed to any colour with a suitable liquid dye. The main places to use these dyed maggots are waters where the fish have been subjected to a lot of angling pressure and become wary of the white or bronze varieties.

Anglers fishing for small fish will often use other varieties of maggot, such as squatts (housefly larvae) and pinkies (greenbottle fly larvae). These are smaller and lighter than bluebottle maggots and are particularly good for fishing on the drop.

Caster (pupated maggots) are an excellent bait for most species and tend to attract bigger fish. They are good where fish have become maggot-shy, and are very effective when fished as a hookbait over a bed of hempseed. They become darker in colour and lighter in weight as they age, and old, floating casters are a splendid bait for surface-feeding species such as rudd.

Casters

Maggots

Pinkies

Dyed maggots

MAGGOT

HOOKING MAGGOTS (*above*)
Hook a maggot through the blunt end and as lightly as possible to ensure that it remains livelier for longer. Use maggots singly on hook sizes 16 to 18, or in bunches on a size 12. When fish are proving wary, it can pay to hook maggots halfway along their bodies. This will make them sink horizontally, and therefore more slowly and naturally.

HOOKING CASTERS (*right*)
To hook a single caster, pierce the thick end and push the hook in, completely burying it inside. Use hook sizes 14 to 18. Casters can also be presented singly, or in twos or threes, by lightly hooking them through their blunt ends.

CASTER

WORMS & SLUGS

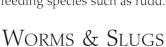

SLUGS

WORMS

Carp, tench, and chub will gulp down a whole lobworm in seconds, while smaller species find half a lob or a smaller worm, such as a branding, more manageable. Slugs are adored by chub, carp, and roach. On mild, damp nights, lobworms can be collected from lawns, and slugs emerge from rockeries and hedgerows; brandlings and redworms can be found in compost heaps.

LOBWORM

HOOKING WORMS
When using lobworms, either thread the hook a good way through the body, or hook it twice, top and bottom, to prevent it from flying off during casting or being torn off by a lunging fish. Use hook sizes 4 to 8 for lobworms, and 10 to 14 for worm sections or brandlings. Lightly hook small worms once when fish are confident, but thread the hook some way through the body when fish are only plucking tentatively at the bait.

HOOKING SLUGS
Use a big hook, size 2 or 4, and nick it gently through the body. A slug's weight enables it to be cast a long way and because of its tough skin, more than one fish can be caught on it.

SLUG

BRANDLING WORM

FISH

MACKEREL

HERRING

SARDINE

Many fish species include other fish in their diet. Pike, for instance, will eat just about any fish bait offered to them, although some are undoubtedly preferred: herring, sprat, smelt, sardine, mackerel, trout, and grayling are all good pike baits, as is freshwater eel. Where pike become used to certain fish baits, try painting theses baits with liquid dyes to make them different.

Other freshwater species regularly taken on fish baits include catfish, perch, zander, bass, muskellunge, and trout, and in recent years some big chub have fallen to deadbaits intended for pike.

Fish baits can be freelined for legered static, trotted beneath a float, or spun or wobbled like an artificial lure. Being relatively soft-fleshed, sea fish tend not to last too long when continually cast out and retrieved. Freshwater baits are preferable for this, and none is better than small trout.

HOOKING FISH
Fish deadbaits on a pair of semi-barbless trebles, size 8 or 10. Set the uptrace treble in the tail root and the other no more than 8 cm (3 in) from it, with both facing the tail. For spinning, set the uptrace treble in the mouth, the other in the flank.

SHRIMPS & PRAWNS

SHRIMPS

These baits, when peeled, are excellent for catching just about every freshwater species. Unpeeled, they are best known as salmon baits, but they will also account for catfish, chub, bass, barbel, carp, tench, and crappies. They can be used raw or boiled, and are readily available canned, frozen, or fresh from most supermarkets.

HOOKING PRAWNS
Peeled prawns are best presented singly on a size 8 or 10 hook pushed through the thick end of the tail. Mount unpeeled prawns on a size 2 or 4 hook, threaded through the tail or through and out of the underside of the body.

CADDIS LARVAE

CADDIS LARVAE

A caddis grub is simply the larva of any one of many types of caddis fly, especially the sedges. The caddis grub is of particular interest as bait, and you'll find them living in tubes they make out of grains of sand or small pieces of twig, leaves, shells, and other bottom-debris material. You'll find caddis clinging to the sides of stones in the water, especially in the shallow margins. Carefully take each case off the rock and prise the grub from its shelter. Caddis are brilliant baits for virtually every type of fish that swim. Try two caddis, for example, on a size 12 hook for species like barbel, chub, or roach. Sometimes a bunch of caddis works well, or even try a single caddis on a 16 for shy fish.

EELS

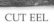

CUT EEL

Freshwater eels are a fine pike bait and can be used whole, if small, or in sections. They are tough-skinned, which often allows several fish to be caught on the same bait, and can be cast a long way. Eels up to 30 cm (12in) long make good baits for wobbling, while smaller eels and cut sections are generally fished on a freeline or legered.

HOOKING EELS
For wobbling and legering, mount an eel or eel portion on a standard snap tackle of two size 8 or 10 semi-barbless trebles on a 50-cm (20-in) wire trace. Small sections of eel can be fished on a large single hook threaded through the flesh with only part of the bend and point visible.

PROCESSED BAITS

Most of the large number of processed baits are common foodstuffs such as bread, cheese, meat, and vegetables, and while most are very unlikely to feature naturally in the diets of fish, they are nonetheless eaten when offered. In addition to these household foods, there is one group of processed baits that is produced exclusively for fishing: the high-protein (HP) baits. They were originally developed for carp fishing but are now widely used for many other non-predatory species, such as tench.

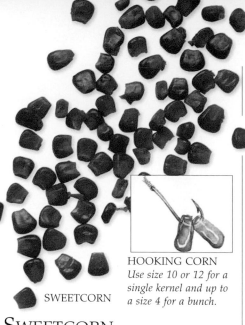

HOOKING CORN
Use size 10 or 12 for a single kernel and up to a size 4 for a bunch.

SWEETCORN

CHEESE

PROCESSED CHEESE

STRONG CHEESE

CHEDDAR CHEESE

In summer, cheese can be used straight from the pack. However, cold water hardens cheeses such as cheddar, so in winter grate these and mix them into a stiff paste with breadcrumbs and a sprinkling of water and cooking oil.

HOOKING CHEESE
For large baits, such as for carp or chub, use a size 4; for small ones use a 10, bury the hook point inside the cheese.

SWEETCORN

Available either canned or frozen, corn is liked by many species. The kernels are relatively tough-skinned, enabling them to be cast a fair distance without flying off the hook. They are also fairly dense and sink quite quickly to the bottom, which is useful on rivers. On waters where corn has been used extensively, it can still be an effective bait if you liven it up with a tiny amount of edible flavouring such as clove oil or dye it a different colour.

BREAD

BREAD PASTE BALLS

BREAD CRUSTS

BREAD FLAKE

BREAD CUBES

Bread provides a number of different baits that can be fished in a variety of ways. The crust can be trotted, legered, or even freelined, on lakes for carp and rudd and on rivers for roach and chub. The soft flake (inner crumb) can be used both as a hookbait and as a groundbait. For the hook, the best flake to use is from a really fresh loaf as it will stay on longer. It can also be turned into a paste by mixing with water then kneading in a porous cloth.

HOOKING BREADFLAKE
Use hook sizes 4 to 14, depending on the size of fish you are after. Fold the flake right around the hook, then squeeze it together to ensure it stays on.

CANNED MEAT

Canned pork and ham, cut into small cubes, are fine bait for chub and barbel, and work well for some other species, including carp. When fixed properly on the hook, this is a bait that stays on well and survives distance casting. Tinned cat food is liked by carp and catfish: mix it into a paste with breadcrumbs, and then shape it into small balls.

LUNCHEON MEAT

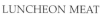

HOOKING MEAT
Use a hook size 4 to 8, threaded carefully through the meat so that the point shows, and secure the bait with a piece of leaf.

CAT & DOG BISCUITS

CAT
BISCUITS

DOG BISCUITS

WET DOG
BISCUITS

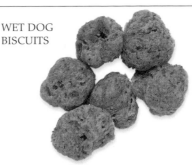

Dry cat and dog biscuits make the basis of a highly effective floating bait for carp, working much like other floating particle baits. Their strength lies in the attractive scented oils that they give off. In order to make them soft enough

to put on the hook, try soaking them in boiling water for a couple of minutes. The use of a controller float will provide sufficient casting weight to give the distance you need, and additional biscuits can be catapulted

upwind of the fish and allowed to drift down. Don't be in a hurry to strike if your bait disappears – wait until the line tightens. If the carp are wary about the line in open water, fish the biscuits over weed or lily pads to disguise the line.

CARP PELLETS

These are a useful bait, but before using them you should check the local rules, as pellets are not allowed on all waters. This is because some kinds of pellet are thought to be indigestible to species such as trout. There are, however, a number of commercially-available pellets that have been thoroughly field tested and are definitely non-harmful. Choose a brand of soft pellets, as these are

malleable and much easier to hook than the harder type. Alternatively, hard pellets can be boiled and made into a paste that can be moulded onto the hook. Pellets can be catapulted out as free offerings, or you can fill a PVA bag with pellets and cast it out with the hook bait.

CARP PELLETS
These can be used singly on the hook, and catapulted or cast out in larger quantities as attractive ground bait.

SEEDS & GRAINS

RICE   MAIZE   RAW TARES   PROCESSED HEMP   COOKED TARES   PEANUTS

Many seeds and grains make excellent particle baits, but all must be boiled to soften them before use, because fish cannot digest them uncooked. The most widely used seed is hemp, which sends many cyprinid species into a feeding frenzy. It is often used as groundbait,

with the bigger tare, a reddish brown berry, fished on the hook. Boiled peanuts have proved a very effective bait for carp, and maize, wheat, and barley (all boiled) are good roach baits. Boiled rice is useful to supplement a meagre supply of maggots.

HOOKING SEEDS
AND GRAINS
Most seeds and grains are simply pushed onto the hook (size 6 to 14). Boiled hemp splits and the hook is inserted into the split.

HIGH-PROTEIN (HP) BAITS

HP baits are made of milk proteins, eggs, animal proteins, soy flour, wheat-germ, colourings, and flavourings. The mixture is either used as a paste or rolled into balls and boiled, producing "boilies". These have a thick skin that is impervious to the attentions of small nuisance fish. Most boilies produced are sinkers, but floaters are also made.

BOILIES

HOOKING BOILIES
Use a hook size 2 to 8 and ensure that the hook point and gape are not impeded, or use a hair rig or a boilie bayonet.

FRESHWATER GROUNDBAIT

Groundbait is a bait or mixture of baits introduced into the water to draw fish to the vicinity of the baited hook, and to keep them feeding in the area long enough for them to notice and take the hookbait. The key to successful groundbaiting is to use a bait that will attract the species you are after, and to use enough to hold their attention without offering them so much food that they are likely to miss or ignore the hookbait.

USING GROUNDBAIT

Groundbait can be used both in rivers and in stillwaters. In rivers with moderate or swift currents, and in waters where bottom-feeding species are the quarry, use balls of stiff, heavy, bread-based groundbait that sink quickly to the bottom before breaking up.

In still or slow-moving waters, and for fish feeding in the upper layers, use the lighter, finer type of groundbait known as cloudbait. This is made of finely crushed dried breadcrumbs, dampened with water and squeezed into small balls immediately before use. When they are thrown into the water, the balls break up into a slowly sinking cloud of tiny bread particles.

The effectiveness of cloudbait can be enhanced by mixing a little powdered milk with the crumbs before forming them into balls.

Mixing groundbait
When mixing groundbait, the first step is to prepare the base. For a fast-sinking groundbait, soak stale bread in cold water for at least half an hour (do not use warm water because it makes the bread go slimy). Then pour away the water in which it was standing, and remove some of the water it has soaked up by gently squeezing it – the more you squeeze, the firmer the mixture will be. Mash the wet bread into a smooth paste consisting of tiny particles of flake and crust with no lumps. Stiffen the paste with bran or a coarse cereal meal, such as maize meal.

This mixture can be formed into balls, preferably with the addition of hookbait samples such as maggots or cut worms, and perhaps something to enhance their flavour. For example, many members of the carp family have a sweet tooth, and find groundbait laced with small amounts of sweet flavourings highly palatable.

GROUNDBAIT BASES
The simplest bases for groundbait are soaked, mashed-up stale bread, and bread that has been heated in an oven to dry it and then crushed into crumbs. Both can be used alone or mixed with hookbaits and other additives. Many anglers consider that brown bread makes a more effective groundbait than white.

Mashed bread / Bread crumb

Commercial groundbait and additives
Commercially made groundbaits need little or no preparation, and many are formulated specifically for particular species or fishing methods. Additives, either liquid or powder, add colour, flavour, and scent to baits and groundbaits and revitalize their attractiveness when fish have become suspicious of them. These additives should be used sparingly, because too high a concentration in a bait will repel fish rather than attract them.

CATAPULTS

A good way to deliver balls of ground-bait into distant swims is to use a catapult, preferably one designed specifically for the task. To prevent the balls from breaking up in flight, form them from a stiff groundbait mixture and make the firing action as smooth as possible. For consistent accuracy when baiting a swim at long range, aim towards a feature on the far bank, such as a tree, and pull the catapult pouch back the same distance on each firing. When you are using a catapult, always hold it at arm's length and chest height. This will ensure that if the elastic breaks and flies back, it will not injure your eyes.

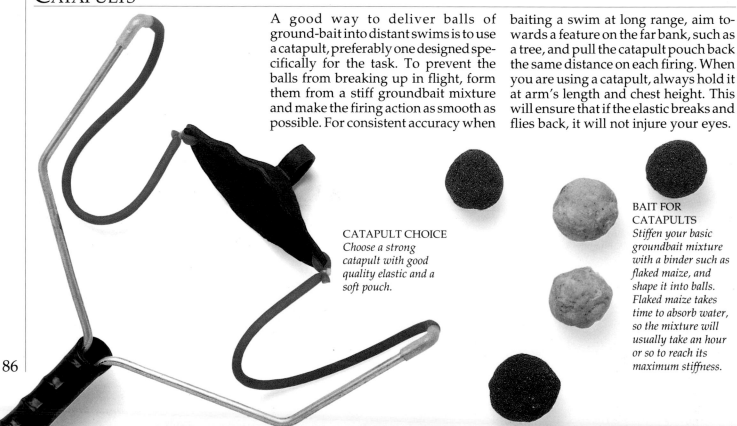

CATAPULT CHOICE
Choose a strong catapult with good quality elastic and a soft pouch.

BAIT FOR CATAPULTS
Stiffen your basic groundbait mixture with a binder such as flaked maize, and shape it into balls. Flaked maize takes time to absorb water, so the mixture will usually take an hour or so to reach its maximum stiffness.

SWIMFEEDERS

Swimfeeders, or feeders, are widely used in legering for presenting either groundbait or samples of the hookbait close to the baited hook, and are attached to the terminal tackle in place of the leger weight. Most are simple perforated plastic or wire-mesh cylinders, and are weighted to aid casting and to ensure that they remain on the bed of the lake or river after their contents have been released. This weighting can take the form of a weight or weights at the base of the feeder, or may be a metal strip running along one side.

Open-ended feeders

Open-ended feeders are plastic tubes, open at both ends and usually perforated to hasten the inflow of water, thus speeding up dispersal of the bait contained inside. They are usually weighted with strips of lead, folded over and stapled at either end. Because the weight is not adjustable, these feeders are produced in a range of different sizes with different widths of lead strip.

Open-ended feeders are generally used with groundbait, although they can also be filled with hookbait samples, held inside by a plug of groundbait at each end. They are particularly suitable for bream and other species that roam in big shoals and need large quantities of bait to hold them in a swim.

Blockend feeders

As their name suggests, these feeders are blocked (closed) at each end by caps. On some models, both caps are removable, while on others only the top cap can be taken off for the feeder to be filled with bait.

They are normally used with maggots, casters, or hempseed; the plastic tube is liberally perforated to allow the maggots to crawl out and the static casters and hemp to be washed out by the water. The release of bait can be slowed by winding insulating tape around part of the feeder to seal some of the holes.

The position of the weight on blockend feeders varies. On some, it is located below the base, on others in one of the end caps, while on others flat lead strip is used. Most blockends are tubular, but some are oval in cross-section to hold bottom in fast water.

OPEN-ENDED FEEDERS
These are used with straight or bait-laced groundbait, or samples of hookbait held in by plugs of groundbait pushed into each end.

FEEDER WEIGHT
When you are using a swimfeeder, make sure that its weight when filled with bait is not too great for the rod and line you are using.

WIRE CAGE FEEDERS
These are made of wire mesh and filled quickly and easily by simply pushing them into groundbait.

SIDE VIEW

DAIWA HARRIER FEEDERS
The aerodynamic shape of these feeders permits accurate, long-range casting and helps them to rise quickly to the surface for a rapid retrieve. Slots instead of holes speed up the inflow of water and therefore groundbait release.

BAIT DROPPER
The hinged front face of the bait dropper opens to release the groundbait when the weighted plunger hits bottom. It is sometimes cast out and retrieved on a separate rod and line.

DRENNAN FLAT BLOCKEND
This feeder has a flattened shape (rather like that of a hip flask) and lead strip weight to help it stay in place on the bottom in fast-flowing water.

DRENNAN FEEDERLINK
The Feederlink has a removable top cap, and interchangeable weights that are clipped onto the base.

THAMESLEY BLOCKEND
Both end caps of this versatile feeder are removable. This facility enables it to be quickly and easily converted from a blockend to an open-ended feeder.

SPINNERS & SPOONS

Spinners and spoons are artificial baits designed to provoke a response from predatory fish as they pass through their line of vision, either because the fish are hungry or because they are defending their territory. They can be made of a variety of materials and come fitted with single or treble hooks.

SPINNERS

On a spinner, a vane or blade rotates around a central bar as the lure is retrieved. Some have lifelike worms or fish of soft rubber that encourage fish to hang on after grabbing the lure. Others, including buzz baits, have plastic skirts over their hooks that imitate swimming crayfish: the throbbing action of the blade attracts the fish, which then lunge at the plastic tassels.

LIL' HUSTLER SPOILER (above)
A spinner bait. Being virtually weedless, it is at its best when worked in fish-holding vegetation. Fish it shallow on a continuous retrieve or by sink and draw.

SPRAT (DEVON MINNOW)
Made in both floating and sinking versions for a variety of water conditions, this is a traditional salmon and trout lure that takes many other species.

TEASER (above)
An in-line spinner bait, best fished at a medium to fast pace. Its sleek, aerodynamic shape ensures that it casts well.

GOLD WING (above)
A buzz bait, at its best when retrieved on or just under the surface. Virtually weedless, it can be fished among lily pads where pike often lurk.

FLYING CONDOM
This unique lure produces a tremendously heavy throbbing action on the retrieve, and it has proved highly effective for many species including salmon, bass, pike, and perch.

SNAGLESS SALLY (left)
Fitted with a double-pronged weed guard, this lure can be cast right into and pulled through dense fish-holding weedbeds without fear of snagging.

MEPPS COMET (left)
A small lure with an attractive fluttering action that works well for trout, chub, pike, and perch. It fishes best in lakes or slow rivers.

BIG FISH
This variation on the Flying Condom lure is equipped with a highly natural, soft rubber fish below the spinning blade.

SPOONS

Spoons wobble through the water in a fishlike manner, and are often trolled behind boats as well as being cast and retrieved. Most are oval, and cast well due to their all-metal construction. Their action depends on the style of retrieve: winding in erratically can give the impression of a fish in distress, while twitching the rod tip when winding in gives extra "life" to the lure.

ABU ATOM
The Atom's rippled finish catches and reflects light as it is pulled through the water. It has an irregular action and is particularly good for pike in clear water.

ATLANTIC
This is a well-proven spoon for pike and other predatory fish. It is at its most effective when fished very slowly, just off the bottom, in lakes and gravel pits.

CISCO
A lure with a realistic action, designed for salmon, trout, and pike. Equally at home trolled, even up to 13 km/h (8 mph), or fished from the bank, where sink-and-draw is recommended.

HERON
A king-sized spoon designed specifically for big pike, this is perfect for distance casting on large, deep waters as well as for trolling or downrigging.

ABU TOBY SALMO
A highly effective gamefish lure that imitates the movement of a small fish as it twists and turns on its way through the water. The Salmo is a good lure to use in moving water.

HEDDON MOSS BOSS (left)
Designed to be used in well-weeded waters where other lures can foul up. Its interesting action helps it to glide over dense weed.

ABU LILL-ÖRINGEN (below)
This is a small, streamlined, and lightweight spoon, good for fishing near the surface or in shallow water.

ABU GLIMMY
An excellent pike and salmon lure with an undulating swing produced by its double-curve profile. Surfaces rapidly when retrieved at speed.

ABU STOR-ÖRINGEN
A lively big brother to the Lill-Öringen, this is a productive lure for salmon and zander. Displaces a lot of water during the retrieve.

KILTY KERRYMAN
This Irish salmon lure has also proved to be an enticer of pike. Its fluttering action often produces hard takes.

TOBY FAT
The elliptical shape and double curve of this spoon induce a lively but undulating action. A good lure for long casts. Retrieve slowly for best results.

PLUGS

Plugs are made of materials such as wood, plastic, and metal, and designed to either float, dive below the surface, or sink when retrieved. Floating plugs are fished across the surface, and they often have features that create extra fish-attracting surface disturbance, such as propellers or plastic skirts. Floating plugs that dive when cranked in are very versatile, because the speed of retrieve determines how deep they dive, allowing a great variety of depths to be explored. The diving action is produced by an angled vane or lip at the head, and some plugs contain balls that rattle to enhance their attractiveness. Sinking plugs are made in a variety of densities to fish at different depths.

FLOATING PLUGS

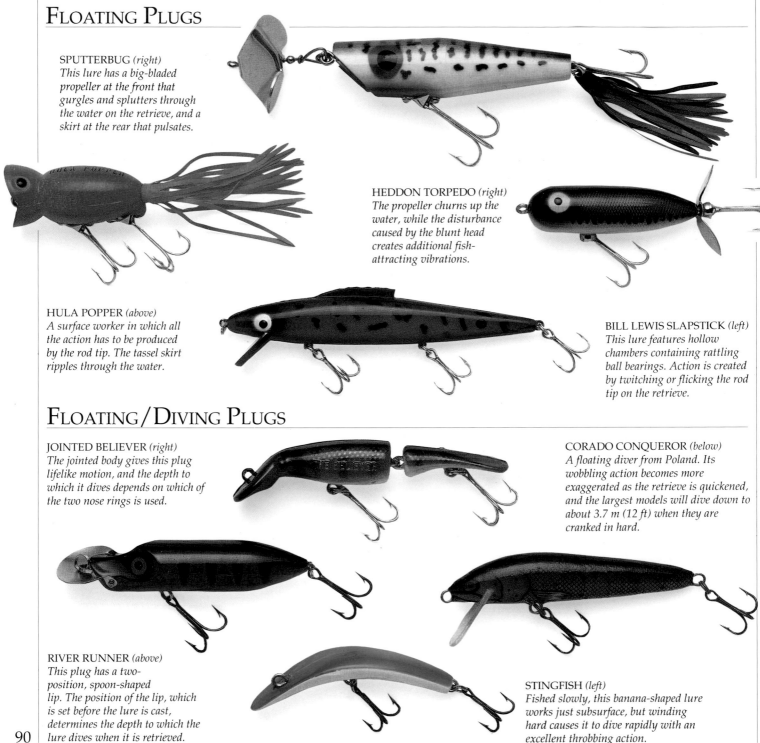

SPUTTERBUG (right)
This lure has a big-bladed propeller at the front that gurgles and splutters through the water on the retrieve, and a skirt at the rear that pulsates.

HULA POPPER (above)
A surface worker in which all the action has to be produced by the rod tip. The tassel skirt ripples through the water.

HEDDON TORPEDO (right)
The propeller churns up the water, while the disturbance caused by the blunt head creates additional fish-attracting vibrations.

BILL LEWIS SLAPSTICK (left)
This lure features hollow chambers containing rattling ball bearings. Action is created by twitching or flicking the rod tip on the retrieve.

FLOATING/DIVING PLUGS

JOINTED BELIEVER (right)
The jointed body gives this plug lifelike motion, and the depth to which it dives depends on which of the two nose rings is used.

RIVER RUNNER (above)
This plug has a two-position, spoon-shaped lip. The position of the lip, which is set before the lure is cast, determines the depth to which the lure dives when it is retrieved.

CORADO CONQUEROR (below)
A floating diver from Poland. Its wobbling action becomes more exaggerated as the retrieve is quickened, and the largest models will dive down to about 3.7 m (12 ft) when they are cranked in hard.

STINGFISH (left)
Fished slowly, this banana-shaped lure works just subsurface, but winding hard causes it to dive rapidly with an excellent throbbing action.

SINKING PLUGS

SMITHWICK DEVIL'S HORSE *(right)*
This wooden lure can be cast and retrieved or trolled. Its twin propellers churn up the water, creating a disturbance similar to the thrashing of an injured baitfish.

LEROY BROWN *(below)*
A lifelike vibrating lure with a busy, wobbling action that is a very effective fish attractor.

SHIMMY *(right)*
A darting lure with a built-in wriggle. This slow-sinking plug is designed to be fished sink-and-draw at varying speeds of retrieve.

CORDELL RATT'L SPOT *(above)*
The shiny finish of this lure makes it more easily visible in poor light, and its vibrating action is enhanced by rattling ball bearings that are housed inside the body.

JOINTED WIGGLER *(left)*
A heavy, fast-sinking plug from Canada that is excellent for fishing large stillwaters and deep, swift-flowing rivers.

DEEP-DIVING PLUGS

BAGLEY DIVING BANG-O-B *(right)*
A large, tough, hardwood trolling lure with a big lip that will take it down to depths of 6 to 9 m (20 to 30 ft). It can be used for marine species as well as for freshwater fish.

THE HUNTER *(below)*
A pike lure designed to be fished slowly just off the bottom, especially in winter when the fish are lying deep and torpid.

HEDDON MAGNUM HELLBENDER *(above)*
This classic lure will dive rapidly down to 11 m (35 ft) when trolled. Effective along deep banks, marginal ledges, and drop-offs.

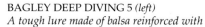

BAGLEY DEEP DIVING 5 *(left)*
A tough lure made of balsa reinforced with hardwood. Designed for use in the deeper parts of lakes and reservoirs and in powerful rivers.

NATURAL BAITS

In addition to fish baits, such as cut or whole mackerel and herring, the saltwater angler has a wide range of natural baits to choose from. There are probably more species of fish reliant on non-fish meals than species regularly eating other fish, so the broader the range of natural baits used, the greater the chances of angling success. Fresh, good-quality bait has no equal, but it must be kept cool and moist at all times during storage, and should, if possible, be presented naturally when used.

CUTTLEFISH

SQUID

RAGWORMS

Anglers classify the various species of ragworm (*Nereis* spp.) by colour and size. Red ragworms can be dug from shellfish beds and stone patches in estuaries, and kept for up to a week if loosely wrapped in damp newspaper and refrigerated. King ragworm are the largest reds, used in portions or whole for stingrays, pollack, and similar large predators. Smaller reds are popular general-purpose baits, while tiny harbour ragworms, dug from estuarine mud, are much loved by flounders and mullet. White ragworms, the favourite bait of match anglers, are found on clean sands.

KING RAGWORM

RAGWORM

HOOKING RAGWORMS
Feed the worm up the shank until the hook is full, or push it up onto the trace leaving nothing hanging free for fish to tug at. Beware of the nippers at the head end when handling ragworm.

LUGWORMS

There are two common species of lugworm (*Arenicola* spp.), and both leave telltale heaps of debris at their burrow entrances. Brown lug can be dug from the middle shore sands. They will keep for a few days if loosely wrapped in damp newspaper and put in a refrigerator, or they can be kept in tanks. The larger black lug live beneath the lower shore and can be frozen. Many species of fish find them irresistible.

LUGWORM

HOOKING LUGWORMS
To hook a lugworm, carefully thread the hook through the head and the centre of the body, taking care not to burst the worm. Nip off any surplus tail that might give small fish a starting point for tearing the bait from the hook.

BROWN LUGWORM

SANDEELS

SANDEELS

The various sandeel species (family Ammodytidae) are small, elongate, gregarious fish that form vast shoals for protection and also burrow into the sand to escape predation. They are a major link in the marine food chain – most predatory fish feed on them and some, such as sandbank turbot and bass, are almost reliant on them. They are netted in areas of strong tidal activity (which seem to attract them) or dug from surf beaches, and kept in aerated tubs.

THREE WAYS TO HOOK A SANDEEL

LIPPING

TAILING

HEADING

HOOKING SANDEELS
To be at their most effective as a bait, sandeels must be alive and swimming and fished on the drift. The most natural presentation is lipping, with the point also nicked into the skin under the gill cover. Heading and tailing can also be used but appear less natural.

SQUID AND CUTTLEFISH

Squid and cuttlefish are cephalopods, tentacled molluscs with small internal shells. They are highly intelligent and active predators in their own right, but, either strip-cut or whole, they make excellent baits for a very wide range of species. If they have a fault as baits it is their lack of fish-attracting scent, but fish will take them avidly once they find them. Small squid are available from retail fish outlets, cuttle and large squid from inshore fishing boats.

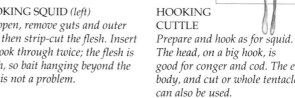

CUTTLEFISH HEAD

HOOKING SQUID (left)
Cut open, remove guts and outer skin, then strip-cut the flesh. Insert the hook through twice; the flesh is tough, so bait hanging beyond the hook is not a problem.

SQUID STRIP

HOOKING CUTTLE
Prepare and hook as for squid. The head, on a big hook, is good for conger and cod. The entire body, and cut or whole tentacles, can also be used.

OCTOPUS

OCTOPUS TENTACLE

HOOKING OCTOPUS
Strips are hooked as for squid; to hook a whole tentacle, insert the hook down the centre, bringing it out a shank's length down.

OCTOPUS

Octopus are more common in inshore waters than many people realize, and are taken on rod and line in some areas. Like squid and cuttlefish, they are predatory cephalopods, and as baits they are prepared and used in much the same way; small ones can be used whole. Long strips of octopus flesh, when fished fluttering in the tide, will attract fish by their visual appeal. When using long strips, give a taking fish enough time to get the whole bait down before striking to set the hook.

RAZORSHELLS

Several species of razorshell (*Ensis* spp. and *Solen* spp.) inhabit the sands of the extreme lower shore. Razorshells move too quickly to be dug up, so are either speared or coaxed from the sand by squirting a strong salt solution into their keyhole-shaped burrow apertures. They appeal to many fish, including those usually taken on fish strips. Take care not to damage the flesh when taking it from the shell, and remove the tough foot, which fish dislike.

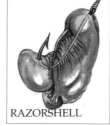

RAZORSHELL

HOOKING RAZORSHELLS
Cut a suitably firm section of flesh, and pass the hook through it as many times as possible because it is soft and tears easily.

CRABS

As crabs grow, they shed their shells and grow larger ones. At such times, the crab crawls out, then takes on water to expand a soft, wrinkled outer skin that hardens in a few days to form the new shell. Crabs about to shed are called peelers; those without hard shells, softbacks. Both make excellent baits for a wide range of fish, but the peeler is the more effective.

PEELER CRABS

HOOKING CRABS
Peel fully, then cut into halves. Pile these onto the hook and bind in place with thread. Appearance is unimportant: the appeal lies in the smell.

PEELER CRAB

Foot

RAZORSHELL

93

SALTWATER GROUNDBAIT

Saltwater groundbaiting, also known as chumming or swimfeeding, is a very effective means of attracting fish into the vicinity of a baited hook, and of delaying the passage of passing fish so that you can place baits in front of them. It can also be used to give fish a taste for whatever bait you intend to put on your hook, and to encourage them to feed when they otherwise might not. The secret lies in using measured amounts appropriate to the species and the prevailing conditions, and in using enough to tempt the fish without feeding them so much that they have no appetite for the hookbait.

RUBBY DUBBY

This is a very effective particulate groundbait, based on the flesh of oily fish, which is released into the water and carried along by the tide to create a long, continuous slick of particles, blood, and body juices. The heavier particles sink, making the slick three-dimensional, and the baits are set at appropriate depths within it. For pelagic fish, such as sharks, it is normally used when drift fishing but can also be used from an anchored boat.

When fishing at anchor for bottom-feeding fish, some anglers tie a mesh bag full of minced mackerel to the anchor in the belief that the ensuing trail will pass beneath the boat, but this will not always be the case. On a dying tide with a stiff breeze cutting across it, the boat will be pushed out of line, and fish following the slick through to its source will not pass beneath it. It is better to hang the bag over the stern on a short, weighted rope.

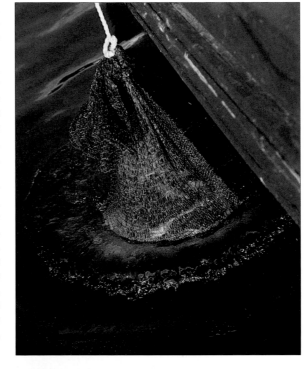

RUBBY DUBBY *(above)*
The best rubby dubby is made from stale mackerel mixed with bran and pilchard oil. Some anglers mince the mackerel, but this produces particles of uniform size that will disperse in a uniform manner, which fails to exploit the technique's full potential. It is far better to pulp the fish in a tub or bucket with a lump of wood. This gives a variety of particle sizes, which will sink to different depths, and some of them will not wash out of the bag but stay there to draw fish right up to the boat.

USING RUBBY DUBBY *(left)*
The mixture is packed in a mesh bag and hung over the side of the boat. It should be shaken and topped up regularly to maintain the consistency of the slick.

BAIT DROPPERS

Bait droppers are lowered on a rope, or by rod and line, to place large portions of bait on the seabed. These attract sharks and other large predators, and draw territorial species such as conger from their lairs. Because a strong tide will tend to disperse the bait portions away from the hookbaits, this technique works best on neap tides.

A bait dropper usually consists of a weighted plastic tube with a flap that opens when the dropper hits the bottom. A cheaper alternative is a plastic bag with a sinker tied inside one corner. On a fast drop, water pressure keeps the bag closed around its contents, which are released by raising the rod tip a couple of times when the sinker has touched the bottom.

LOWERING DROPPERS *(left)*
Lower a custom-made dropper carefully so as not to trigger the flap prematurely.

BAITS FOR DROPPERS *(above)*
When using a dropper, choose a bait or baits that are likely to attract the species of fish you hope to catch. Suitable baits to use in droppers include large pieces of fish or squid, whole or cut worms, whole or crushed shellfish, and broken crabs; you can also use pulped or minced fish.

BIG-GAME GROUNDBAITING

CHUMMING FOR SHARKS
Cruising sharks can be attracted towards the baited hooks by chumming – dropping chopped stale fish and squid into the water. Oily fish, such as mackerel and herring, are the most effective.

Big-game groundbaiting can take a number of forms, but all are intended either to draw fish towards the hooks or to stir them into a feeding frenzy.

Rubby dubby and bait droppers are good ways of attracting fish to the baited hooks when fishing with natural baits. Another method is to drop chum (small pieces of fish) into the water, but to be effective this needs one person constantly cutting and dropping the chum.

When trolling with natural baits, one way of attracting fish up from the depths is to space twenty link swivels along a length of mono, then clip a live pilchard to each. This rig is trailed astern, and more live pilchard are thrown in loose to form a school with those on the links. If you are trolling lures, you can create the impression of a small school of fish by using multiple lures or by trailing a team of teaser lures. These are hookless lures designed simply to attract species such as marlin and sailfish into the vicinity of the hooked lures.

SHORE GROUNDBAITING

Rock and pier anglers cannot normally reach the areas where fish are feeding, but they can draw feeding fish within casting range by groundbaiting with shirvy. When this paste is put into deep water, such as that below rock ledges, it is carried out to sea by the tide, creating a scent trail that will entice fish right up to the shore. Mullet and bass are among the species readily attracted by shirvy, and conger respond well to a bag of rubby dubby hung over a harbour wall at night.

Fish also gather to feed on bits of fish washed from the decks of trawlers, and on refuse from pier restaurants and moored boats.

USING SHIRVY
When using shirvy, it is essential to create a continuous slick to keep the fish moving inshore. You can do this by putting it into a mesh bag and lowering it into the sea, or by throwing in small amounts with an old serving spoon. The slick makes an oily line on the surface, showing where the baits should be placed. When this fades, throw in another spoonful.

SHIRVY
Shirvy is a thick paste that can be made by mixing finely minced meat and meat fat with bran and fish blood, or by mixing boiled pulped oily fish with bread and pilchard oil. Like rubby dubby, its variously sized particles and its oil and juices are carried along by the tide to form a three-dimensional slick.

LURES

Artificial lures, used alone or in conjunction with natural baits, will take most species of saltwater gamefish. As in freshwater fishing, the size and type of lure to use depends mainly on the species you intend to catch and the style of fishing you are going to employ, such as trolling or spinning. There are thousands of different lures on the market, but if you equip yourself with a small range of each of the basic patterns you will have a selection to cover most of your normal fishing requirements.

TROLLING FEATHER (*above*)
This is a loose lure, one that is threaded onto the line before the hook is attached. This allows it to be used with your personal choice of hook and trace. It can be used weightless and skipping the surface, lightly weighted with a trolling weight, or sent deeper on a downrigger.

PLASTIC SQUID (*below*)
Known informally as "muppets", these lures first proved their value in wreck fishing. They are very attractive to cod, but will take many other species, including ling and pollack, and are especially effective when baited. Like feathers, they are put onto short droppers above a sinker or pirk, but they are fished only at the bottom. The dropper is passed through a small hole in the head of the lure, then a bead is added to prevent it from sliding down over the hook.

FEATHERS (*above*)
When feathers are strung out on short droppers above a sinker, there are few fish they cannot catch. The original versions, devised for mackerel fishing, were simply bunches of feathers, sometimes dyed, whipped to the shank of a hook. These are still used, but bright synthetic materials are increasingly popular. For mackerel, they should be worked up and down repeatedly at all levels until the shoal has been located.

SALTWATER FLIES (*above*)
Small saltwater fish, such as shad, mackerel, and bass, can be taken on many freshwater fly patterns, including the Dog Nobbler. Streamers and bucktails, some based on freshwater flies and others designed specifically for saltwater species, are used for fish such as tarpon, sharks, and sailfish.

MARLIN LURE (*above*)
This large plastic lure is one of many on the market that are similar in appearance and action to the original Kona Head design. The Kona Head, which originated in Hawaii, is a big-fish trolling lure with a big reputation. It is one of the standard big-game lures and will take a wide range of species including marlin, tuna, dolphinfish, and bonito.

LARGE SQUID (*above*)
The large version of the plastic squid is often used in conjunction with a trolled deadbait, or as an additional skirt for another lure, when fishing for open-ocean gamefish such as marlin. On its own, with a big single hook, a large plastic squid is a good trolling lure for species such as sailfish.

SPOONS (*right*)
The fixed-hook spoon is designed specifically to attract fish to within detection range of a natural bait, which induces the fish to take the hook. The metal blade wobbles as it moves through the water, sending out eyecatching glints of light that attract species such as cod, snapper, and grouper.

TROLLING LURE (above)
There are many variations on this basic theme, which is essentially a loose lure with a plastic skirt and a drilled head that allows it to be rigged to personal taste. Skirts are made of turkey marabou, feathers, or plastic, and coloured to imitate a particular baitfish or to trigger an aggressive response from predatory fish.

SPINNER (above)
In saltwater, as in freshwater, a spinner is fished by casting and retrieving. Spinners can be used with light spinning tackle for small species such as bass, barracuda, and jack.

MACKEREL SPINNER (above)
This spinner has a blade that rotates like a propeller when the lure is retrieved or trolled. It is an excellent lure for mackerel and most small predatory species.

TWO-TAILED EEL (below)
This version of the rubber sandeel has two tails to give it a lively, attractive action when worked through the water. When fished on a flying collar rig (see page 249) it is good for pollack, bass, and cod.

ATTRACTOR SPOON (above)
A small attractor spoon is a useful flatfish lure when the water is clear and long drifts over clean ground are possible. When mounted just above a baited hook on a long trace, and fished along the bottom, it glints and stirs up puffs of sand as it rotates.

PLUGS (below)
In warm waters, slowly trolled plugs are very effective lures for a wide range of shallow-reef and open-ocean species. In cooler temperate waters, bass that are hunting around shallow offshore reefs will take them without hesitation.

RUBBER SANDEELS (above)
Since Alex Ingram designed his legendary Redgill rubber sandeel, imitations, which are reputedly the sincerest form of flattery, have been legion. The trace line passes down the body via the mouth to the hook, which appears from the vent. The tail is thin, flat, and flexible, with an angled end, and provides a lifelike swimming action and enticing vibrations that few fish can resist. Most species will take rubber sandeels, and they are fished on long traces, retrieved slowly from bottom to top, for free-swimming species such as pollack and bass.

PLASTIC EELS (above)
These simple but effective jigging lures are made of lengths of coloured plastic tube, crimped to swivels attached to long, twisted-shanked hooks. The lures are fished on short droppers above the sinker, which is bounced along the bottom. Plastic eels are excellent lures for cod, coalfish, and shoaling reef pollack.

PIRKS (above and right)
These metal jigging lures were developed from cod lures used by commercial handliners. They range in size from tiny lures weighing as little as 28 g (1 oz), which are used to catch baitfish, to huge slabs of metal weighing 910 g (2 lb) or more for use in deep water with strong currents. Pirks are used unbaited for cod and pollack, and baited for ling and halibut.

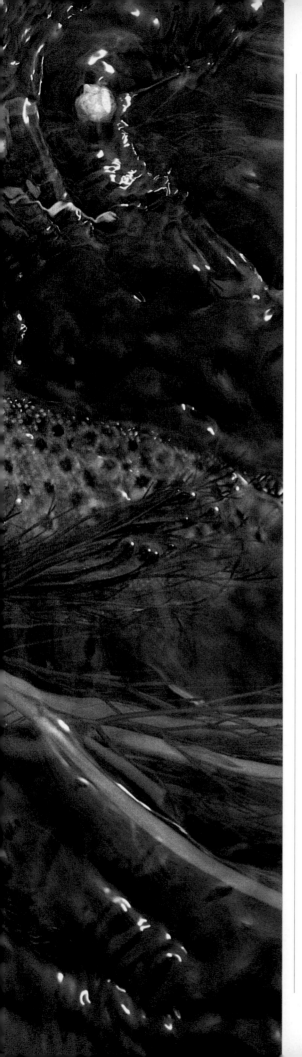

THE FLY

THE CAPTURE, ON ARTIFICIAL FLY, of a fish
instilled with all the cunning that evolution
bestows, is to many the ultimate angling
challenge. Where other methods, such as
fishing with a natural bait, may be more
effective, fly fishing offers an experience that
has tested the angler's skill for many
hundreds of years.

Today, except where local fishing rules
dictate, our choice of fly is extremely wide
but essentially practical. We simply choose
the most effective for the prevailing
conditions, be it a large streamer or a tiny
dry fly. Many new materials, including man-
made products, ensure that the development
of the artificial fly carries on at a pace more
rapid than at any time in its history.

This chapter looks at the various fly
classifications, from the gaudiest of
attractors to the most delicate of imitative
patterns. The major fly groups, including
streamers, hairwings, nymphs, wet flies, and
dry flies, are all covered, and effective
examples are illustrated. The groups include
patterns that appeal to a wide range of
species, from trout and salmon to pike, bass,
and grayling. The link between artifice and
nature is also covered, with a review of the
main prey items and insect groups that are
so important to the angler intent on an
imitative approach. This
craft of mimicry is further
illustrated by an outline
of flytying and the relevant
tools and materials.

FLY PATTERNS
*The earliest flies were tied to catch the brown trout, but today there are
patterns designed for a wide range of freshwater and saltwater species.*

NATURALS 1

For the fly fisher intent on an imitative approach, a comprehensive knowledge of the fish's prey is extremely important. Even for the less dedicated, a basic understanding of it provides an important insight into the way that a fish will respond to an artificial fly. There are seven main groups of creatures of interest to the fly fisher and imitated or suggested by artificial flies: mayflies (Ephemeroptera); caddis flies (Trichoptera); stoneflies (Plecoptera); chironomids or non-biting midges (Diptera); damselflies and dragonflies (Odonata); crustaceans and fish; and terrestrials, creatures that find their way inadvertently onto the water.

FEEDING TROUT
Brown trout will take full advantage of whatever food is available. Try to use a fly pattern that corresponds to the naturals that the fish are feeding on at the time.

MAYFLIES

The order Ephemeroptera encompasses the up-wing flies and olives that are among the most important insects to the fly fisher. They are called "up-wing" because they fold their wings vertically when at rest, as a butterfly does.

The life cycle begins with the egg hatching into a larva or nymph. This is the longest-lived stage, which (depending on the species) feeds on detritus, small organisms, or algae until fully developed. Once mature, it rises to the water's surface, emerging as the subimago, or dun. Although winged, it is not yet sexually mature, and it must cast its skin one more time to become the imago, or spinner. Its task then is simply to reproduce.

The largest of all the up-wings are the mayflies, genus *Ephemera*, which measure 2.5 cm (1 in) or so in body length. Although the mayflies are the largest of the group, smaller species, including the medium olive, blue-winged olive, iron blue, and spurwings, have longer seasons and are taken more often by fish. Some, such as *Caenis*, are so small that imitations are tied on hooks as tiny as size 24.

FEMALE MAYFLY SPINNER
The imago, or spinner, of the mayfly Ephemera danica is a handsome creature with sparkling, dark-veined wings. After mating, the female returns to the water to lay her eggs. With this task accomplished, her life is over, and she falls spent upon the water's surface. The trout are quick to take advantage.

FEMALE MAYFLY DUN
The subimago, or dun, of the mayfly emerges towards mid-day, when it may elicit a spectacular rise of fish.

GREENWELL'S GLORY
This, perhaps the most famous of all up-wing imitations, was devised in 1854 by Canon Greenwell and James Wright to tempt large brown trout on Scotland's River Tweed.

POND OLIVE NYMPH
This has the typical profile of nymphs of the family Baetidae, which also includes the medium olive and large dark olive. They are all basically olive in colour, well camouflaged to avoid detection by predators, and because of their ability to move quickly when necessary are called "agile darters".

OLIVE NYMPH
This is a simple, general tying to suggest a wide range of up-wing nymphs. It uses a pale olive fur body plus dark pheasant tail fibres to mimic the coloration of the natural close to emergence. It should be fished dead-drift or with a slow retrieve.

CADDIS FLIES

Caddis or sedge flies are to be found on both still and running water, and their life cycle includes larval, pupal, and adult stages. They are mothlike insects belonging to the order Trichoptera, which means "hairy-winged"; caddis flies have hairs on their wings, whereas the wings of moths are covered in tiny, dustlike scales.

The larva is soft bodied, and many species build protective cases from stones, sand, weed, even small snail shells. There are also caseless caddis fly larvae, however, and these include species of *Hydropsyche* and *Rhyacophila*. The larva is an active creature with a pair of specially adapted, hair-fringed legs that enable it to swim strongly.

When pupation occurs, even the caseless species build a protective case, which is usually anchored to a large rock. When fully developed, the pupa uses its strong jaws to cut itself free of its case. It then rises to the surface, at which point its skin splits along the thorax and the adult emerges. The adult has four wings, which lie along the body when at rest, and these give the caddis its typical roof-winged profile.

CADDIS LARVA CASES
The protective cases built by the larvae of many caddis species are bonded together by a tough material that is secreted by the creatures.

CADDIS PUPA
This imitation of a medium-sized caddis pupa mimics the natural's curved body and antennae.

ADULT SEDGE
The adult sedge has long antennae and four wings. Species range in size from 6 mm (¼ in) up to 38 mm (1½ in) in the case of the great red sedge Phryganea grandis.

FISH & CRUSTACEANS

The diet of trout and bass is not restricted to insects; various baitfish also make up a proportion of their diet. Many not only provide a substantial meal but are to be found in convenient, tightly packed shoals, just there for the taking. Silvery flanked species such as roach and bream are very important on stillwaters, where trout can go into a veritable feeding frenzy as they charge into the shoals. On rivers, minnows and small, bottom-dwelling species are the selected prey.

Crustaceans, too, rank high on the dietary list. Most numerous are the freshwater shrimps or scuds, such as *Gammarus*, which are bottom-dwelling creatures ranging in length from 6 mm (¼ in) to 18 mm (¾ in) and varying in colour from a pale, washed-out olive to a rusty brown. Imitations should reflect this if they are to be effective. Another common food item, the water hoglouse (*Asellus*), is similar in size to a freshwater shrimp. This crustacean is most often found in stillwaters, where it occurs in prolific numbers, living and feeding in the bottom detritus.

MILLER'S THUMB
Sculpins such as the miller's thumb are heavily preyed upon, particularly by large brown trout.

WATER HOGLOUSE
This dull, insignificant-looking creature inhabits many lakes and slow rivers in huge numbers.

FRESHWATER SHRIMP
The freshwater shrimp, Gammarus, forms an important part of the diet of both stillwater and river trout. Imitations should be well weighted, and similar in colour to the naturals.

HOGLOUSE
Hare fur, brown partridge, and dark turkey tail make an effective copy of the natural.

NATURALS 2

DAMSELFLIES & DRAGONFLIES

Summer would not really be the same without the sight of these large, predatory insects darting around marginal vegetation as they quarter their territories. Both belong to the order Odonata but are grouped into suborders, the damselflies being Zygoptera while the dragonflies are Anisoptera.

Both suborders have an aquatic nymphal stage, which is also predatory and feeds on tiny aquatic creatures. The adults of damselflies may be distinguished from adult dragonflies by their slimmer bodies and by the way they fold their wings along their bodies when at rest; the dragonflies hold their wings out horizontally. Both nymphs and adults are taken by fish such as bass and trout, and good imitations can prove very successful when cast around weedbeds and partly submerged timber.

DAMSELFLY NYMPH (*left*)
The damselfly nymph may be distinguished from the dragonfly nymph by its much slimmer appearance and the three leaflike gills on the tip of the abdomen. It comes in a wide range of shades of olive and brown to mimic its habitat.

COMMON BLUE DAMSELFLY (*below*)
The common blue damselfly, Enallagma cyathigerum, is a well-known sight around lakes. When mature, the nymph climbs free of the water, its skin splits along the back, and the adult emerges.

DAMSELFLY
A dry damselfly imitation can prove effective in summer, when trout and bass leap to take the natural insects.

STONEFLIES

Stoneflies, which are insects of the order Plecoptera, are creatures of stony or gravel-bottomed rivers. On these waters, particularly in their nymphal form, they form an important part of the diet of trout and other fish.

Most species are dark brown or black but a few are much brighter, notably the aptly named Yellow Sally. At rest, the hard, shiny, heavily veined wings are held flat along the top of the body. The aquatic nymphal stage (or creeper) of the stonefly is an active creature, scuttling over the rocks that are its habitat. When mature, it clambers free of the water, usually onto marginal rock. The skin along the back of the thorax splits and the adult emerges.

Although trout will take the female returning to lay her eggs, the nymph is the most important stage to the fly fisher. A heavily weighted nymph imitation, allowed to drift just off the bottom, can prove very effective during high water conditions.

STONEFLY NYMPH
The stonefly nymph differs from the nymphs of up-winged flies in having two tails rather than three.

DRY STONEFLY
When female stoneflies return to lay their eggs, flopping along on the water's surface, trout feeding on them will often take a dry imitation of the correct size.

ADULT STONEFLY
Stoneflies vary in length from less than 6 mm (¼ in), in the case of small species such as needle flies, to the 5 cm (2 in) of the Pteronarcys species. Although they are capable of flight, many stoneflies are happy to crawl through bankside cover.

CHIRONOMIDS

The various species of chironomid, or non-biting midge, belonging to the genus *Chironomus* make up a very large proportion of the stillwater trout's diet. The life cycle begins when the egg hatches into a small, wormlike larva that burrows into the bottom mud. Chironomid larvae vary in colour from pale olive and brown to the vivid blood-red of the *Chironomus plumosus* larva, known as the bloodworm. The bloodworm receives its colour from haemoglobin, a substance that enables it to thrive in the black, oxygen-poor mud of lakebeds.

When the larvae pupate, the pupae remain within their mud burrows until fully developed, a period that can be as little as 36 hours. Then they rise to the surface to transform into adults, where they are at the mercy of the trout, which take them in truly prodigious quantities. The pupae are taken not only as they rise but also at the very point of emergence as adults.

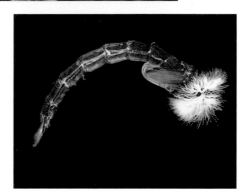

ADULT CHIRONOMID
The adults of the chironomids have slim bodies and two wings, and range in size from the merest wisp up to 12 mm (½ in) or more. They vary in colour from black and brown to bright green.

MIDGE PUPA
Imitations of chironomid pupae should mimic the bulbous-thoraxed profiles of the naturals.

CHIRONOMID PUPA
Although varying in size, all chironomid pupae have slim abdomens, bulbous thoraxes, and white breathing filaments. Black is the most common colour.

TERRESTRIALS

Not all creatures that find themselves engulfed by large predatory fish are aquatic: many are terrestrials, which are non-aquatic insects and other life forms that are carried or fall onto the water's surface. Many, such as spiders, beetles, hoverflies, ants, and aphids, are blown onto the water by the wind. On large, windswept expanses of water, it is common for winged insects to be blown out over the surface. Many of them succumb to the waves, or are simply weak fliers that have to touch down on the water.

The large, gangling-legged crane fly is one such insect. Also known as the daddy longlegs, it is usually at its most numerous during the damp days of autumn, when it can produce a confident rise of feeding fish. Earlier in the year, the hawthorn fly and related species can find their way onto rivers and lakes with similar results.

Terrestrials make up a large part of the diet of many fish, including trout, in rainfed rivers. The water in this type of river is often deficient in nutrients, resulting in a poor aquatic biomass. In such waters the trout are opportunist feeders, quick to snap up caterpillars, beetles, and indeed any unfortunate small creature that happens to fall from bankside vegetation.

CRANE FLY
To be effective, imitations of the crane fly, or daddy longlegs, should always include the long, trailing legs of the natural.

HAWTHORN FLY
This large, jet-black fly is on the wing during late spring, when the long-legged males hover in small swarms around bankside vegetation.

BLACK ANT
This pattern is useful during the sultry days of late summer, when swarms of flying ants often appear.

GUM BEETLE
The iridescent gum beetle is very popular with Australian brown and rainbow trout.

103

THE ARTIFICIAL FLY

The artificial fly is the link between the fly fisherman and the fish, and designing it offers the angler the challenge of creating the illusion of a delicate insect or other small creature from a handful of inanimate objects. The fly and the skill of presentation then come together to seduce the fish into taking that fly, either from aggression or from the belief that it is a living creature. It is this pitting of the angler's abilities against the natural guile of the fish that gives fly fishing its special appeal.

ORANGE
BUSTARD

GOLDEN
DRAKE

FLY HISTORY
The first stirrings of modern fly design began in 1676 with Charles Cotton's chapter in The Compleat Angler *listing 65 effective fly patterns. The creation of new patterns reached its peak in the late 19th and early 20th centuries.*

ATTRACTORS & DECEIVERS

Artificial flies fall into two main groups: attractors and deceivers. Attractors are usually gaudy, bright creations designed to stimulate a predatory fish's aggression; they suggest nothing edible but provoke a predatory response. Orange and yellow are favourite colours for attractor flies. Deceivers are intended to fool the fish into mistaking them for natural food items, such as nymphs, crustaceans, or small fish. This group includes dry flies, nymphs, and some wet fly patterns, particularly those that are direct imitations of a fish's food. Deceivers are usually subtle in coloration, mimicking the hues of the naturals.

DECEIVER

ATTRACTOR

TYPES OF FLY

WINGED
WET FLY

WINGED
DRY FLY

NYMPH

HAIRWING

Wet flies
Wet flies are effective on a wide range of water types, from rivers and streams to vast, windswept lakes, but all have one thing in common: they are fished beneath the water's surface. Some wet flies are subtly coloured deceivers, while the more gaudy types of dressing work as attractors.

Wet fly types vary from simple spider patterns, with merely a few turns of hackle at the eye, to intricate dressings with hackles both along the hook and at the throat, plus a wing. Many of the winged wet flies used for stillwater boat fishing are of this latter type.

Another type, palmers, have rough, dubbed bodies with hackles running the entire length.

Dry flies
The dry fly is designed to float on the water's surface. To prevent it sinking, water-repellent hackles are wound around the hook to distribute the weight over the surface of the water. The hackles also simulate the legs and "buzz" of an aquatic or terrestrial insect trapped on the water.

Most dry flies are deceivers, and many patterns are designed to imitate specific insects; examples include the Blue Winged Olive, Grannom, and Crane Fly. Others, such as the Wickham's Fancy and the Adams, are more general designs that are intended just to look edible.

Dry flies may be simply hackled, or tied with wings, depending on the level of imitation required.

Nymphs
A nymph is the immature stage of certain aquatic insects such as mayflies and damselflies. Imitations of this stage are likewise termed nymphs, and the term is also applied to wingless patterns that suggest the larval and pupal stages of insects. Natural nymphs have sombre hues, so the artificials are similarly coloured. Browns, olives, and greens are especially effective, as are mottled shades.

Emergers
Emergers are tied to imitate that stage of an aquatic insect's life when it actually emerges, at the water's surface, from its nymphal or pupal skin. While trapped on the surface, emerging insects are particularly vulnerable to fish predation.

Streamers and hairwings
Streamer and hairwing flies, which are generally large and tied on long-shanked hooks, include the majority of salmon and steelhead patterns. The difference between streamers and hairwings is simply that the wings of streamers are tied with feathers, such as marabou or cock hackles, while those of hairwings are tied with hair, including bucktail and squirrel tail.

Like wet flies, streamers and hairwings may be brightly coloured attractors or more subtle deceivers, and many have an imitative role. For example, some are tied to imitate the small fish that are eaten by predators such as trout and pike. These patterns often incorporate white and silver materials.

PARTS OF A FLY

The head
The head is normally the last part of the fly to be tied, and usually consists of turns of tying thread that hold in place the wing, the hackle, and the loose ends of both rib and body materials. Because it secures these other components it is the weak point of the fly, and therefore it is important that the thread is finished off correctly and that the bare turns are well protected. The head is protected by coats of cellulose varnish, which are applied with either the tip of a fine needle or a specially designed applicator. When coloured threads are used, clear varnish gives the best results, though for streamers and other large flies, two or three coats of black or red varnish produce a smooth, glossy effect.

The wing
In both dry and wet flies the wing often suggests that of a natural insect, but may be added simply to provide movement. This is particularly the case in those wet flies and streamers that use mobile wing materials, such as cock hackles, to give "life" to the fly. Many feathers and furs are used to produce fly wings, one of the most popular materials being slips taken from the primary feathers of game birds. Duck feathers are especially useful, and the smoky shades of mallard and teal closely match the wing coloration of many species of mayfly.

The tail
In dry flies the tail not only acts in an imitative way, suggesting that of the natural, but, by becoming trapped on the surface of the water, it balances the fly and helps it to float. In wet flies and streamers the tail is usually decorative rather than functional; often brightly coloured, it is added to give the fly extra fish-attracting allure.

Cock hackle fibres are often used for imitative tails, while for a brighter effect, wool, fluorescent floss, hair, and golden pheasant toppings and tippets are all very popular. Highly mobile materials are also widely used; marabou, dyed in a variety of colours, gives a wonderfully sinuous action to a wide range of large nymphs and lead-headed patterns.

The wing

The head

The rib

The tail

The hackle

The body

Hook

Hooks
Fly hooks range from the tiny midge-sized models to giant long-shanks, with single, double, or treble points, depending on their use. Worldwide, singles are by far the most popular for all types of fly.

The hackle
Hackles, in their various forms, are the basis of the vast majority of fly patterns. Although a range of feathers may be used, it is those taken from the necks or "capes" of domestic poultry that provide the hackle on over 90 per cent of artificial flies. The diversity of colours and stiffnesses, found in both male and female plumage, has shaped the whole development of wet flies and dry flies throughout their history.

In dry flies, it is inevitably the stiffer-fibred, more water-repellent cock hackles that provide the flotation. Conversely, the softer hen hackle is preferred for wet flies and streamers, where its ability to become rapidly waterlogged is a prime factor. Soft hackles also work better in the water, providing movement and a semblance of life to what is an otherwise dead object.

Where softness and mobility are the prerequisite, rather than the ability to float, other types of feather may be used. Feathers from species such as grouse, snipe, partridge, and mallard are all effective examples; their coloration mimics superbly that of many natural nymphs and pupae.

The body
The body of a fly covers the bulk of the hook and provides the substance of a pattern. A wide range of materials is used, from sombre furs to flashy metallic products. On imitative patterns, or those that merely suggest a living creature, fur (or a man-made substitute) gives a wonderful shaggy effect, especially when teased out. Smoother effects are produced by floss, flat metal tinsel, or Lurex. Mylar tubing, with its scaly appearance, is particularly good for imitations of small fish. Feather fibre also gives an interesting texture: goose, turkey, and cock pheasant tail are effective examples.

Detached body
The detached body is the only type that is not formed around the hook: it is created out of plastic, deer hair, or feather and secured to the hook at one end only, projecting back over the bend. Its advantages, even on a large fly, are that it is light and it allows the use of a much smaller hook.

The rib
The function of a rib is threefold. Firstly, it mimics the segmentation of the body of an insect or small crustacean. Secondly, if made from a sparkling material, such as metal tinsel or Lurex, it adds extra flash to a pattern, or, on more imitative dressings, it is used to suggest the gases trapped within an emerging insect's skin. Thirdly, a tough material (metal wire for example) adds to the durability of the fly, holding a delicate body in place or protecting it from the ravages of a predatory fish.

Traditionally, wire and metal twists were used to rib all types of fly. Plain wire is still very popular, and now comes in a variety of colours. While metals are fine for patterns intended to sink, their weight is a disadvantage on flies intended to sit on or in the surface. Here, lighter materials are better. Nylon monofilament is a robust alternative, while Lurex, although more delicate, works superbly on emerger-style patterns. Coloured, translucent plastic strands produce a very lifelike segmented effect on nymph and pupa imitations.

FLY TYING EQUIPMENT

Before you can begin tying your own flies, you need to obtain the basic tools and materials. For tools, a vice, scissors, hackle pliers, and a bobbin holder are all that are really necessary at first, and the other tools can be purchased as you gain experience. The most difficult decision is what to choose from the dazzling array of furs and feathers available. The best solution to this is to take a look at three or four of your favourite patterns, make a note of all the ingredients, and then use this as your shopping list.

Vice jaws

Vice handle

Height adjuster

Bench clamp

BOBBIN HOLDERS
The best bobbin holders are the spigot type, where the bobbin is held by sprung metal arms. The thread is fed off through a tube.

HACKLE PLIERS
Hackle pliers are used to wind hackles, chenille, and other materials. The simplest and best are made of sprung metal, with either smooth metal or rubber-covered jaws to prevent them cutting the hackle material.

DUBBING NEEDLE
A fine, sharp needle has many uses, such as dividing wing slips or picking out dubbed body material to create a ragged effect. You can buy a purpose-made dubbing needle or use a large sewing needle.

SHARP-NOSED SCISSORS
Scissors, with either straight or curved blades, are extremely important to the fly tier. The base of the jaws is used to cut tough materials, leaving the tips sharp enough for precise trimming.

HAIR STACKER
Producing a neat hairwing with all the tips even is not easy: all too often the hairs remain staggered. Using a hair stacker enables you to get the tips neatly aligned.

DUBBING TWISTER
Looping the dubbing produces some interesting effects. This tool uses sprung metal arms to hold the loop open, and its weight helps you to spin the thread.

WHIP FINISH TOOL
The whip finish tool is very useful if you find the hand whip finish difficult, or when materials are very close to the eye of the hook. The standard tool has two wire arms over which the thread is looped.

BOBBIN THREADER
Using this simple tool makes it much easier to feed thread through the thin tube of a spigot bobbin holder.

VICE
Of all the tools used by the fly tier, the vice is certainly the most important. It is the means by which the hook is held stationary while all the threads and materials are added to produce the finished fly. The hook is held between a pair of metal jaws, which can be adjusted to accommodate a wide range of hook sizes and diameters of wire. Various types of vice are available. Some have simple screw-tightened jaws, while on others the jaws are spring loaded or, as in the type shown here, are operated by a single cam lever. Whichever type of mechanism is used, the mark of a good vice is that it holds the hook securely, allowing no movement.

GOLDEN PHEASANT TIPPETS

PHEASANT FEATHERS
The feathers of many species of pheasant are used for tying flies, especially the centre tails of both sexes of the ring-necked pheasant. The most colourful pheasant feathers are used for salmon patterns.

SECTION OF COCK PHEASANT TAIL FEATHER

HEN CAPE

HEN PHEASANT TAIL FEATHERS

TEAL WINGS

CAPES
The hackles from the capes of domestic poultry form the basis of most flies. The soft hackles of hens are good for wet flies, while the more water-repellent cock hackles are better used for dry flies.

COCK CAPE

TEAL WINGS
The primary feathers of a number of duck species, including teal, offer pale grey shades that mimic those found in the wings of many natural up-winged flies.

DYED SQUIRREL TAIL

WOOD DUCK

MARABOU

NATURAL SQUIRREL

MALLARD

MARABOU
Once obtained from the marabou stork, this highly mobile feather now comes from the domestic white turkey.

DUCK FEATHERS
Among the most popular duck feathers used in fly tying are bronze and speckled grey mallard feathers and the barred black-and-white feathers of the teal and pintail. The striking black-and-white and speckled, lemon feathers of the wood duck are also used.

PEACOCK HERL
The herl (barbs) of the male peacock's eye feather produce sparkling, bulbous bodies and thoraxes.

SQUIRREL TAIL
Although the grey, white, and black tail hair of the grey squirrel may be used in its natural state, bleaching it and then dyeing it with pure colours vastly increases its versatility as a fly material.

PEACOCK HERL

TINSEL
Tinsel gives sparkle to the fly and protects delicate body materials.

TYING THREAD
Fly-tying thread was originally made of natural silk, but today silk has been almost entirely superseded by man-made fibres such as nylon, which are much stronger and also rotproof. Tying threads are sold in many colours, either plain or pre-waxed.

RAYON FLOSS
Like tying thread, floss was originally made from silk. Today, fibres such as rayon are used to make multi-stranded, rotproof floss that spreads and flattens as it is wound, helping to produce a neat body.

WOOL
Natural or man-made wool is used to make tails, or wound or teased out and dubbed to form fat, "buggy" fly bodies.

VARNISH
Varnish is used to protect the bare threads at the eye of the hook. Clear or coloured cellulose varnish may be used, but for bonding materials in place an adhesive varnish with a vinyl base is much better.

MYLAR TUBING
This sparkling, metallic-finish tubing has a wonderful scale-effect surface, perfect for producing the bodies of fish fry imitations.

POLYPROPYLENE FLOSS
This light, water-repellent material is ideal for both bodies and for the wings of dry flies that imitate "spent" naturals.

FLY TYING BASICS 1

The ability to tie flies is one of the fly fisher's greatest assets, and fly tying is also a source of considerable pleasure in itself. Tying flies allows the individual angler to develop new and effective patterns, or to make subtle adjustments to an established dressing to increase its fish-catching potential. To the angler-entomologist it is an indispensable skill: to watch a fish taking a particular insect, then to construct an imitation good enough to fool that fish into taking it, elicits a sense of satisfaction rarely found elsewhere in angling.

FLY TYING
The pleasures of fly fishing are greatly enhanced when you use flies that you have tied yourself.

STARTING OFF & WHIP FINISHING

There is obviously little point in beginning to tie a fly if you do not know how to start off the tying thread. What may not be so obvious is that it is equally important to learn how to finish the fly securely: without a robust finish, the fly will simply fall apart during fishing. Starting the thread off properly allows you to build a neat, strong bed to which you will attach the rest of the materials; neatness and strength are the secret of constructing a tidy, robust fly. The whip finish is the most secure way of finishing a fly. It entails winding a loop of thread over itself repeatedly then pulling it tight, and bedding the loose end beneath turns of thread produces a firm finish that will take a good deal of punishment.

Starting off

1 Fix the hook securely in a vice. Next, loop the thread beneath the hook, forming an upright V-shape.

2 Hold the loose end of thread taut and wind the bobbin end over it. Wind until the loose end is trapped.

Whip finishing by hand

1 When the fly is complete, form a figure-4-shaped loop over the first two fingers of your right hand.

2 Flip the fingers around, bringing them beneath the hook. This takes the vertical strand over the loose end.

3 Repeat four or five times, ensuring that the loop is wound neatly over the loose end lying back along the hook.

4 Slip the thread off the fingers, draw the loop tight, and insert a dubbing needle into it to retain tension.

Using a whip finish tool

1 Loop the tying thread around the two prongs of the whip finish tool. Then bring the thread back to form a figure-4 shape.

2 Rotate the tool so that it falls beneath the hook, trapping the loose end. This movement forms the first turn of the whip finish.

3 Repeat the process four or five times. When you are happy with the number of turns, slip the thread off the lower prong of the tool.

4 Retain tension by allowing the thread to catch on the hooked prong. Steadily pull the loose end of the thread to draw the loop tight.

TAILS

A tail may represent that of a natural insect, impart movement to a fly, or just add a flash of colour. The materials used for tails range from cock hackle fibres to fluorescent floss, and on traditional wet fly patterns, the black and gold banding of the golden pheasant tippet feather produces a striking effect.

BODIES

Bodies come in many shapes and sizes, from the slimness of flat tinsel to the ragged effect of dubbed fur. In most patterns, the main task of the body is to provide the substance of the fly.

Most bodies, except those that are detached or of Mylar tubing, are actually wound around the hook shank. Take care to ensure that each turn is as close to the next one as possible, with no gaps.

RIBS

The rib provides sparkle and adds strength, whether it is bedding into a soft body or protecting a delicate body or hackle. The perfect rib forms a neat, open spiral, running the length of the body. Coloured wires and tinsel are the traditional materials, but nylon monofilament is ideal for ribbing dry flies. Lurex and Crystal Hair both give a superb, non-tarnish sparkle effect.

Tying a tail

1 Tie the thread to the hook shank opposite the barb. Select a well-marked golden pheasant tippet feather.

2 Remove five or six fibres from the feather. Offer the bunch up to the hook, extending it beyond the bend.

3 Catch in the tail with turns of thread, ensuring it does not twist. The tail should be about half the hook's length.

Tying a tinsel body

1 Ensure that an even bed has been formed, then cut the tip of the tinsel to a thin "scallop" and catch it in.

2 Take the tying thread to just short of the eye. Wind the tinsel up the body in tight, closely butted turns.

3 Secure the loose end with turns of thread; remove excess tinsel. Wind rib over the body in an open spiral.

Dubbing a body

1 With the rib caught in, offer a small pinch of dubbing up to prewaxed thread. Ensure that the spread is even.

2 Gently twist the dubbing between forefinger and thumb into an even rope. Wind over hook in close turns.

3 Finish the body just short of the eye. Wind the rib, then tease out the fibres of fur with a dubbing needle.

Tying a rib

1 Run the tying thread down the hook to a point opposite the barb. There, catch in the ribbing material with several turns of thread.

2 Allow the waste end of the ribbing to lie along almost the full length of the hook shank to produce an even underbody.

3 Add the body material. Then wind the ribbing material firmly around and along the body so that it forms a neat, open spiral.

FLY TYING BASICS 2

HACKLES

The exact function of a hackle depends on the type of fly it is tied on. In wet flies, nymphs, streamers, and in fact any pattern that is fished subsurface, the hackle represents the legs of a nymph or the twitching fins of a small fish. In dry flies and emergers, the hackle is used to suggest the legs and wings of an insect and also to keep the fly afloat. Palmered flies not only have a hackle at the head but also one wound along the body. This produces a dense "bumble" effect, providing great floatability in dry flies and a superb action in wet flies.

Most hackles are made of feathers, but various types of hair may also be adapted into a hackle: rabbit, hare, and squirrel may all be spun in a dubbing loop, then wound over the hook to form a thorax-cum-hackle. It is a technique that lends itself particularly well to nymph and pupa imitations.

Wet-fly hackle

1 Catch in the hackle feather just behind the eye. Make four full turns, using hackle pliers, then secure the tip.

2 Stroke the hackle fibres beneath the hook, fastening them in place with turns of tying thread.

3 Remove any hackle fibres still above the hook or not lying back properly. Finally, add a wing and a whip finish.

Dubbing-loop hackle

1 With the body covering the rear two-thirds of the hook, insert a pinch of hare's fur into a loop of tying thread.

2 Take hold of the loop with a pair of hackle pliers and twist it until the fur spins into a fluffy rope.

3 Wind the fur over the hook up to the eye; trim the thorax top and sides, but leave some hairs beneath the hook.

Dry-fly hackle

1 With the body complete, prepare a cock hackle by stripping the butt, leaving a short, bare stem.

2 Catch in the hackle and take hold of the tip with a pair of hackle pliers. Make three or four full turns.

3 Ensure that the turns are butted together. Secure the hackle tip, remove the waste end, and tie a whip finish.

Palmered hackle

1 With body in place prepare a cock hackle by stripping the butt, leaving a short, bare stem. Catch in the hackle.

2 Using pliers, wind the hackle down the body to the bend. Ensure each turn is evenly spaced.

3 Wind the ribbing material up through the hackle in the opposite spiral. This will fix the hackle in place.

4 Remove excess hackle at the bend and ribbing at the eye. Add a second, slightly longer-fibred hackle at the eye.

WINGS

Wings can give movement to a fly or, when used in a more imitative role, suggest those of a real insect. In streamers, the traditional wing material is cock hackle, taken either from the neck or saddle of the bird, but dyed turkey marabou, with its superb, pulsating action, is now the firm favourite. Hairwings use a variety of hair types to provide their profile and to create a stiff, robust appearance well suited to fast water.

Imitative wet-fly and dry-fly wings may be tied in a variety of positions, such as paired, split, advanced, or pent, depending on the insect stage being copied. Paired slips of duck primary feather are the most widely used, but other materials, including hackle points, polypropylene yarn, feather fibre, and even hair, all have their place.

Hackle-point wing

1 With tail and body complete, select two well-marked hackle points with fibres the same length as the hook gape.

2 Remove the base fibres from the bottom of each hackle, leaving two points approximately the same length as the hook shank.

3 Catch the hackle points in by their bare stems and bring them to a vertical position with a few turns of tying thread.

Feather wing

1 With body and hackle in place, remove two equal-sized slips from duck primaries taken from opposite sides of the bird.

2 Place the slips together, curves inward, so the curves cancel each other out. Secure the wing with several turns of thread.

3 With the wing in place, remove the excess stubs of feather before building up a neat head and finally adding a whip finish.

Single wing case

1 When the tail and body are complete, catch in a slip of feather fibre at the rear of the thorax position.

2 Add the thorax (here it is dubbed fur) then stretch the fibre over the back, securing it at the eye.

Hair wing

1 Leaving a space behind the eye, take a small bunch of hair, removing broken hairs before judging for length.

2 With the hair projecting slightly past the bend, fix it in position with locking turns of thread around the base.

HEADS

The head may simply be the finishing point of a fly or it may have an extra function: it can be weighted to make the fly sink, or else made buoyant to enable the fly to be "waked" through the water's surface. The Muddler, with its buoyant deer-hair head, is a famous example of this latter group.

Muddler head

1 With body and wing in place, offer up a bunch of deer hair to the hook shank, securing it in place with two loose turns of thread.

2 Pull the thread tight. This makes the hair flare and spin. Add further bunches, if required, and then carefully trim the hair to shape.

3 Using a sharp pair of scissors, clip the hair into a neat bullet shape. Allow a ruff of hair tips to remain as a sort of hackle.

SIMPLE HEAD

DRY FLIES

The term "dry fly" covers a vast and structurally diverse range of patterns, from the merest speck intended to imitate a midge right up to something as bulky as a large caddis fly, mayfly, or dragonfly imitation. The main prerequisite of all dry flies is that they should float on or in the surface, and so they are tied with various light or water-repellent materials. Cock hackles are the most often-used aid to flotation, but other materials such as deer hair and polypropylene are also used to good effect.

GREY WULFF
This is one of a series of large, well-hackled patterns, devised by the late Lee Wulff, which ride high even in fast-flowing or broken water. This version is a representation of the mayfly Ephemera danica.

IRON BLUE (*right*)
This imitates a number of small, dark, up-winged flies of the genus Baetis, *including B. muticus. This hackled pattern is effective during the naturals' main emergence periods of early summer and autumn.*

LETORT HOPPER
Pennsylvania's Letort River gives its name to this simple grasshopper imitation. As in many other imitations of this chunky terrestrial, deer body hair is used for the head and overwing to give the required buoyancy.

TRAUN-WING CADDIS
Traun River Products manufactures meshed, lifelike wing material, which mimics the veining of a caddis fly's wing. Used in conjunction with softer materials, it produces good imitations of many caddis species.

DADDY LONGLEGS
The daddy longlegs, or crane fly, is a large, gangling terrestrial and is common in late summer and early autumn. Imitations fished dry or wet often produce better-than-average fish.

CUT-WING GREEN DRAKE
This pattern uses shaped mallard breast feathers to imitate the wings of a mayfly dun or green drake. The realistic profile makes the fly effective even when the trout have seen everything else.

POLY-WING SPINNER
The water-repellent properties of polypropylene are put to good use here, where the material forms the wing of a small imitation of a spent spinner.

GODDARD SEDGE
This highly buoyant imitation of an adult caddis, devised by John Goddard, is made almost entirely of deer hair. It works well on both stillwaters and streams.

ADAMS
The Adams has gradually become the most widely used up-winged dun pattern. Its grey fur body, grizzle hackle-point wings, and mixed grizzle and brown hackle give the subtle coloration of a freshly emerged olive dun. It may be tied on hooks ranging in size from a 10 right down to a 24.

HUMPY
The Humpy uses the buoyancy of deer body hair to keep it riding high even in fast, broken water. It is an excellent general pattern that will take anything from trout in small streams to salmon on wide, powerful rivers.

IRRESISTIBLE
The Irresistible, dressed in a range of sizes, is a truly adaptable pattern that will take trout from small, broken streams and even salmon and steelhead. The key to its effectiveness is the body of spun and clipped deer hair, which produces an almost unsinkable fly.

BLACK KLINKHAMMER
Hans van Klinken, of the Netherlands, devised this novel variation on the parachute hackle theme. It is tied large on an emerger hook to give it the bent effect typical of an emerging chironomid.

COMPARA-DUN
The easily tied Compara-dun, which was devised by American fly tiers Al Caucci and Bob Nastasi, offers a very lifelike profile of a newly emerged olive dun mayfly.

TROTH CADDIS
Al Troth is the originator of this very effective imitation of an adult caddis fly. It uses a wing of bleached elk hock to create the correct silhouette and make it very buoyant, and is effective on both still and running water.

DUCK'S DUN
Cul de canard feathers, which are taken from around the preen glands of ducks such as mallard, make effective wings for up-wing imitations. The Duck's Dun suggests a wide range of species including the blue-winged olive, medium olive, and lake olive.

EPHEMERELLA SPINNER
This imitates the spent imago or spinner of up-wings of the genus Ephemerella, *such as the blue-winged olive. Its hackle suggests the insect's wings trapped in the surface of the water.*

HARE'S FACE MIDGE
Charles Jardine devised this fine representation of an adult chironomid midge. It uses the sandy fur from a hare's mask to suggest the shading of the natural, plus a wing of cul de canard feather for good visibility.

HAWTHORN FLY
This is a specific imitation of the hawthorn fly Bibio marci, *a terrestrial that gathers in small swarms around bankside vegetation in middle to late spring. Imitations should mimic the size, colour, and trailing legs of the natural.*

THORAX MAYFLY
The speckled, lemon feathers from wood duck are used to mimic the wing colour and markings in this imitation of the larger mayfly species such as Ephemera danica.

CLARET HOPPER
The Hopper series has taken the stillwater fishing scene by storm. Dry-fly fishing was once seldom considered an effective technique on lakes and reservoirs, but the Hopper, with its devastating effectiveness even in calm conditions, has changed all that.

GINGER QUILL
This traditional pattern imitates the dun of small to medium-sized olives or up-wings. A strand of peacock eye feather represents segmentation, and slips of grey mallard or starling primary imitate the wing coloration of the natural. Similar patterns include Olive Quill and Red Quill.

BEACON BEIGE
This fly, popularized by fly tier Peter Deane, is one of the best general imitations of an olive dun. It uses a mixed hackle of grizzle and brown to give a lifelike "buzz", and the body is of stripped peacock quill.

DAVE'S HOPPER
The Dave in this instance is American fly tier Dave Whitlock, an angler who has put his name to many very effective trout and bass patterns. This wonderful imitation of a grasshopper uses knotted slips of turkey feather to imitate the large jumping legs of the natural.

113

WET FLIES

The wet fly is designed to fish below the water's surface. In order to accomplish this, many wet flies are tied slim, with wing and hackle swept back to minimize water resistance. Exceptions to this include the palmers, which are dense, bushy-hackled flies created for use on large natural waters. These are designed to make an attractive disturbance in the water's surface as they are retrieved. Other winged wet-fly patterns are tied as general attractors or as the suggestion of an adult insect.

DARK CAHILL
This is the dark member of a pair of patterns created by American fly tier Dan Cahill. With its dark grey body and lemon wood-duck wing it is a fair representation of a number of darker medium-sized species of Ephemeroptera, including members of the genus Stenonema. It may be fished upstream or in the classic down-and-across style.

INVICTA
The Invicta, created back in the late 19th century by James Ogden, is as popular today as ever. With its yellow seal-fur substitute body and palmered brown hackle, it makes a fair imitation of an emerging sedge pupa.

PARTRIDGE AND ORANGE
The best known of the Partridge series, and an excellent fly for rough-stream trout and grayling. In this variation, the body is of fur instead of the silk of the original version.

OLIVE BUMBLE
The doyen of Irish fly tiers, T. Kingsmill Moore, created this as part of a range of bumbles designed for the wild conditions found on large Irish waters. It is a big, bushy representation of a mayfly.

MALLARD AND CLARET
A traditional wet-fly pattern, and the most popular and enduring of a large series with bodies and hackles of various colours. The wing of the Mallard and Claret comes from the shoulder feathers of the drake mallard, and the body is of seal-fur substitute. Good for brown trout and sea trout.

BUTCHER
A fly with a long pedigree dating back at least 150 years, when it was known as Moon's Fly. Its name was changed to Butcher in the early 19th century. A fine pattern for both stillwater and river, and good for sea trout.

DUNKELD
Originally the Dunkeld was a fully dressed salmon fly with a married wing. This much-simplified version is an effective attractor pattern for trout, and it works well when fished on the point of a three-fly cast.

SOLDIER PALMER
Although this pattern should really be known as the Red Palmer, it is the dressing most stillwater trout fishers recognize as the Soldier Palmer. A superb top-dropper pattern for fishing the drift, it works well throughout the season and particularly during early summer. An indispensable pattern.

OLIVE QUILL
A wet-fly member of the popular Quill series, all of which use stripped peacock quill to give the body a striking segmented effect. This version suggests a medium-sized olive such as a lake olive or a large dark olive. Good on both lakes and rivers.

BREADCRUST
Not an imitation of a piece of bread, but a general hackled wet-fly-cum-nymph. Seal-fur substitute or wool is used to build the succulent body, which is ribbed with a stripped brown cock hackle stem. It provides a fair imitation of a caddis pupa.

DARK WATCHETT
This version of the Dark Watchett, by T. E. Pritt, is a traditional soft-hackled fly that has proved very effective on trout streams.

TEAL, BLUE, AND SILVER
With its barred wing and silver body, this member of the Teal series is a fine representation of a small fish. Good for stillwater and river trout, and large versions (up to a size 2 hook) are excellent for night fishing for sea trout.

BIBIO
This highly effective pattern is a good general representation of a number of terrestrials of the Bibionidae family, especially the heather fly, whose red legs are imitated by the brighter central section.

MARCH BROWN
An effective imitation of the natural March brown, Rhithrogena germanica, *this is a very edible-looking fly that works well even on trout that have never seen the natural. It may also be tied in a silver-bodied version.*

SOOTY OLIVE
The lake olives (Cloeon simile) *that hatch from the large limestone loughs of western Ireland are of a particularly dark hue. This pattern uses a dark olive seal-fur substitute body and a brown mallard wing to mimic their coloration. A great fly for early season.*

ROYAL COACHMAN
This definitive American pattern is the gaudy cousin of the Coachman. This, the wet-fly version, is a derivative of John Haily's 1878 dry fly and has spawned a whole range of variants including streamers and hairwings. Although the wings may vary, all have the same red central body section, butted either side with peacock herl. It often works when nothing else will.

GOSLING *(right)*
The Gosling is the epitome of the Irish stillwater fly. It is tied to represent the dun of the mayfly Ephemera danica, *which is distributed throughout Europe and hatches in impressive numbers from limestone lakes. It uses an orange cock hackle, overwound with one of speckled grey mallard flank, to suggest the wings. The colour match is hardly perfect, but it certainly does work.*

GREEN PETER
The Green Peter (Phryganea varia) *is a beautiful caddis species. The imitation is effective even when there are no naturals in evidence, and is a good point fly.*

OAKHAM ORANGE
During the warmer summer months, stillwater rainbows experience what can only be described as "orange madness". As the water warms they become more and more willing to chase bright flies, and little could be brighter than hot orange. This palmered fly, with its tag of fluorescent orange floss, is a very effective pattern either on a floating line or fished slightly deeper.

KATE MCLAREN
A sombre, heavily hackled pattern, this fly is named after the wife of Charles McLaren, a truly great sea-trout angler. It is a very effective pattern on large lakes, taking brown trout, sea trout, and salmon, and works well as a top-dropper fly.

DOOBRY
The Scottish angler and fly tier, Stan Headley, devised the Doobry for fishing in clear water on overcast days or in coloured water in brighter conditions. It is very successful in peaty water, where its combination of black, orange, and gold not only looks very good, but also catches fish.

NYMPHS

Although the word "nymph" refers to the larval stages of a number of aquatic insect species, to the fly fisher it has become a far more general term. Along with the true nymphs, it includes insect pupae, small crustaceans, and even general patterns used to suggest something small and edible. The diversity of flies classified as nymphs is truly astounding, ranging from tiny imitations of larval up-wings and midge pupae to the veritable giants that mimick creatures as different as dragonfly and stonefly nymphs.

SUSPENDER BUZZER
This Brian Leadbetter pattern imitates the chironomid pupa at the point of emergence. It uses a thorax of buoyant, closed-cell foam to keep the fly floating in the water's surface.

DISTRESSED DAMSEL
The long, mobile tail of olive marabou adds a wonderful sinuous action to this oversized imitation of a damselfly nymph. Devised by Charles Jardine, it works well on small stillwater trout, either fished blind on a slow-sinking or intermediate line, or cast to individual fish.

FOX-SQUIRREL NYMPH
This effective general nymph pattern was devised by Dave Whitlock and suggests a wide range of naturals such as stonefly nymphs and caddis larvae. It is constructed almost entirely from fox-squirrel fur.

GOLDEN STONE
The nymphs or creepers of the stonefly species vary widely in size and colour. This dressing mimics the medium to large, golden types, and should be heavily weighted to fish hard along the riverbed.

MARABOU NYMPH
Mobile turkey marabou works well in both tails and wings, and it may also be dubbed to produce an effect that is especially good for nymph imitations. The Marabou Nymph is one such pattern, and the buoyant back of deer hair makes it a very slow-sinking fly.

GOLD-HEAD DAMSEL
This effective pattern resembles a damselfly nymph, and has a gold bead at the head plus a tail of dyed olive arctic fox. The weighted bead and highly mobile tail impart a ducking, diving action to the fly that trout find irresistible. This olive form works particularly well when the natural damselfly nymphs are in abundance, but it will take fish throughout the season.

CASUAL DRESS
The Casual Dress, a highly effective general nymph pattern, was devised in the early Sixties by E. H. (Polly) Rosborough for fishing the Upper Big Deschutes in Oregon. It is made almost entirely from muskrat fur; even the thorax-hackle consists of spun muskrat, and the only exception is the ruff of black ostrich herl at the head. It is a very good suggestion of medium to large stonefly nymphs, and may be fished weighted.

DRAGONFLY NYMPH
Large, sluggish dragonfly nymphs form an important part of the diet of trout and bass in late summer. This pattern incorporates lead eyes to help work the pattern along the lakebed. Fish it around sunken timber and weedbeds.

GE NYMPH
This Charles Jardine pattern suggests a general range of up-wing or ephemerid nymphs, hence GE for "general ephemerid". It is tied in many sizes, from 20 to 10, mimicking the Baetidae and other nymphs of similar form.

LONGSHANK PHEASANT TAIL
A much smaller version of this fly is used on rivers and streams, but this large, heavy nymph is a useful addition to the stillwater angler's armoury. It works best when fished from midwater down, and is often weighted.

OLIVE FLASHBACK

This is part of a range of patterns that have a strip of pearl Lurex along the back to impart sparkle. The Lurex mimics the effect created by subcutaneous gases trapped within a nymph about to change into an adult.

WOOLY WORM

The Wooly Worm is an easily dressed pattern that has the appearance of a hairy caterpillar but is used more as a general bottom-grubbing nymph. It is tied in various natural colours including olives and browns.

JORGENSEN'S FUR THORAX PUPA

The Fur Thorax Pupa is Poul Jorgensen's superb caddis pupa imitation. The interesting part of this fly is that, by spinning in a dubbing loop, hare, rabbit, or squirrel fur is used to form a very lifelike combined thorax and hackle.

WALKER'S MAYFLY NYMPH

Richard Walker was without doubt one of the greatest contemporary designers of trout flies, with many well-thought-out patterns to his credit. His Mayfly Nymph is one of the best; observing the natural mayfly, he noted that it was not olive, as some authorities stated, but a pale ivory.

TRUE-TO-LIFE MIDGE PUPA

This is a highly lifelike imitation of the pupal stage of the non-biting midge, or chironomid. It includes the most important features of the natural, including the bulbous thorax, slim body, and breathing filaments.

PHEASANT TAIL NYMPH

All of the great many versions of this pattern use the glossy chestnut tail feather fibres of the cock ring-necked pheasant.

LARGE DARK STONE

This imitates many of the largest stonefly nymphs, particularly the darker types such as Pteronarcys californica. Since it is fished in fast water it should be tied with a heavily weighted underbody.

FOUR WATER FAVOURITE

This variation of the Hare's Ear nymph is a specific stillwater pattern developed by Gordon Fraser, and uses a small tuft of rabbit fur in the tail to provide extra movement. It should be tied weighted, using either a weighted underbody or a gold bead.

THE GOLDHEAD

Hans van Klinken originated this novel but highly effective bottom-grubbing pattern. It is a very good suggestion of a cased caddis fly, and uses a combination of a weighted underbody and a gold bead at the head to allow it to be bumped along the riverbed.

EMERGENT PUPA

This is part of a range developed by Gary LaFontaine to imitate the various stages of the caddis pupa. It uses a man-made material, Antron, to give a sparkling layer over the duller dubbed body. The Antron is added as a loose sheath so that it traps bubbles of air, giving a great impression of life. The pattern is dressed in a range of colours including brown and amber.

CASED CADDIS

This Bob Carnill dressing is a great early-season fly, imitating the cased caddis larva as it trundles along the bottom. Its weighted underbody helps it fish deep and slow.

SHRIMP

This is a specific imitation of the freshwater shrimp Gammarus pulex. The natural tends to skulk along the bottom among stones and weeds, so the imitation should be fished similarly.

BIRD'S STONEFLY NYMPH

This very good suggestion of the larger species of stonefly nymph was created by Calvert T. Bird. It is not as obviously lifelike as some imitations, but Bird's philosophy of producing a fly that is suggestive of something for the trout to eat, rather than an exact imitation of a natural, has produced a classic pattern.

117

SALMON & STEELHEAD FLIES

With a few exceptions, migratory salmonids cease feeding as they return to freshwater to spawn, but salmon and steelhead can be tempted or provoked into taking a general attractor pattern or an impression of something that they were feeding upon in the open ocean. Shrimp or prawn patterns are very effective, but curiously few dressings are produced to imitate sandeels or other baitfish. Often, however, a salmon will succumb to something as nondescript as a tiny black hairwing, having totally ignored a whole procession of larger, more colourful patterns.

SILVER RAT
The Rat series of patterns has proved extremely effective for Atlantic salmon throughout their range. The silver version uses grey fox guard hairs for the wing and has a soft grizzle hackle. It is a truly universal fly and a great favourite on Canadian rivers such as the Restigouche and Matapedia.

SILVER DOCTOR (right)
The Silver Doctor is one of the fully dressed patterns much loved by salmon anglers of the 19th and early 20th centuries. The dressings of these patterns are extremely complicated, and the original dressings included strips of dyed swan feather, married together, plus exotic plumage such as Indian crow, blue chatterer, and toucan, many of which materials are no longer available.

BLACK BRAHAN
This fly is ideal for salmon in early summer, when the water is at a reasonable level. A good fly at both dawn and dusk, its only sparkle comes from the red (or sometimes green) Lurex body.

EGG-SUCKING LEECH
This large, dark pattern suggests the big leeches that feed on the eggs of Pacific salmon. The weighted head and the pulsating body and tail of dyed black rabbit fur give this pattern a superb action, and salmon, steelhead, and rainbows find it very attractive, attacking it with gusto.

ALLY'S SHRIMP
Alistair Gowans created this pattern to simulate the translucent, shrimplike crustaceans he had observed in a trawler catch. The pattern has proved successful for salmon on large rivers.

TEENY NYMPH
Jim Teeny rates among the very best of salmon and steelhead anglers, and any pattern of his design is worth a second look. The Teeny Nymph is not really a nymph at all, but it is a very effective pattern. It uses natural or dyed pheasant tail for the body.

SPARKLE SHRIMP
A direct imitation of a shrimp, the Sparkle Shrimp uses a strip of pearl Lurex tied as a shell back to add extra fish attraction. It has proved a good fly for Pacific salmon.

GENERAL PRACTITIONER
This was developed in the early Fifties by Esmond Drury as an imitation of a prawn, for use where the natural is banned. It consists of golden-pheasant body feathers and orange fur, and has proved effective on a wide range of waters in Britain, Canada, and Iceland.

CHARTREUSE STREAMER
Steelhead and Pacific salmon find chartreuse a very attractive colour, and this pattern works well in coloured water even when fished near the bottom. Its mobile tail and weighted bead chain eyes give a superb action.

PURPLE ZONKER
The strip of rabbit fur used for the wing gives the Purple Zonker great movement, which is attractive to steelhead and salmon. However, although purple is a good colour to use during dull conditions or when light levels are low, it can either prove very effective or actually spook the fish.

COMET
During the early season, when the water is cold, tube flies offer the fly fisher a lure large enough to tempt what can be very dour fish. The Comet is a dark fly that has a wing of black bucktail, and may be tied up to 8 cm (3 in) long on plastic or brass tubes, depending on how deep it is to be fished.

GREEN HIGHLANDER
This is the hairwing version of the famous fully dressed Green Highlander pattern, and mixes various colours of bucktail to form the wing, rather than feathers as in the original. This method is used to update many traditional patterns.

WILLIE GUNN (right)
The Willie Gunn is named after the Sutherland Estate's head keeper on the River Brora in Scotland, and its wing is a mixture of yellow, red, and black bucktail. This tube-fly version may be tied on plastic or metal tubing, and works well in high or cold water.

TWO-EGG SPERM FLY (below)
Egg flies are effective patterns for steelhead and salmon, and this fly develops the idea by imitating two salmon eggs in tandem. Fluorescent orange chenille mimics the roe being shed, and a white turkey marabou wing imitates the flow of sperm over them.

UMPQUA SPECIAL
This classic pattern was developed by Don Hunter in the Thirties to tempt the steelhead of Oregon's Umpqua River. It is a bright fly, ideal for coloured water where the red-and-white combination of the hair wing is particularly deadly for steelhead. It is tied in a range of sizes, most commonly on up-eyed salmon hooks sizes 2 to 8.

SPRUCE
The Spruce was originally designed for sea-run cutthroat trout and rainbows, but it has also proved to be very successful for steelhead. It has become one of the most popular West Coast streamer patterns.

EGG FLY
This is one of the simplest of all flies, being formed from a clipped ball of Glo-Bug yarn. It is extremely effective for steelhead, Pacific salmon, and rainbow trout, and it should be weighted and fished dead-drift to imitate the movement of real eggs.

119

STREAMERS & HAIRWINGS

Streamers and hairwings differ in one obvious way: the wing of the streamer is made of feather, while that of the hairwing is made of hair. Most streamers and hairwings are large and usually dressed on long-shank hooks, and tend to be attractors or suggestive of something alive and edible for a predatory fish. The major exceptions are the imitations of coarse fish or baitfish, which include representations of species such as miller's thumbs, sculpins, or more active shoaling fish such as perch or roach.

ORANGE BOOBY
This is the lure version of Gordon Fraser's original Booby nymph. All Boobies have buoyant eyes of closed-cell foam, and this buoyancy plus a turkey marabou tail gives a tremendous action. Fish it on a fast-sinking line and an ultra-short leader.

GOLDIE
Black, gold, and yellow is an effective colour combination where brown trout are concerned, and Bob Church used it when he devised this pattern to tempt big stillwater browns. It may be tied on a single hook or as a tandem, and is a good fly for sea trout as well as browns.

BLACK GHOST
This is a typical streamer, using pairs of white cock hackle back-to-back for the wing. A good general pattern for trout and steelhead on both rivers and stillwaters, and an effective fry imitation.

DAHLBERG DIVER
This Muddler variation, created by Larry Dahlberg of Minnesota, is designed to dive by means of an angled vane trimmed from the collar of the head. It has terrific action, popping along the surface as well as diving at each pull of the retrieve. A great pattern for big trout and bass.

JAFFA
This orange mini-lure, tied with dyed turkey marabou, is very effective for stillwater rainbows in high summer, and is tied to fall within the size limit for international-rules fly-fishing competitions.

THUNDER CREEK MINNOW
This was designed by Keith Fulsher as a specific imitation of a range of small baitfish species. It offers a slim profile using brown and white bucktail, tied forward and then drawn back and secured along the hook, to provide it with the all-important countershading.

FLOATING FRY
When small baitfish are dying off, trout often take them rather than chase a more elusive meal, and an imitation designed to float can prove extremely effective. Deer hair is the perfect material for this type of buoyant pattern.

MUDDLER MINNOW
This is the original Don Gapen dressing, tied with a wing and tail of oak turkey and a head of deer body hair to imitate a small sculpin. From this pattern has developed the vast range of Muddlers we have today.

RABBIT
This effective Australian pattern uses a small strip of rabbit fur to produce a highly mobile wing. The body colour may be varied to give a wide range of patterns of an impressionistic nature.

WOOLLY BUGGER
Tied in a variety of sizes and colours, this big streamer is used as a general bottom-grubbing pattern, as an imitation of a leech, and as a general representation of large nymphs such as those of stoneflies and dragonflies.

TIN HEAD
Flies with weighted heads and long, mobile tails are much in vogue on the British stillwater scene. The Tin Heads come in a variety of tail, body, and head colour combinations. These include olive with a silver head, and black with a grizzle hackle and either a red or a fluorescent green head.

ZONKER
Rabbit fur on the skin provides a robust wing for a large range of Zonker variations, not least those that imitate small baitfish. This example has a weighted keel that keeps the hook inverted, allowing the fly to be fished around sunken timber and weedbeds without snagging.

MINKIE
This pattern is similar to the Zonker, but uses mink fur rather than the more mundane rabbit. It is tied weighted or plain and with or without a Muddler head, and is excellent as a fry imitation fished in slow draws or with a figure-of-eight retrieve.

WHITE TANDEM
Trout will at times concentrate on quite large fish fry, sometimes as large as 15 cm (6 in), to the exclusion of all other food forms. It is then important to use a pattern similar in size to the prey fish, and by joining two long-shank hooks together in tandem, a large, lightweight, and easily cast streamer is created.

PINK NASTY
Pink is a curious colour, sometimes proving almost totally ineffective, but often triggering a response in the fish that no other colour will. Gordon Fraser is responsible for this garish pattern, which combines striking fluorescent pink with a mobile tail.

BADGER MATUKA
The idea of binding the hackle wing of a streamer along the top of the hook shank originated in New Zealand. It is a technique that makes for a very robust wing resembling an elongated dorsal fin.

SOFT HACKLE STREAMER
American fly tier Jack Gartside came up with the idea of using a marabou feather as a hackle rather than as a bunched wing or tail. This simple but very effective turkey marabou tying works as a general attractor or fry imitation.

VIVA
Black and green is a very effective colour combination for a stillwater trout fly, especially when fished slowly in the early season. This Viva is a compact hairwing version of the Victor Furse original.

121

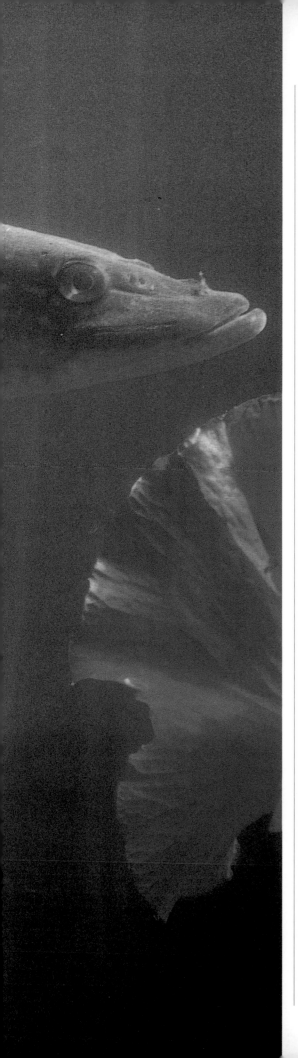

SPECIES

A SPECIES OF FISH (or any other organism) is a genetically distinct group, consisting of related individuals that resemble each other in appearance and behaviour, and can breed among themselves but not – with some exceptions – with other species. Closely related species are grouped together into genera (or genuses), and related genera are grouped into families.

Because the common names of fish can vary greatly from one region or country to another, biologists refer to them by their scientific names to avoid confusion. The scientific name of a species consists of two words, usually derived from Latin; the first of these defines the genus, and the second identifies the species. The brown trout, *Salmo trutta*, is thus the species *trutta* of the genus *Salmo*. It is also described as a salmonid, because it belongs to the Salmonidae family, which includes the salmon, trout, and char.

There are about 22,000 known species of fish, of which relatively few are of interest to anglers. This chapter gives brief descriptions of major sporting species, together with notes on the sort of techniques, tackle, and bait that may be used to catch them. They are grouped, as far as is practicable, into freshwater and saltwater species, and arranged within these groups alphabetically by family name.

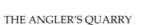

THE ANGLER'S QUARRY
The fish pursued by anglers range from small species that feed mainly on insects to voracious predators such as pike and shark.

ANATOMY

Fish can be divided broadly into two groups: those that
have skeletons made of bone (the bony fish) and those
with skeletons made of cartilage (the cartilaginous fish). In addition to
having different skeletal materials, the two groups differ in their
means of reproduction. In bony fish, with a few exceptions, the females
discharge their eggs into the water, where they are fertilized by milt (semen)
from the males. In cartilaginous fish, as in mammals, the eggs are fertilized within
the bodies of the females. (Brief explanations of the anatomical terms used here
are given in the glossary on pages 280–281.)

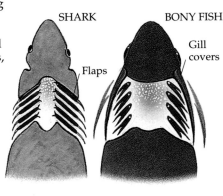

Caudal fin
or tail

Skin

BONY FISH (OSTEICHTHYES)

A typical bony fish has two sets of paired fins (pectoral and
pelvic) and a set of vertical fins (dorsal, anal, and tail). The
four gill openings on each side of the head are covered by
flattened bones, of which the operculum is the largest, and
most species possess a gas-filled swim bladder. By altering
the amount of gas (usually oxygen) in this bladder, a bony
fish can adjust its buoyancy and maintain its chosen depth
in the water without constantly swimming. Cartilaginous
fish (*see opposite*) lack swim bladders and must keep
swimming or sink to the bottom.

GILLS
A fish "breathes" by drawing
water into its mouth, then
forcing it through its gill
chambers and out via the gill
slits. Inside the gill chambers,
delicate filaments absorb
oxygen from the water and
pass it into the blood, and
remove carbon dioxide
from the blood and then
discharge it
into the
water.

SHARK   BONY FISH

Gill
covers

Flaps

ANATOMY OF A BONY FISH

First dorsal fin
(spiny rays)

Second dorsal fin
(soft rays)

Spinal column
(cut away)

Spiny first ray

Vertebra

Nerve cord

Kidney

Brain

Eye

Throat cavity

Gill rakers

Heart

Liver

Spleen

Spiny
first
ray

Pelvic
fin

Pyloric caeca

Stomach

Intestine

Swim
bladder

Gonad

Anus

Spiny
first
ray

Anal fin
(soft rays)

Muscle
segments

Front view of vertebra
*Each segment, or vertebra,
of the flexible backbone is
hollow, with a plug of
gristle at its centre.*

ANATOMY OF A CARTILAGINOUS FISH

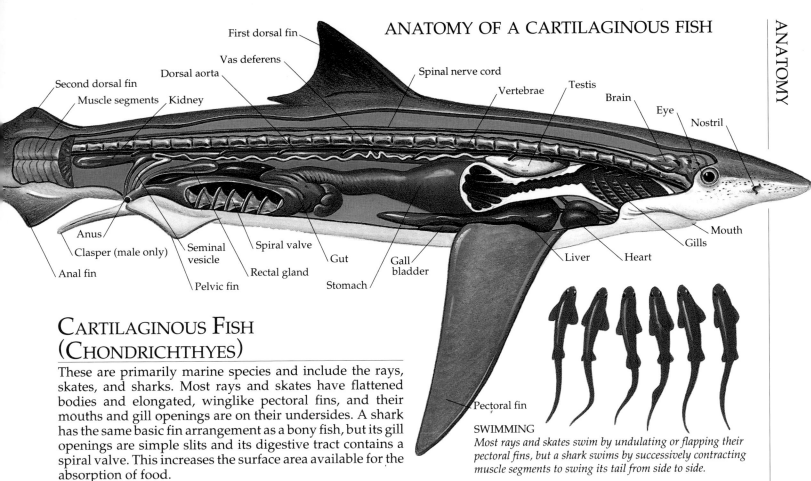

First dorsal fin
Vas deferens
Dorsal aorta
Second dorsal fin
Muscle segments Kidney
Spinal nerve cord
Vertebrae
Testis
Brain
Eye
Nostril
Anus
Clasper (male only)
Seminal vesicle
Spiral valve
Rectal gland
Gut
Gall bladder
Stomach
Liver
Heart
Gills
Mouth
Pectoral fin
Anal fin
Pelvic fin

CARTILAGINOUS FISH (CHONDRICHTHYES)

These are primarily marine species and include the rays, skates, and sharks. Most rays and skates have flattened bodies and elongated, winglike pectoral fins, and their mouths and gill openings are on their undersides. A shark has the same basic fin arrangement as a bony fish, but its gill openings are simple slits and its digestive tract contains a spiral valve. This increases the surface area available for the absorption of food.

SWIMMING
Most rays and skates swim by undulating or flapping their pectoral fins, but a shark swims by successively contracting muscle segments to swing its tail from side to side.

LATERAL LINE
The lateral line running along each side of the body is a canal lined with sensory organs. These detect vibrations and changes in temperature and pressure, and help the fish to maintain its balance.

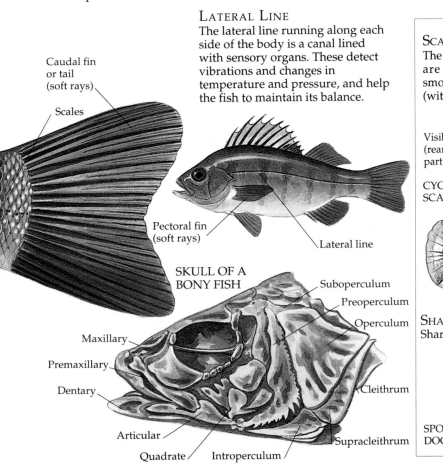

Caudal fin or tail (soft rays)
Scales
Pectoral fin (soft rays)
Lateral line

SKULL OF A BONY FISH
Suboperculum
Preoperculum
Operculum
Maxillary
Premaxillary
Dentary
Cleithrum
Articular
Quadrate Introperculum
Supracleithrum

SCALES
The scales of most bony fish are either cycloid (with smooth rear edges) or ctenoid (with serrated rear edges).

The scales are usually layered in rows, like roof tiles. Scales lost through injury are soon replaced, but often they do not grow back in the same pattern as existing scales.

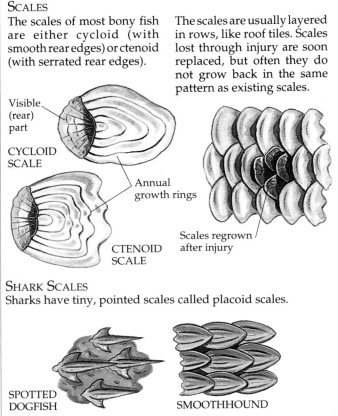

Visible (rear) part
CYCLOID SCALE
Annual growth rings
CTENOID SCALE
Scales regrown after injury

SHARK SCALES
Sharks have tiny, pointed scales called placoid scales.

SPOTTED DOGFISH
SMOOTHHOUND

CENTRARCHIDAE

BLACK BASS

The species collectively known as black bass include two of the most important sporting species in North America: the smallmouth bass and the largemouth bass. Black bass are the largest members of the Centrarchidae family, which also includes the bluegill, the crappies, and the sunfish (*see page 128*).

SUWANNEE BASS
Micropterus notius

SUWANNEE BASS
This small bass, which rarely exceeds 340 g (12 oz), is found in the Suwannee and Ochlockonee river drainages of Florida and Georgia. Its overall coloration is brownish, with dark markings along the back and sides; the adult male has blue cheeks, breast, and belly.

Male has blue cheeks, breast, and belly

GUADALUPE BASS
Micropterus treculi

SPOTTED BASS
This bass gets its name from the rows of small, dark spots on its pale flanks and belly. It is found mainly in the Ohio and Mississippi river systems and has two localized subspecies, the Alabama spotted bass and the Wichita spotted bass, *Micropterus punctulatus henshalli* and *M. p. wichitae*. It grows to about 2.27 kg (5 lb).

GUADALUPE BASS
The Guadalupe bass is similar to the spotted bass, but has distinctive dark bars along each side and is smaller, seldom reaching 454 g (1 lb). Its range is restricted to the Guadalupe, Colorado, Brazos, San Antonio, and Nueces river systems of central Texas.

SPOTTED BASS
Micropterus punctulatus

LARGEMOUTH BASS
The largemouth bass is so named because its upper jaw extends to behind its eye; that of the smallmouth bass does not extend beyond the eye. The northern largemouth seldom exceeds 4.54 kg (10 lb), but the southern subspecies, the Florida largemouth (*M. s. floridanus*), can reach more than 9.1 kg (20 lb).

REDEYE BASS
The red eyes and white-tipped orange caudal (tail) fin of the redeye bass make it easy to distinguish from other bass; young redeyes also have brick-red dorsal and anal fins. The redeye is one of the smaller bass species, and although it can exceed 3.6 kg (8 lb) it usually does not grow to more than about 454 g (1 lb).

REDEYE BASS
Micropterus coosae

White tip to caudal fin

FISHING NOTES

Techniques
Spinning or baitcasting with artificial lures, fly fishing, and trolling with livebaits will all prove successful.

Tackle
For lure fishing, try a 1.7 m to 2.1 m (5½ to 7 ft) spinning or baitcasting rod and a fixed-spool or multiplier reel with 2.7 to 4.54 kg (6 to 10 lb) mono line. A good rod to use for fly fishing is a 2.1 to 2.7 m (7 to 9 ft) bass fly rod with a fast taper, fitted with a single-action fly reel carrying a floating #7 to #9 line with a 2.7 to 3.6 kg (6 to 8 lb) leader. For trolling, use a 2.7 or 3 m (9 or 10 ft) stiff-action rod with a 1.1 kg (2½ lb) test curve, and a multiplier reel with 4.5 to 9.1 kg (10 to 20 lb) mono line, a nylon or Dacron trace, and hook sizes 2/0 to 5/0.

Bait
Black bass, being active predators that feed on a wide variety of creatures, can be tempted to strike at practically any kind of bait, either artificial or natural. Artificials such as spinners, spoons, crankbaits, surface plugs, and plastic worms are particularly effective. For fly fishing, bass bugs, streamers, and bucktails have all proved their worth; for trolling, try worms, crayfish, leeches, and minnows.

SMALLMOUTH BASS

The hard-fighting smallmouth is the most highly regarded black bass. It is slightly larger than the northern largemouth, reaching a maximum of about 5.4 kg (12 lb), and it prefers clear lakes and streams with rocky or gravel bottoms. The largemouth favours weedy, mud-bottomed waters.

SMALLMOUTH BASS
Micropterus dolomieui

LARGEMOUTH BASS
Micropterus salmoides

DISTRIBUTION
Smallmouth: from North Dakota to Quebec, Oklahoma, and Alabama; also widely introduced elsewhere.
Largemouth: from Minnesota to Quebec and south to the Gulf; widely introduced elsewhere.
Spotted: Mississippi basin from southern Ohio to the Gulf; introduced elsewhere.
Guadalupe: central Texas.
Suwanee: Florida and Georgia.
Redeye: Alabama, Georgia, South Carolina; introduced elsewhere.

Feeding
All the black bass are active predators. When young, they feed at first on tiny crustaceans, insects and their larvae, worms, and tadpoles, but they soon progress to larger prey such as fish, crayfish, and frogs. The largest bass will even take small waterfowl.

LARGEMOUTH BASS

SMALLMOUTH BASS

Dorsal fins
In addition to the different lengths of their upper jaws, largemouth and smallmouth bass have different dorsal fin structures. The spiny first dorsal fin of the largemouth bass is highest at its midpoint and is almost separated from the soft-rayed second dorsal. The smallmouth bass has a somewhat flatter first dorsal fin, which is connected to the second dorsal, and the second dorsal has a patch of scales at its base.

Size comparison

Largemouth bass   Smallmouth bass   Spotted bass   Redeye bass   Guadalupe bass   Suwanee bass

CENTRARCHIDAE

BLUEGILL, CRAPPIES, PUMPKINSEED, & SUNFISH

These small relatives of the black bass are among the most popular American panfish, which are fish that are too small to be considered true gamefish but still provide considerable angling (and eating) pleasure. The range of each of these species has been considerably extended by widespread stocking programmes.

Sharply arched back and dip above eye

PUMPKINSEED
This attractive little fish lives among the weeds in lakes, ponds, and quiet river pools. Its maximum weight is about 482 g (1 lb 1 oz), but most individuals are much smaller.

BLUEGILL
This the most widely distributed panfish, and probably the most fished-for species in North America. It prefers quiet, weedy waters and averages about 113g (4 oz), although it can grow to over 1.8 kg (4 lb).

Dark spot on dorsal fin

BLUEGILL
Lepomis macrochirus

PUMPKINSEED
Lepomis gibbosus

REDBREAST SUNFISH
The redbreast sunfish, which reaches a maximum weight of about 454 g (1 lb), is most abundant in the creeks and small to medium-sized rivers of the Atlantic Slope. It is also sometimes found in ponds and lake margins.

Gill covers
Sunfish of the genus Lepomis *can be identified by examining the shape and markings of their gill covers.*

REDBREAST SUNFISH

REDBREAST SUNFISH
Lepomis auritus

GREEN SUNFISH
The green sunfish has a more elongated body than most other sunfish, and the upper jaw of its large mouth extends back to below the midpoint of the eye. Like the redbreast sunfish, it is primarily a stream fish but is also found in stillwaters. It can attain a weight of over 910 g (2 lb).

PUMPKINSEED

REDEAR SUNFISH

GREEN SUNFISH
Lepomis cyanellus

REDEAR SUNFISH
Lepomis microlophus

REDEAR SUNFISH
The plump redear sunfish is also called the "shellcracker", because its diet includes snails and clams, which it crushes up with powerful grinding teeth. It can grow to over 2.15 kg (4 lb 12 oz).

128

WHITE CRAPPIE
Pomoxis annularis

WHITE CRAPPIE
The white crappie is generally a little larger than the closely related black crappie, and its overall coloration is usually paler. The most reliable way to distinguish between the two is to count the spines in the first dorsal fin: the white crappie has six, while the black crappie has seven or eight. The white crappie usually reaches 454 to 680 g (1 lb to 1 lb 8 oz), but it can grow to over 2.27 kg (5 lb).

DISTRIBUTION
Pumpkinseed: the Dakotas and Iowa to the Atlantic drainages.
Bluegill: from the Great Lakes to the Gulf and New Mexico; widely introduced elsewhere.
Redbreast sunfish: the Atlantic drainages.
Green sunfish: From the Great Lakes to Texas.
Redear sunfish: Indiana to the Gulf; introduced elsewhere.
Crappies: eastern North America from southern Canada to the Gulf; widely introduced.
Rock bass: From Manitoba to New England and northern Alabama.

BLACK CRAPPIE
Pomoxis nigromaculatus

BLACK CRAPPIE
The black crappie is often found together with the white, and both species are widely distributed in ponds, lakes, and rivers, although the black tends to prefer larger, clearer waters than those tolerated by the white. Its average weight is in the 340 to 680 g (12 oz to 1 lb 8 oz) range, with a maximum of up to 2.27 kg (5 lb).

ROCK BASS
Ambloplites rupestris

ROCK BASS
The mottled, dark olive rock bass has distinctive red eyes and a large mouth, and there is usually a white or gold margin to the dark spot on its gill cover. It is most common in clear, rocky streams and is also found in lake margins where the bottom is rocky and there is ample vegetation. Its maximum weight is about 1.36 kg (3 lb), but it typically weighs around 227 g (8 oz).

FISHING NOTES

Techniques
Float fishing, fly fishing, and baitcasting, all with light tackle.

Tackle
For float fishing, a 3 to 4.3 m (10 to 14 ft) pole, 2.7 to 6.8 kg (6 to 15 lb) mono line, and a small jig or livebait fished below a small float; or a 1.8 to 2.1 m (6 to 7 ft) ultralight spinning rod with a fixed-spool reel, 1.36 kg (3 lb) mono line, and a small float. Use hook sizes 10 to 14, and weight the rig with split shot about 30 cm (12 in) from the hook. For fly fishing, use a fly rod up to 113 g (4 oz) in weight, with matching reel and line. When baitcasting, use a 1.4 to 1.8 m (4½ to 6 ft) rod, a baitcasting reel, and 910 g to 1.8 kg (2 to 4 lb) line.

Bait
Small minnows, worms, maggots, and jigs for float fishing; tiny wet flies, nymphs, and dry flies for fly fishing; miniature spinners and crankbaits for baitcasting.

Size comparison

White crappie

Black crappie

Rock bass

Bluegill

Pumpkinseed

Green sunfish

Redear sunfish

Redbreast sunfish

CYPRINIDAE

BARBEL, TENCH, & ASP

The tench is a very popular angling species in its native Eurasian waters and has been introduced into North America and Australia. It is mainly a stillwater species, although it also inhabits the lower reaches of rivers. The asp is found in large lakes and, like barbel, in the middle reaches of clean rivers where the current is relatively fast and the water well oxygenated. Asp and barbel are often found together in those areas of Europe where their ranges overlap, asp in midwater and barbel on the bottom.

FEMALE   MALE

Male and female tench
The sex of a tench can be determined from its pelvic fins. Those of the male are much longer and broader than those of the female, and they extend to beyond the anal vent.

TENCH

The tiny scales of the tench are covered with a layer of protective slime and set flat against its thick-set body, making it appear almost scaleless. The fins are smoothly rounded, and the wrist of the barely forked tail is distinctively thick. Large individuals of up to 8.5 kg (18 lb 12 oz) have been reported, but the tench is slow-growing, and the usual maximum is about 1.8 kg (4 lb).

TENCH
Tinca tinca

GOLDEN TENCH
Tinca tinca

Golden Tench
The rare golden variety of tench is stocked as an ornamental fish in private ponds and park lakes. It has an orange or yellow body with scattered black markings, and its pink-tinged fins are less rounded than those of the common tench.

Natural food
Tench and barbel have a varied diet that includes plants, insects, molluscs, and crustaceans. When young, the asp eats insects and small crustaceans, but as an adult it preys on small fish such as bleak.

Spawning male asp
At spawning time the male asp develops numerous tough, wartlike lumps (tubercles) on its head, which help it to fend off rivals. Asp spawn in spring over gravel beds.

ASP

The slender, streamlined body of the predatory asp gives it the speed and agility it needs to capture its food, which is primarily small midwater and near-surface fish. A popular angling species that fights strongly when hooked, it favours deep water and is often found in weir pools. Asp average about 3.5 kg (7 lb 11 oz), but can reach a maximum of around 12 kg (26 lb 7 oz).

ASP
Aspius aspius

Size comparison

Asp   Barbel   Tench   Southern barbel

SOUTHERN BARBEL

The southern or Mediterranean barbel inhabits fast-flowing upland rivers and streams in southern Europe. It is much smaller than the common barbel, averaging only about 250 g (9 oz).

SOUTHERN BARBEL
Barbus meridionalis

BARBEL

In the fast-flowing water that it prefers, the barbel's streamlined, flat-bellied body helps it to stay close to the river bed, where it feeds. When hooked, it will use its considerable strength and stamina to the full and fight hard until it is exhausted, and its power is comparable with that of a salmon of similar weight. It usually grows to about 2.27 kg (5 lb), but it can reach a maximum of around 7.3 kg (16 lb).

BARBEL
Barbus barbus

DISTRIBUTION
Tench: throughout Europe with the exception of northern Scandinavia; introduced into North America and Australia.
Barbel: from southern England and Wales to southern Europe.
Southern barbel: northern Spain, southern France, and northern Italy; Danube basin.
Asp: from eastern Holland east through northern and central Europe to the Caspian Sea.

Mouth and barbels
The barbel's downturned mouth and fleshy lips are beautifully adapted for bottom feeding. The four barbels (or barbules) that give the fish its name carry a large number of taste and touch cells, and act like external tongues with which the fish can examine potential food items.

Gudgeon and tench each have two barbels

Barbel (barbule)

Barbel and carp each have four barbels

A stone loach has six barbels

Young barbel
Up to a weight of around 227 to 340 g (8 to 12 oz) and a length of 15 to 20 cm (6 to 8 in), young barbel often have speckled flanks, and their overall coloration tends to be more olive-green than that of their parents.

Identification
Count the barbels to distinguish young barbel and carp from similar fish.

FISHING NOTES

Techniques
Float fishing, legering, and freelining for tench; lure fishing and deadbaiting for asp; for barbel, float fishing and legering, especially legering with a swimfeeder.

Tackle
When float fishing for tench, use a 3.7 m (12 ft) medium-action rod, with a fixed-spool reel, 4.54 kg (10 lb) line, and hook sizes 6 or 8. To leger for tench, try a 3.7 m (12 ft) Avon rod with a fixed spool reel, 3.2 kg (7 lb) line, size 6 to 12 hook, and a swimfeeder. For asp, try a 2.7 m (9 ft) medium-action spinning rod with a fixed-spool reel, 6.8 kg (15 lb) line, and a small spoon. To leger for barbel, use a 3.7 m (12 ft) rod with quivertip, a fixed-spool reel, 3.6 kg (8 lb) line, hook sizes 8 to 12, and a swimfeeder.

Bait
Good tench baits include bread, maggots, corn, worms, meat, and small boilies. Asp can be taken on spoons, especially if a small piece of red wool is tied to the hook to provide extra attraction, and on small fish baits such as bleak. For barbel, try maggots, meat, tares, hempseed, corn, worms, bread, and cheese.

131

BREAM, NASE, & VIMBA

These European members of the carp family are all primarily bottom-feeders. Bream are widely distributed in stillwaters, canals, and deep, slow-flowing rivers, the nase prefers the faster-flowing waters of the middle reaches of rivers, and the vimba is found in the middle and lower reaches of large, slow rivers. The most widespread of these species, and the most popular with anglers, is the bronze bream.

YOUNG BREAM

Young bream
When young, bronze bream are silvery with black fins. In Britain, these little fish are known as tinplate bream or skimmers.

NASE
Chondrostoma nasus

NASE
The silvery, slender-bodied nase has red-tinged fins and a smallish head with a noticeably protuberant snout. It feeds on algae and diatoms, which it scrapes from rocks and stones with its hard, horny lower lip, and can reach a maximum weight of about 1.8 kg (4 lb). The toxostome, or soiffe (*Chondrostoma toxostoma*), is similar to the nase, but smaller.

Roach/bream hybrids
Where spawning schools of bream and roach (see page 137) occur in the same waters, roach/bream hybrids are common. To identify a hybrid, count the number of rays in the anal fin: a roach has 9 to 12, a bream has 23 to 29, and a hybrid 14 to 19.

VIMBA *Vimba vimba*

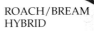

ROACH/BREAM HYBRID

Hybr anal fin

Bream anal fin

VIMBA
For most of the year, the vimba (known in Germany as the Zährte) has silvery sides and a blue-grey back, but at spawning time (in early summer) the male becomes very dark on the back with an orange-red belly. The vimba's staple diet consists of worms, molluscs, and crustaceans, and its weight ranges from around 910 g (2 lb) to 3 kg (6 lb 10 oz).

Feeding bream
When feeding, a bream upends itself and its mouth protrudes down to suck in worms, molluscs, crustaceans, and insect larvae. A school of feeding bream will betray its presence by stirring up clouds of silt from the bottom.

SILVER BREAM
Blicca bjoerkna

Size comparison

Bronze bream   Vimba   Nase   Silver bream   Danubian bream

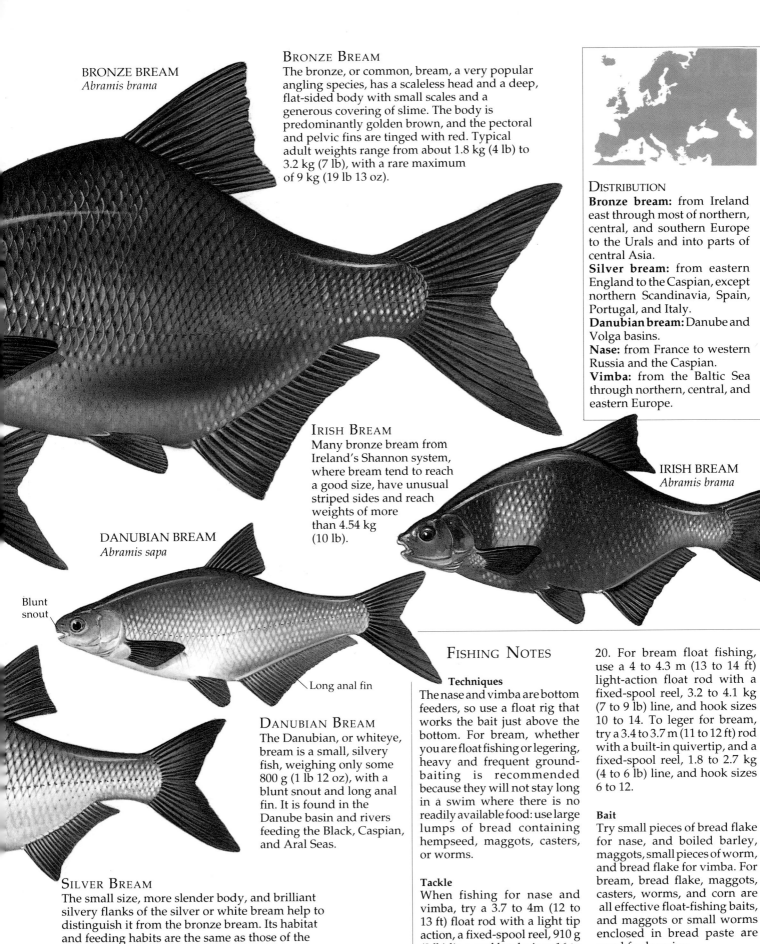

BRONZE BREAM
Abramis brama

BRONZE BREAM
The bronze, or common, bream, a very popular angling species, has a scaleless head and a deep, flat-sided body with small scales and a generous covering of slime. The body is predominantly golden brown, and the pectoral and pelvic fins are tinged with red. Typical adult weights range from about 1.8 kg (4 lb) to 3.2 kg (7 lb), with a rare maximum of 9 kg (19 lb 13 oz).

DISTRIBUTION
Bronze bream: from Ireland east through most of northern, central, and southern Europe to the Urals and into parts of central Asia.
Silver bream: from eastern England to the Caspian, except northern Scandinavia, Spain, Portugal, and Italy.
Danubian bream: Danube and Volga basins.
Nase: from France to western Russia and the Caspian.
Vimba: from the Baltic Sea through northern, central, and eastern Europe.

IRISH BREAM
Many bronze bream from Ireland's Shannon system, where bream tend to reach a good size, have unusual striped sides and reach weights of more than 4.54 kg (10 lb).

IRISH BREAM
Abramis brama

DANUBIAN BREAM
Abramis sapa

Blunt snout

Long anal fin

DANUBIAN BREAM
The Danubian, or whiteye, bream is a small, silvery fish, weighing only some 800 g (1 lb 12 oz), with a blunt snout and long anal fin. It is found in the Danube basin and rivers feeding the Black, Caspian, and Aral Seas.

SILVER BREAM
The small size, more slender body, and brilliant silvery flanks of the silver or white bream help to distinguish it from the bronze bream. Its habitat and feeding habits are the same as those of the bronze, but it is much smaller, its usual maximum weight being only 454 g (1 lb).

FISHING NOTES

Techniques
The nase and vimba are bottom feeders, so use a float rig that works the bait just above the bottom. For bream, whether you are float fishing or legering, heavy and frequent groundbaiting is recommended because they will not stay long in a swim where there is no readily available food: use large lumps of bread containing hempseed, maggots, casters, or worms.

Tackle
When fishing for nase and vimba, try a 3.7 to 4m (12 to 13 ft) float rod with a light tip action, a fixed-spool reel, 910 g (2 lb) line, and hook sizes 16 to 20. For bream float fishing, use a 4 to 4.3 m (13 to 14 ft) light-action float rod with a fixed-spool reel, 3.2 to 4.1 kg (7 to 9 lb) line, and hook sizes 10 to 14. To leger for bream, try a 3.4 to 3.7 m (11 to 12 ft) rod with a built-in quivertip, and a fixed-spool reel, 1.8 to 2.7 kg (4 to 6 lb) line, and hook sizes 6 to 12.

Bait
Try small pieces of bread flake for nase, and boiled barley, maggots, small pieces of worm, and bread flake for vimba. For bream, bread flake, maggots, casters, worms, and corn are all effective float-fishing baits, and maggots or small worms enclosed in bread paste are good for legering.

CARP

The wild carp was being farmed for food in Asia by about 400 BC. Since then, selective breeding on eastern European fish farms has produced a number of variants such as the common, leather, and mirror forms. These and the wild carp have spread throughout Europe both naturally and by introduction, and have been introduced elsewhere, including North America and Australia.

FISHING NOTES

Techniques
Float fishing, legering, and freelining for common carp; float fishing for crucian.

Tackle
For common carp float fishing, use a 3.7 m (12 ft), 680 g (1½ lb) test curve rod with a fixed-spool reel, 3.6 kg (8 lb) line, and hook sizes 8 to 12. Legering calls for heavier tackle, for instance a 3.7 m (12 ft), 910 g (2 lb) test curve rod, fixed-spool reel, 5.4 kg (12 lb) line, and hook sizes 6 to 10. For crucian carp, use a 4 m (13 ft) light-action rod with a fixed-spool reel, 680 g to 1.1 kg (1½ to 2½ lb) line, and hook sizes 12 to 18.

Bait
The range of baits used by carp fishermen is enormous and constantly growing. It extends from simple, traditional baits, such as bread, worms, and maggots, through luncheon meat, sweetcorn, and potatoes, to the numerous commercially prepared baits such as boilies, and bait additives such as aromatic meat-, spice-, and fruit-flavoured oils.

WILD CARP
The wild carp is a strong, slow-growing fish with a scaleless head and a fully scaled body. Smaller and less deep-bodied than the common carp, its average weight is 910 g to 2.27 kg (2 to 5 lb) and it seldom exceeds 9.1 kg (20 lb).

WILD CARP
Cyprinus carpio

Breeding
Wild and common carp spawn in late spring and early summer, when the water temperature exceeds 18°C (64°F). The eggs are laid in shallow water that has abundant dense vegetation and good exposure to sunlight, and are attached to the leaves and stems of water plants. They hatch in five to eight days, the hatchlings initially remaining attached to the plants. The young fish grow very quickly.

Eggs

Hatchling

Larva

Feeding
The common carp feeds at the surface, on the bottom, or in midwater on plants, algae, snails, worms, insect larvae, shrimps, mussels, and many other organisms. It opens its mouth wide and sucks its food in like a vacuum cleaner, and often rummages through the bottom detritus, sending up clouds of silt and uprooting plants.

CRUCIAN CARP
Carassius carassius

CRUCIAN CARP
This small, deep-bodied carp is more closely related to the goldfish than to the wild carp, but will interbreed with both species. It averages about 255 g (9 oz), but can exceed 2.5 kg (5 lb 8 oz), and it will tolerate a wide range of temperatures, low oxygen levels, acidity, and dense vegetation.

Size comparison

Grass carp   Common carp   Mirror carp   Leather carp   Wild carp   Crucian carp   Goldfish

GRASS CARP

The wide mouth of the grass carp is superbly adapted for feeding on plants, and because of its huge appetite it has been introduced into many canals, ponds, and drains in Europe and North America for weed clearance. Its growth rate is very rapid, and in warm waters it can reach 35 kg (77 lb).

GRASS CARP
Ctenopharyngodon idella

DISTRIBUTION
Common carp: through most of Eurasia; North America, South Africa, India, Australia, and New Zealand.
Crucian, grass, and **goldfish:** native to Eurasia and widely introduced elsewhere.

GOLDFISH
Carassius auratus

GOLDFISH

Within a few generations of release into the wild, the domestic goldfish reverts to its natural carplike coloration and can grow to a weight of about 3 kg (6lb 10 oz).

COMMON (OR KING) CARP

The heavy, deep-bodied common, or king, carp, together with its leather and mirror varieties, is the result of centuries of selective breeding by fish farms. Like the wild carp from which it derives, the common carp has a scaleless head and a fully scaled body, and its coloration is variable. It can reach a weight of 36 kg (80 lb) and a length of about 1.5 m (5 ft).

Mirror carp scale
The scales of the mirror carp are much larger than those of the common carp. A typical mirror carp scale might be 5 cm (2 in) long and 3 cm (1.2 in) wide, compared with a length of 3 cm (1.2 in) and a width of 2.5 cm (1 in) for a scale of a similar-sized common carp.

COMMON (OR KING) CARP
Cyprinus carpio

MIRROR CARP
Cyprinus carpio

LEATHER CARP

The scaleless or almost-scaleless leather carp is a variety of common carp. Any scales that are present are large and few in number, and usually near the fins and tail. Like the common and mirror varieties, it has been introduced around the world.

MIRROR CARP

The mirror variety of common carp occurs in a number of forms. The fully scaled is covered in large, irregular scales; the scattered has individual, randomly sited scales; the linear has a continuous line of scales along the lateral line; and the plated has just a few, very large, scales along the lateral line.

LEATHER CARP
Cyprinus carpio

135

CYPRINIDAE
CHUB, DACE, ROACH, & RUDD

These popular angling species are widespread in the rivers and stillwaters of Europe. Chub and dace prefer moderate to fast flows of clean water, but they are also found in slow lowland rivers and sometimes in lakes. Roach and rudd thrive in canals, slow-flowing rivers, and stillwaters where there is plenty of vegetation. The roach has been introduced into Australia, where it is found in Victoria and southern New South Wales, and the rudd has been introduced into the northeastern United States, where there are breeding populations in Maine and in the lower Hudson basin in New York.

Chub food
Young chub eat mostly insect larvae and aquatic invertebrates. Adults will take anything edible that comes their way, opening their large, wide mouths to engulf small fish, frogs, crayfish, and small water voles, and snapping up berries that fall from overhanging trees and bushes.

Convex dorsal fin

CHUB
Leuciscus cephalus

Convex anal fin is pink, becoming darker with age

DACE
Leuciscus leuciscus

Concave dorsal fin

Pink pelvic fin

Slim body

CHUB
The body of the chub is thickset, with rounded fins and a blunt snout, and the dark edges of its scales give its back and sides an attractive, latticed appearance. In British waters the maximum weight is probably about 5.4 kg (12 lb), but in mainland Europe it can reach 7.26 kg (16 lb).

Concave anal fin

Protruding lower jaw

Large eye

DACE
The slim, silvery dace is one of the smallest species to be of serious angling interest: its maximum weight is only about 600 g (1 lb 5 oz), and a fish of 170 to 227 g (6 to 8 oz) would be a good catch. It feeds on insects, crustaceans, and plants.

BLEAK
Alburnus alburnus

Long anal fin

FISHING NOTES

Techniques
Float fishing and legering are the most usual techniques for these species, but fly fishing is an enjoyable alternative.

Tackle
To leger for chub, use a 3.7 m (12 ft) rod with a built-in quivertip, a fixed-spool reel, 2.27 kg (5 lb) line, hook sizes 8 to 16, and a suitable blockend

feeder. For float fishing, try a 3.7 to 4m (12 to 13 ft) rod with fixed-spool reel, 1.36 kg (3 lb) line, and hook sizes 14 to 20. To float fish for dace, use a 3.7 m (12 ft) rod with a light tip action, a fixed-spool reel, 910 g (2 lb) line, and hook sizes 16 to 20. To float fish for roach or rudd, try a 3.7 m (12 ft) rod with a light tip action, a fixed-spool reel, 1.1 kg (2½ lb) line, and hook sizes 14 to 20. When legering for roach or rudd, use

a 3 to 3.7 m (10 to 12 ft) rod with quivertip, a fixed-spool reel, 1.36 to 1.8 kg (2½ to 4 lb) line, and hook sizes 10 to 16.

Bait
For all these species, good float fishing or legering baits include maggots, casters, bread flake, and worms, and large slugs are especially effective for chub. These species can also be taken on fly tackle, using either wet or dry flies.

Chub, dace, or bleak?
Young chub are similar in size and general appearance to dace and bleak, but each has its own distinguishing features. The chub has convex dorsal and anal fins, and its pelvic and anal fins are pink. In comparison, the greyish dorsal fin and pale, yellowish anal fins of the dace are concave, and the greyish, concave anal fin of the bleak is much longer than that of either the chub or the dace. The bleak also has a protruding lower jaw and large, prominent eyes.

DANUBIAN ROACH

This relatively slender-bodied roach has a small head and large, silvery scales, and occurs as two subspecies: *Rutilus pigus pigus* of the Po basin in northern Italy, and *R. p. virgo* of the Danube basin. It can reach a weight of 1 kg (2 lb 3 oz) or more, but most are much smaller.

DANUBIAN ROACH
Rutilus pigus

ROACH
Rutilus rutilus

ROACH

The silvery, deep-bodied roach has red eyes, reddish pectoral fins, red pelvic and anal fins, and dusky dorsal and tail fins. It is the most popular angling species in Europe, mainly because it is extremely common and catching it requires skill. It reaches about 1.8 kg (4 lb), and often hybridizes with bream *(see page 132)*.

DISTRIBUTION

Chub: Europe, except Ireland, the snowbelt of Scandinavia, and southern Italy.
Dace: from Ireland to Siberia, but not south of the Pyrenees and the Alps.
Roach: Europe from Ireland to the Urals, but not found in the Scandinavian snowbelt or south of the Pyrenees and the Alps; has been introduced into Australia.
Rudd: Europe from Ireland to the Urals and from southern Sweden to northern Italy and Greece; introduced into the northeastern United States.

RUDD
Scardinius erythrophthalmus

Upturned mouth

Orange pectoral fins

Golden flanks

Bright red or orange anal fin

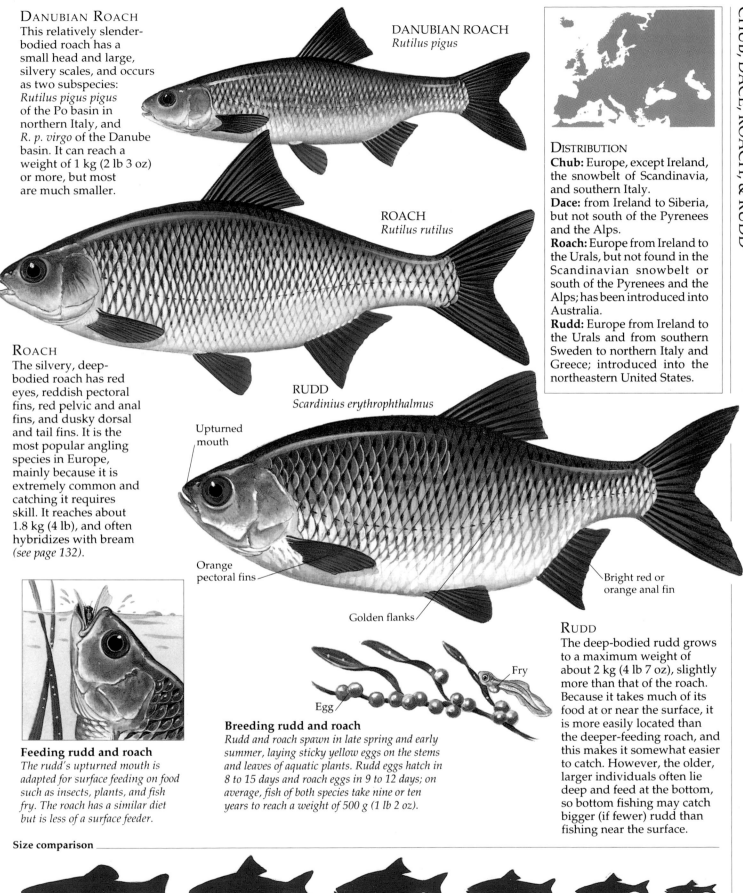

Feeding rudd and roach
The rudd's upturned mouth is adapted for surface feeding on food such as insects, plants, and fish fry. The roach has a similar diet but is less of a surface feeder.

Egg

Fry

Breeding rudd and roach
Rudd and roach spawn in late spring and early summer, laying sticky yellow eggs on the stems and leaves of aquatic plants. Rudd eggs hatch in 8 to 15 days and roach eggs in 9 to 12 days; on average, fish of both species take nine or ten years to reach a weight of 500 g (1 lb 2 oz).

RUDD

The deep-bodied rudd grows to a maximum weight of about 2 kg (4 lb 7 oz), slightly more than that of the roach. Because it takes much of its food at or near the surface, it is more easily located than the deeper-feeding roach, and this makes it somewhat easier to catch. However, the older, larger individuals often lie deep and feed at the bottom, so bottom fishing may catch bigger (if fewer) rudd than fishing near the surface.

Size comparison

Chub

Roach

Rudd

Danubian roach

Dace

Bleak

137

ESOCIDAE

PIKE, PICKEREL, & MUSKELLUNGE

The members of the pike family are voracious predators, disliked and even feared by some anglers but greatly admired by others because of their size and the tenacious fight they put up when hooked. They inhabit rivers, streams, and stillwaters with clear water but with plenty of vegetation in which to lurk in wait for their prey. The pike itself, known in North America as the northern pike, is one of the few freshwater species to be native to both Eurasia and North America. Pickerel and muskellunge are purely North American species.

REDFIN PICKEREL
Esox americanus americanus

GRASS PICKEREL
Esox americanus vermiculatus

CHAIN PICKEREL
Esox niger

PICKEREL
The chain pickerel averages only 910 g (2 lb) but has been known to reach 4.25 kg (9 lb 6 oz). Despite being relatively small, it provides good sport on light tackle, as do the even smaller grass and redfin pickerels, which are less than half its size. Apart from the difference in their sizes, the chain pickerel can be distinguished from the grass and redfin by its markings. The chain pickerel has a distinctive dark, chainlike pattern on its sides, while the grass and redfin are both marked with dark bars; the redfin, as its name implies, also has red fins.

MUSKELLUNGE
The mighty muskellunge is a powerful, fast-growing fish that can reach a length of 30 cm (12 in) in only four months and grows to 1.83 m (6 ft) or more. Its maximum weight is at least 31.75 kg (70 lb), and weights in excess of 45 kg (100 lb) have been reported. The most visible difference between the muskellunge and the northern pike is in their markings: the "muskie" has dark bars or blotches on its sides, while the pike has a series of pale bars and spots.

MUSKELLUNGE
Esox masquinongy

FEEDING
The principal food of the pike family is fish, including smaller fish of their own kind. They are, however, great opportunists and will take any available small prey including frogs, snakes, crayfish, rodents, and ducklings. Their markings provide excellent camouflage as they hide among the weeds, waiting to pounce on passing fish, which they swallow head first.

FISHING NOTES

Techniques
These active predators are usually caught by spinning, baitcasting, and trolling, using lures, deadbaits, and livebaits. Fish for them from the bank, or use a boat to reach weedbeds that are otherwise inaccessible.

Tackle
For pickerel, try a 1.7 m (5½ ft) baitcaster with a multiplier reel or a 1.8 to 2.1 m (6 to 7 ft) spinning rod with a fixed-spool reel; use 2.7 to 3.6 kg (6 to 8 lb) line with a short wire trace. When lure fishing from the bank or a boat for pike or muskellunge, try a 1.8 to 2.7 m (6 to 9 ft) spinning or baitcasting rod with a multiplier or a fixed-spool reel, 4.54 to 6.8 kg (10 to 15 lb) line, and a 9.1 kg (20 lb) wire trace. When you are downrigger trolling for pike or muskellunge, use a 1.8 to 2.1 m (6 to 7 ft) fast-taper rod with a multiplier reel, 6.8 to 9.1 kg (15 to 20 lb) line, and a 11.3 kg (25 lb) wire trace.

Bait
Small spinners and spoons are ideal baits for pickerel. For pike and muskellunge, use large spinners, spoons, and plugs, cut fish baits (especially herring, mackerel, and eel), and whole minnows.

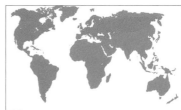

DISTRIBUTION
Pike: northern Europe south to the Pyrenees, east to Siberia; Labrador west to Alaska, south to Pennsylvania, Missouri, and Nebraska.
Muskellunge: Great Lakes region, Mississippi basin, Atlantic drainages south to Georgia and Virginia.
Chain pickerel: Atlantic drainages from Nova Scotia to Florida, Mississippi basin from Missouri south.
Redfin pickerel: Atlantic drainages.
Grass pickerel: Mississippi basin and Great Lakes.

Jaws
The members of the pike family have abundant sharp teeth and very complex skull and jaw structures. These enable them to seize and swallow relatively large fish and other prey; the pike, for example, tends to select prey that is 10 to 25 per cent of its own body weight.

PIKE
Esox lucius

PIKE
Like the other members of the family, the pike is an aggressive, solitary hunter, and its torpedo-shaped body is built for short bursts of acceleration rather than sustained speed. It is usually found in or near weedbeds that provide it with cover, but in large lakes it ventures into open water to feed on salmon, trout, or other fish. Growth rates for pike vary enormously and are directly dependent on the available food supply, but an annual weight gain of 910 g to 1.4 kg (2 to 3 lb) is fairly typical. The maximum weight is thought to be about 34 kg (75 lb), but most are much smaller and a pike of 4.54 to 9.1 kg (10–20 lb) is a worthwhile catch.

Size comparison

Muskellunge   Pike   Chain pickerel   Grass pickerel   Redfin pickerel

ICTALURIDAE

BULLHEAD

The North American bullhead and freshwater catfish *(see page 142)* are members of the Ictaluridae, which, with some 40 species, is the largest family of freshwater fish native to North America; some have been introduced into Europe and elsewhere. Bullhead are omnivorous, bottom-feeding fish, found mostly in still and slow-flowing waters and characterized by a scaleless body, four pairs of barbels, an adipose fin, and stiff, sharp spines at the leading edges of the pectoral and dorsal fins.

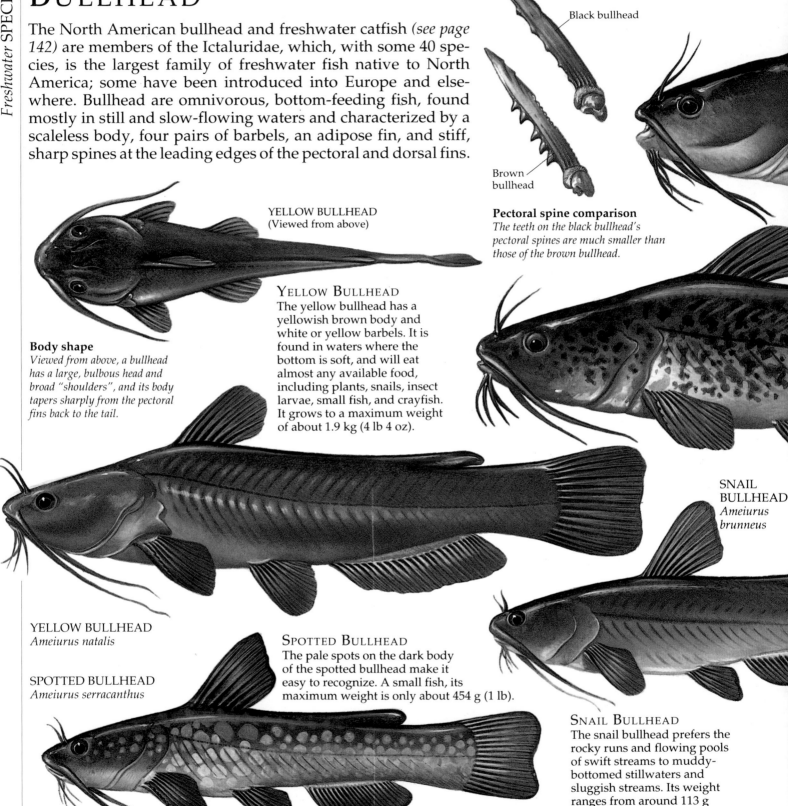

PECTORAL SPINES

Black bullhead

Brown bullhead

Pectoral spine comparison
The teeth on the black bullhead's pectoral spines are much smaller than those of the brown bullhead.

YELLOW BULLHEAD
(Viewed from above)

Body shape
Viewed from above, a bullhead has a large, bulbous head and broad "shoulders", and its body tapers sharply from the pectoral fins back to the tail.

YELLOW BULLHEAD
The yellow bullhead has a yellowish brown body and white or yellow barbels. It is found in waters where the bottom is soft, and will eat almost any available food, including plants, snails, insect larvae, small fish, and crayfish. It grows to a maximum weight of about 1.9 kg (4 lb 4 oz).

YELLOW BULLHEAD
Ameiurus natalis

SPOTTED BULLHEAD
Ameiurus serracanthus

SPOTTED BULLHEAD
The pale spots on the dark body of the spotted bullhead make it easy to recognize. A small fish, its maximum weight is only about 454 g (1 lb).

SNAIL BULLHEAD
Ameiurus brunneus

SNAIL BULLHEAD
The snail bullhead prefers the rocky runs and flowing pools of swift streams to muddy-bottomed stillwaters and sluggish streams. Its weight ranges from around 113 g (4 oz) up to about 454 g (1 lb).

Size comparison

Black bullhead

Brown bullhead

Yellow bullhead

Snail bullhead

Flat bullhead

Spotted bullhead

BLACK BULLHEAD
Ameiurus melas

BROWN BULLHEAD
Ameiurus nebulosus

Fins edged
with black

BLACK BULLHEAD
Also known as the horned pout, the black bullhead is a popular angling species that will tolerate very poor water quality. It is broadly similar in appearance to the brown bullhead, but lacks the mottled coloration and large pectoral spine teeth of that species. The black is the largest of the bullheads, but although it can grow to about 3.6 kg (8 lb) it seldom exceeds 910g (2 lb).

BROWN BULLHEAD
The brown bullhead has a mottled coloration, and sharp teeth on its pectoral spines. Its maximum weight of around 2.5 kg (5 lb 8 oz) is less than that of the black, but its average of about 1.36 kg (3 lb) is slightly more. Both have been introduced into many European waters, with the brown now common in Holland and Germany and the black thriving in southern France.

FLAT BULLHEAD
Ameiurus platycephalus

DISTRIBUTION
Black: from Montana east to the Great Lakes and south to the Gulf Slope drainages; introduced into Europe.
Brown: the Great Lakes and Maine south to Mexico and Florida; introduced into Europe and New Zealand.
Yellow: Dakotas to Atlantic and Gulf Slope drainages.
Spotted: Florida, Georgia, and Alabama.
Snail: southern Virginia to eastern Alabama and northern Florida.
Flat: Virginia to Georgia.

FLAT BULLHEAD
In profile, the flat bullhead has a flattened head and relatively straight snout. Its coloration is a mottled yellow to dark brown, with a light belly, and it averages about 454 g (1 lb) with a maximum of 910 g (2 lb).

Spawning bullhead
Bullhead spawn in spring and early summer, laying their eggs in depressions in the mud or among stones or other cover. One or both parents will then guard the eggs until they hatch.

FISHING NOTES

Techniques
Bullhead can be caught on most natural or processed baits by float fishing or legering, and also on small artificial lures by spinning or baitcasting.

Tackle
For float fishing, try a 3.7 m (12 ft) rod with a tip action, a fixed-spool reel, 1.1 kg (2½ lb) line, and hook sizes 10 to 16. For legering, use a 3 to 3.7m (10 to 12 ft) rod with a quivertip, a fixed-spool reel, 1.1 to 1.8 kg (2½ to 4 lb) line, and hook sizes 10 to 16. For spinning or baitcasting, try a 1.5 to 2.1 m (5 to 7 ft) medium-action rod with a multiplier or small closed-face fixed-spool reel, and 1.36 or 1.8 kg (3 or 4 lb) line.

Bait
Like their larger relatives the freshwater catfish, bullhead will take a wide range of natural and processed baits. These include worms, meat, bread, cheese, cut fish, tiny minnows, mussels, snails, shrimps, and freshwater clams. Adding small amounts of flavourings, such as spice oils, helps to make bread and other relatively bland baits more attractive. When baitcasting or spinning, try lightweight spinners and spoons, plastic worms, tiny jigs, and small wet flies.

ICTALURIDAE; SILURIDAE; PLOTOSIDAE

FRESHWATER CATFISH

Worldwide, there are over 30 families of freshwater and marine catfish, containing about 2,250 species. These families include the Ictaluridae of North America (see also page 140), the Siluridae of Europe, and the Plotosidae of Australasia, all of which have scaleless bodies, broad heads, and "whiskers" around their mouths. They generally inhabit still or slow-flowing waters, and are most active at night and on cloudy days.

Head shows distinctive flattening

YOUNG ADULT FISH

CHANNEL CATFISH
The channel catfish, one of the larger North American catfish species, is the only one to have both spots and a deeply forked tail; the spots tend to fade in old, large fish. Its maximum size is about 27 kg (60 lb).

CHANNEL CATFISH
Ictalurus punctatus

WHITE CATFISH
The coloration of the white catfish varies from white to silvery beige or blue, with a white belly. It is very popular as an angling and food fish, and usually grows to about 1.36 kg (3 lb) although it has been known to reach weights of over 7.7 kg (17 lb).

WELS
Also known as the Danubian catfish, the wels is native to central and eastern Europe but has been widely introduced into western European waters. The reason for these introductions is that the wels is one of the largest of all freshwater fish, reliably known to reach a length of 3 m (9 ft 10 in) and a weight of 200 kg (441 lb); individuals weighing over 320 kg (700 lb) have been reported.

WELS
Silurus glanis

WHITE CATFISH
Ameiurus catus

TANDAN
Tandanus tandanus

TANDAN
The tandan is a member of the Plotosidae family, which comprises about 30 marine and freshwater species that are widely distributed throughout Australasia and the Indo-Pacific. It inhabits stillwaters and slow-flowing streams, typically reaching a weight of up to 2 kg (4 lb 7 oz) with a maximum of about 6 kg (13 lb 4 oz).

FISHING NOTES

Techniques
Freshwater catfish are usually taken on natural or processed baits by float fishing, legering, or freelining, but spinning with artificial lures is also effective, particularly for channel and blue catfish.

Tackle
Use a 2.7 to 3m (9 to 10 ft) rod, such as a heavy bass rod, with a fixed-spool reel, 2.7 to 5.4 kg (6 to 12 lb) line, and hook sizes 6 to 1/0. To freeline for the larger species, such as the wels, use a 3 to 3.7 m (10 to 12 ft) rod with a powerful all-through action, a fixed-spool reel, 6.8 kg (15 lb) line, 9.1 kg (20 lb) Dacron trace, and hook sizes 4 to 2/0.

Bait
Freshwater catfish can be taken on practically any type of bait or lure, even a bare, shiny hook. Every catfish angler has a personal preference when it comes to a choice of bait, but the best results are said to come with "stink" baits. These baits include soured clams and ripened chicken entrails, beef liver, pig liver, and rabbit liver, coagulated blood, and even pieces of scented soap.

FLATHEAD CATFISH
Pylodictis olivaris

FLATHEAD CATFISH
The preferred habitat of the flathead is the deep, sluggish pools of large rivers, but it is also found in smaller streams and stillwaters. It averages about 1.8 kg (4 lb) but may reach 45 kg (100 lb).

Front view of a wels showing its very wide and flattened head

Whiskers
The barbels or "whiskers" around the mouth of a catfish are highly sensitive organs with which the fish can taste, smell, and feel its food. The wels has six whiskers, and the American catfish and the tandan have eight.

DISTRIBUTION
Wels: southern Sweden to the Danube basin and Amu Darya; introduced into England, France, Spain, Italy.
Channel: Great Lakes to Gulf Slope drainages.
White: Atlantic and Gulf Slope drainages.
Flathead: lower Great Lakes, Mississippi basin, Gulf Slope drainages.
Blue: Mississippi basin, Gulf Slope drainages.
Tandan: Queensland, New South Wales, Victoria, and South Australia.

BLUE CATFISH
Ictalurus furcatus

BLUE CATFISH
The blue catfish is the largest North American catfish, averaging up to 22.7 kg (50 lb) and capable of exceeding 45 kg (100 lb). Unlike most catfish it prefers swift-flowing and relatively clear streams to slow, turbid waters, and is found over rock, sand, or gravel bottoms rather than mud or silt.

Feeding
Blue catfish feed mainly at night, when they move from deep water into shallow, swift-flowing rapids and chutes to hunt for fish and crayfish.

Size comparison

Wels   Blue catfish   Channel catfish   Flathead catfish   White catfish   Tandan

143

BASS & MURRAY COD

Until recently, these perchlike species were all classified as members of the Percichthyidae family, but those of the genus *Morone* are now considered to be a separate family, the Moronidae. Both families are widely distributed in temperate and tropical waters, some being exclusively freshwater fish, others exclusively marine, and some migrating from the sea into freshwater to spawn. They feed mainly on small fish, crustaceans, worms, and insects.

AUSTRALIAN BASS

This is one of the most important gamefish of the coastal rivers, estuaries, and lakes of southeastern Australia. It grows to a weight of 1 kg (2 lb 3 oz) or more, and spawns in estuaries during the winter. The eggs hatch in about three days, and by around three months of age the young fish resemble small adults but are marked with faint vertical bars on the back and sides.

AUSTRALIAN BASS
Macquaria novemaculeata

YELLOW BASS
Morone mississippiensis

WHITE PERCH
Morone americana

WHITE PERCH

The white perch can reach a weight of about 2.2 kg (4 lb 12 oz), but averages only about 454 g (1 lb). It is found in the Atlantic Slope drainages of northeastern North America, primarily in brackish water near the mouths of rivers. It is also found in the quiet pools of medium to large rivers, and close inshore in shallow coastal waters.

YELLOW BASS

This little freshwater bass has silvery yellow sides, and the lower stripes along them are broken and offset. It rarely exceeds 1 kg (2 lb 3 oz) and usually weighs only 113 to 340 g (4 to 12 oz), but despite its small size it offers good sport on light tackle.

WHITE BASS
Morone chrysops

WHITE BASS

The white bass is very similar to the yellow bass, but its coloration is silvery white, the stripes along its sides are not broken and offset, and its lower jaw is more protuberant. It is found mainly in large, relatively clear waters, and although it grows to over 3 kg (6 lb 10 oz) most of those caught are in the 227 to 910 g (8 oz to 2 lb) range.

Size comparison

Striped bass   Murray cod   European sea bass   Spotted sea bass   Australian bass   Yellow bass   White bass   White perch

MURRAY COD
Maccullochella peeli

MURRAY COD
With a maximum length of 1.8 m (6 ft) and a weight of up to 113.5 kg (250 lb), the Murray cod is the largest Australian freshwater fish. Its preferred habitat is deep holes in muddy, slow-flowing water, and it is fished for commercially as well as for sport. It is widely distributed through the Murray-Darling River system, and has been introduced into many lakes in New South Wales and Victoria.

DISTRIBUTION
Australian bass, Murray cod: Queensland to Victoria.
White perch: from Quebec to South Carolina.
Yellow bass: from Montana and Wisconsin south to the Gulf of Mexico.
White bass: Manitoba and Quebec to the Gulf.
Spotted sea bass: western France to North Africa.
European sea bass: southern Norway to the Black Sea.

SPOTTED SEA BASS
Dicentrarchus punctatus

EUROPEAN SEA BASS
Dicentrarchus labrax

SPOTTED SEA BASS
The spotted sea bass is similar in size and habits to the European sea bass, from which it may be distinguished by its spotted sides. Its range overlaps that of the European sea bass, but it is not found as far north.

EUROPEAN SEA BASS
The European sea bass is found in coastal waters and the brackish water of estuaries, and reaches a weight of about 8.6 kg (19 lb). It spawns in the sea in spring and early summer, and young fish often have spots on their sides like those of the spotted bass; these spots fade and disappear as the fish mature.

STRIPED BASS
Morone saxatilis

STRIPED BASS
This large bass, which can grow to 2 m (6 ft 7 in) long and a weight of 57 kg (126 lb), is found along the Atlantic and Gulf coasts of North America, and was introduced into the Pacific coastal waters in 1886. It migrates into freshwater to spawn during late spring and early summer, and there are a number of landlocked, lake-dwelling populations. It will readily take baits such as mullet, sandeels, squid, crabs, clams, worms, and lures, and is fished for commercially as well as for sport.

FISHING NOTES

Techniques
In freshwater, try spinning or trolling for striped bass and Murray cod, and spinning or fly fishing for the smaller species. In saltwater, try surfcasting, trolling, or uptide fishing.

Tackle
For freshwater striped bass and Murray cod, use a heavy spinning rod with 9.1 to 18.1 kg (20 to 40 lb) line. For the smaller freshwater fish, use a 2.1 to 2.7 m (7 to 9 ft) light spinning or fly rod. For striped bass in saltwater, try a 13.6 kg (30 lb) class boat rod for trolling and a 3.7 m (12 ft) rod for surfcasting; when fishing for the smaller species in saltwater, use a 3.4 m (11 ft) light surfcasting rod or a 5.4 kg (12 lb) class uptide rod.

Bait
These fish are all active predators, and will therefore take most suitably sized natural baits or artificial lures.

Freshwater SPECIES

AUSTRALIAN PERCH & GRUNTERS

The Macquarie, golden, and estuary perches are members of the Percichthyidae family *(see page 144)*, while the jungle perch belongs to the Kuhliidae, a small family of fish that are similar to the Centrarchidae of North America *(see pages 126–9)*. The silver perch and sooty grunter are members of the Teraponidae (grunter) family, which consists of about 45 Indo-Pacific marine and freshwater species.

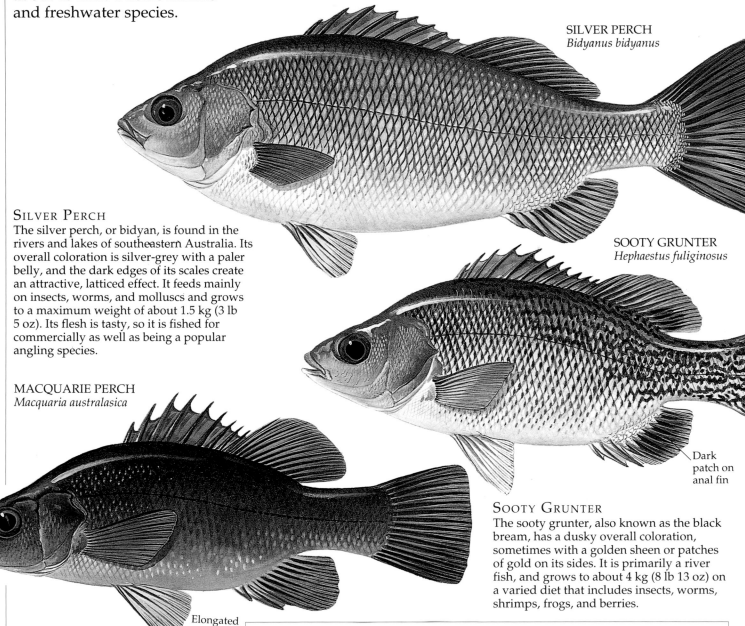

SILVER PERCH
Bidyanus bidyanus

SOOTY GRUNTER
Hephaestus fuliginosus

Dark patch on anal fin

Elongated rays

SILVER PERCH
The silver perch, or bidyan, is found in the rivers and lakes of southeastern Australia. Its overall coloration is silver-grey with a paler belly, and the dark edges of its scales create an attractive, latticed effect. It feeds mainly on insects, worms, and molluscs and grows to a maximum weight of about 1.5 kg (3 lb 5 oz). Its flesh is tasty, so it is fished for commercially as well as being a popular angling species.

MACQUARIE PERCH
Macquaria australasica

MACQUARIE PERCH
The colour of the Macquarie perch varies from greenish brown to almost black, with a pale, sometimes yellowish, belly. It occurs in cool rivers and deep lakes, and has been introduced into reservoirs. Its diet consists mainly of insects, molluscs, and crustaceans, and it reaches a weight of around 1.5 kg (3 lb 5 oz). It spawns in spring and early summer.

SOOTY GRUNTER
The sooty grunter, also known as the black bream, has a dusky overall coloration, sometimes with a golden sheen or patches of gold on its sides. It is primarily a river fish, and grows to about 4 kg (8 lb 13 oz) on a varied diet that includes insects, worms, shrimps, frogs, and berries.

FISHING NOTES

Techniques
Spinning or baitcasting with artificial lures, fly fishing, and trolling with livebaits will all prove successful.

Tackle
For lure fishing, try a 2.1 m (7 ft) spinning or baitcasting rod, a fixed-spool or multiplier reel and 2.7 kg (6 lb) mono line. For fly fishing, use a 2.7 m (9 ft) rod with a fast taper, a fly reel, and a floating #7 to #9 line with a 2.7 kg (6 lb) leader. For trolling, use a 2.7 m (9 ft) stiff-action rod with a 1.1 kg (2½ lb) test curve, and a multiplier reel with 4.54 to 9.1 kg (10 to 20 lb) mono line, a nylon or Dacron leader attached by a swivel, and hook sizes 2/0 to 5/0.

Bait
These fish will take a wide range of lures and flies, and trolled natural baits such as worms, minnows, and crayfish.

146

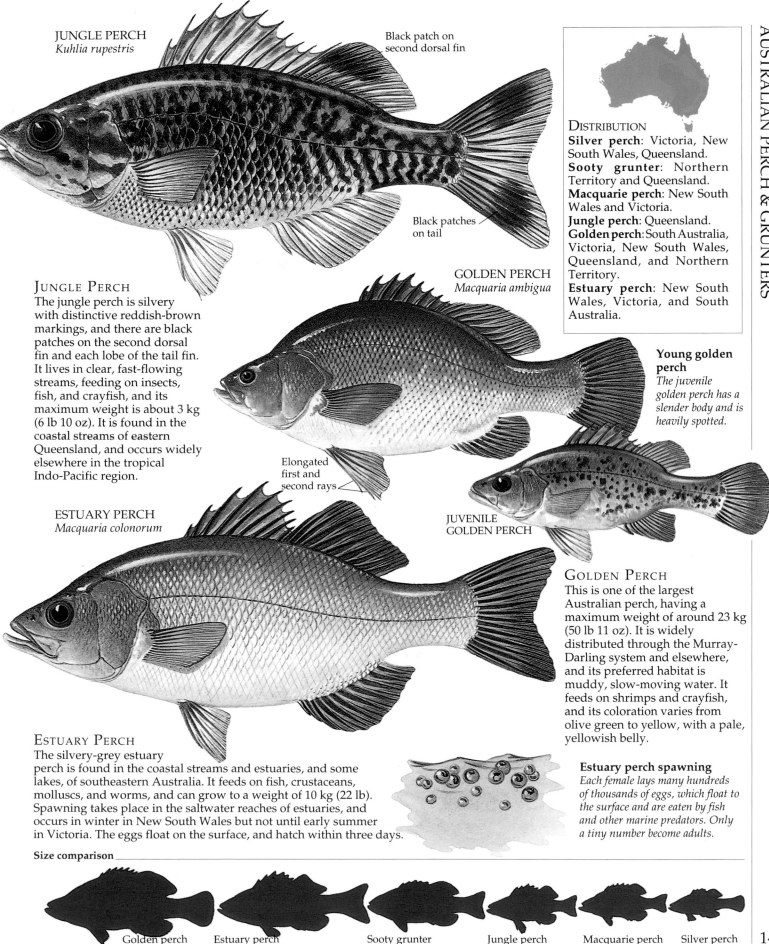

JUNGLE PERCH
Kuhlia rupestris

Black patch on second dorsal fin

Black patches on tail

DISTRIBUTION
Silver perch: Victoria, New South Wales, Queensland.
Sooty grunter: Northern Territory and Queensland.
Macquarie perch: New South Wales and Victoria.
Jungle perch: Queensland.
Golden perch: South Australia, Victoria, New South Wales, Queensland, and Northern Territory.
Estuary perch: New South Wales, Victoria, and South Australia.

JUNGLE PERCH
The jungle perch is silvery with distinctive reddish-brown markings, and there are black patches on the second dorsal fin and each lobe of the tail fin. It lives in clear, fast-flowing streams, feeding on insects, fish, and crayfish, and its maximum weight is about 3 kg (6 lb 10 oz). It is found in the coastal streams of eastern Queensland, and occurs widely elsewhere in the tropical Indo-Pacific region.

GOLDEN PERCH
Macquaria ambigua

Young golden perch
The juvenile golden perch has a slender body and is heavily spotted.

Elongated first and second rays

JUVENILE GOLDEN PERCH

ESTUARY PERCH
Macquaria colonorum

GOLDEN PERCH
This is one of the largest Australian perch, having a maximum weight of around 23 kg (50 lb 11 oz). It is widely distributed through the Murray-Darling system and elsewhere, and its preferred habitat is muddy, slow-moving water. It feeds on shrimps and crayfish, and its coloration varies from olive green to yellow, with a pale, yellowish belly.

ESTUARY PERCH
The silvery-grey estuary perch is found in the coastal streams and estuaries, and some lakes, of southeastern Australia. It feeds on fish, crustaceans, molluscs, and worms, and can grow to a weight of 10 kg (22 lb). Spawning takes place in the saltwater reaches of estuaries, and occurs in winter in New South Wales but not until early summer in Victoria. The eggs float on the surface, and hatch within three days.

Estuary perch spawning
Each female lays many hundreds of thousands of eggs, which float to the surface and are eaten by fish and other marine predators. Only a tiny number become adults.

Size comparison

Golden perch   Estuary perch   Sooty grunter   Jungle perch   Macquarie perch   Silver perch

PERCIDAE

PERCH, SAUGER, WALLEYE, & ZANDER

The Percidae is a large and diverse family of fish comprising perch and related species. These are characterized by their long, slender bodies and their two dorsal fins, separate in some species but joined in others, with the first dorsal having spines and the second having soft rays. The members of the Percidae are found both in streams and in stillwaters. The small species and the young of the large ones feed on insect larvae and other invertebrates; the adults of the large species are fish-eaters.

Perch scales
Perch feel rough to the touch because they have ctenoid scales – scales that have fine teeth on their exposed edges. Smooth scales with no teeth, such as those of the carp family, are called cycloid scales.

Perch eggs
The European perch and the yellow perch both spawn in spring and lay their eggs in long, lacelike ribbons. These are deposited on stones, or woven among water plants and tree roots, in the shallows of still or slow-flowing waters.

Joined dorsal fins

RUFFE
Gymnocephalus cernuus

Many dark marks on first dorsal fin

SAUGER
Stizostedion canadense

RUFFE
The diminutive ruffe, or pope, is one of the smallest of the perch family to be of interest to anglers as a quarry. It usually grows to about 170 g (6 oz), but can reach 750 g (1 lb 10 oz).

WALLEYE
Stizostedion vitreum

ZANDER
The zander, or pikeperch, preys heavily on small fish such as bream, ruffe, and roach, and can reach a weight of over 12 kg (26 lb 8 oz). It was originally found in the Danube and other waters of northern and central Europe, but it has been introduced as far west as England and its range is slowly spreading. Some introductions have been controversial, with the zander being blamed for drastic reductions in local fish populations, but in many waters the introductions seem to have caused no major problems.

SAUGER
The genus *Stizostedion* includes the sauger, walleye, and zander, collectively known as pikeperch, which have only slight genetic differences and are very similar in appearance and habits. Like all pikeperch, the sauger is a predator; it can reach a maximum weight of more than 3.6 kg (8 lb).

WALLEYE
The walleye is so named because of its large, glassy eyes, which are distinctive in daylight and glow at night when a light is shone on them, like the eyes of a cat. It is the largest of the North American perches, typically reaching 1.36 kg (3 lb) with a maximum of 11.3 kg (25 lb), and is a prized food fish as well as being a favourite quarry of anglers.

Size comparison

Zander   Walleye   Sauger   European perch   Volga zander   Yellow perch   Ruffe

YELLOW PERCH
Perca flavescens

EUROPEAN PERCH
Perca fluviatilis

DISTRIBUTION
Sauger, walleye: Northwest Territories east to Quebec, southeast to Alabama.
Zander: northern and central Europe; also introduced into western Europe and England.
Volga zander: river systems entering the northern Black and Caspian Seas.
Ruffe: eastern England to Asia; introduced into Scotland and the Great Lakes.
European perch: from Ireland to Siberia; has been introduced into Australia.
Yellow perch: found from the Northwest Territories to the Atlantic drainages as far south as South Carolina.

YELLOW PERCH
The North American yellow perch is very similar to the European perch in appearance and habits, and the two species are closely related. Like all the large members of the Percidae, they make excellent eating and are among the tastiest of freshwater fish.

EUROPEAN PERCH
This perch is widespread in stillwaters and slow-flowing lowland rivers throughout Europe. It is a shoaling fish that feeds on insects and small fish, including perch fry, and in some waters of the European mainland it can attain a weight of up to 6.5 kg (14 lb).

ZANDER
Stizostedion lucioperca

Eggs

VOLGA ZANDER
Stizostedion volgensis

Spawning zander
Zander spawn in spring and early summer, laying clumps of pale yellow eggs on plants or on sand and stones. The larvae hatch after a few days and live on their yolk sacs until their teeth develop and they can feed themselves. Young zander feed on small prey, such as insect larvae and fish fry.

FISHING NOTES

Techniques
Legering, float fishing, and spinning are all effective.

Tackle
For legering and float fishing, try a 3 to 3.7 m (10 to 12 ft) slow or medium-action rod with a fixed-spool reel. Use 2.27 kg (5 lb) mono line and hook sizes 4 to 10 for ruffe and perch, and 2.7 to 4.45 kg (6 to 10 lb) mono with a 50 cm (20 in) wire trace and size 10 treble hook for walleye, sauger, and zander. When spinning, for perch use a 2.1 to 2.7 m (7 to 9 ft) light spinning rod with a fixed-spool reel, 2.27 or 2.7 kg (5 or 6 lb) mono line, and a swivelled trace; for walleye, sauger, and zander, use a 2.4 m (8 ft) medium-action spinning rod, fixed-spool reel, 2.7 to 3.6 kg (6 to 8 lb) mono line, and a short, fine-wire trace.

Bait
Worms and maggots for perch, small fish for walleye, sauger, and zander. Spinning: spinners, spoons, jigs, plugs.

VOLGA ZANDER
The appearance of the Volga zander is similar to that of the zander, but the dark markings on its back are much more well defined. It is also generally smaller, and lacks the long fangs of the zander, although its mouth is well equipped with small, sharp teeth. The Volga zander is found in rivers flowing into the Caspian and Black seas, including the Volga itself and the Danube as far upstream as Vienna. It prefers open, deep water to vegetated areas, and grows to about 2 kg (4 lb 6 oz).

149

SALMONIDAE

CHAR

The most obvious difference between char (salmonids of the genus *Salvelinus*) and salmon and trout (genera *Salmo* and *Oncorhynchus*) lies in their coloration: char have light markings on a darker background; salmon and trout have dark markings on a lighter background. Char feed on invertebrates and small fish, and they are native to the cool waters of the northern parts of the Northern Hemisphere; they are all excellent angling species. Lake and brook trout have been widely introduced elsewhere.

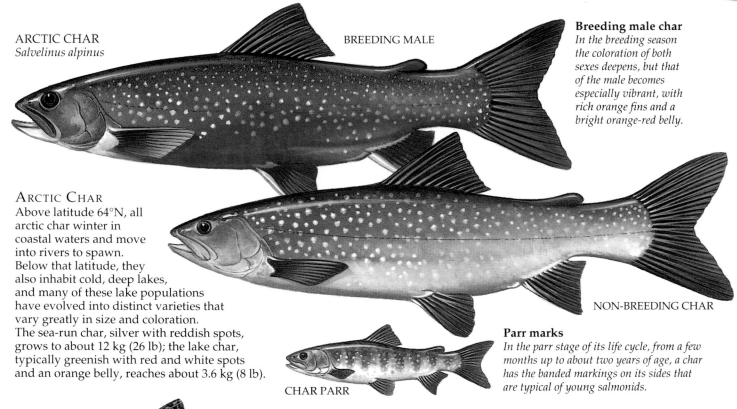

ARCTIC CHAR
Salvelinus alpinus

BREEDING MALE

Breeding male char
In the breeding season the coloration of both sexes deepens, but that of the male becomes especially vibrant, with rich orange fins and a bright orange-red belly.

ARCTIC CHAR
Above latitude 64°N, all arctic char winter in coastal waters and move into rivers to spawn. Below that latitude, they also inhabit cold, deep lakes, and many of these lake populations have evolved into distinct varieties that vary greatly in size and coloration. The sea-run char, silver with reddish spots, grows to about 12 kg (26 lb); the lake char, typically greenish with red and white spots and an orange belly, reaches about 3.6 kg (8 lb).

NON-BREEDING CHAR

Parr marks
In the parr stage of its life cycle, from a few months up to about two years of age, a char has the banded markings on its sides that are typical of young salmonids.

CHAR PARR

Hybrids
Hybridization among members of the Salmonidae family occurs both naturally and as a result of selective breeding by fish farms. Natural hybrids include Atlantic salmon × sea trout and rainbow × cutthroat; farmed crossbreeds include the splake (brook trout × lake trout), the tiger trout (brook × brown), and the cheetah trout (brook × rainbow).

SPLAKE (HYBRID)

FISHING NOTES

Techniques
Fly fishing, spinning, and trolling for arctic char and lake trout; fly fishing and spinning for brook trout and Dolly Varden.

Tackle
For fly fishing use a 2.4 to 3.4 m (8 to 11 ft) fly rod with a fly reel, floating or sinking line as appropriate, and flies dressed on hook sizes 10 to 14. For spinning and for shallow trolling try a 2.7 m (9 ft), medium spinning rod with a fixed-spool reel, and use 1.8 to 2.7 kg (4 to 6 lb) line for spinning and 4.54 to 6.8 kg (10 to 15 lb) line for shallow trolling.

For deep trolling, use a 1.8m (6ft), fast-taper trolling rod with braided wire line; the rod should have hardened rings or roller guides to resist the abrasive action of the wire line.

Bait
For arctic char, use small, bright spinners or spoons, or wet fly patterns that incorporate a flashy material such as gold or silver tinsel, for example Butcher or Mallard and Claret. Use large, trolled spoons or livebait for lake trout in deep water, and spoons, spinners, plugs, or streamer flies when the fish are close inshore. Brook trout and Dolly Varden may be taken on lures, dry flies, wet flies, and nymphs.

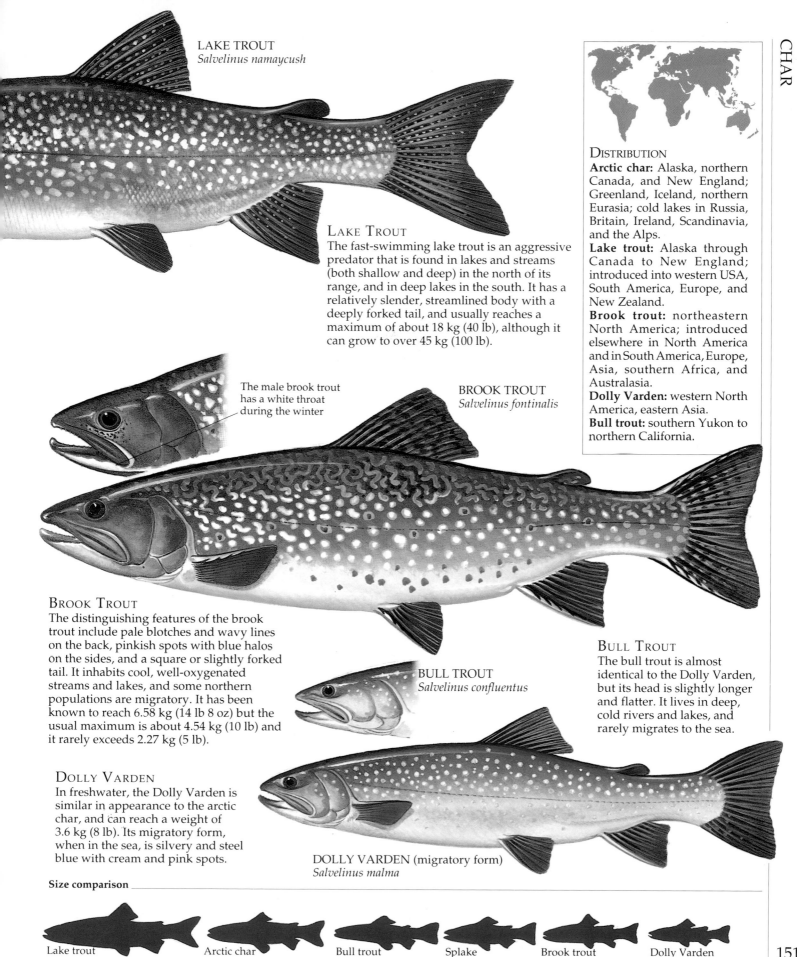

LAKE TROUT
Salvelinus namaycush

LAKE TROUT
The fast-swimming lake trout is an aggressive predator that is found in lakes and streams (both shallow and deep) in the north of its range, and in deep lakes in the south. It has a relatively slender, streamlined body with a deeply forked tail, and usually reaches a maximum of about 18 kg (40 lb), although it can grow to over 45 kg (100 lb).

DISTRIBUTION
Arctic char: Alaska, northern Canada, and New England; Greenland, Iceland, northern Eurasia; cold lakes in Russia, Britain, Ireland, Scandinavia, and the Alps.
Lake trout: Alaska through Canada to New England; introduced into western USA, South America, Europe, and New Zealand.
Brook trout: northeastern North America; introduced elsewhere in North America and in South America, Europe, Asia, southern Africa, and Australasia.
Dolly Varden: western North America, eastern Asia.
Bull trout: southern Yukon to northern California.

The male brook trout has a white throat during the winter

BROOK TROUT
Salvelinus fontinalis

BROOK TROUT
The distinguishing features of the brook trout include pale blotches and wavy lines on the back, pinkish spots with blue halos on the sides, and a square or slightly forked tail. It inhabits cool, well-oxygenated streams and lakes, and some northern populations are migratory. It has been known to reach 6.58 kg (14 lb 8 oz) but the usual maximum is about 4.54 kg (10 lb) and it rarely exceeds 2.27 kg (5 lb).

BULL TROUT
The bull trout is almost identical to the Dolly Varden, but its head is slightly longer and flatter. It lives in deep, cold rivers and lakes, and rarely migrates to the sea.

BULL TROUT
Salvelinus confluentus

DOLLY VARDEN
In freshwater, the Dolly Varden is similar in appearance to the arctic char, and can reach a weight of 3.6 kg (8 lb). Its migratory form, when in the sea, is silvery and steel blue with cream and pink spots.

DOLLY VARDEN (migratory form)
Salvelinus malma

Size comparison

| Lake trout | Arctic char | Bull trout | Splake | Brook trout | Dolly Varden |

151

SALMONIDAE

SALMON

Salmon are some of the most important commercial and sport fish in the world. All begin their lives in freshwater and most migrate to the sea to mature, returning to freshwater to spawn. The principal exceptions are the landlocked varieties of the Atlantic and sockeye salmon, and two Eurasian landlocked species, the huchen (*Hucho hucho*) and the taimen (*Hucho taimen*). The huchen, a fish of the Danube basin, is now a protected species in many of its native waters but has been introduced successfully into some French rivers; the taimen is common in the Volga basin and Siberia.

ATLANTIC SALMON LIFE CYCLE

ALEVIN (12 to 15 weeks) WITH YOLK SAC

EGG

BREEDING MALE (3 to 8 years)

ATLANTIC SALMON
Salmo salar

Life cycles
The life cycles of all the salmon species are broadly similar. The main differences are that the Pacific species die after spawning but many Atlantic salmon spawn more than once; the landlocked species do not migrate to the sea but mature in freshwater; and there are some differences in timing. The eggs are laid in redds (nests) scooped out of gravel by the female, and take from 70 to 200 days to hatch.

BREEDING MALE

COHO SALMON
Oncorhynchus kisutch

Spots on upper lobe only

Coloration
The coloration of a salmon changes when it is ready to breed, and the male develops a hook (kype) on its lower jaw.

BREEDING MALE CHINOOK

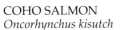

COHO SALMON
The coho or silver salmon is an important sport fish both in its native waters and those to which it has been introduced, such as the Great Lakes. It is similar to the chinook, but has white gums rather than black, less extensive spotting on the tail, and is smaller, reaching a maximum of around 15 kg (33 lb).

MASU SALMON
The relatively small and stocky masu, or cherry salmon, is an Asian species with both migratory and freshwater forms. It reaches maturity in three or four years, growing to about 4.54 kg (10 lb), and is fished for commercially as well as for sport.

MASU SALMON
Oncorhynchus masou

BREEDING MALE PINK

PINK SALMON
Oncorhynchus gorbuscha

FISHING NOTES

Techniques
The Atlantic salmon is fished for in freshwater. The most usual technique is fly fishing, but it is also taken on spoons, plugs, and natural baits on waters (and at times of the year) where these methods are permitted. Pacific salmon, of which the chinook and coho are the most important species for the sport fisherman, are usually taken by trolling just offshore and in estuaries, but they are also caught by fly fishing and spinning (as are the landlocked varieties) when they move into freshwater to spawn.

Tackle
Fly tackle for freshwater salmon fishing is typically a 3.7 to 4.9 m (12 to 16 ft) rod, a fly reel, and weight-forward fly line. For spinning and bait fishing, try a heavy 3 m (10 ft) spinning rod with a multiplier reel and 6.8 to 9.1 kg (15 to 20 lb) line. The usual saltwater rig for chinook and coho is a boat or trolling rod with a star-drag multiplier reel and 9.1 to 20.4 kg (20 to 45 lb) line.

Bait
In freshwater, use flies, lures, worms, or prawns. In saltwater, use streamers, lures, or fish baits.

PINK SALMON
Because of the distinctively humped back of the spawning male, the pink salmon is also known as the humpback or humpy. It is the most abundant of the Pacific species and is of considerable commercial importance, but it is a small fish, usually averaging 1.36 to 2.27 kg (3 to 5lb) with a maximum of 5.4 kg (12 lb).

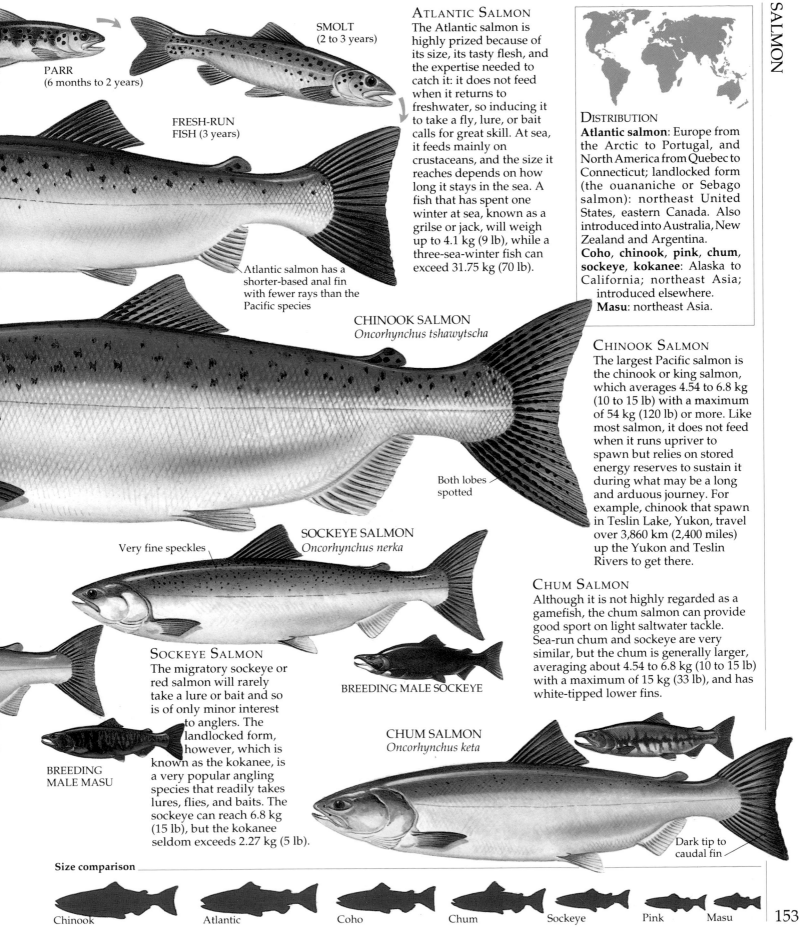

PARR
(6 months to 2 years)

SMOLT
(2 to 3 years)

FRESH-RUN
FISH (3 years)

ATLANTIC SALMON

The Atlantic salmon is highly prized because of its size, its tasty flesh, and the expertise needed to catch it: it does not feed when it returns to freshwater, so inducing it to take a fly, lure, or bait calls for great skill. At sea, it feeds mainly on crustaceans, and the size it reaches depends on how long it stays in the sea. A fish that has spent one winter at sea, known as a grilse or jack, will weigh up to 4.1 kg (9 lb), while a three-sea-winter fish can exceed 31.75 kg (70 lb).

Atlantic salmon has a shorter-based anal fin with fewer rays than the Pacific species

DISTRIBUTION

Atlantic salmon: Europe from the Arctic to Portugal, and North America from Quebec to Connecticut; landlocked form (the ouananiche or Sebago salmon): northeast United States, eastern Canada. Also introduced into Australia, New Zealand and Argentina.
Coho, **chinook**, **pink**, **chum**, **sockeye**, **kokanee**: Alaska to California; northeast Asia; introduced elsewhere.
Masu: northeast Asia.

CHINOOK SALMON
Oncorhynchus tshawytscha

Both lobes spotted

CHINOOK SALMON

The largest Pacific salmon is the chinook or king salmon, which averages 4.54 to 6.8 kg (10 to 15 lb) with a maximum of 54 kg (120 lb) or more. Like most salmon, it does not feed when it runs upriver to spawn but relies on stored energy reserves to sustain it during what may be a long and arduous journey. For example, chinook that spawn in Teslin Lake, Yukon, travel over 3,860 km (2,400 miles) up the Yukon and Teslin Rivers to get there.

CHUM SALMON

Although it is not highly regarded as a gamefish, the chum salmon can provide good sport on light saltwater tackle. Sea-run chum and sockeye are very similar, but the chum is generally larger, averaging about 4.54 to 6.8 kg (10 to 15 lb) with a maximum of 15 kg (33 lb), and has white-tipped lower fins.

SOCKEYE SALMON
Oncorhynchus nerka

Very fine speckles

SOCKEYE SALMON

The migratory sockeye or red salmon will rarely take a lure or bait and so is of only minor interest to anglers. The landlocked form, however, which is known as the kokanee, is a very popular angling species that readily takes lures, flies, and baits. The sockeye can reach 6.8 kg (15 lb), but the kokanee seldom exceeds 2.27 kg (5 lb).

BREEDING MALE SOCKEYE

BREEDING MALE MASU

CHUM SALMON
Oncorhynchus keta

Dark tip to caudal fin

Size comparison

Chinook   Atlantic   Coho   Chum   Sockeye   Pink   Masu

SALMONIDAE

TROUT

The brown trout and the rainbow trout are two of the world's most important gamefish species, and because of the high-quality sport they offer their distribution has been increased by extensive introduction schemes. The cutthroat trout, despite its qualities as a gamefish, has not been widely introduced beyond its natural range for a number of reasons, such as its tendency to hybridize with the rainbow trout. Trout thrive in cool, clean streams and lakes and feed mainly on insects, insect larvae, crustaceans, and fish. When at sea, the migratory forms eat fish and crustaceans.

RAINBOW TROUT
The rainbow trout varies greatly in appearance and size, and there are many different races and subspecies such as the Kamloops, Shasta, and Kern River rainbows. Most, however, have a pink stripe along the lateral line and small black speckles on the sides, back, upper fins, and tail. In North America, rainbows weighing more than 22.7 kg (50 lb) have been recorded, but the usual maximum in European waters is only around 11 kg (24 lb).

STEELHEAD
Steelhead are rainbow trout that migrate to sea before returning to rivers to spawn, or live in lakes and move into streams to spawn. Fresh-run steelhead are silvery, but their coloration soon changes to resemble that of non-migratory rainbows.

Sharply squared-off tail

SEA TROUT
Migratory form of brown trout

BROWN TROUT
Salmo trutta

SEA TROUT
The sea trout, the silvery migratory form of the brown trout, enters the sea at about two years old but returns to rivers to spawn. A large sea trout resembles an Atlantic salmon (see page 152), but its tail has a thicker "wrist" and is more squared-off.

BROWN TROUT
The brown trout is highly variable in appearance and size, and these variations are caused by environmental and genetic factors. In general, the body is brownish and sprinkled with black and red spots, and its weight ranges from under 454 g (1 lb) in small streams to over 13.6 kg (30 lb) in large waters.

FISHING NOTES

Techniques
Trout are taken on natural baits and on spinners, but fly fishing is without any doubt the pre-eminent trout-fishing technique.

Tackle
For fly fishing, use a 1.8 to 3.4 m (6 to 11 ft) fly rod, a fly reel, and floating or sinking line as appropriate. To fish for trout with naturals such as worms, use a 2.1 to 3 m (7 to 10 ft) medium-action rod

with a fixed spool reel, 1.8 to 3.6 kg (4 to 8 lb) line, and hook sizes 6 to 14. For spinning with artificial lures, try a 2.1 to 2.7 m (7 to 9 ft) spinning rod with a fixed-spool reel and 1.8 to 3.6 kg (4 to 8 lb) line.

Bait
For fly fishing, use whichever pattern is appropriate for the water, the style of fishing, and the prevailing conditions. For spinning, use small spinners, spoons, and plugs. Suitable naturals for trout include larvae and worms.

Hooked jaw

Cannibal trout
Although all brown trout are carnivorous, large individuals will even eat smaller members of their own species. These cannibal trout, which develop a distinctly hooked lower jaw, lurk in deep water waiting to pounce on their prey as it swims past.

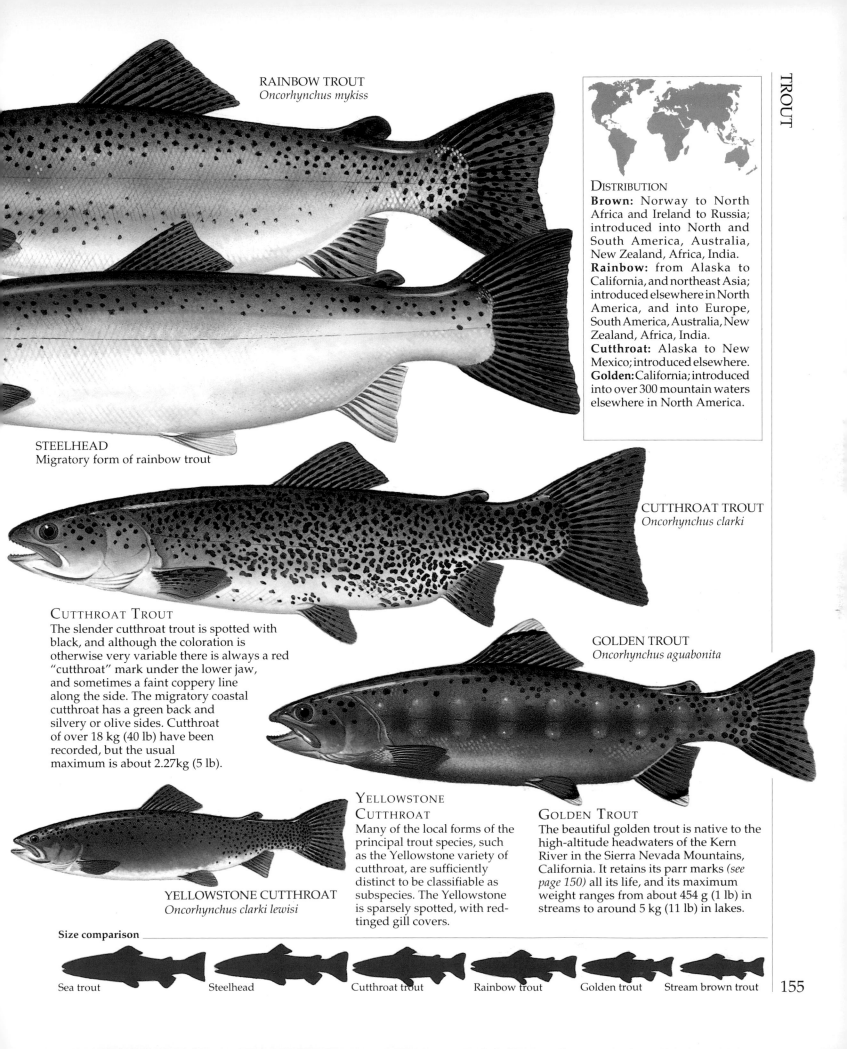

RAINBOW TROUT
Oncorhynchus mykiss

STEELHEAD
Migratory form of rainbow trout

DISTRIBUTION

Brown: Norway to North Africa and Ireland to Russia; introduced into North and South America, Australia, New Zealand, Africa, India.
Rainbow: from Alaska to California, and northeast Asia; introduced elsewhere in North America, and into Europe, South America, Australia, New Zealand, Africa, India.
Cutthroat: Alaska to New Mexico; introduced elsewhere.
Golden: California; introduced into over 300 mountain waters elsewhere in North America.

CUTTHROAT TROUT
Oncorhynchus clarki

CUTTHROAT TROUT

The slender cutthroat trout is spotted with black, and although the coloration is otherwise very variable there is always a red "cutthroat" mark under the lower jaw, and sometimes a faint coppery line along the side. The migratory coastal cutthroat has a green back and silvery or olive sides. Cutthroat of over 18 kg (40 lb) have been recorded, but the usual maximum is about 2.27kg (5 lb).

GOLDEN TROUT
Oncorhynchus aguabonita

YELLOWSTONE CUTTHROAT

Many of the local forms of the principal trout species, such as the Yellowstone variety of cutthroat, are sufficiently distinct to be classifiable as subspecies. The Yellowstone is sparsely spotted, with red-tinged gill covers.

YELLOWSTONE CUTTHROAT
Oncorhynchus clarki lewisi

GOLDEN TROUT

The beautiful golden trout is native to the high-altitude headwaters of the Kern River in the Sierra Nevada Mountains, California. It retains its parr marks (*see page 150*) all its life, and its maximum weight ranges from about 454 g (1 lb) in streams to around 5 kg (11 lb) in lakes.

Size comparison

Sea trout   Steelhead   Cutthroat trout   Rainbow trout   Golden trout   Stream brown trout

WHITEFISH & GRAYLING

Whitefish and grayling are widely distributed in the colder lakes and streams of the Northern Hemisphere. Grayling are popular angling species, as are several of the whitefish, but many whitefish species are threatened with extinction *(see page 279)* and it is illegal to fish for them in many countries and on certain waters. Grayling feed mainly on bottom-dwelling creatures such as insect larvae, crustaceans, and worms, but will also take insects at the surface. The whitefish's diet ranges from plankton to fish.

INCONNU

The large, powerful inconnu, or sheefish, is the only predatory whitefish in North America. Its average weight is about 2.27 kg (5 lb), but it can live for over 20 years and has been known to reach weights of up to 25 kg (55 lb). Most inconnu live in the estuaries and lower reaches of rivers and migrate upstream to spawn, but there are some non-migratory lake populations. The young fish feed on plankton at first, and then on small, bottom-dwelling creatures before becoming predatory during their second year.

INCONNU
Stenodus leucichthys

Protruding lower jaw

EUROPEAN WHITEFISH
Coregonus sp.

EUROPEAN WHITEFISH

In Europe, the many whitefish species, subspecies, races, and local variants have yet to be classified definitively. In general, they are at best of minor interest to anglers, but many are netted commercially because of their tasty flesh. Common names include vendace, houting, powan, and schelly; they are slender, silvery fish that range in size from about 454 g (1 lb) *(Coregonus albula)* to around 5 kg (11 lb) *(C. pallasi).*

CISCO

Because of its herringlike size, shape, and general appearance, the cisco is also known as the lake herring. Despite being a small fish, rarely exceeding 910 g (2 lb), it is popular with anglers because it will readily take a wide range of lures and baits, including flies.

CISCO
Coregonus artedi

Size comparison

| Inconnu | Lake whitefish | Grayling | Cisco | European whitefish |

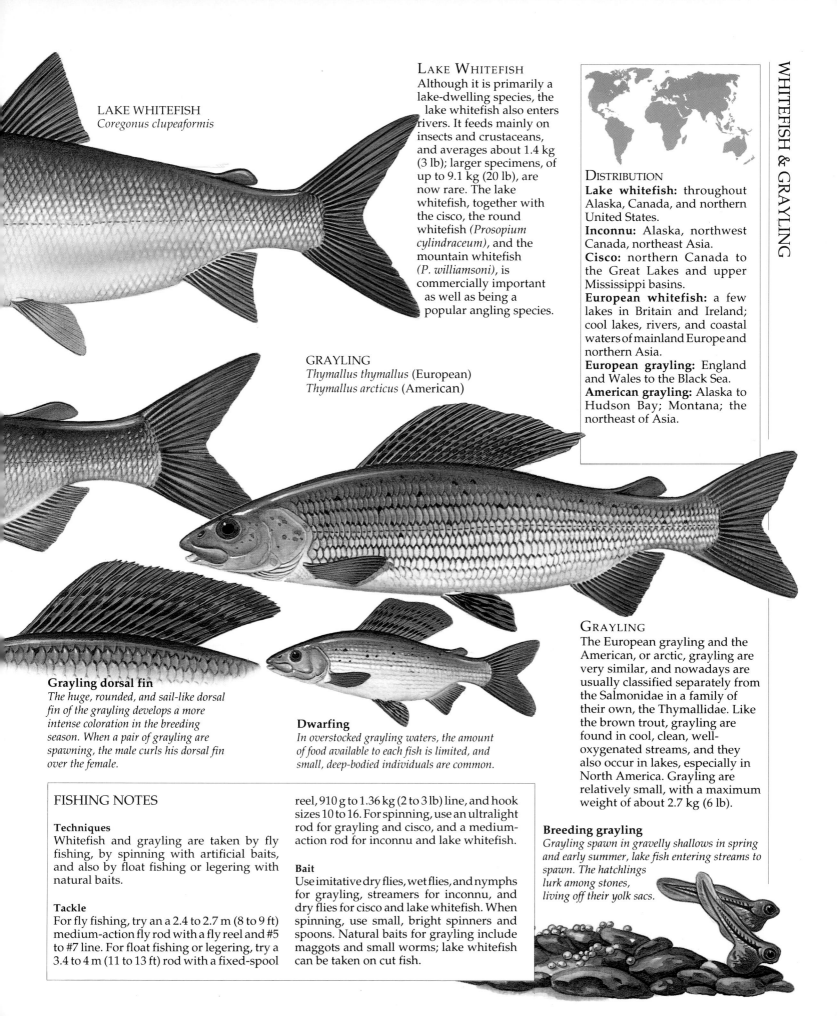

LAKE WHITEFISH
Coregonus clupeaformis

LAKE WHITEFISH

Although it is primarily a lake-dwelling species, the lake whitefish also enters rivers. It feeds mainly on insects and crustaceans, and averages about 1.4 kg (3 lb); larger specimens, of up to 9.1 kg (20 lb), are now rare. The lake whitefish, together with the cisco, the round whitefish (*Prosopium cylindraceum*), and the mountain whitefish (*P. williamsoni*), is commercially important as well as being a popular angling species.

DISTRIBUTION

Lake whitefish: throughout Alaska, Canada, and northern United States.
Inconnu: Alaska, northwest Canada, northeast Asia.
Cisco: northern Canada to the Great Lakes and upper Mississippi basins.
European whitefish: a few lakes in Britain and Ireland; cool lakes, rivers, and coastal waters of mainland Europe and northern Asia.
European grayling: England and Wales to the Black Sea.
American grayling: Alaska to Hudson Bay; Montana; the northeast of Asia.

GRAYLING
Thymallus thymallus (European)
Thymallus arcticus (American)

Grayling dorsal fin
The huge, rounded, and sail-like dorsal fin of the grayling develops a more intense coloration in the breeding season. When a pair of grayling are spawning, the male curls his dorsal fin over the female.

Dwarfing
In overstocked grayling waters, the amount of food available to each fish is limited, and small, deep-bodied individuals are common.

GRAYLING

The European grayling and the American, or arctic, grayling are very similar, and nowadays are usually classified separately from the Salmonidae in a family of their own, the Thymallidae. Like the brown trout, grayling are found in cool, clean, well-oxygenated streams, and they also occur in lakes, especially in North America. Grayling are relatively small, with a maximum weight of about 2.7 kg (6 lb).

Breeding grayling
Grayling spawn in gravelly shallows in spring and early summer, lake fish entering streams to spawn. The hatchlings lurk among stones, living off their yolk sacs.

FISHING NOTES

Techniques

Whitefish and grayling are taken by fly fishing, by spinning with artificial baits, and also by float fishing or legering with natural baits.

Tackle

For fly fishing, try an a 2.4 to 2.7 m (8 to 9 ft) medium-action fly rod with a fly reel and #5 to #7 line. For float fishing or legering, try a 3.4 to 4 m (11 to 13 ft) rod with a fixed-spool reel, 910 g to 1.36 kg (2 to 3 lb) line, and hook sizes 10 to 16. For spinning, use an ultralight rod for grayling and cisco, and a medium-action rod for inconnu and lake whitefish.

Bait

Use imitative dry flies, wet flies, and nymphs for grayling, streamers for inconnu, and dry flies for cisco and lake whitefish. When spinning, use small, bright spinners and spoons. Natural baits for grayling include maggots and small worms; lake whitefish can be taken on cut fish.

ALBULIDAE; ELOPIDAE; POMATOMIDAE

BONEFISH, BLUEFISH, & TARPON

These fish haunt the shallow coastal waters of the tropical and warm-temperate regions of the world, and are among the most exciting and popular marine sports species. The food of bonefish (the Albulidae) and tarpon (the Elopidae) consists mainly of crustaceans and small fish, but the bluefish (a member of the Pomatomidae) is a savage predator that will eat virtually anything edible that crosses its path.

Vertical bars fade with age

BONEFISH
Albula vulpes

TARPON
Megalops atlanticus

BONEFISH
The bonefish is a bottom feeder that grubs in the mud or sand for food such as shrimps and crabs. In very shallow water, the tails of feeding bonefish often break the surface, betraying their presence to stalking anglers who wade the mudflats in pursuit of them. Adult bonefish typically weigh up to 4.54 kg (10 lb) but can reach 8.6 kg (19 lb).

BLUEFISH
Pomatomus saltatrix

BLUEFISH
The highly migratory bluefish can grow to over 23 kg (50 lb), and travels in huge schools that go into a feeding frenzy when they encounter shoals of prey fish such as herring or menhaden. They have been known to come close inshore and attack bathers, and their sharp, prominent, triangular teeth can inflict painful wounds. They should be handled with care when caught, especially when they are being unhooked.

TARPON
The large, silvery tarpon is usually caught in tidal creeks, estuaries, mangrove swamps, and lagoons, and can sometimes be taken offshore. Its scales are large and tough, with a bright, metallic sheen, and the last ray of the dorsal fin is greatly elongated. Most tarpon landed by anglers weigh between 9.1 and 36.3 kg (20 and 80 lb), but the maximum weight is much higher and individuals of over 136 kg (300 lb) have been reported.

FISHING NOTES

Techniques
The usual techniques are trolling for bluefish, and spinning and fly fishing for bonefish and tarpon.

Tackle
For bluefish, use a 9.1 kg (20 lb) class boat rod with a 4/0 multiplier, 9.1 kg (20 lb) nylon or Dacron line, a trolling weight, a wire terminal trace, and hook sizes 4/0 to 6/0. When spinning for bonefish and tarpon, try a 2 to 2.1 m (6½ to 7 ft) medium-action rod and fixed-spool reel. Use 3.6 kg (8 lb) mono line with a mono leader for bonefish, and 6.8 kg (15 lb) mono line with a short wire trace for tarpon. Suitable fly tackle for bonefish and tarpon would be a 2.7 to 3 m (9 to 10 ft) saltwater fly rod and a 10 cm (4 in) reel, with 3.6 kg (8 lb) backing for bonefish and 12.2 kg (27 lb) backing for tarpon; hook sizes are 6 to 1/0 for bonefish, 2 to 5/0 for tarpon.

Bait
Bluefish are usually taken on plugs or baitfish. For bonefish, spin with small leadhead lures and use shrimp imitator patterns, bucktails, and small imitation marabou streamers for fly fishing. For tarpon, spin with medium-sized plugs, and use yellow or orange splayed-wing streamers for fly fishing.

Hard fighter
The hard-fighting tarpon is justifiably regarded as one of the world's most exciting gamefish. As soon as it feels the hook being set, it begins a series of spectacular, twisting leaps in an effort to free itself, and it very often succeeds in doing so.

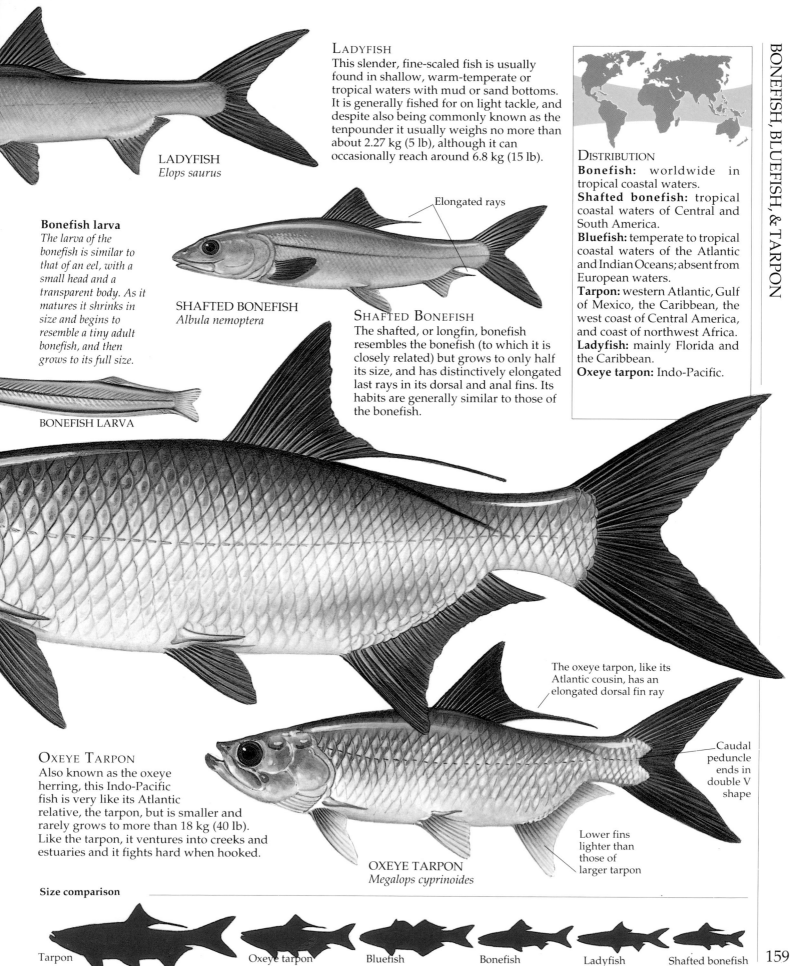

LADYFISH
This slender, fine-scaled fish is usually found in shallow, warm-temperate or tropical waters with mud or sand bottoms. It is generally fished for on light tackle, and despite also being commonly known as the tenpounder it usually weighs no more than about 2.27 kg (5 lb), although it can occasionally reach around 6.8 kg (15 lb).

LADYFISH
Elops saurus

Bonefish larva
The larva of the bonefish is similar to that of an eel, with a small head and a transparent body. As it matures it shrinks in size and begins to resemble a tiny adult bonefish, and then grows to its full size.

BONEFISH LARVA

Elongated rays

SHAFTED BONEFISH
Albula nemoptera

SHAFTED BONEFISH
The shafted, or longfin, bonefish resembles the bonefish (to which it is closely related) but grows to only half its size, and has distinctively elongated last rays in its dorsal and anal fins. Its habits are generally similar to those of the bonefish.

DISTRIBUTION
Bonefish: worldwide in tropical coastal waters.
Shafted bonefish: tropical coastal waters of Central and South America.
Bluefish: temperate to tropical coastal waters of the Atlantic and Indian Oceans; absent from European waters.
Tarpon: western Atlantic, Gulf of Mexico, the Caribbean, the west coast of Central America, and coast of northwest Africa.
Ladyfish: mainly Florida and the Caribbean.
Oxeye tarpon: Indo-Pacific.

The oxeye tarpon, like its Atlantic cousin, has an elongated dorsal fin ray

Caudal peduncle ends in double V shape

OXEYE TARPON
Also known as the oxeye herring, this Indo-Pacific fish is very like its Atlantic relative, the tarpon, but is smaller and rarely grows to more than 18 kg (40 lb). Like the tarpon, it ventures into creeks and estuaries and it fights hard when hooked.

Lower fins lighter than those of larger tarpon

OXEYE TARPON
Megalops cyprinoides

Size comparison

Tarpon   Oxeye tarpon   Bluefish   Bonefish   Ladyfish   Shafted bonefish

159

EELS

There are more than 20 families of eel, including the Muraenidae (morays) and Congridae (congers), and all but one of them comprise exclusively saltwater fish. The exception is the family Anguillidae, which includes the American, European, and longfinned eels, all of which mature in freshwater and travel to the sea to spawn. The American and European eels travel to the Sargasso Sea, an area in the North Atlantic; the longfinned eel and the other Australasian species of Anguillidae migrate to the Indian Ocean.

CONGER
Conger conger

MORAY

The European moray *Muraena helena*, found in the eastern Atlantic and the Mediterranean, is one of the more than 80 species of moray. All are notoriously short-tempered and quick to use their razor-sharp teeth when they feel threatened. They are rarely fished for, but are sometimes hooked when other species are being sought. *M. helena* can reach 1.3 m (4 ft 3 in) but is usually much smaller.

MORAY
Muraena helena

CALIFORNIA MORAY

This moray is found in shallow water along the coasts of California and Baja California, from Point Conception south. It attains a maximum length of about 1.5 m (5 ft).

CALIFORNIA
MORAY
*Gymnothorax
mordax*

AMERICAN EEL
Anguilla rostrata

AMERICAN EEL

Adult American eels usually spend several years in freshwater, the males staying near the mouths of rivers and the females travelling far upstream. The females grow to 1 m (3 ft 3 in) or more and a weight of over 5 kg (11 lb), but the males are much smaller, generally around 30 cm (1 ft) in length.

EUROPEAN EEL
Anguilla anguilla

EUROPEAN EEL

The European eel is very similar to its American counterpart, and the two may be a single species. After spawning, the adults die; the journey to freshwater takes young American eels about a year, and young European eels three or four years.

LONG-
FINNED EEL
Anguilla reinhardtii

LONGFINNED EEL

This is one of a number of freshwater eels found in Australasia. Like the American and European eels, it migrates to the sea to spawn, possibly in the Coral Sea. It grows to 14 kg (31 lb).

Eel larvae
In the early stages of their development, eel larvae are strange, transparent, leaflike creatures called leptocephali. Later, they become elvers, miniature versions of their parents, and it is as elvers that freshwater eels arrive in rivers.

EARLY STAGE

LATER STAGE

Size comparison

Conger   California moray   Moray   Longfinned eel   American eel   European eel

CONGERS

The various species of conger differ from morays in having pectoral fins (morays have none) and from freshwater eels in being scaleless (freshwater eels have minute, embedded scales). A conger may also have a dark fringe to its dorsal and anal fins. *Conger conger*, found in the Atlantic, Mediterranean and Baltic, grows to about 2.7 m (9 ft) and 65 kg (143 lb).

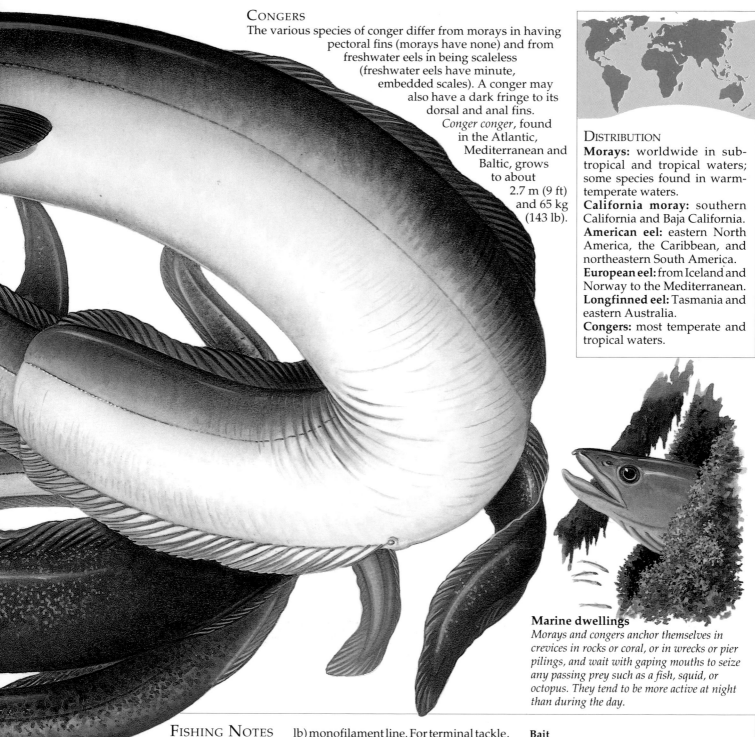

DISTRIBUTION
Morays: worldwide in subtropical and tropical waters; some species found in warm-temperate waters.
California moray: southern California and Baja California.
American eel: eastern North America, the Caribbean, and northeastern South America.
European eel: from Iceland and Norway to the Mediterranean.
Longfinned eel: Tasmania and eastern Australia.
Congers: most temperate and tropical waters.

Marine dwellings
Morays and congers anchor themselves in crevices in rocks or coral, or in wrecks or pier pilings, and wait with gaping mouths to seize any passing prey such as a fish, squid, or octopus. They tend to be more active at night than during the day.

FISHING NOTES

Techniques
The migratory eels are usually fished for in freshwater, by legering. Marine eels (conger and moray) are taken by fishing with natural baits from rocky shores, piers, jetties, and sea walls, and from boats over rocks and wrecks.

Tackle
For migratory eels, use a 3 to 3.7 m (10 to 12 ft), 910 g (2 lb) test curve, carp or pike rod, with a fixed-spool reel, and 2.27 kg (5 lb) monofilament line. For terminal tackle, use a running leger or fish the bait freelined, with a size 4 to 8 hook tied direct to the line. When fishing from the shore for marine eels, use a 9.1 to 22.7 kg (20 to 50 lb) class surfcasting rod with a 4/0 multiplier reel, 13.6 to 15.9 kg (30 to 35 lb) line, a running leger wire trace, a pear- or pyramid-shaped weight, and a 6/0 hook. To fish from a boat for marine eels, try a 22.7 kg (50 lb) boat rod, 8/0 multiplier reel, and 22.7 to 27.2 kg (50 to 60 lb) line. Use a wire trace, a size 8/0 hook, and a pear-or pyramid-shaped weight.

Bait
Worms are good bait for freshwater eels, as are small, dead fish. Fish baits are very effective for large eels, and they should be whole, about 13 cm (5 in) long, and punctured so that they sink. Pungent baits such as fish liver and smoked fish are also effective, and it is worth using an oily, smelly, non-floating groundbait to attract eels into the swim you are going to fish.

The marine eels can be caught on large natural baits, such as whole or cut fish, squid, and cuttlefish, and these baits should be fished on the bottom.

SEA CATFISH & BARRACUDA

The Ariidae family of sea catfish consists of about 80 species, widely distributed around the world in warm coastal waters and estuaries, and also (in the tropics) in freshwater. When caught, a sea catfish must be handled carefully, because the dorsal and pectoral fins have sharp spines that can inflict painful wounds. Barracuda belong to the Sphyraenidae family, which contains about 20 species. They are all fierce predators that feed voraciously on small, schooling species, and because they are attracted to their quarry by sight rather than smell they tend to concentrate on bright, silvery coloured prey.

Mouth brooding
In most species of sea catfish, the male keeps the marble-sized fertilized eggs in his mouth until they hatch, which can take up to a month.

HARDHEAD CATFISH
The hardhead catfish, also called the sea catfish, is common in coastal and brackish waters from Massachusetts to Mexico. It has four barbels on its chin and two on its upper jaw, and can reach a weight of 5.4 kg (12 lb) although it usually does not exceed 910 g (2 lb). Several related species are found in the coastal waters, rivers, and lakes of northern Australia, including the blue catfish or salmon catfish (*Arius graeffei*).

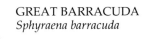

HARDHEAD CATFISH
Arius felis

GUAGUANCHE
Like other barracuda, the guaguanche has a slender, cigar-shaped body, two widely separated dorsal fins, and a protruding lower jaw; it is identifiable by the yellow stripe along its lateral line. It is found on both sides of the Atlantic, and grows to a length of about 60 cm (2 ft).

GUAGUANCHE
Sphyraena guachancho

NORTHERN SENNET
Sphyraena borealis

SENNETS
The northern sennet and southern sennet are almost identical, and may in fact be a single species.
These little barracuda have the same overall coloration and both grow to about 45 cm (18 in), but the southern sennet has fewer scales on its lateral line (107 to 116 as opposed to 118 to 135) and its eyes are larger. The northern sennet is found from New England to Florida and the Gulf of Mexico, and the southern sennet from Florida to Uruguay. In the eastern Atlantic and the Mediterranean, barracuda are represented by the European barracuda (*Sphyraena sphyraena*).

Large eye

SOUTHERN SENNET
Sphyraena picudilla

GREAT BARRACUDA
Sphyraena barracuda

PACIFIC BARRACUDA
Sphyraena argentea

FISHING NOTES

Techniques
Catfish are caught by bottom fishing from the shore or piers. For barracuda fishing try trolling, or spinning from a boat or from the shore.

Tackle
For catfish, try a 3.4 or 3.7 m (11 or 12 ft) medium-action rod, with a fixed-spool reel, 3.2 to 6.8 kg (7 to 15 lb) mono line, size 4 to 6/0 hook, and a 28 g (1 oz) weight. To troll for barracuda, use a 5.4 to 13.6 kg (12 to 30 lb) class boat rod with a multiplier reel, 5.4 to 13.6 kg (12 to 30 lb) nylon line with a wire trace, a size 4/0 to 8/0 hook, and a banana-shaped trolling weight. Spinning calls for a medium spinning rod with a fixed-spool reel, 5.4 to 13.6 kg (12 to 30 lb) nylon line with a wire trace, and hook sizes 4/0 to 8/0.

Bait
Cut fish and livebaits such as sandworms are ideal for catfish, which can also be taken on jigs and plugs. For barracuda, use bright, flashy spinners, wooden plugs, strips of fish, and whole fish such as sardines, anchovies, and queenfish.

Barracuda in shallows
Barracuda are often found in shallow water, where their natural curiosity leads them to follow (and sometimes attack) swimmers.

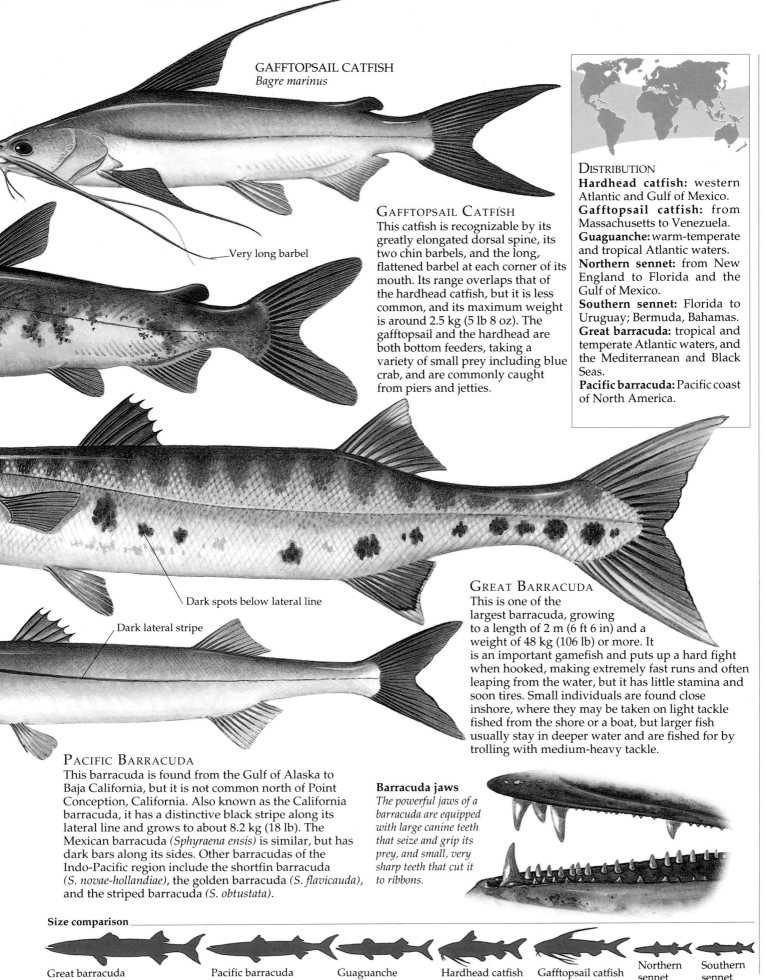

GAFFTOPSAIL CATFISH
Bagre marinus

Very long barbel

DISTRIBUTION
Hardhead catfish: western Atlantic and Gulf of Mexico.
Gafftopsail catfish: from Massachusetts to Venezuela.
Guaguanche: warm-temperate and tropical Atlantic waters.
Northern sennet: from New England to Florida and the Gulf of Mexico.
Southern sennet: Florida to Uruguay; Bermuda, Bahamas.
Great barracuda: tropical and temperate Atlantic waters, and the Mediterranean and Black Seas.
Pacific barracuda: Pacific coast of North America.

GAFFTOPSAIL CATFISH
This catfish is recognizable by its greatly elongated dorsal spine, its two chin barbels, and the long, flattened barbel at each corner of its mouth. Its range overlaps that of the hardhead catfish, but it is less common, and its maximum weight is around 2.5 kg (5 lb 8 oz). The gafftopsail and the hardhead are both bottom feeders, taking a variety of small prey including blue crab, and are commonly caught from piers and jetties.

Dark spots below lateral line

Dark lateral stripe

GREAT BARRACUDA
This is one of the largest barracuda, growing to a length of 2 m (6 ft 6 in) and a weight of 48 kg (106 lb) or more. It is an important gamefish and puts up a hard fight when hooked, making extremely fast runs and often leaping from the water, but it has little stamina and soon tires. Small individuals are found close inshore, where they may be taken on light tackle fished from the shore or a boat, but larger fish usually stay in deeper water and are fished for by trolling with medium-heavy tackle.

PACIFIC BARRACUDA
This barracuda is found from the Gulf of Alaska to Baja California, but it is not common north of Point Conception, California. Also known as the California barracuda, it has a distinctive black stripe along its lateral line and grows to about 8.2 kg (18 lb). The Mexican barracuda (*Sphyraena ensis*) is similar, but has dark bars along its sides. Other barracudas of the Indo-Pacific region include the shortfin barracuda (*S. novae-hollandiae*), the golden barracuda (*S. flavicauda*), and the striped barracuda (*S. obtustata*).

Barracuda jaws
The powerful jaws of a barracuda are equipped with large canine teeth that seize and grip its prey, and small, very sharp teeth that cut it to ribbons.

Size comparison

Great barracuda   Pacific barracuda   Guaguanche   Hardhead catfish   Gafftopsail catfish   Northern sennet   Southern sennet

AMBERJACK & JACK

The Carangidae is a large family of predatory marine fish, and has over 200 members including amberjack, jack, and pompano (*see page 166*). They have streamlined bodies with deeply forked tails, the spiny and soft parts of their dorsal fins are separate, and they feed on fish and invertebrates such as squid. Their flesh is tasty, but you should seek local advice before eating any you catch because they can be a source of ciguatera, a distressing type of food poisoning that can be fatal.

Dark band

ALMACO JACK
The almaco jack is distributed worldwide in warm waters and grows to a weight of 57 kg (126 lb) or more. It is similar to the greater amberjack and the yellowtail, but the dark bands through its eyes are more pronounced, and the front lobe of its soft dorsal fin is longer and sickle-shaped. The almaco jack of the eastern Pacific is sometimes classified as a separate species, the Pacific amberjack (*Seriola colburni*).

Dark band more pronounced than in amberjack

ALMACO JACK
Seriola rivoliana

Schooling fish
Young fish of the Carangidae family often form small schools beneath floating objects such as jellyfish. Older fish of most species roam the seas in large, fast-swimming schools, but the oldest, largest fish tend to be solitary. The carangids are widely distributed in temperate and tropical seas, and are usually at their most abundant in inshore waters.

BLUE RUNNER
Caranx crysos

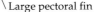
Large pectoral fin

BLUE RUNNER
The blue runner is a small Atlantic jack, very closely related to the Pacific green jack (*Caranx caballus*). It grows to over 3.6 kg (8 lb) but averages less than 454 g (1 lb); like most carangids, its flesh is tasty and it is fished for commercially. It is a popular angling species, and makes a very good bait for big-game fish.

Size comparison

Greater amberjack   Almaco jack   California yellowtail   Crevalle jack   Blue runner   Lesser amberjack

GREATER AMBERJACK
Seriola dumerili

LESSER AMBERJACK
Seriola fasciata

YOUNG FISH

Young lesser amberjack
The young of the lesser amberjack are distinctively marked with several broad, dark brown bands, usually separated by paler areas. These dark bands fade as the fish mature.

Large, domed head

Dark blotches

Faint yellow stripe

CALIFORNIA YELLOWTAIL
Seriola lalandi dorsalis

GREATER AMBERJACK

This fish is widely distributed in warm waters and is the largest amberjack in the Atlantic, averaging about 6.8 kg (15 lb) but capable of exceeding 80 kg (176 lb). Its overall coloration is silvery, and there is often a broad, yellow or coppery stripe along each side. The dark bands that run from its upper jaw through its eyes meet at the point where the dorsal fin begins, forming an inverted V-shape.

LESSER AMBERJACK

The adult lesser amberjack is similar in appearance to the greater amberjack, but the dark bands on its head converge well in front of the first dorsal fin. The lesser amberjack is a relatively small fish, reaching a maximum weight of only about 4.54 kg (10 lb). It is found in the warm waters of the western Atlantic.

CREVALLE JACK

The hard-fighting crevalle jack is widely distributed in warm waters, and is found both inshore and in the open ocean. It averages under 910 g (2 lb), but can reach 25 kg (55 lb). The crevalle jack found in the Pacific is often regarded as a separate species, *Caranx caninus*; other Pacific and Indo-Pacific members of the genus *Caranx* include the trevally (*Caranx georgianus*), the ulua (*C. stellatus*), and the pauu'u (*C. ignobilis*).

DISTRIBUTION

Almaco jack: most tropical and warm-temperate waters.
Blue runner: tropical and warm-temperate Atlantic.
Greater amberjack: most tropical and warm-temperate waters.
Lesser amberjack: western Atlantic from Massachusetts south to Brazil.
Crevalle jack: most tropical and warm-temperate waters.
California yellowtail: eastern Pacific from British Columbia south to Chile.

CREVALLE JACK
Caranx hippos

CALIFORNIA YELLOWTAIL

This subspecies of the yellowtail (*Seriola lalandi*) has a maximum weight of about 36 kg (80 lb), and is one of the most highly prized gamefish of the Pacific coast of North America. The closely related southern yellowtail, *S. grandis*, which is abundant in Australian and New Zealand waters, can reach a weight of 52 kg (114 lb 10 oz).

FISHING NOTES

Techniques
Trolling, drifting, and spinning are the usual methods of fishing employed for amberjack and jack.

Tackle
For trolling and drifting, use a 13.6 kg (30 lb) class rod with a 4/0 multiplier reel, 13.6 kg (30 lb) mono line, a wire or heavy mono leader, and a 6/0 or 8/0 single hook. For spinning, use a heavy spinning rod with a large fixed-spool reel, 6.8 to 9.1 kg (15 to 20 lb) mono line, a wire leader, and a 4/0 or 6/0 single hook.

Bait
Chumming (groundbaiting) will attract and hold schools of fish near the boat. When trolling or drifting, use artificial lures, such as plugs and spinners, or natural baits such as squid and cut or whole fish. Good fish baits for these species include mullet, pinfish, sardines, and anchovies. For spinning, use plugs, spinners, or spoons.

Saltwater SPECIES

POMPANO, JACKMACKEREL, & ROOSTERFISH

The jackmackerel and the four species of pompano shown here (including the permit) are members of the Carangidae family, which also includes the amberjack and jack *(see page 164)*. The roosterfish is sometimes classified as a member of the Carangidae, but is usually placed in a separate family, the Nematistiidae. Pompano have deep, almost diamond-shaped bodies, while the jackmackerel and roosterfish are more elongated and streamlined. All except the African pompano venture close inshore, often into very shallow water within easy reach of shore anglers, and they offer good sport on light tackle.

Large, oval spots

LARGESPOT POMPANO
Trachinotus botla

PERMIT
The permit is found in large numbers along the coasts of the Bahamas and southern Florida, and is regarded as one of the finest light-tackle gamefish. Like the bonefish *(see page 158)*, it feeds in the shallow waters of coral flats. Its diet includes crabs, molluscs, shrimps, and sea urchins, and it grows to a weight of over 23 kg (51 lb).

JUVENILE PERMIT

LARGESPOT POMPANO
The largespot pompano is widely distributed in coastal waters of the Indian Ocean from Africa to Australia. It is found in the surf zones of sandy beaches, and when feeding it will often swim on its side so that it can move into very shallow water. It grows to a weight of more than 2 kg (4 lb 6 oz).

PERMIT
Trachinotus falcatus

FLORIDA POMPANO
Trachinotus carolinus

FLORIDA POMPANO
This pompano puts up a good fight on light tackle, and is renowned for its fine-tasting flesh. Like the permit, it enters very shallow water, and is taken from beaches, piers, jetties, bridges, and drifting or anchored boats. It averages 910 g (2 lb), with a maximum weight of 3.6 kg (8 lb).

FISHING NOTES

Techniques
Because most of these species come close inshore, they can be taken by surfcasting or by spinning from the shore or a boat. The African pompano prefers deeper water and is caught by trolling.

Tackle
For surfcasting, try a 3.7 m (12 ft) rod that is capable of handling 85 to 142 g (3 to 5 oz) sinkers. For spinning and trolling, try a 2 to 2.4 m (6½ to 8 ft) medium spinning rod with 2.7 to 5.4 kg (6 to 12 lb) mono line, a short, 9.1 kg (20 lb) mono leader, and hook sizes 2 to 2/0.

Bait
The usual baits are crabs, clams, sand fleas, small bucktails, and jigs; anchovies are an excellent bait for jackmackerel.

166

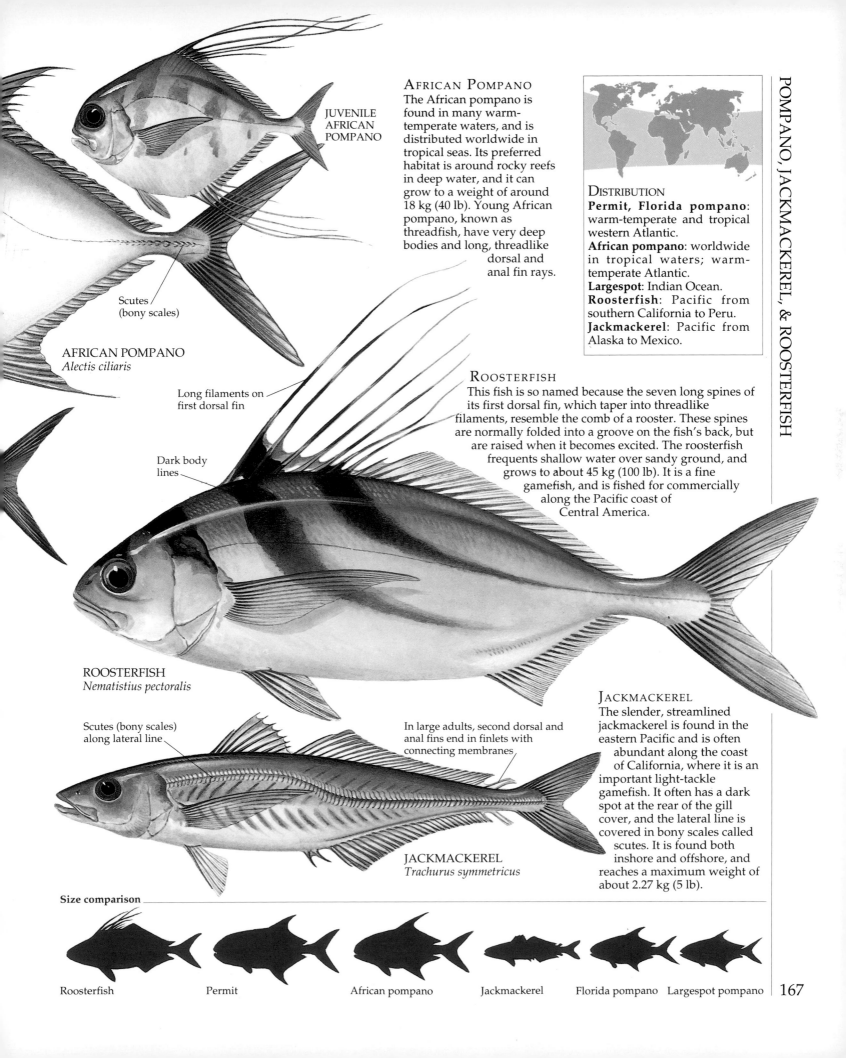

JUVENILE
AFRICAN
POMPANO

AFRICAN POMPANO

The African pompano is found in many warm-temperate waters, and is distributed worldwide in tropical seas. Its preferred habitat is around rocky reefs in deep water, and it can grow to a weight of around 18 kg (40 lb). Young African pompano, known as threadfish, have very deep bodies and long, threadlike dorsal and anal fin rays.

Scutes
(bony scales)

AFRICAN POMPANO
Alectis ciliaris

Long filaments on
first dorsal fin

Dark body
lines

DISTRIBUTION

Permit, Florida pompano: warm-temperate and tropical western Atlantic.
African pompano: worldwide in tropical waters; warm-temperate Atlantic.
Largespot: Indian Ocean.
Roosterfish: Pacific from southern California to Peru.
Jackmackerel: Pacific from Alaska to Mexico.

ROOSTERFISH

This fish is so named because the seven long spines of its first dorsal fin, which taper into threadlike filaments, resemble the comb of a rooster. These spines are normally folded into a groove on the fish's back, but are raised when it becomes excited. The roosterfish frequents shallow water over sandy ground, and grows to about 45 kg (100 lb). It is a fine gamefish, and is fished for commercially along the Pacific coast of Central America.

ROOSTERFISH
Nematistius pectoralis

Scutes (bony scales)
along lateral line

In large adults, second dorsal and
anal fins end in finlets with
connecting membranes

JACKMACKEREL

The slender, streamlined jackmackerel is found in the eastern Pacific and is often abundant along the coast of California, where it is an important light-tackle gamefish. It often has a dark spot at the rear of the gill cover, and the lateral line is covered in bony scales called scutes. It is found both inshore and offshore, and reaches a maximum weight of about 2.27 kg (5 lb).

JACKMACKEREL
Trachurus symmetricus

Size comparison

Roosterfish   Permit   African pompano   Jackmackerel   Florida pompano   Largespot pompano

167

Saltwater SPECIES

COBIA, SNOOK, & BARRAMUNDI

The cobia, the only member of the Rachycentridae family, is a prized gamefish. It is also fished for commercially for its fine flesh, which is often sold smoked. Snook and barramundi belong to the Centropomidae family, which contains about 30 species. Some of the Centropomidae are exclusively marine, others are marine but move into brackish water and even into rivers; some live in rivers and spawn in brackish estuaries, while a few are found only in freshwater.

TARPON SNOOK
Centropomus pectinatus

Dark-tipped
pelvic fin

COBIA

This long, slim-bodied fish occurs in most warm seas, from coastal waters to the open ocean, but is not found along the Pacific coast of North America. It has a flat head, a large mouth with a slightly protruding lower jaw, and a first dorsal fin that consists of eight separate spines. Fish and crustaceans make up the bulk of its diet, and it grows to a weight of about 68 kg (150 lb). It is usually solitary but sometimes forms small schools.

FAT SNOOK
Centropomus parallelus

FAT SNOOK

The fat snook is a small, rather deep-bodied fish that rarely exceeds about 1.36 kg (3 lb). The most reliable way to distinguish it from other small snook is to count the number of scales along the lateral line: the fat snook has 80 to 90, the tarpon snook 65 to 70, and the black about 60.

First dorsal fin reduced
to eight spines

COBIA
Rachycentron canadum

FISHING NOTES

Techniques
Cobia are usually taken by bottom fishing with lures or natural baits. Lure fishing is an effective technique for barramundi and for snook, which can also be taken on fly tackle.

Tackle
For cobia, use a heavy spinning rod with 6.8 to 9.1 kg (15 to 20 lb) mono line and a 90 cm (3 ft) leader of wire or 27.2 to 36.3 kg (60 to 80 lb) mono, and hook sizes 2/0 to 4/0. Try a 1.8 m (6 ft) surfcaster with 4.54 to 5.4 kg (10 to 12 lb) mono when lure

fishing for snook, and a fast, 2.7 m (9 ft) tip-action rod for fly fishing. For barramundi, use a 2.7 to 3 m (9 to 10 ft) spinning rod with 9.1 to 13.6 kg (20 to 30 lb) mono line.

Bait
Good baits for cobia include natural baits such as fish, crabs, and shrimps, and artificials including large plugs with bright blue or silver finishes, and 42 to 85 g (1½ to 3 oz) jigs with yellow or white skirts. Try plugs, spoons, jigs, shrimps, streamer flies, and fish (especially mullet) for snook, and jointed, 15 cm (6 in) shallow-diving plugs for barramundi.

Cobia habitat
Cobia like to lurk in the cover of pilings and wrecks, and beneath buoys, floating wreckage, and other flotsam. They are also often found in the company of cruising sharks.

BLACK SNOOK
Centropomus nigrescens

DISTRIBUTION

Cobia: most warm seas, but not along the Pacific coast of North America.
Fat snook, tarpon snook: southern Florida and West Indies to Brazil.
Black snook: eastern Pacific from Baja California to Peru.
Snook: western Atlantic from South Carolina to Brazil.
Barramundi: Asian coastal regions and islands from the Persian Gulf to China, and around the northern half of the Australian coast.

TARPON SNOOK

This little fish has a noticeably upturned snout, like that of a tarpon *(see page 158)*, and its pelvic fins are orange or orange-yellow with dark tips. Its preferred habitat is brackish, well-shaded lakes and lagoons, and its maximum weight is usually less than about 1 kg (2 lb 3 oz).

BLACK SNOOK

The black snook, which is found along the Pacific coast of tropical America, grows to a weight of over 1.36 kg (3 lb). It is common in shallow coastal waters and also occurs in brackish estuaries, the lower reaches of rivers and streams, and in coastal canals.

SNOOK

This large, pikelike fish has a protruding lower jaw and a distinctive black lateral stripe that extends into its tail. It is an active predator, feeding on fish, shrimps, and crabs, and averages 2.27 to 3.6 kg (5 to 8 lb) with a maximum of over 24 kg (53 lb). Although it is usually found in shallow coastal waters, it also explores estuaries, mangrove swamps, and creeks, and sometimes travels well inland along rivers and canals. It should be handled with care when caught, because the edges of its gill covers are very sharp.

SNOOK
Centropomus undecimalis

BARRAMUNDI (GIANT PERCH)
Lates calcarifer

Large pelvic fin

BARRAMUNDI

The barramundi, or giant perch, lives in rivers, creeks, and mangrove swamps, and spawns in estuaries and coastal waters. It feeds on fish, crayfish, crabs, shrimps, and insects, and grows to a weight of 60 kg (132 lb); the closely related Nile perch (*Lates niloticus*), an African freshwater fish, can reach 91 kg (200 lb).

Size comparison

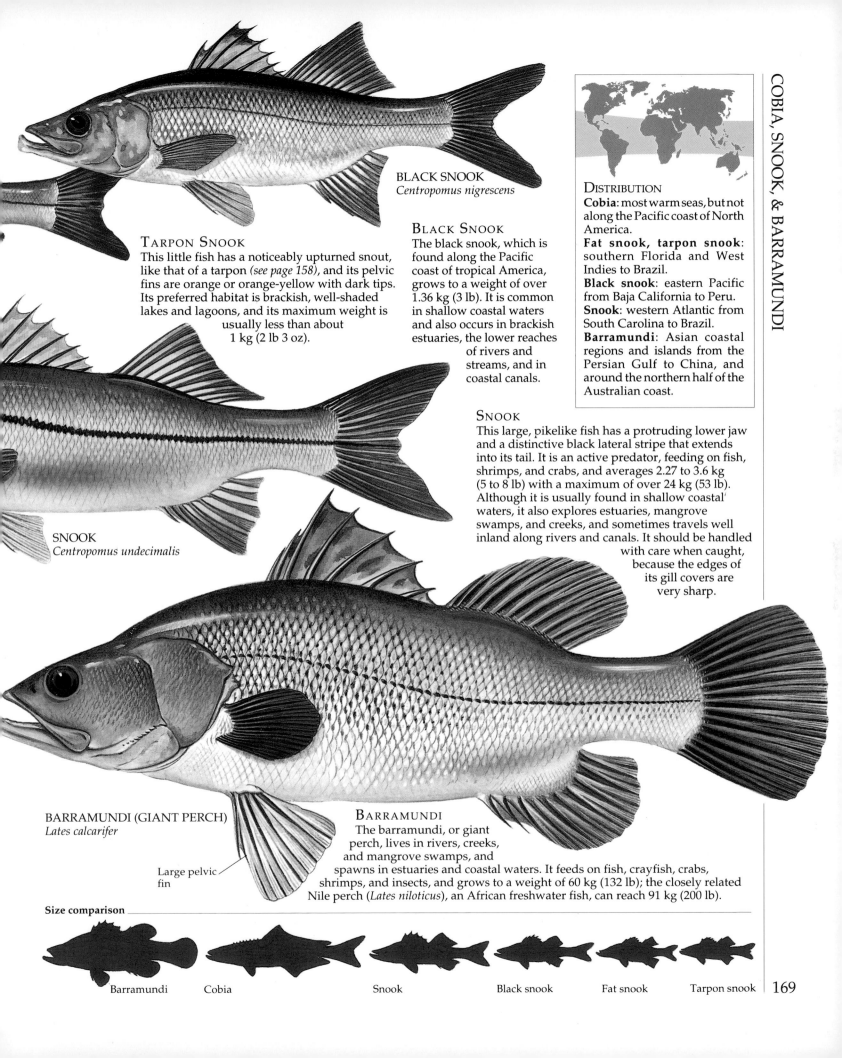

Barramundi   Cobia   Snook   Black snook   Fat snook   Tarpon snook

SURFPERCH

The Embiotocidae family consists of 21 species, of which two occur in Japan and Korea; the rest are found along the Pacific coast of North America, and all but one are marine species. The exception is the tule perch (*Hysterocarpus traski*), a freshwater fish that has a limited distribution in central California. Surfperch males use their anal fins to transfer sperm to the females, which give birth to live young. Their food includes algae, invertebrates, and fish, and they range in length from 10 to 45 cm (4 to 18 in).

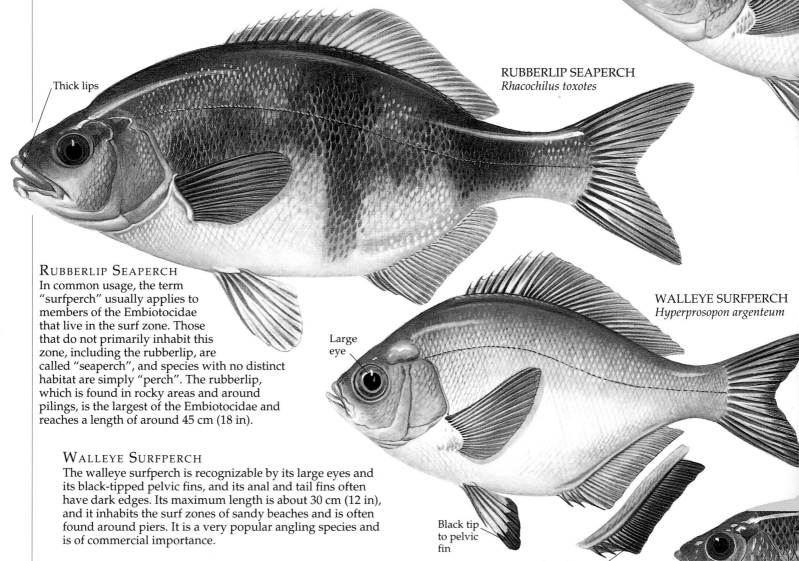

Thick lips

RUBBERLIP SEAPERCH
Rhacochilus toxotes

WALLEYE SURFPERCH
Hyperprosopon argenteum

Large eye

Black tip to pelvic fin

Breeding female has dark anal fin

RUBBERLIP SEAPERCH
In common usage, the term "surfperch" usually applies to members of the Embiotocidae that live in the surf zone. Those that do not primarily inhabit this zone, including the rubberlip, are called "seaperch", and species with no distinct habitat are simply "perch". The rubberlip, which is found in rocky areas and around pilings, is the largest of the Embiotocidae and reaches a length of around 45 cm (18 in).

WALLEYE SURFPERCH
The walleye surfperch is recognizable by its large eyes and its black-tipped pelvic fins, and its anal and tail fins often have dark edges. Its maximum length is about 30 cm (12 in), and it inhabits the surf zones of sandy beaches and is often found around piers. It is a very popular angling species and is of commercial importance.

FISHING NOTES

Techniques
Surfperch are usually caught by light surfcasting or by bottom fishing.

Tackle
For surfcasting, use a light surfcaster with a small multiplier reel, 4.54 to 6.8 kg (10 to 15 lb) monofilament line, a size 1/0 hook (or smaller, depending on species sought), and a grip or bomb-shaped sinker. For bottom fishing, try a spinning rod or a 5.4 kg (12 lb) class boat rod, fitted with a fixed-spool reel or small multiplier reel, 4.54 to 6.8 kg (10 to 15 lb) monofilament line, a size 1/0 hook (or smaller), and a bomb-shaped sinker.

Bait
Surfperch baits include cut fish and crab, ghost shrimps, clams, and mussels.

SHINER PERCH
This little surfperch, which grows to about 18 cm (7 in), is abundant and easily caught from piers, which makes it very popular with young anglers. Its habitat ranges from shallow water, where it frequents weedbeds, pilings, and piers, to depths of about 146 m (480 ft), and it will also venture into brackish areas and sometimes into freshwater. There is often a dark spot above its upper lip.

REDTAIL SURFPERCH
Amphistichus rhodoterus

REDTAIL SURFPERCH
This is one of the most common surfperch species. It grows to a length of around 41 cm (16 in), and is recognizable by its red fins and the brownish bars on its sides. The calico surfperch (*Amphistichus koelzi*) has a similar coloration, but is smaller, and its dorsal fin spines are not longer than the soft rays, as they are in the redtail.

STRIPED SEAPERCH
This beautiful fish grows to 38 cm (15 in) and is found over rocky ground and kelp beds from shallow water out to depths of about 21 m (70 ft). Although it occurs as far south as Baja California, it is most common in the cooler waters north of Point Conception.

DISTRIBUTION
Rubberlip seaperch: from northern California to central Baja California.
Walleye surfperch: from Vancouver Island to Baja California.
Shiner perch: southeast Alaska to Baja California.
Redtail surfperch: Vancouver Island to Monterey Bay.
Striped seaperch: southeast Alaska to Baja California.
Barred surfperch: northern California to Baja California.

BARRED SURFPERCH
The barred surfperch is usually silvery or brassy, with eight to ten brownish bars on each side, but in some individuals these bars are absent. It is found in the surf zones of sandy beaches and also further out, to depths of 70 m (230 ft) or more. It is an important angling species, and can reach 43 cm (17 in) and 2 kg (4 lb 6 oz), but most of those caught are less than 30 cm (12 in) and 454 g (1 lb).

STRIPED SEAPERCH
Embiotoca lateralis

BARRED SURFPERCH
Amphistichus argenteus

Males lose yellow bars in summer

SHINER PERCH
Cymatogaster aggregata

All species give birth to live young, usually 3 to 10 per litter

Size comparison

Rubberlip seaperch   Barred surfperch   Redtail surfperch   Striped seaperch   Walleye surfperch   Shiner perch

GADIDAE

COD, HAKE, LING, & BURBOT

The members of the Gadidae, the codfish family, are distributed widely around the world, especially in the colder waters of the Northern Hemisphere. Most live at or near the bottom, feeding on fish and invertebrates, and many of them have great commercial importance as well as being popular quarry for sea anglers. Unfortunately, the commercial value of many species has led to serious overfishing in some areas, particularly the North Atlantic. As a result, there has been a serious decline in the numbers and sizes of these species.

Dark spot on flank behind gill cover

Heavily toothed jaw

POLLACK
Like many other members of the Gadidae, such as the Atlantic cod, the pollack has three dorsal and two anal fins. It is most easily identified by its protruding lower jaw and the distinct curve of its lateral line. Small pollack are found over sandy bottoms, but the larger ones, which can reach a weight of about 13 kg (29 lb), prefer rocky ground.

SAITHE
The saithe is similar to the pollack, but its upper and lower jaws are approximately the same size, and its lateral line is only slightly curved. Its maximum size is about 32 kg (71 lb), and the largest individuals are usually found in the vicinity of reefs.

POLLACK
Pollachius pollachius

Downward-curving lateral line

SAITHE
Pollachius virens

Protruding lower jaw

BURBOT
This is the only member of the codfish family that lives exclusively in freshwater. It is widely distributed in deep, cold waters in northern latitudes, and although it averages about 910 g (2 lb) it can grow much larger, and specimens weighing in at around 32 kg (71 lb) have been taken from European waters. It is probably now extinct in the British Isles.

BURBOT
Lota lota

FISHING NOTES

Techniques
The marine codfish may be fished for from the shore by surfcasting or by fishing from rocks, piers, and jetties with natural baits, and from a boat with natural baits or by feathering, jigging (pirking), or using attractor spoons in conjunction with baited hooks. The burbot, the freshwater member of the codfish family, is a slow-moving fish that feeds mostly at night and may be caught by static legering in shallow water.

Tackle
When shore fishing for the marine species, try a 3.7 m (12 ft) surfcasting rod with a multiplier reel, 13.6 kg (30 lb) nylon line, hook sizes 2/0 to 8/0, and a bomb-shaped or grip weight. To fish for the marine species from a boat, use a 13.6 kg (30 lb) class boat rod with a 4/0 to 6/0 multiplier reel, 13.6 kg (30 lb) wire or nylon line, and hook sizes 2/0 to 8/0. When using natural baits and when feathering, use a bomb-shaped weight. For burbot, try a 3 to 3.7 m (10 to 12 ft) leger rod with a fixed-spool reel, 2.7 kg (6 lb) mono line, and size 10 to 14 hook.

Bait
The wide range of effective natural baits for the marine species includes many invertebrates, such as mussels, lugworms, ragworms, clams, razorshells, and squid. Fish baits, either cut or whole, are also worth trying, especially the oily fish such as herring, mackerel, sprat, and pilchard. Among the artificial baits, leadhead jigs, metal pirks, and plastic sandeels will get results, and a bunch of orange or white feather hackles on a 5/0 hook is excellent as a boat fishing lure. Burbot will take a bunch of large worms or a small fish.

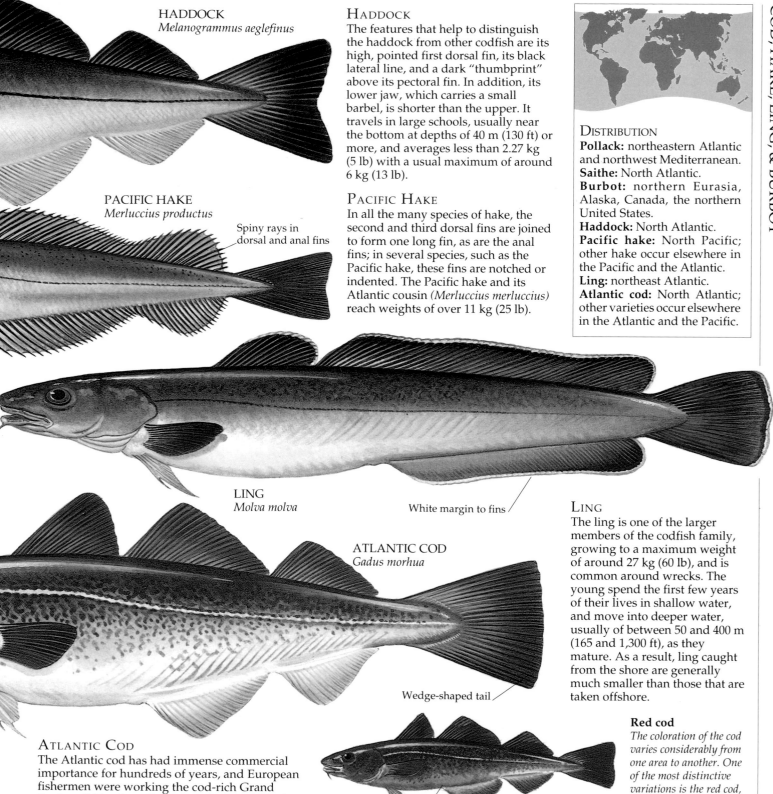

HADDOCK
Melanogrammus aeglefinus

PACIFIC HAKE
Merluccius productus

Spiny rays in dorsal and anal fins

LING
Molva molva

White margin to fins

ATLANTIC COD
Gadus morhua

Wedge-shaped tail

Pink underside

RED COD

HADDOCK
The features that help to distinguish the haddock from other codfish are its high, pointed first dorsal fin, its black lateral line, and a dark "thumbprint" above its pectoral fin. In addition, its lower jaw, which carries a small barbel, is shorter than the upper. It travels in large schools, usually near the bottom at depths of 40 m (130 ft) or more, and averages less than 2.27 kg (5 lb) with a usual maximum of around 6 kg (13 lb).

PACIFIC HAKE
In all the many species of hake, the second and third dorsal fins are joined to form one long fin, as are the anal fins; in several species, such as the Pacific hake, these fins are notched or indented. The Pacific hake and its Atlantic cousin *(Merluccius merluccius)* reach weights of over 11 kg (25 lb).

DISTRIBUTION
Pollack: northeastern Atlantic and northwest Mediterranean.
Saithe: North Atlantic.
Burbot: northern Eurasia, Alaska, Canada, the northern United States.
Haddock: North Atlantic.
Pacific hake: North Pacific; other hake occur elsewhere in the Pacific and the Atlantic.
Ling: northeast Atlantic.
Atlantic cod: North Atlantic; other varieties occur elsewhere in the Atlantic and the Pacific.

LING
The ling is one of the larger members of the codfish family, growing to a maximum weight of around 27 kg (60 lb), and is common around wrecks. The young spend the first few years of their lives in shallow water, and move into deeper water, usually of between 50 and 400 m (165 and 1,300 ft), as they mature. As a result, ling caught from the shore are generally much smaller than those that are taken offshore.

Red cod
The coloration of the cod varies considerably from one area to another. One of the most distinctive variations is the red cod, which is red-gold with a paler belly and is occasionally found in rocky waters that have abundant weed growth.

ATLANTIC COD
The Atlantic cod has had immense commercial importance for hundreds of years, and European fishermen were working the cod-rich Grand Banks, off Newfoundland, long before Columbus reached America. It usually reaches about 4.54 kg (10 lb), but it can grow to over 45 kg (100 lb) and has been known to attain 95.7 kg (211 lb).

Size comparison

Ling   Atlantic cod   Pollack   Haddock   Pacific hake   Burbot   Saithe

173

BILLFISH & SWORDFISH

Saltwater SPECIES

Highly prized by big-game anglers, the spectacularly hard-fighting billfish and swordfish roam widely through the world's tropical and warm-temperate seas, occasionally venturing into higher latitudes in summer. In all of these huge, fast-swimming fish – marlin, spearfish, sailfish, and swordfish – the upper jaw is elongated into a "bill" or "sword".

SHORTBILL SPEARFISH
Tetrapturus angustirostris

SPEARFISH
Spearfish are the smallest of the billfish, reaching 2.1 to 2.4 m (7 to 8 ft) and a weight of 40 to 52 kg (90 to 115 lb). The upper jaw of the shortbill (a Pacific species) is only about 50 per cent longer than the lower, whereas in the longbill (an Atlantic fish) the upper jaw is at least twice the length of the lower. A third species of spearfish, *Tetrapturus belone*, is found in the Mediterranean. Spearfish are seldom found in coastal waters, except in areas that have steep drop-offs.

LONGBILL SPEARFISH
Tetrapturus pfluegeri

SAILFISH
Istiophorus platypterus

SAILFISH
The Atlantic and Pacific sailfish are classified as the same species, but the Pacific variety is much the heavier of the two, growing to about 110 kg (240 lb) and 3.3 m (10 ft 10 in) as opposed to the 58 kg (128 lb) and 2.4 m (8 ft) of the Atlantic fish. A sailfish is easily recognizable by its long bill and huge, sail-like dorsal fin; the length of the longest ray of this fin is some 150 per cent or more of the maximum depth of the body.

STRIPED MARLIN
Tetrapturus audax

SWORDFISH
Xiphias gladius

SWORDFISH
The swordfish is the only member of the Xiphiidae family. Like the billfish, it has a greatly elongated upper jaw, but unlike that of a billfish the swordfish's upper jaw is flat in cross-section rather than round. Other features distinguishing the swordfish from the billfish are body shape and scales. A billfish has a body that is compressed in cross-section and has narrow, pointed scales; the body of a swordfish is nearly round, and the adult fish has no scales. In size, the swordfish is comparable to the largest billfish, reaching 4.6 m (15 ft) and weighing up to 590 kg (1,300 lb).

Natural food
Billfish and swordfish feed on fish (particularly tuna and herring), crustaceans, and squid. Once pursued, the quarry has little chance of escaping these powerful, fast-swimming predators.

174

FISHING NOTES

Techniques

Trolling at or close to the surface is the usual technique for these species, but swordfish and blue marlin may also be taken by deep still-fishing using live or dead natural baits. In addition, the sailfish offers exciting sport to the saltwater fly fisherman. A billfish must be handled carefully when it is brought to the boat to be hauled on board or cut free, because the bill can inflict nasty wounds, and it is wise to wear gloves to protect your hands because the bill is very rough.

Tackle

For the smaller species, use a 9.1 to 22.7 kg (20 to 50 lb) class boat rod with a 20- to 50-class lever drag reel or a 6/0- or 7-class star drag reel. For larger fish use a 36.3 to 59 kg (80 to 130 lb) class rod with an 80- to 130-class lever drag or 12/0 or 14/0 star drag. Use 9.1 to 59 kg (20 to 130 lb) nylon or Dacron line with a heavy wire or nylon trace. Hooks should be flat forged, 8/0 to 14/0. When fly fishing for sailfish, use a heavy fly rod with a suitable saltwater fly reel, a weight-forward #10 line with a 9.1 kg (20 lb) leader, and a streamer fly on a 2/0 to 5/0 hook.

Bait

Live or dead fish, such as mullet, mackerel, herring, and squid, and lures such as Kona Heads, feathered jigs, and plastic squids.

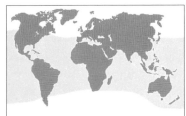

DISTRIBUTION

Blue marlin, sailfish, and swordfish: worldwide.
Black and **striped marlins:** Pacific and Indian Oceans.
Shortbill spearfish: Pacific.
White marlin, longbill spearfish: Atlantic.

BLUE MARLIN
Makaira nigricans

BLUE MARLIN

The blue marlin, the biggest of the billfish, may exceed 4.6 m (15 ft) and 910 kg (2,000 lb). It is rivalled in size by the black marlin (*Makaira indicus*), and fish of both species weighing over 455 kg (1,000 lb) have been taken on rod and line. Once hooked, a marlin of any size will put up a tremendous fight.

Marlinsuckers

Marlins are often accompanied by remoras (suckers), which cling to their hosts with suction discs on the tops of their heads. They feed on scraps of the marlins' food.

STRIPED MARLIN

The striped marlin is an important sport fish of the Pacific and Indian Oceans. It grows to more than 4 m (13 ft) and about 313 kg (690 lb), but in the waters accessible to anglers those caught are usually 91 to 113 kg (200 to 250 lb). Some of the best striped marlin fishing is to be found off the coasts of Chile and New Zealand, where fish in the 180 to 227 kg (400 to 500 lb) range have been taken.

Size

The billfish and the swordfish range in maximum size from the 2.4 m (8 ft) of the shortbill spearfish to the 4.6 m (15 ft) of the blue marlin.

0   Blue marlin   5 m (16 ft 5 in)

Size comparison

Blue marlin   Swordfish   Striped marlin   Sailfish   Longbill spearfish   Shortbill spearfish

WRASSE & DOLPHINFISH

Wrasse belong to the Labridae family, which has more than 400 members distributed widely in coastal tropical and temperate waters. A typical wrasse has thick lips and strong teeth, which it uses to crush shellfish, and swims by flapping its pectoral fins rather than by using its tail. Wrasse range in size from small species about 10 cm (4 in) long up to the 2.3 m (7 ft 6 in) giant maori wrasse (*Cheilinus undulatus*) of Indo-Pacific waters. The dolphinfish is one of the two members of the Coryphaenidae family.

CALIFORNIA SHEEPHEAD

The coloration of the California sheephead varies with age and sex. Adult males are typically a striking black and red, but females are usually pinkish overall; both sexes have white throats. Young fish are red, with a dark spot on each fin. This wrasse is found along the coast of southern California, usually over rocky ground and kelp beds, at depths of about 3 to 55 m (10 to 180 ft). It grows to a maximum of around 90 cm (3 ft) and 16.4 kg (36 lb 4 oz).

SENORITA
Oxyjulis californica

SENORITA

This small, cigar-shaped fish inhabits kelp beds and rocky ground off the coast of southern California, and is best known to anglers as an expert bait stealer. It feeds on small invertebrates, and larger fish come to it to be cleaned of their parasites. Its maximum size is about 25 cm (10 in), and like many other small wrasse it buries itself in the sand at night.

FEMALE

MALE

CALIFORNIA SHEEPHEAD
Semicossyphus pulcher

MALE

DOLPHINFISH
Coryphaena hippurus

DOLPHINFISH

The dolphinfish, also known as the dolphin or dorado, grows to about 40 kg (88 lb). Its diet consists mainly of fish (especially flying fish) plus squid and crustaceans, and it puts up a tremendous fight when hooked, making fast, powerful runs and leaping and tailwalking over the surface. The flesh of the dolphinfish is delicious, and is often sold under its Hawaiian name, *mahi mahi*. The much smaller pompano dolphin (*Coryphaena equisetis*), which resembles the female dolphinfish, reaches a weight of about 2.27 kg (5 lb).

FISHING NOTES

Techniques
Most wrasse are taken by bottom fishing from the shore or cliffs. The usual techniques for dolphinfish are drift fishing, trolling, and spinning.

Tackle
For wrasse, try a 3 to 3.7 m (10 to 12 ft) light surfcasting or heavy spinning rod with 5.4 to 6.8 kg (12 to 15 lb) mono line. Terminal tackle should be a size 1/0 or 2/0

hook on a paternoster or running leger, with the sinker attached by a sacrificial weak link. For dolphinfish, try a heavy spinning rod or a 9.1 kg (20 lb) class boat rod, with 9.1 kg (20 lb) mono line and a 4/0 hook.

Bait
Wrasse will take a wide range of natural baits, including worms, crabs, molluscs, and crustaceans, and dolphinfish take fish, plugs, and spoons.

FEMALE

Head shape
The heads of female dolphinfish, and of young of both sexes, are more rounded than those of adult males.

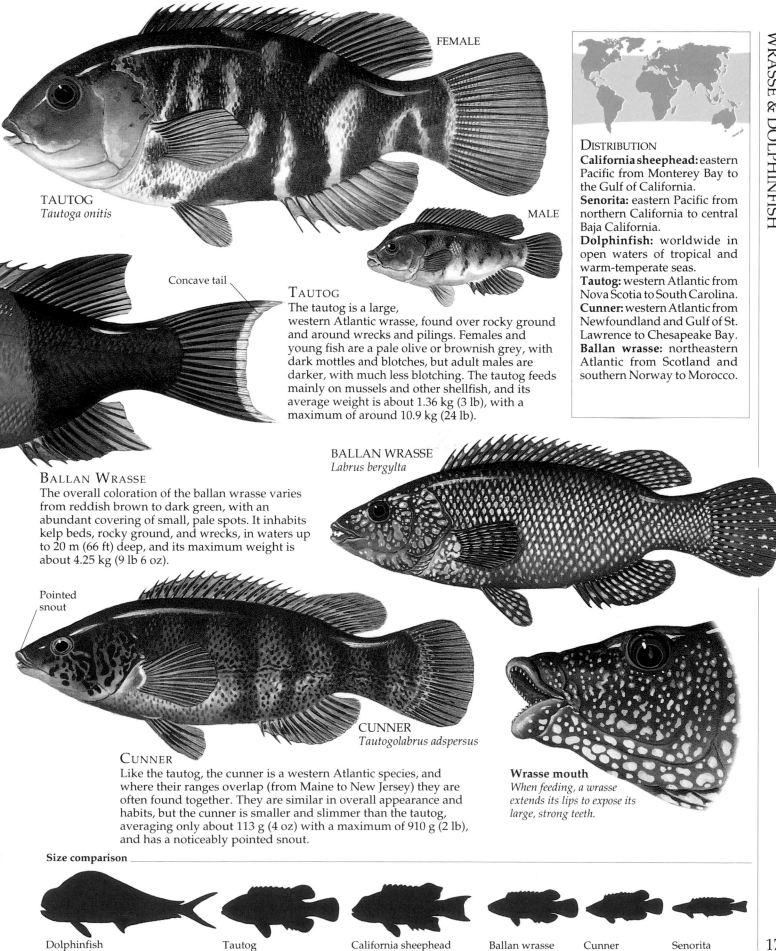

FEMALE

TAUTOG
Tautoga onitis

MALE

Concave tail

TAUTOG
The tautog is a large, western Atlantic wrasse, found over rocky ground and around wrecks and pilings. Females and young fish are a pale olive or brownish grey, with dark mottles and blotches, but adult males are darker, with much less blotching. The tautog feeds mainly on mussels and other shellfish, and its average weight is about 1.36 kg (3 lb), with a maximum of around 10.9 kg (24 lb).

DISTRIBUTION
California sheephead: eastern Pacific from Monterey Bay to the Gulf of California.
Senorita: eastern Pacific from northern California to central Baja California.
Dolphinfish: worldwide in open waters of tropical and warm-temperate seas.
Tautog: western Atlantic from Nova Scotia to South Carolina.
Cunner: western Atlantic from Newfoundland and Gulf of St. Lawrence to Chesapeake Bay.
Ballan wrasse: northeastern Atlantic from Scotland and southern Norway to Morocco.

BALLAN WRASSE
Labrus bergylta

BALLAN WRASSE
The overall coloration of the ballan wrasse varies from reddish brown to dark green, with an abundant covering of small, pale spots. It inhabits kelp beds, rocky ground, and wrecks, in waters up to 20 m (66 ft) deep, and its maximum weight is about 4.25 kg (9 lb 6 oz).

Pointed snout

CUNNER
Tautogolabrus adspersus

CUNNER
Like the tautog, the cunner is a western Atlantic species, and where their ranges overlap (from Maine to New Jersey) they are often found together. They are similar in overall appearance and habits, but the cunner is smaller and slimmer than the tautog, averaging only about 113 g (4 oz) with a maximum of 910 g (2 lb), and has a noticeably pointed snout.

Wrasse mouth
When feeding, a wrasse extends its lips to expose its large, strong teeth.

Size comparison

Dolphinfish   Tautog   California sheephead   Ballan wrasse   Cunner   Senorita

SNAPPER

Most of the 230 or so species of snapper that make up the Lutjanidae family are found in tropical seas, but a few also occur in warm-temperate waters. They are predatory fish, with sharp, conical teeth, including one or two large canine teeth on either side of the front of each jaw. These canine teeth help to distinguish the snappers from the groupers *(see page 200)*, many species of which are similar in overall appearance. Large numbers of snapper are taken in shallow coastal waters and over reefs by anglers and spearfishers, and some species are fished for commercially.

Long canine teeth

MUTTON SNAPPER

This is one of the most common snappers in the Caribbean and the waters off southern Florida, and is found near coral heads, in shallow channels and tidal creeks, on coral flats, and in blue holes – deep, circular holes or pits in the seabed. Its coloration is variable, but there is a blue stripe beneath each eye and a small dark spot on each side. Adults usually weigh from 2.27 to 4.54 kg (5 to 10 lb), and the maximum weight is about 11.3 kg (25 lb).

Blue stripe

MUTTON SNAPPER
Lutjanus analis

GRAY SNAPPER
Lutjanus griseus

GRAY SNAPPER

The gray snapper, also known as the mangrove snapper, is found in the same waters as the mutton snapper and also occurs along the coast of tropical western Africa. It is most common along mangrove shores, but also lives over reefs, and grows to about 4.54 kg (10 lb). The overall coloration is greyish, sometimes tinged with red or copper, and there is often a dark stripe running from the snout through each eye.

LANE SNAPPER

This little snapper is identifiable by its pink and yellow stripes, the black edge of its tail fin, and the large dark spot on each side between the dorsal fin and the lateral line. It is found in shallow water throughout the tropical west Atlantic, and although it usually weighs less than 454 g (1 lb) it is popular with anglers because it can be caught from piers and the shore and is good to eat.

LANE SNAPPER
Lutjanus synagris

FISHING NOTES

Techniques
Cubera, mutton snapper, and red snapper are taken by slow bottom trolling. Cubera and mutton snapper are also brought to the surface by chumming, and then taken by spinning with artificial lures. Spinning, with either artificial lures or natural baits, will take gray snapper, lane snapper, and mangrove jack.

Tackle
For trolling, try a medium spinning rod with a fixed-spool reel, 6.8 to 9.1 kg (15 to 20 lb) mono line, a 30 cm (12 in) wire or heavy mono leader, and a size 2/0 hook. For spinning, use a light or medium spinning rod with a multiplier reel, 6.8 to 9.1 kg (15 to 20 lb) mono line, a 30 cm (12 in) wire or heavy mono leader (use transparent mono for gray snapper), and a size 2/0 treble hook.

Bait
Good natural baits for cubera, mutton, red, and lane snapper include shrimp and cut fish such as mullet. Artificial lures used for cubera snapper, mutton snapper, and mangrove jack include bucktails, feathers, and jigs, and plugs with a flashy, silvery finish. These often work best when fished with a jerky retrieve. The best bait to use when fishing for gray snapper is live shrimp.

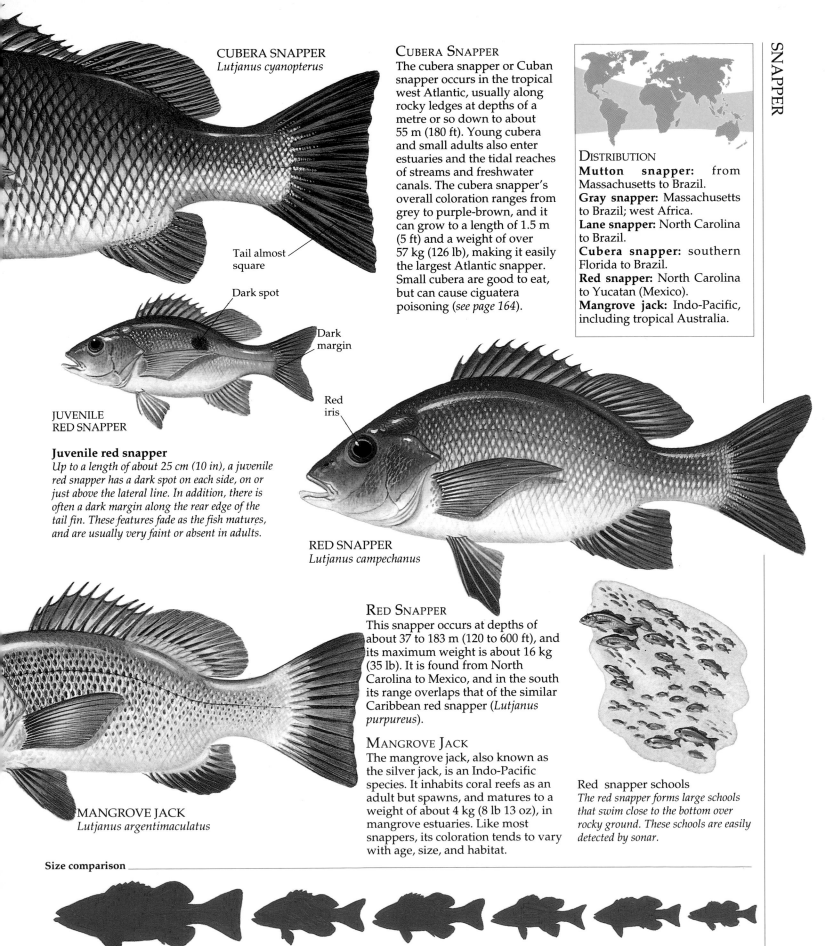

CUBERA SNAPPER
Lutjanus cyanopterus

Tail almost square

Dark spot

Dark margin

Red iris

CUBERA SNAPPER

The cubera snapper or Cuban snapper occurs in the tropical west Atlantic, usually along rocky ledges at depths of a metre or so down to about 55 m (180 ft). Young cubera and small adults also enter estuaries and the tidal reaches of streams and freshwater canals. The cubera snapper's overall coloration ranges from grey to purple-brown, and it can grow to a length of 1.5 m (5 ft) and a weight of over 57 kg (126 lb), making it easily the largest Atlantic snapper. Small cubera are good to eat, but can cause ciguatera poisoning (*see page 164*).

DISTRIBUTION

Mutton snapper: from Massachusetts to Brazil.
Gray snapper: Massachusetts to Brazil; west Africa.
Lane snapper: North Carolina to Brazil.
Cubera snapper: southern Florida to Brazil.
Red snapper: North Carolina to Yucatan (Mexico).
Mangrove jack: Indo-Pacific, including tropical Australia.

JUVENILE
RED SNAPPER

Juvenile red snapper
Up to a length of about 25 cm (10 in), a juvenile red snapper has a dark spot on each side, on or just above the lateral line. In addition, there is often a dark margin along the rear edge of the tail fin. These features fade as the fish matures, and are usually very faint or absent in adults.

RED SNAPPER
Lutjanus campechanus

RED SNAPPER

This snapper occurs at depths of about 37 to 183 m (120 to 600 ft), and its maximum weight is about 16 kg (35 lb). It is found from North Carolina to Mexico, and in the south its range overlaps that of the similar Caribbean red snapper (*Lutjanus purpureus*).

MANGROVE JACK

The mangrove jack, also known as the silver jack, is an Indo-Pacific species. It inhabits coral reefs as an adult but spawns, and matures to a weight of about 4 kg (8 lb 13 oz), in mangrove estuaries. Like most snappers, its coloration tends to vary with age, size, and habitat.

MANGROVE JACK
Lutjanus argentimaculatus

Red snapper schools
The red snapper forms large schools that swim close to the bottom over rocky ground. These schools are easily detected by sonar.

Size comparison

Cubera snapper	Red snapper	Mangrove jack	Mutton snapper	Gray snapper	Lane snapper

179

MULLET

There are about 70 species of mullet in the Mugilidae family, distributed worldwide in temperate and tropical waters. Most live close to the shore and often move into estuaries and rivers, and some, including the Australian mullet, inhabit freshwater. They are primarily bottom-feeders, living on algae, organic detritus, and small, mud-dwelling organisms, and are fished for commercially as well as by anglers. The red mullet belongs to the Mullidae family (the goatfish), which consists of over 50 species widely distributed in warm waters.

STRIPED MULLET

This is one of the largest and most widely distributed of the mullet family, reaching a weight of about 6.8 kg (15 lb) and occurring in most warm seas. It is the only species of mullet found along the Pacific coast of North America. Its stripes are formed by horizontal rows of small dark spots, and there is a dark patch at the base of each pectoral fin. The origin of the second dorsal fin is in line with that of the anal fin.

STRIPED MULLET
Mugil cephalus

FRESHWATER MULLET

The freshwater mullet, also known as the pinkeye, lives in the coastal rivers of southeast Australia, and migrates downstream to estuaries to spawn. It usually grows to about 40 cm (16 in), but can reach twice that length and a weight of 7.5 kg (16 lb 8 oz). Like marine mullet, it feeds mainly on algae and detritus.

FRESHWATER MULLET
Myxus petardi

Dark fins

Chin barbels

DAYTIME COLORATION

RED MULLET
Mullus surmuletus

WHITE MULLET
Mugil curema

RED MULLET

The red mullet is renowned for its fine-tasting flesh and is one of the ingredients of *bouillabaisse*, the classic French fish stew. It uses its long chin barbels to probe in the bottom mud for its food, which is mainly worms, molluscs, and crustaceans, and at night its coloration changes from striped to mottled and barred. Its maximum weight is about 1.64 kg (3 lb 10 oz).

NIGHTTIME COLORATION

Very broad lips

THICK-LIPPED
GREY MULLET
Chelon labrosus

First dorsal fin set well back

Narrow lips

Dark spot

THIN-LIPPED
GREY MULLET
Liza ramada

DISTRIBUTION
Striped: almost worldwide in warm waters.
Freshwater: Burnett River, Queensland, to Georges River, New South Wales.
Red: Mediterranean; eastern Atlantic from southern Norway to the Canary Islands.
Thick-lipped, thin-lipped, golden: Mediterranean; eastern Atlantic from southern Norway to the Canary Islands.
White: warm-temperate and tropical Atlantic; eastern Pacific from Mexico to Chile.

THICK-LIPPED GREY MULLET

The large lips of this European mullet help to distinguish it from the very similar thin-lipped grey mullet, which is found in the same waters where their ranges overlap. The thick-lipped grey mullet, which forms small schools that cruise near the surface, is found close inshore and enters harbours and estuaries. Its maximum weight is around 6.4 kg (14 lb).

THIN-LIPPED GREY MULLET

In addition to having thinner lips than the thick-lipped grey mullet, this fish has a dark spot at the base of each pectoral fin and its first dorsal fin is set further back. Its habits are similar to those of the thick-lipped grey, but it is more likely to enter freshwater and is the most abundant mullet in European estuaries. It grows to a maximum of about 3.2 kg (7 lb).

GOLDEN MULLET

The golden mullet, sometimes called the golden grey mullet, resembles the thin-lipped grey but has an overall bronze hue and golden blotches on its cheeks. It is also smaller, with a maximum weight of under 1.36 kg (3 lb).

GOLDEN MULLET
Liza aurata

WHITE MULLET

This mullet is found in warm Atlantic waters and in the tropical eastern Pacific. It has a dark spot at the base of each pectoral fin, and often one or two gold patches on each side of its head. It usually grows to a weight of about 1.36 kg (3 lb).

FISHING NOTES

Techniques
Float fishing, spinning, or freelining. These fish have soft, relatively small mouths and are easily spooked, so light tackle, delicate bait presentation, and a careful approach are required.

Tackle
Use a 3 to 3.7 m (10 to 12 ft) float rod for float fishing and freelining, with a fixed-spool reel, 2.27 kg (5 lb) mono line, and hook sizes 6 to 16; for float fishing, use a peacock, Avon, or slider float and split shot. For spinning, try a 2.1 to 3 m (7 to 10 ft) light spinning rod with a fixed-spool reel, 2.27 kg (5 lb) mono line, and size 10 treble hook.

Bait
Mullet will take a wide range of small, soft, natural and processed baits, including small or cut worms, maggots, banana, corn, cut fish, bread, cheese, peas, minced meat, and pasta. For spinning, use tiny spoons and spinners, baited with small or cut ragworm.

Size comparison

Striped mullet   Freshwater mullet   Thick-lipped grey mullet   Thin-lipped grey mullet   Golden mullet   Red mullet   White mullet

PLEURONECTIDAE; BOTHIDAE; SOLEIDAE

FLATFISH

For a few days after hatching from the egg, the larva of a flatfish resembles that of any other fish, but then it begins to change into the compressed, asymmetrical shape that makes flatfish superbly adapted to a bottom-hugging life. There are over 500 species, the main families being the Pleuronectidae or righteyed flatfish, in which both eyes are on the right side of the body; the Bothidae or lefteyed flatfish, in which both eyes are on the left; and the Soleidae or sole family, which contains mostly righteyed species.

PACIFIC HALIBUT
This huge, righteyed flatfish and its Atlantic counterpart (*Hippoglossus hippoglossus*) are among the largest fish in the sea, probably capable of exceeding 360 kg (800 lb). However, most caught by anglers are young fish weighing less than 4.54 kg (10 lb), the largest adults being found in very deep water.

SUMMER FLOUNDER
Paralichthys dentatus

Black and yellow bands on fins

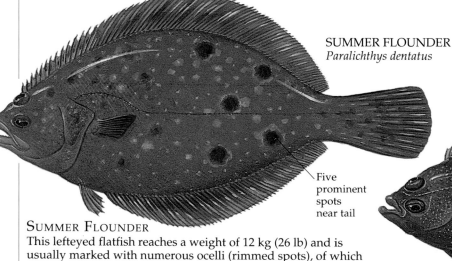

Five prominent spots near tail

SUMMER FLOUNDER
This lefteyed flatfish reaches a weight of 12 kg (26 lb) and is usually marked with numerous ocelli (rimmed spots), of which five near the tail are large and prominent. It is found along the Atlantic coast of the United States, and from the Carolinas south its range overlaps that of the southern flounder (*Paralichthys lethostigma*), which is often marked with spots but not with ocelli.

STARRY FLOUNDER
Platichthys stellatus

SOLE
The sole, a common flatfish of the eastern Atlantic and the Mediterranean, is brown with dark patches on its upper side and creamy white below. It spends the day buried in the sand, feeding at night in midwater, and grows to 3 kg (6 lb 10 oz).

EUROPEAN PLAICE
Pleuronectes platessa

STARRY FLOUNDER
This flatfish, which can be righteyed or lefteyed, is common on the Pacific coast of North America. Its fins are marked with black and yellow bands, and the upper side of its body has patches of shiny, star-shaped scales. It grows to 9.1 kg (20 lb), and hybridizes with the English sole (*Parophrys vetulus*) to produce the "hybrid sole."

EUROPEAN PLAICE
The righteyed European plaice is found in the eastern Atlantic from the tidal shallows out to depths of about 200 m (650 ft). It is marked with bold red or orange spots and grows to a weight of over 4.54 kg (10 lb). The American plaice (*Hippoglossoides platessoides*) is similar, but lacks the red spotting and reaches 6.4 kg (14 lb).

Eggs and larvae
Female flatfish lay up to 500,000 eggs. These float in the water, as do the symmetrically shaped larvae.

SOLE
Solea solea

Size comparison

Pacific halibut   Turbot   Summer flounder   Starry flounder   Winter flounder   Plaice   Sole

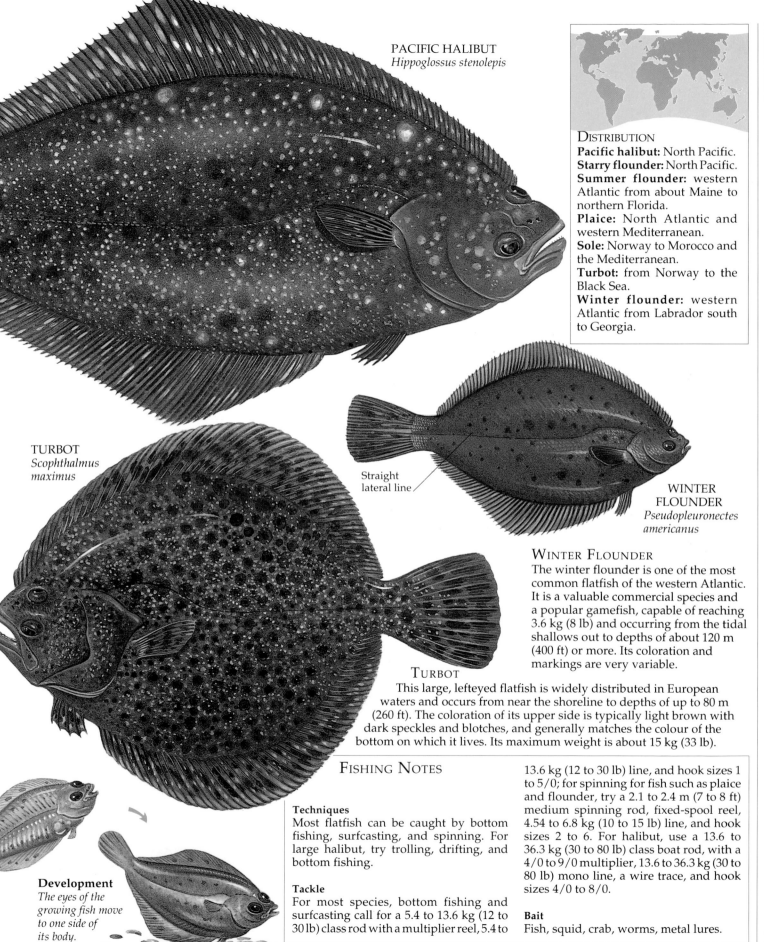

PACIFIC HALIBUT
Hippoglossus stenolepis

DISTRIBUTION
Pacific halibut: North Pacific.
Starry flounder: North Pacific.
Summer flounder: western Atlantic from about Maine to northern Florida.
Plaice: North Atlantic and western Mediterranean.
Sole: Norway to Morocco and the Mediterranean.
Turbot: from Norway to the Black Sea.
Winter flounder: western Atlantic from Labrador south to Georgia.

TURBOT
Scophthalmus maximus

Straight lateral line

WINTER FLOUNDER
Pseudopleuronectes americanus

WINTER FLOUNDER
The winter flounder is one of the most common flatfish of the western Atlantic. It is a valuable commercial species and a popular gamefish, capable of reaching 3.6 kg (8 lb) and occurring from the tidal shallows out to depths of about 120 m (400 ft) or more. Its coloration and markings are very variable.

TURBOT
This large, lefteyed flatfish is widely distributed in European waters and occurs from near the shoreline to depths of up to 80 m (260 ft). The coloration of its upper side is typically light brown with dark speckles and blotches, and generally matches the colour of the bottom on which it lives. Its maximum weight is about 15 kg (33 lb).

FISHING NOTES

Development
The eyes of the growing fish move to one side of its body.

Techniques
Most flatfish can be caught by bottom fishing, surfcasting, and spinning. For large halibut, try trolling, drifting, and bottom fishing.

Tackle
For most species, bottom fishing and surfcasting call for a 5.4 to 13.6 kg (12 to 30 lb) class rod with a multiplier reel, 5.4 to 13.6 kg (12 to 30 lb) line, and hook sizes 1 to 5/0; for spinning for fish such as plaice and flounder, try a 2.1 to 2.4 m (7 to 8 ft) medium spinning rod, fixed-spool reel, 4.54 to 6.8 kg (10 to 15 lb) line, and hook sizes 2 to 6. For halibut, use a 13.6 to 36.3 kg (30 to 80 lb) class boat rod, with a 4/0 to 9/0 multiplier, 13.6 to 36.3 kg (30 to 80 lb) mono line, a wire trace, and hook sizes 4/0 to 8/0.

Bait
Fish, squid, crab, worms, metal lures.

ORDER RAJIFORMES

RAYS

The order Rajiformes consists of eight families of cartilaginous fish and includes the rays, mantas, sawfish, and skates *(see page 186)*. These fish are characterized by flattened bodies and wide, often winglike, pectoral fins; their mouths and gill openings are on the undersides and their eyes on the upper. In most families, the eggs are fertilized and hatch within the body of the female; the exception is the Rajidae, in which the internally fertilized eggs are laid before hatching.

MANTA

The mantas or devil rays belong to the Mobulidae family, which contains about a dozen species. These range in size from the Australian mobula *(Mobula diabola)*, which measures about 60 cm (2 ft) across its wings, to the manta *(Manta birostris)*, which reaches 6.7 m (22 ft) across the wings and a weight of 1,820 kg (4,000 lb). Despite its tremendous size, the manta is a generally harmless fish that feeds on small fish and crustaceans, which it steers into its mouth with its cephalic fins, the pair of "horns" on its head. Mantas cruise between midwater and the surface, and frequently leap into the air, perhaps to rid themselves of parasites or maybe just for fun.

THORNBACK RAY

The thornback is the most common ray in European waters. A member of the Rajidae family, it is a bottom-dweller found at depths of 10 to 60 m (about 30 to 200 ft), and gets its name from the numerous thorny spines on its tail, back, and pectoral fins. Young thornbacks live in shallow water and feed on small crustaceans, and as they grow they move into deeper water and begin feeding on larger prey including crabs and fish. They grow to about 18 kg (40 lb).

SPOTTED RAY
Raja montagui

THORNBACK RAY
Raja clavata

Colour variation
The colour of the thornback is very variable, but most individuals are a mottled brown.

SPOTTED RAY

Like the thornback, the spotted ray is a European member of the Rajidae family. It lives in deeper water than the thornback, preferring depths of 60 to 120 m (about 200 to 400 ft), and is a smaller fish, with a maximum weight of around 3.8 kg (8 lb 6 oz). Its diet consists mainly of crustaceans but it will also take small fish.

Spines
The thorny spines of the thornback and many other species have a strong, buttonlike base.

Egg cases
The eggs laid by members of the Rajidae family are each enclosed in a tough case known as a "mermaid's purse".

MANTA
Manta birostris

Size comparison

Manta

Sawfish

Bat ray

Thornback ray

Round stingray

Spotted ray

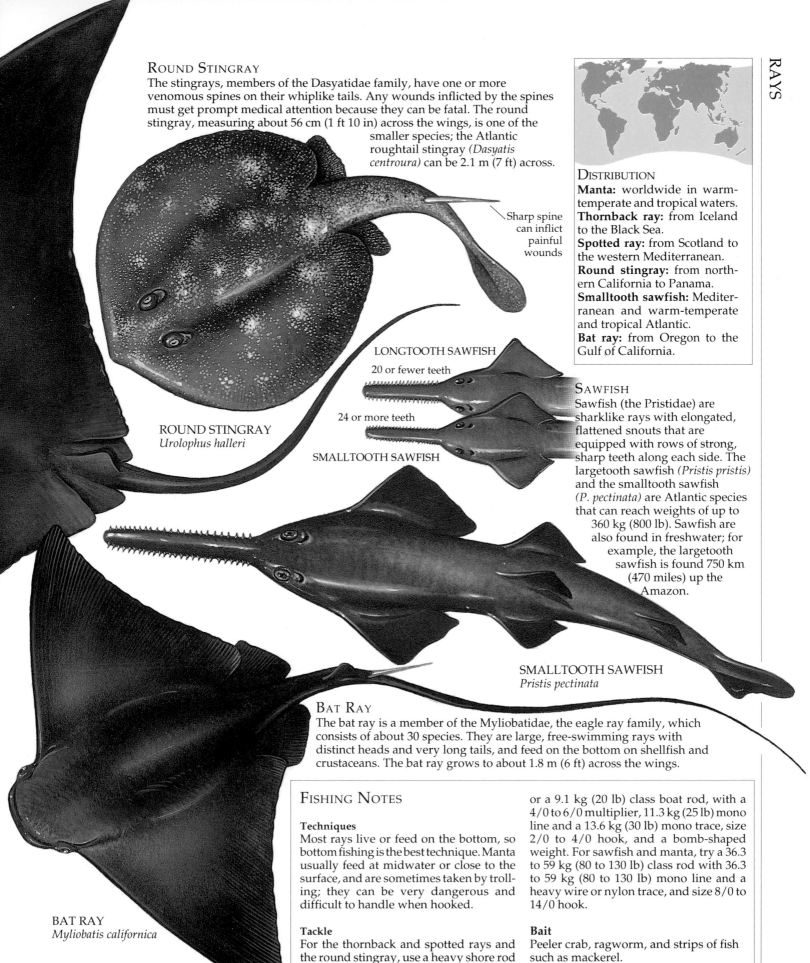

ROUND STINGRAY

The stingrays, members of the Dasyatidae family, have one or more venomous spines on their whiplike tails. Any wounds inflicted by the spines must get prompt medical attention because they can be fatal. The round stingray, measuring about 56 cm (1 ft 10 in) across the wings, is one of the smaller species; the Atlantic roughtail stingray (*Dasyatis centroura*) can be 2.1 m (7 ft) across.

Sharp spine can inflict painful wounds

ROUND STINGRAY
Urolophus halleri

LONGTOOTH SAWFISH
20 or fewer teeth

24 or more teeth

SMALLTOOTH SAWFISH

DISTRIBUTION
Manta: worldwide in warm-temperate and tropical waters.
Thornback ray: from Iceland to the Black Sea.
Spotted ray: from Scotland to the western Mediterranean.
Round stingray: from northern California to Panama.
Smalltooth sawfish: Mediterranean and warm-temperate and tropical Atlantic.
Bat ray: from Oregon to the Gulf of California.

SAWFISH

Sawfish (the Pristidae) are sharklike rays with elongated, flattened snouts that are equipped with rows of strong, sharp teeth along each side. The largetooth sawfish (*Pristis pristis*) and the smalltooth sawfish (*P. pectinata*) are Atlantic species that can reach weights of up to 360 kg (800 lb). Sawfish are also found in freshwater; for example, the largetooth sawfish is found 750 km (470 miles) up the Amazon.

SMALLTOOTH SAWFISH
Pristis pectinata

BAT RAY

The bat ray is a member of the Myliobatidae, the eagle ray family, which consists of about 30 species. They are large, free-swimming rays with distinct heads and very long tails, and feed on the bottom on shellfish and crustaceans. The bat ray grows to about 1.8 m (6 ft) across the wings.

BAT RAY
Myliobatis californica

FISHING NOTES

Techniques
Most rays live or feed on the bottom, so bottom fishing is the best technique. Manta usually feed at midwater or close to the surface, and are sometimes taken by trolling; they can be very dangerous and difficult to handle when hooked.

Tackle
For the thornback and spotted rays and the round stingray, use a heavy shore rod or a 9.1 kg (20 lb) class boat rod, with a 4/0 to 6/0 multiplier, 11.3 kg (25 lb) mono line and a 13.6 kg (30 lb) mono trace, size 2/0 to 4/0 hook, and a bomb-shaped weight. For sawfish and manta, try a 36.3 to 59 kg (80 to 130 lb) class rod with 36.3 to 59 kg (80 to 130 lb) mono line and a heavy wire or nylon trace, and size 8/0 to 14/0 hook.

Bait
Peeler crab, ragworm, and strips of fish such as mackerel.

Saltwater SPECIES

SKATES

The skates are members of the Rajidae *(see also page 184)*, which contains over a hundred species and is the largest family within the order Rajiformes. Most skates are a mottled brownish colour with whitish undersides, and their tails are relatively thick, rather than whiplike. Skates usually rest on the bottom during the day, lying partly buried in sand or mud, and become active at night to feed on shellfish, crustaceans, and sometimes small fish. They swim by making smooth undulations of their pectoral fins.

BIG SKATE
Raja binoculata

Eye spot

BARNDOOR SKATE
Raja laevis

BARNDOOR SKATE
This large, aggressive skate of the northwestern Atlantic grows to a length of around 1.5 m (5 ft) and a weight of 18 kg (40 lb). It is found from the tidal shallows out to depths of 430 m (1,410 ft), and will sometimes enter brackish water. It has a noticeably pointed snout, large, black pores on its underside, and a smooth skin. Its wings (pectoral fins) have concave leading edges and sharply angled corners. It feeds mainly on large crustaceans, molluscs, and fish such as herring, and it will readily take a baited hook.

Sharp-angled corner of wing

Dark bars and streaks

BIG SKATE
The big skate, as its name indicates, is a large fish and can reach a length of 2.4 m (8 ft) and weigh over 91 kg (200 lb). It has a triangular snout, and there is a large eyespot on the upper surface of each wing. The big skate is found at depths of 3 to 110 m (10 to 360 ft) along the Pacific coast of North America, and the southern part of its range overlaps that of the California skate *(Raja inornata)*. This skate is much smaller, about 76 cm (2 ft 6 in) long, with a sharply pointed snout and usually no eyespots.

CLEARNOSE SKATE
Raja eglanteria

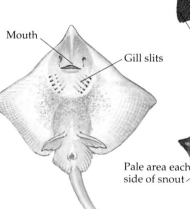

Mouth

Gill slits

Pale area each side of snout

CLEARNOSE SKATE
The clearnose skate, which grows to a length of about 90 cm (3 ft), gets its name from the pale, translucent areas at either side of its snout. The overall coloration of its upper side is light brown to reddish brown, marked with dark bars, streaks, and spots. It migrates inshore to breed during the spring, and in summer it is the most abundant skate in the western Atlantic from Long Island to the Carolinas.

Skate underside
The underside of a skate is usually a pale, whitish colour. The mouth is just below the snout, and just above the two sets of five gill slits.

Size comparison

Common skate

Big skate

Barndoor skate

Winter skate

Clearnose skate

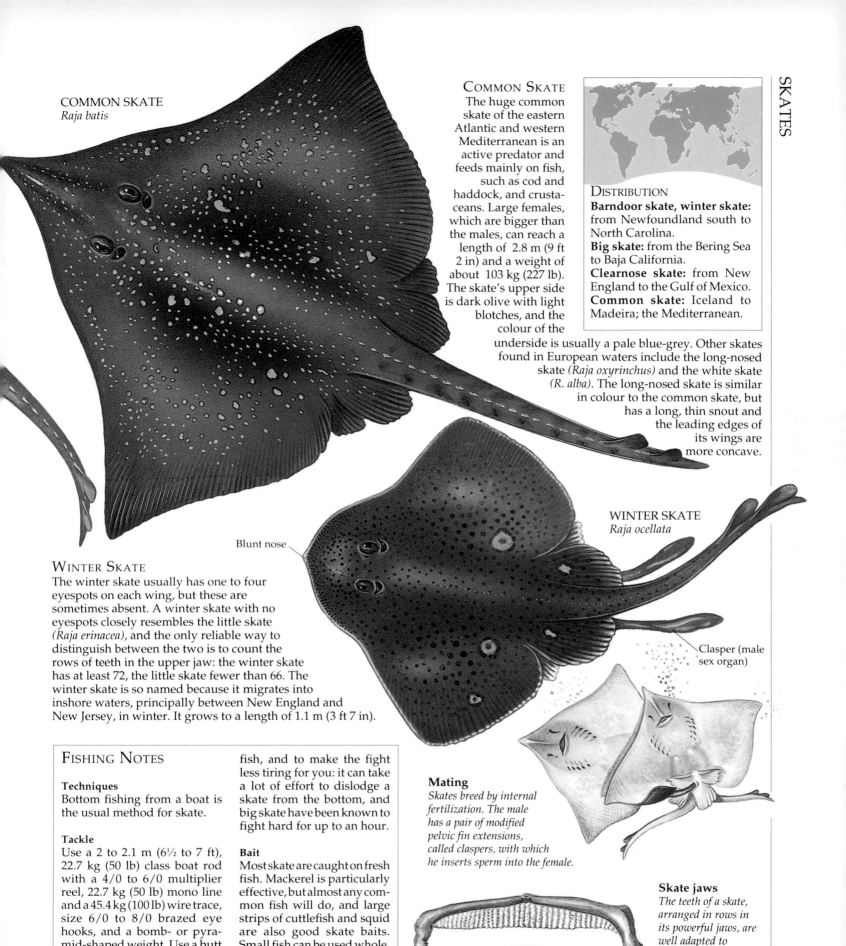

COMMON SKATE
Raja batis

COMMON SKATE

The huge common skate of the eastern Atlantic and western Mediterranean is an active predator and feeds mainly on fish, such as cod and haddock, and crustaceans. Large females, which are bigger than the males, can reach a length of 2.8 m (9 ft 2 in) and a weight of about 103 kg (227 lb). The skate's upper side is dark olive with light blotches, and the colour of the underside is usually a pale blue-grey. Other skates found in European waters include the long-nosed skate *(Raja oxyrinchus)* and the white skate *(R. alba)*. The long-nosed skate is similar in colour to the common skate, but has a long, thin snout and the leading edges of its wings are more concave.

DISTRIBUTION

Barndoor skate, winter skate: from Newfoundland south to North Carolina.
Big skate: from the Bering Sea to Baja California.
Clearnose skate: from New England to the Gulf of Mexico.
Common skate: Iceland to Madeira; the Mediterranean.

WINTER SKATE
Raja ocellata

Blunt nose

Clasper (male sex organ)

WINTER SKATE

The winter skate usually has one to four eyespots on each wing, but these are sometimes absent. A winter skate with no eyespots closely resembles the little skate *(Raja erinacea)*, and the only reliable way to distinguish between the two is to count the rows of teeth in the upper jaw: the winter skate has at least 72, the little skate fewer than 66. The winter skate is so named because it migrates into inshore waters, principally between New England and New Jersey, in winter. It grows to a length of 1.1 m (3 ft 7 in).

FISHING NOTES

Techniques
Bottom fishing from a boat is the usual method for skate.

Tackle
Use a 2 to 2.1 m (6½ to 7 ft), 22.7 kg (50 lb) class boat rod with a 4/0 to 6/0 multiplier reel, 22.7 kg (50 lb) mono line and a 45.4 kg (100 lb) wire trace, size 6/0 to 8/0 brazed eye hooks, and a bomb- or pyramid-shaped weight. Use a butt socket or full harness to help you exert maximum leverage on the rod when fighting the fish, and to make the fight less tiring for you: it can take a lot of effort to dislodge a skate from the bottom, and big skate have been known to fight hard for up to an hour.

Bait
Most skate are caught on fresh fish. Mackerel is particularly effective, but almost any common fish will do, and large strips of cuttlefish and squid are also good skate baits. Small fish can be used whole, because skate have big mouths and readily gulp them down.

Mating
Skates breed by internal fertilization. The male has a pair of modified pelvic fin extensions, called claspers, with which he inserts sperm into the female.

Skate jaws
The teeth of a skate, arranged in rows in its powerful jaws, are well adapted to crushing and grinding up the fish, lobsters, crabs, and molluscs that it feeds on.

187

DRUM & KAHAWAI

The widely distributed Sciaenidae (drum) family consists of over 200 tropical and warm-temperate marine species – including drum, croaker, seatrout, seabass, and weakfish – plus the freshwater drum (*Aplodinotus grunniens*) of North America. Many species can make drumming sounds by contracting muscles on the walls of their swim bladders (gas-filled bladders that help to give them buoyancy). The kahawai, one of the two members of the Arripidae family, is also known as the Australian salmon because its juveniles bear a superficial resemblance to the Atlantic salmon.

BLACK DRUM

The black drum grows to a weight of over 52 kg (115 lb), and its deep body is marked with four or five dark bars on each side. It is a bottom feeder, and uses the barbels on its chin to help it locate the crustaceans and molluscs that make up the bulk of its diet. It is an important gamefish, commonly caught from the shore and piers.

Large chin barbels

RED DRUM

This large drum, also known as the redfish or channel bass, has a reddish overall coloration and one or more dark spots at the base of the tail. Its body is not as deep as that of the black drum, and it lacks chin barbels. It feeds at the bottom on crustaceans and molluscs and also takes small fish, especially mullet. The usual adult weight is under 18 kg (40 lb) but it can reach about 43 kg (95 lb).

RED DRUM
Sciaenops ocellatus

WHITE SEABASS
Atractoscion nobilis

WHITE SEABASS

The white seabass is one of a number of important gamefish of the drum family found along the Pacific coast of North America. Others include the white croaker (*see opposite page*), the California corbina (*Menticirrhus undulatus*), the spotfin croaker (*Roncador stearnsii*), and the yellowfin croaker (*Umbrina roncador*). The white seabass is found over rocks, near kelp, and in the surf zone, feeding on fish and squid and growing to about 41 kg (90 lb).

Black bars

JUVENILE
WHITE SEABASS

KAHAWAI

The two members of the Arripidae family, the kahawai and the ruff (*Arripis georgianus*), are related to the Sciaenidae and resemble them in overall appearance. During the summer, kahawai form huge schools that cruise inshore near the surface, feeding on small fish and krill. Its average weight is 1.36 to 4.54 kg (3 to 10 lb), with a maximum of around 7.3 kg (16 lb).

KAHAWAI
Arripis trutta

Size comparison

| Black drum | White seabass | Red drum | Spotted seatrout | Kahawai | Weakfish | White croaker |

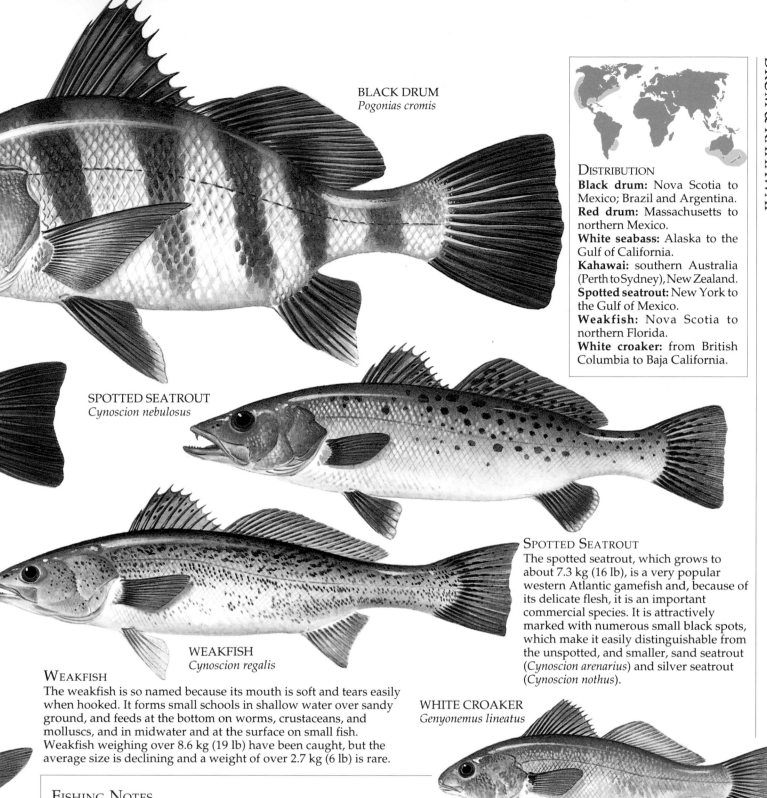

BLACK DRUM
Pogonias cromis

DISTRIBUTION

Black drum: Nova Scotia to Mexico; Brazil and Argentina.
Red drum: Massachusetts to northern Mexico.
White seabass: Alaska to the Gulf of California.
Kahawai: southern Australia (Perth to Sydney), New Zealand.
Spotted seatrout: New York to the Gulf of Mexico.
Weakfish: Nova Scotia to northern Florida.
White croaker: from British Columbia to Baja California.

SPOTTED SEATROUT
Cynoscion nebulosus

WEAKFISH
Cynoscion regalis

SPOTTED SEATROUT

The spotted seatrout, which grows to about 7.3 kg (16 lb), is a very popular western Atlantic gamefish and, because of its delicate flesh, it is an important commercial species. It is attractively marked with numerous small black spots, which make it easily distinguishable from the unspotted, and smaller, sand seatrout (*Cynoscion arenarius*) and silver seatrout (*Cynoscion nothus*).

WHITE CROAKER
Genyonemus lineatus

WEAKFISH

The weakfish is so named because its mouth is soft and tears easily when hooked. It forms small schools in shallow water over sandy ground, and feeds at the bottom on worms, crustaceans, and molluscs, and in midwater and at the surface on small fish. Weakfish weighing over 8.6 kg (19 lb) have been caught, but the average size is declining and a weight of over 2.7 kg (6 lb) is rare.

FISHING NOTES

Techniques
These fish are taken by a number of methods, the most usual being bottom fishing, surfcasting, and spinning.

Tackle
For bottom fishing, try a 13.6 kg (30 lb) class boat rod with a size 4/0 multiplier reel, 13.6 kg (30 lb) mono line, size 4/0 hook, and a bomb-shaped sinker. When surfcasting, use a 3.7 m (12 ft) surfcasting rod with a fixed-spool or multiplier reel, 9.1 kg (20 lb) mono line, size 4/0 hook, and a grip sinker. For spinning, use a 2.4 to 2.7 m (8 to 9 ft) spinning rod with a fixed-spool reel, 6.8 to 9.1 kg (15 to 20 lb) mono line, and size 1/0 to 4/0 hook.

Bait
Good baits include shrimp, fish, crab, clams, mussels, worms, and most types of artificial lure.

WHITE CROAKER

The white croaker is most reliably distinguished from other species of drum found along the Pacific coast of North America by the number of spines in its first dorsal fin: the white croaker has 12 to 16, the others 11 or fewer. It is found from close inshore to depths of 183 m (600 ft), and grows to about 454 g (1 lb).

MACKEREL

The Scombridae family consists of about 45 species and includes the many species of mackerel plus tuna, bonito, and wahoo. The typical scombrid is a fast-swimming predator with a beautifully stream-lined, spindle-shaped body and a large, deeply forked or lunate (crescent-shaped) tail. Many scombrids are able to fold some of their fins into slots in their bodies to make them more streamlined and enable them to swim faster. The bluefin tuna, for example *(see page 193)*, withdraws its pectoral, pelvic, and first dorsal fins in this way when travelling at speed.

CHUB MACKEREL

The chub mackerel or Pacific mackerel can reach a weight of 2.9 kg (6 lb 5 oz) but usually does not exceed 1 kg (2 lb 3 oz). It occurs in temperate and subtropical waters worldwide but its distribution is uneven, and there are minor differences between the Atlantic and Pacific varieties. Both, however, have widely separated first and second dorsal fins and about 30 wavy, dark bars on the back. This species is a very important commercial fish, especially in the Pacific region, and is found in large schools in inshore waters.

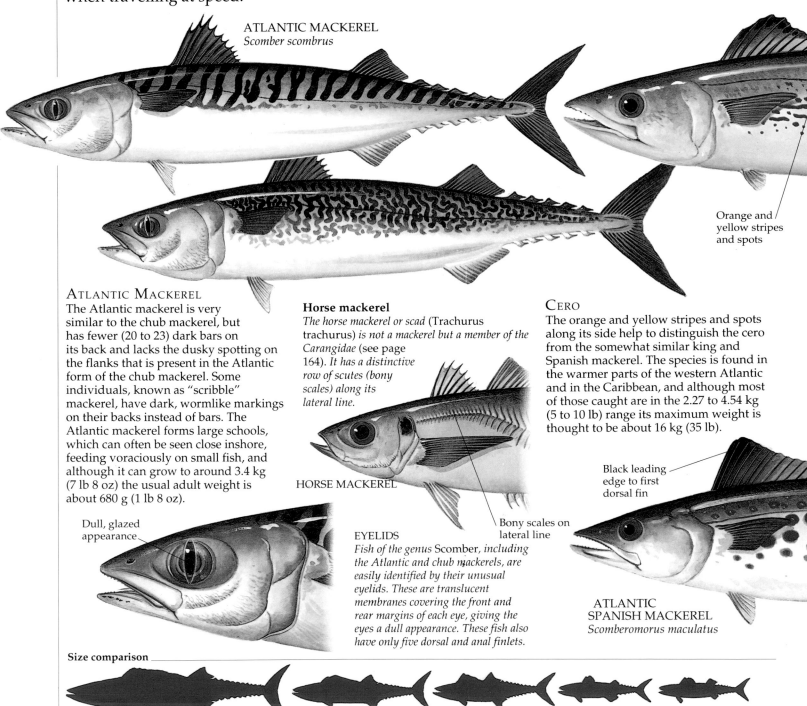

ATLANTIC MACKEREL
Scomber scombrus

Orange and yellow stripes and spots

ATLANTIC MACKEREL

The Atlantic mackerel is very similar to the chub mackerel, but has fewer (20 to 23) dark bars on its back and lacks the dusky spotting on the flanks that is present in the Atlantic form of the chub mackerel. Some individuals, known as "scribble" mackerel, have dark, wormlike markings on their backs instead of bars. The Atlantic mackerel forms large schools, which can often be seen close inshore, feeding voraciously on small fish, and although it can grow to around 3.4 kg (7 lb 8 oz) the usual adult weight is about 680 g (1 lb 8 oz).

Horse mackerel
The horse mackerel or scad (Trachurus trachurus) is not a mackerel but a member of the Carangidae (see page 164). It has a distinctive row of scutes (bony scales) along its lateral line.

HORSE MACKEREL

CERO

The orange and yellow stripes and spots along its side help to distinguish the cero from the somewhat similar king and Spanish mackerel. The species is found in the warmer parts of the western Atlantic and in the Caribbean, and although most of those caught are in the 2.27 to 4.54 kg (5 to 10 lb) range its maximum weight is thought to be about 16 kg (35 lb).

Black leading edge to first dorsal fin

Dull, glazed appearance

EYELIDS
Fish of the genus Scomber, *including the Atlantic and chub mackerels, are easily identified by their unusual eyelids. These are translucent membranes covering the front and rear margins of each eye, giving the eyes a dull appearance. These fish also have only five dorsal and anal finlets.*

Bony scales on lateral line

ATLANTIC SPANISH MACKEREL
Scomberomorus maculatus

Size comparison

King mackerel   Cero   Spanish mackerel   Atlantic mackerel   Chub mackerel

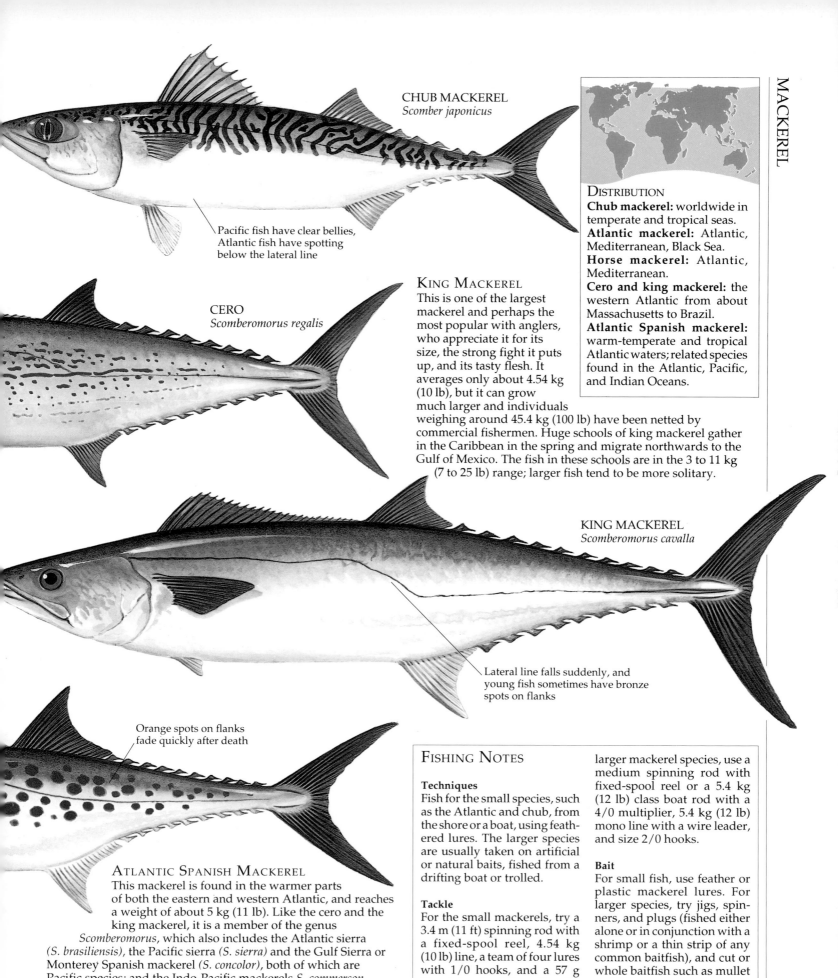

CHUB MACKEREL
Scomber japonicus

Pacific fish have clear bellies, Atlantic fish have spotting below the lateral line

CERO
Scomberomorus regalis

DISTRIBUTION
Chub mackerel: worldwide in temperate and tropical seas.
Atlantic mackerel: Atlantic, Mediterranean, Black Sea.
Horse mackerel: Atlantic, Mediterranean.
Cero and king mackerel: the western Atlantic from about Massachusetts to Brazil.
Atlantic Spanish mackerel: warm-temperate and tropical Atlantic waters; related species found in the Atlantic, Pacific, and Indian Oceans.

KING MACKEREL
This is one of the largest mackerel and perhaps the most popular with anglers, who appreciate it for its size, the strong fight it puts up, and its tasty flesh. It averages only about 4.54 kg (10 lb), but it can grow much larger and individuals weighing around 45.4 kg (100 lb) have been netted by commercial fishermen. Huge schools of king mackerel gather in the Caribbean in the spring and migrate northwards to the Gulf of Mexico. The fish in these schools are in the 3 to 11 kg (7 to 25 lb) range; larger fish tend to be more solitary.

KING MACKEREL
Scomberomorus cavalla

Lateral line falls suddenly, and young fish sometimes have bronze spots on flanks

Orange spots on flanks fade quickly after death

ATLANTIC SPANISH MACKEREL
This mackerel is found in the warmer parts of both the eastern and western Atlantic, and reaches a weight of about 5 kg (11 lb). Like the cero and the king mackerel, it is a member of the genus *Scomberomorus*, which also includes the Atlantic sierra (*S. brasiliensis*), the Pacific sierra (*S. sierra*) and the Gulf Sierra or Monterey Spanish mackerel (*S. concolor*), both of which are Pacific species; and the Indo-Pacific mackerels *S. commerson* and *S. guttatus*, which are very common in Australian waters.

FISHING NOTES

Techniques
Fish for the small species, such as the Atlantic and chub, from the shore or a boat, using feathered lures. The larger species are usually taken on artificial or natural baits, fished from a drifting boat or trolled.

Tackle
For the small mackerels, try a 3.4 m (11 ft) spinning rod with a fixed-spool reel, 4.54 kg (10 lb) line, a team of four lures with 1/0 hooks, and a 57 g (2 oz) bomb sinker. For the larger mackerel species, use a medium spinning rod with fixed-spool reel or a 5.4 kg (12 lb) class boat rod with a 4/0 multiplier, 5.4 kg (12 lb) mono line with a wire leader, and size 2/0 hooks.

Bait
For small fish, use feather or plastic mackerel lures. For larger species, try jigs, spinners, and plugs (fished either alone or in conjunction with a shrimp or a thin strip of any common baitfish), and cut or whole baitfish such as mullet and balao.

191

TUNA & WAHOO

These members of the Scombridae family are widespread in temperate and tropical waters, and have considerable commercial importance as well as being important gamefish. The commercial value of tuna led to them being fished for with enormous driftnets, especially in the Pacific, but use of these nets has been restricted by international agreements because they took a heavy toll not only of tuna but also of unsought-for species including dolphins, sunfish, billfish, and Ray's bream.

ALBACORE
Because of its very long pectoral fins, which extend beyond the front of the anal fin, the albacore is also known as the longfin tuna. These fins help to distinguish the albacore from other tuna such as the bluefin. The Atlantic and the Pacific albacore were once considered to be separate species but are now known to be identical, and reach weights of around 43 kg (95 lb).

BLACKFIN TUNA
The blackfin of the western Atlantic is one of the smaller tuna, averaging less than 4.54 kg (10 lb) with a maximum of about 19 kg (42 lb). It is renowned more for its delicious flesh than for its sporting qualities, and large numbers are taken by blue marlin as well as by commercial fishermen.

BLACKFIN TUNA
Thunnus atlanticus

Dark finlets edged with white

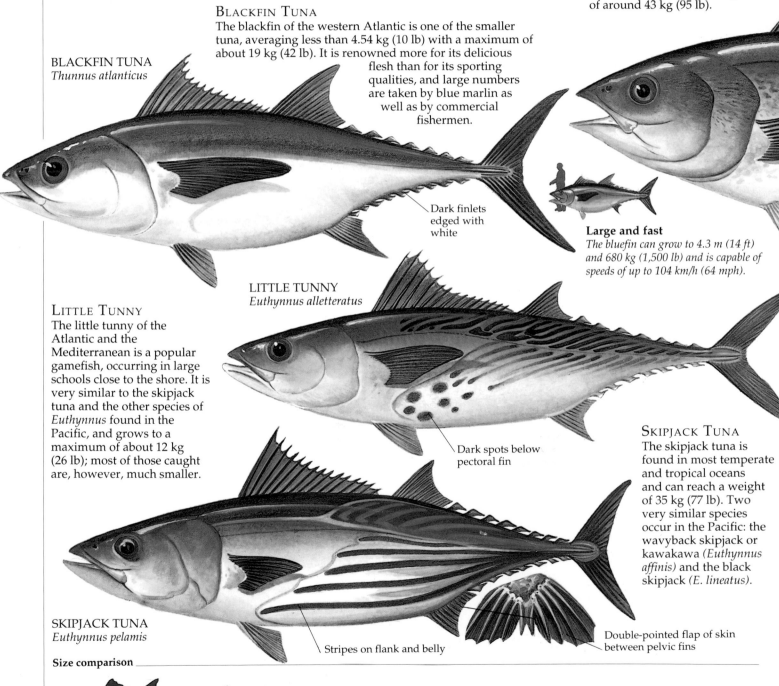

Large and fast
The bluefin can grow to 4.3 m (14 ft) and 680 kg (1,500 lb) and is capable of speeds of up to 104 km/h (64 mph).

LITTLE TUNNY
The little tunny of the Atlantic and the Mediterranean is a popular gamefish, occurring in large schools close to the shore. It is very similar to the skipjack tuna and the other species of *Euthynnus* found in the Pacific, and grows to a maximum of about 12 kg (26 lb); most of those caught are, however, much smaller.

LITTLE TUNNY
Euthynnus alletteratus

Dark spots below pectoral fin

SKIPJACK TUNA
The skipjack tuna is found in most temperate and tropical oceans and can reach a weight of 35 kg (77 lb). Two very similar species occur in the Pacific: the wavyback skipjack or kawakawa (*Euthynnus affinis*) and the black skipjack (*E. lineatus*).

SKIPJACK TUNA
Euthynnus pelamis

Stripes on flank and belly

Double-pointed flap of skin between pelvic fins

Size comparison

Bluefin tuna   Wahoo   Albacore   Skipjack tuna   Little tunny   Blackfin tuna

ALBACORE
Thunnus alalunga

Very long
pectoral fin

BLUEFIN TUNA
Thunnus thynnus

BLUEFIN TUNA
The bluefin is a highly migratory fish, which is found in subtropical seas during winter and moves into cooler waters in summer. Bluefin of up to about 45 kg (100 lb) travel in huge schools, but larger fish form smaller schools and the biggest individuals are often solitary. North Atlantic bluefin and those found in the Pacific and Indian Oceans are sometimes classified as separate species or subspecies, but the differences between them are very slight.

DISTRIBUTION
Albacore: in most temperate and tropical waters; more abundant in the Pacific than in the Atlantic.
Blackfin tuna: Atlantic from Massachusetts to Brazil.
Little tunny: warm-temperate and tropical Atlantic waters and the Mediterranean.
Skipjack tuna, bluefin tuna: worldwide in temperate and tropical waters.
Wahoo: most warm-temperate and tropical waters.

Finlets
One of the distinctive features of the members of the Scombridae, including the wahoo, is the presence of delicate, soft-rayed finlets between the tail, dorsal, and anal fins.

Long dorsal fin

Long, torpedo-shaped body

WAHOO
Acanthocybium solanderi

FISHING NOTES

Techniques
Trolling with lures and drift fishing with natural baits are the usual methods of fishing for tuna, little tunny, and albacore. When fishing for wahoo, try trolling with lures and natural baits, and drift fishing with natural baits. Wahoo are usually taken on flatlines that are fished quite near to the boat, rather than lines on outriggers.

Tackle
For tuna, use a 36.3 to 59 kg (80 to 130 lb) class rod with full roller rings, a lever drag multiplier, and 36.3 to 59 kg (80 to 130 lb) nylon line with a 181 to 272 kg (400 to 600 lb) nylon leader. Use hook sizes 10/0 to 12/0, flat for trolling and offset for drifting. For wahoo, use a 13.6 to 22.7 kg (30 to 50 lb) class rod with a 6/0 star drag or 30- to 50-class multiplier reel, 13.6 to 22.7 kg (30 to 50 lb) nylon line with a heavy wire leader, and a flat hook size 5/0 to 10/0.

Bait
Use a Kona Head lure when trolling for tuna, and try live mackerel or dead herring when drifting. When trolling for wahoo, use a Kona Head or other large artificial, or try a natural bait, such as a whole mullet or balao, mounted for trolling. For drift fishing, use a live baitfish on hook sizes 5/0 to 8/0.

WAHOO
The long, slender-bodied wahoo makes tremendous runs with abrupt changes of direction when hooked, sometimes leaping from the water, and this makes it one of the most exciting fish to catch. Its long, heavily toothed jaws form a beaklike snout, and its first dorsal fin is long, low, and spiny. The average weight is about 6.8 to 9 kg (15 to 20 lb), but it can grow to 83 kg (183 lb) and a length of 2.1 m (6 ft 11 in).

HEAD OF WAHOO

Wahoo jaws
The wahoo is a predatory fish (as are tuna), and its jaws contain rows of flat-sided, razor-sharp teeth that enable it to rip into squid and shoals of baitfish. An unusual feature of the wahoo is that both its jaws are movable.

BONITO & SHAD

Bonito, like mackerel and tuna *(see pages 190–193)*, belong to the Scombridae family. They are fast-swimming predators that feed on squid and small schooling fish, including mackerel, taken just below the surface. Shad, fish of the genus *Alosa*, are members of the herring family, the Clupeidae. They are marine fish that spawn in freshwater (some species also have landlocked populations), and differ from most other herring species in having a "keel" or "sawbelly", a ridge of sharp-edged scales along the belly.

PACIFIC BONITO

The Pacific bonito is a medium-sized fish that averages less than 5.4 kg (12 lb) but can grow to over 11 kg (24 lb). The northern and southern populations of the eastern Pacific are regarded as separate subspecies. Those north of Baja California are classified as *Sarda chiliensis lineolata*, and those off Peru and Chile as *S. c. chiliensis*. The striped bonito, *S. orientalis*, occurs from Baja to Peru, and in the western Pacific.

TWAITE SHAD
Alosa fallax

TWAITE SHAD
This shad differs from the Atlantic herring (*Clupea harengus*) in having a notch in its upper jaw, into which the lower jaw fits, a keel of sharp scales along its belly, and often has dark blotches along each side. Its maximum weight is about 1.4 kg (3 lb 2 oz).

ALLIS SHAD
Alosa alosa

ALLIS SHAD
The allis shad is similar to the twaite shad, but its keel is more pronounced and there may be a single dark blotch on each side, just behind the gill cover. It is also larger, reaching a weight of 2.7 kg (6 lb). Populations of both species have been severely depleted, mainly by pollution and damming of their spawning rivers.

AMERICAN SHAD
The American shad, which is capable of reaching a weight of over 5.5 kg (12 lb), has a large, dark spot behind each gill cover and usually one or two rows of dark spots along each side. It feeds almost entirely on plankton, and the adults have no jaw teeth.

Two rows of spots

Shad diet
The diet of shad consists mainly of plankton, both animal and plant, plus insect larvae and copepods (tiny crustaceans). Skipjack herring and twaite, allis, and hickory shad also feed on small fish.

AMERICAN SHAD
Alosa sapidissima

SKIPJACK HERRING
Alosa chrysochloris

SKIPJACK HERRING
The skipjack herring is also known as the river herring, and when in freshwater it prefers the open water of medium to large rivers and stillwaters. It is very similar to the hickory shad, but its flanks have a brassy tinge and no dark spots. Its maximum weight is about 1.6 kg (3 lb 8 oz).

FISHING NOTES

Techniques
Trolling and spinning for bonito, spinning and fly fishing for shad.

Tackle
To troll for bonito, use a 5.4 kg (12 lb) class boat rod with a size 2/0 multiplier reel, 5.4 kg (12 lb) mono line, and a size 2/0 hook. When spinning for bonito, try a light spinning rod with a fixed-spool reel, 5.4 kg (12 lb) mono line, and size 2/0 hook.

When spinning for shad, use a light spinning rod with a fixed-spool reel, 3.6 kg (8 lb) mono line, and small lures with treble hooks. For fly fishing, try a 2.7 m (9 ft) trout rod, weight-forward floating line, and flies tied on size 6 to 8 hooks.

Bait
For bonito, good baits include plugs, spoons, plastic squid, and whole or cut squid and fish. For shad, try small spinners and bar spoons, and small, white-coloured flies.

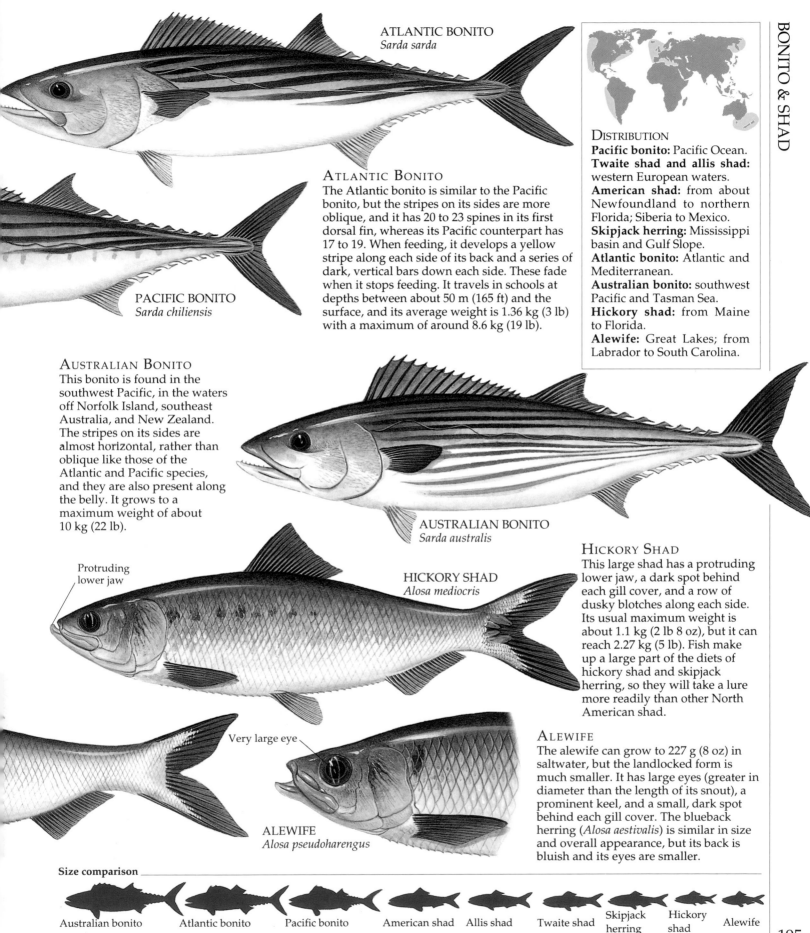

ATLANTIC BONITO
Sarda sarda

PACIFIC BONITO
Sarda chiliensis

ATLANTIC BONITO
The Atlantic bonito is similar to the Pacific bonito, but the stripes on its sides are more oblique, and it has 20 to 23 spines in its first dorsal fin, whereas its Pacific counterpart has 17 to 19. When feeding, it develops a yellow stripe along each side of its back and a series of dark, vertical bars down each side. These fade when it stops feeding. It travels in schools at depths between about 50 m (165 ft) and the surface, and its average weight is 1.36 kg (3 lb) with a maximum of around 8.6 kg (19 lb).

DISTRIBUTION
Pacific bonito: Pacific Ocean.
Twaite shad and allis shad: western European waters.
American shad: from about Newfoundland to northern Florida; Siberia to Mexico.
Skipjack herring: Mississippi basin and Gulf Slope.
Atlantic bonito: Atlantic and Mediterranean.
Australian bonito: southwest Pacific and Tasman Sea.
Hickory shad: from Maine to Florida.
Alewife: Great Lakes; from Labrador to South Carolina.

AUSTRALIAN BONITO
This bonito is found in the southwest Pacific, in the waters off Norfolk Island, southeast Australia, and New Zealand. The stripes on its sides are almost horizontal, rather than oblique like those of the Atlantic and Pacific species, and they are also present along the belly. It grows to a maximum weight of about 10 kg (22 lb).

AUSTRALIAN BONITO
Sarda australis

Protruding lower jaw

HICKORY SHAD
Alosa mediocris

HICKORY SHAD
This large shad has a protruding lower jaw, a dark spot behind each gill cover, and a row of dusky blotches along each side. Its usual maximum weight is about 1.1 kg (2 lb 8 oz), but it can reach 2.27 kg (5 lb). Fish make up a large part of the diets of hickory shad and skipjack herring, so they will take a lure more readily than other North American shad.

Very large eye

ALEWIFE
Alosa pseudoharengus

ALEWIFE
The alewife can grow to 227 g (8 oz) in saltwater, but the landlocked form is much smaller. It has large eyes (greater in diameter than the length of its snout), a prominent keel, and a small, dark spot behind each gill cover. The blueback herring (*Alosa aestivalis*) is similar in size and overall appearance, but its back is bluish and its eyes are smaller.

Size comparison

Australian bonito | Atlantic bonito | Pacific bonito | American shad | Allis shad | Twaite shad | Skipjack herring | Hickory shad | Alewife

Saltwater SPECIES

SHARKS 1

The sharks are a very ancient group of fish, characterized by cartilaginous skeletons, skins covered in tiny, thornlike scales called placoid scales, five to seven gill slits, and powerful jaws equipped with rows of strong, sharp teeth. There are about 300 species, distributed widely throughout the world's seas but particularly in tropical waters, and although most are marine some enter estuaries, rivers, and creeks. They range in size from about 60 cm (2 ft) in length up to at least 18 m (60 ft); those shown here are among the smaller species, up to 3.5 m (11 ft 6 in) long.

PORBEAGLE
Lamna nasus

LEOPARD SHARK
This distinctively patterned shark occurs close inshore along the Pacific coast of the United States, and is especially common in the shallow bays of California. It is usually found in shallow, sandy-bottomed waters less than 3.7 m (12 ft) deep. Males grow to a length of 1.5 m (5 ft), and females reach 2.1 m (7 ft) and 32 kg (71 lb).

Distinctive snout

LEOPARD SHARK
Triakis semifasciata

TOPE
The tope is a member of the largest shark family, the Carcharhinidae or requiem sharks. It has a slender body and prominent snout, long pectoral fins, and a strong tail fin with a large lower lobe. It is found inshore in depths of about 3 m (10 ft) or more, and can attain a length of 1.68 m (5 ft 6 in) and a weight of 34 kg (75 lb). It feeds mainly on fish, such as cod, and also takes squid.

Large second dorsal fin

SMOOTH DOGFISH
Mustelus canis

Tope eyes
The eyes of the tope and most other requiem sharks have translucent membranes (nictitating membranes) that can be drawn across for protection.

SMOOTH DOGFISH
This very common, bottom-dwelling shark of the western Atlantic is usually found at depths of 9 to 360 m (about 30 to 1,200 ft) and will sometimes enter freshwater. It has long pectoral fins and a large second dorsal fin that is almost the same size as the first, and there is a spiracle (a round opening that is the remnant of a first gill slit) behind each eye. It grows to about 1.5 m (5 ft).

Spiracle

Dorsal spines

TOPE
Galeorhinus galeus

SPURDOG
This slender shark, which grows to 1.2 m (4 ft) and 9.5 kg (21 lb), is unusual in having a sharp spine at the leading edge of each dorsal fin. Like the tope, it has a large, strong tail, but it has no anal fin. It lives just above the bottom in depths of 10 to 200 m (about 30 to 650 ft), and it has a very varied diet consisting of schooling fish, such as herring, plus invertebrates such as squid, jellyfish, and worms.

SPURDOG
Squalus acanthias

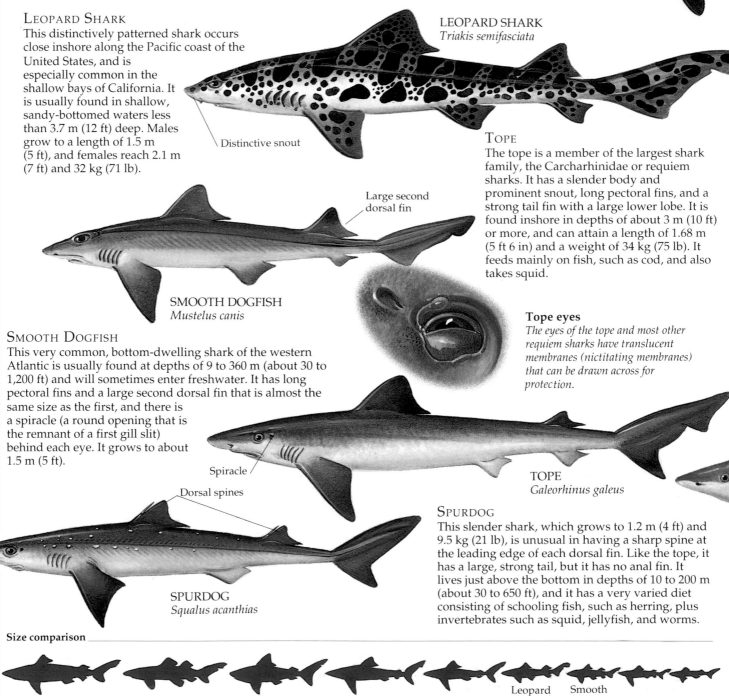

Size comparison

Bull shark   Sand tiger   Porbeagle   Spinner shark   Blacktip shark   Leopard shark   Smooth dogfish   Tope   Spurdog

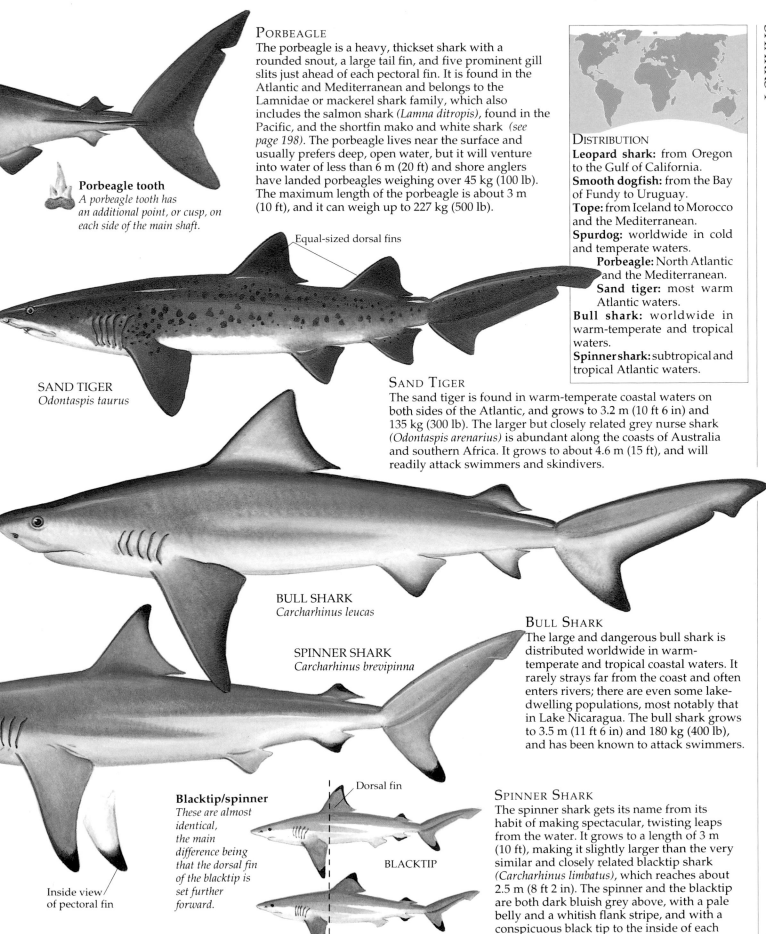

PORBEAGLE

The porbeagle is a heavy, thickset shark with a rounded snout, a large tail fin, and five prominent gill slits just ahead of each pectoral fin. It is found in the Atlantic and Mediterranean and belongs to the Lamnidae or mackerel shark family, which also includes the salmon shark (*Lamna ditropis*), found in the Pacific, and the shortfin mako and white shark *(see page 198)*. The porbeagle lives near the surface and usually prefers deep, open water, but it will venture into water of less than 6 m (20 ft) and shore anglers have landed porbeagles weighing over 45 kg (100 lb). The maximum length of the porbeagle is about 3 m (10 ft), and it can weigh up to 227 kg (500 lb).

Porbeagle tooth
A porbeagle tooth has an additional point, or cusp, on each side of the main shaft.

Equal-sized dorsal fins

SAND TIGER
Odontaspis taurus

DISTRIBUTION

Leopard shark: from Oregon to the Gulf of California.
Smooth dogfish: from the Bay of Fundy to Uruguay.
Tope: from Iceland to Morocco and the Mediterranean.
Spurdog: worldwide in cold and temperate waters.
Porbeagle: North Atlantic and the Mediterranean.
Sand tiger: most warm Atlantic waters.
Bull shark: worldwide in warm-temperate and tropical waters.
Spinner shark: subtropical and tropical Atlantic waters.

SAND TIGER

The sand tiger is found in warm-temperate coastal waters on both sides of the Atlantic, and grows to 3.2 m (10 ft 6 in) and 135 kg (300 lb). The larger but closely related grey nurse shark *(Odontaspis arenarius)* is abundant along the coasts of Australia and southern Africa. It grows to about 4.6 m (15 ft), and will readily attack swimmers and skindivers.

BULL SHARK
Carcharhinus leucas

SPINNER SHARK
Carcharhinus brevipinna

BULL SHARK

The large and dangerous bull shark is distributed worldwide in warm-temperate and tropical coastal waters. It rarely strays far from the coast and often enters rivers; there are even some lake-dwelling populations, most notably that in Lake Nicaragua. The bull shark grows to 3.5 m (11 ft 6 in) and 180 kg (400 lb), and has been known to attack swimmers.

Blacktip/spinner
These are almost identical, the main difference being that the dorsal fin of the blacktip is set further forward.

Dorsal fin

BLACKTIP

SPINNER

Inside view
of pectoral fin

SPINNER SHARK

The spinner shark gets its name from its habit of making spectacular, twisting leaps from the water. It grows to a length of 3 m (10 ft), making it slightly larger than the very similar and closely related blacktip shark *(Carcharhinus limbatus)*, which reaches about 2.5 m (8 ft 2 in). The spinner and the blacktip are both dark bluish grey above, with a pale belly and a whitish flank stripe, and with a conspicuous black tip to the inside of each pectoral fin.

SHARKS 2

The sharks shown here are representative of the larger species, and range in length from just under 4 m (13 ft) up to about 9 m (30 ft) or more. Not shown, because they are too big to be fished for, are the basking shark *(Cetorhinus maximus)* and whale shark *(Rhincodon typus)*, huge but generally placid sharks that feed mainly on plankton. The basking shark is the largest shark in temperate waters, possibly growing to 13.7 m (45 ft) and 20,000 kg (44,000 lb); the whale shark, found in tropical seas, is the world's largest fish and may exceed 15.2 m (50 ft) and 35,000 kg (77,000 lb). The largest verified specimens of these two sharks were a 12.27 m (40 ft 3 in) basking shark and a 12.65 m (41 ft 6 in) whale shark.

Eye

Blunt, very
short snout

Very long tail

THRESHER SHARK

This warmwater shark is immediately recognizable by the exceptionally long upper lobe of its tail, which may be longer than its body. Threshers are found in the open ocean at depths from the surface down to 100 m (330 ft), and they grow to about 6.1 m (20 ft) and 450 kg (1,000 lb). They hunt in packs, using their tails to stun their prey.

THRESHER SHARK
Alopias vulpinus

SHORTFIN MAKO
Isurus oxyrinchus

SHORTFIN MAKO

The shortfin mako, also known as the mako or bonito shark, is probably the fastest-swimming shark, capable of speed bursts of up to 74 km/h (46 mph). Its maximum size is about 3.8 m (12 ft 6 in) and 506 kg (1,115 lb), and it makes spectacular leaps when hooked.

**White
shark bite**
*When a white shark
bites, it opens its
huge jaws wide to
expose its razor-
sharp, serrated teeth,
which can be up to
7.6 cm (3 in) long.*

SIXGILL SHARK

This large, bulky shark is identifiable by its single dorsal fin, which is set near the tail, and the six gill slits just ahead of each pectoral fin. The sixgill is found in temperate waters and lives at or near the bottom, the young in shallow water but the adults preferring depths of 75 m (250 ft) or more. It attains a size of at least 4.9 m (16 ft) and 590 kg (1,300 lb).

FISHING NOTES

Techniques
Trolling and drift fishing are the usual forms of shark fishing, but small sharks that venture into the inshore shallows are also taken by shore anglers, including saltwater fly fishers. Take care to avoid injury when handling sharks.

Tackle
When shore fishing for shark, try a 3.4 to 3.7 m (11 to 12 ft) rod with a multiplier reel, 8.2 kg (18 lb) mono line with a wire leader, a 113 to 170 g (4 to 6 oz) weight, and hook sizes 4/0 to 6/0, or a medium to heavy

saltwater fly outfit with a 30 cm (12 in) wire trace at the end of the tippet, and flies tied on 5/0 or 6/0 hooks. For trolling and drift fishing, the tackle depends on the size of shark you expect to catch. For example, a 9.1 kg (20 lb) class outfit should suffice for small species such as spurdog, but larger fish such as blue shark, porbeagle and mako require 22.7 to 36.3 kg (50 to 80 lb) class tackle.

Bait
Strips of fresh fish (such as mackerel or pollack) for small species, whole fish for the larger ones. For fly fishing, try white streamer flies.

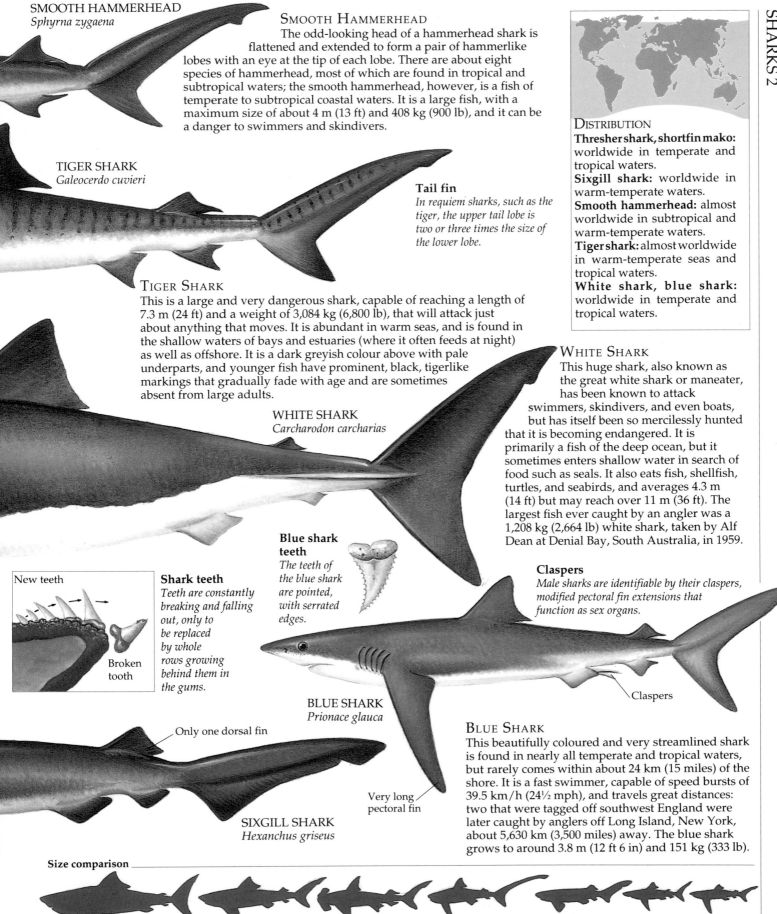

SMOOTH HAMMERHEAD
Sphyrna zygaena

SMOOTH HAMMERHEAD

The odd-looking head of a hammerhead shark is flattened and extended to form a pair of hammerlike lobes with an eye at the tip of each lobe. There are about eight species of hammerhead, most of which are found in tropical and subtropical waters; the smooth hammerhead, however, is a fish of temperate to subtropical coastal waters. It is a large fish, with a maximum size of about 4 m (13 ft) and 408 kg (900 lb), and it can be a danger to swimmers and skindivers.

DISTRIBUTION
Thresher shark, shortfin mako: worldwide in temperate and tropical waters.
Sixgill shark: worldwide in warm-temperate waters.
Smooth hammerhead: almost worldwide in subtropical and warm-temperate waters.
Tiger shark: almost worldwide in warm-temperate seas and tropical waters.
White shark, blue shark: worldwide in temperate and tropical waters.

TIGER SHARK
Galeocerdo cuvieri

Tail fin
In requiem sharks, such as the tiger, the upper tail lobe is two or three times the size of the lower lobe.

TIGER SHARK

This is a large and very dangerous shark, capable of reaching a length of 7.3 m (24 ft) and a weight of 3,084 kg (6,800 lb), that will attack just about anything that moves. It is abundant in warm seas, and is found in the shallow waters of bays and estuaries (where it often feeds at night) as well as offshore. It is a dark greyish colour above with pale underparts, and younger fish have prominent, black, tigerlike markings that gradually fade with age and are sometimes absent from large adults.

WHITE SHARK
Carcharodon carcharias

WHITE SHARK

This huge shark, also known as the great white shark or maneater, has been known to attack swimmers, skindivers, and even boats, but has itself been so mercilessly hunted that it is becoming endangered. It is primarily a fish of the deep ocean, but it sometimes enters shallow water in search of food such as seals. It also eats fish, shellfish, turtles, and seabirds, and averages 4.3 m (14 ft) but may reach over 11 m (36 ft). The largest fish ever caught by an angler was a 1,208 kg (2,664 lb) white shark, taken by Alf Dean at Denial Bay, South Australia, in 1959.

Blue shark teeth
The teeth of the blue shark are pointed, with serrated edges.

New teeth

Shark teeth
Teeth are constantly breaking and falling out, only to be replaced by whole rows growing behind them in the gums.

Broken tooth

Claspers
Male sharks are identifiable by their claspers, modified pectoral fin extensions that function as sex organs.

Claspers

BLUE SHARK
Prionace glauca

BLUE SHARK

This beautifully coloured and very streamlined shark is found in nearly all temperate and tropical waters, but rarely comes within about 24 km (15 miles) of the shore. It is a fast swimmer, capable of speed bursts of 39.5 km/h (24½ mph), and travels great distances: two that were tagged off southwest England were later caught by anglers off Long Island, New York, about 5,630 km (3,500 miles) away. The blue shark grows to around 3.8 m (12 ft 6 in) and 151 kg (333 lb).

Only one dorsal fin

Very long pectoral fin

SIXGILL SHARK
Hexanchus griseus

Size comparison

White shark   Tiger shark   Smooth hammerhead   Thresher shark   Sixgill shark   Shortfin mako   Blue shark

GROUPER

The Serranidae is a large and important family of fish, consisting of more than 375 species. These are mostly temperate and tropical marine fish, ranging in size from less than 30 cm (12 in) to about 3.7 m (12 ft), and are found near rocks, reefs, wrecks, and piers in coastal waters. The larger members of the family are robust, sharp-toothed, basslike fish, which live near the bottom and feed on fish, crustaceans, and shellfish. They tend to be solitary rather than schooling, except at spawning time, and the individuals of many species change sex as they grow: they mature and breed as females, and become males when they grow older and larger.

NASSAU GROUPER
Epinephelus striatus

YELLOWFIN GROUPER
This grouper has distinctive yellow tips to its pectoral fins, dark oval blotches on its head and body, and is speckled with small black spots. Its coloration is otherwise highly variable, but those in shallow water tend to be yellowish or green (yellow phase) and those in deep water red (red phase). Maximum weight is about 9.1 kg (20 lb).

RED PHASE

NASSAU GROUPER
The Nassau grouper is found over rocks, coral reefs, and weedbeds from shallow inshore waters out to depths of around 30 m (100 ft). Its maximum weight is about 25 kg (55 lb), and it is one of the most attractive groupers, having a variable, pale overall coloration marked with dark bars and light spots. It is an important commercial species, as are the red grouper, black grouper, and black seabass, and it fights hard when hooked.

YELLOWFIN GROUPER
Mycteroperca venenosa

FEMALE

YELLOW PHASE

BLACK SEABASS
The black seabass has an average weight of around 680 g (1 lb 8 oz) and a maximum of 3.6 kg (8 lb), but despite its relatively small size it is one of the most popular marine gamefish along the Atlantic coast of the United States. It winters offshore and moves to inshore waters in spring and summer, when it enters sounds and bays where the bottom is hard and there are abundant shellfish. It is caught by bottom fishing from anchored boats, and from piers and docks.

MALE

Three-lobed
tail fin

BLACK SEABASS
Centropristis striata

Size comparison

Jewfish   Black grouper   Red grouper   Yellowfin grouper   Nassau grouper   Black seabass

200

RED GROUPER
Epinephelus morio

RED GROUPER
The red grouper inhabits rocky reefs at depths of 24 to 120 m (80 to 400 ft), but small individuals are sometimes found near the shore in shallow water. This grouper is recognizable by its blotched, reddish coloration, its squared-off tail, and the even top edge of its first dorsal fin; the lining of its mouth is orange or deep red. It can attain a weight of 23 kg (50 lb) or more, and fights hard when hooked on light tackle.

DISTRIBUTION
Yellowfin grouper: Bermuda and Florida to Brazil.
Nassau grouper: Bermuda and North Carolina to Brazil.
Black seabass: from Maine to northeast Florida; eastern Gulf of Mexico.
Red grouper: Bermuda and Massachusetts to Brazil.
Black grouper: Bermuda and Massachusetts to Brazil.
Jewfish: Bermuda; Florida to Brazil; Pacific from the Gulf of California to Panama.

BLACK GROUPER
Mycteroperca bonaci

BLACK GROUPER
The black grouper, which can weigh over 82 kg (180 lb), has a variable overall coloration marked with dark, rectangular blotches. The name "black grouper" is sometimes also used for the warsaw grouper (*Epinephelus nigritus*), which has a uniform dark brown coloration and grows to 263 kg (580 lb).

Rounded tail fin

JEWFISH
Epinephelus itajara

JEWFISH
This huge grouper is known to reach a length of 2.4 m (8 ft) and a weight of 310 kg (680 lb), and may grow to 454 kg (1,000 lb) or more. Despite its size, it lives in shallow water – usually no deeper than 30 m (100 ft) – and is found around rocky ledges, wrecks, and pilings. It is not a hard fighter, but its size and weight, and its habit of bolting into a hole when hooked, make it difficult to land. The Queensland grouper (*Promicrops lanceolatus*), an Indo-Pacific species, is even larger and can grow to 3.7 m (12 ft) and over 500 kg (1,100 lb).

FISHING NOTES

Techniques
Bottom fishing and trolling, using natural or artificial baits, are effective methods for these species. Black seabass are also taken from jetties, docks, breakwaters, and piers on saltwater spinning gear and light, general-purpose tackle.

Tackle
For bottom fishing, use a 13.6 to 22.7 kg (30 to 50 lb) class boat rod with a 4/0 to 6/0 multiplier reel and 13.6 to 22.7 kg (30 to 50 lb) mono line; terminal tackle should be a running leger with an 85 to 227 g (3 to 8 oz) pyramid- or bomb-shaped sinker and 2/0 to 6/0 hook. For trolling, try a 36.3 kg (80 lb) class rod with a 9/0 multiplier reel, 36.3 kg (80 lb) mono line, a heavy wire leader and 10/0 hook.

Bait
Fish, squid, worms, shrimps, clams, and crab are good baits for bottom fishing. These natural baits can also be used for trolling, as can plugs, spinners, spoons, and feathers.

PORGY & SEABREAM

Porgy and seabream are among the 120 species that make up the Sparidae family. The Sparidae have a worldwide distribution in temperate and tropical waters, but are most abundant in warm coastal seas. Most are small to medium-sized fish but some are quite large; in African waters, some species of steenbras (or musselcracker), such as *Pagrus nasutus* and *Petrus repuestris*, can grow to well over 54 kg (120 lb).

RED SEABREAM

The red seabream has red fins and a reddish tinge to its silvery body, and there is a large dark spot behind each gill cover. It is found in depths of 50 to 300 m (160 to 1,000 ft), particularly near reefs and wrecks, and feeds mainly on fish but also takes shrimps, crabs, and squid. Its maximum weight is about 4.54 kg (10 lb).

BLACK SEABREAM

This seabream is silvery grey overall, with a darker back, and usually has six or seven dark vertical bars on each side. Its maximum weight is around 3.2 kg (7 lb). The gilthead (*Sparus aurata*) is somewhat similar, but has a golden stripe across its forehead.

BLACK SEABREAM
Spondyliosoma cantharus

Dark spot

RED SEABREAM
Pagellus bogaraveo

Natural food
Fish make up the bulk of the red seabream's diet, but black seabream and most species of porgy feed mainly on molluscs and crustaceans.

SCUP

This small porgy, which grows to about 1.8 kg (4 lb), is a dull silvery grey overall, often with faint dark bars on its sides and sometimes a blue stripe at the base of its dorsal fin. The front teeth are sharp and incisorlike. The closely related longspine porgy (*Stenotomus caprinus*) is found from North Carolina to Florida and in the Gulf of Mexico.

SCUP
Stenotomus chrysops

Size comparison

| Sheepshead | Jolthead porgy | Red seabream | Black seabream | Whitebone porgy | Scup |

WHITEBONE PORGY
Calamus leucosteus

Blue lines above and below eye

JOLTHEAD PORGY
Calamus bajonado

Blue line below eye

DISTRIBUTION
Red seabream: from Norway to the Mediterranean and the Canary Islands.
Black seabream: Norway to the Mediterranean and Angola.
Scup: Nova Scotia to Florida.
Whitebone porgy: North Carolina to southern Florida; Gulf of Mexico.
Sheepshead: mainland coastal waters from Nova Scotia to the Gulf of Mexico and Brazil.
Jolthead porgy: New England and Bermuda to Brazil.

WHITEBONE PORGY
The overall coloration of the whitebone porgy is a blotched, bluish silver, with small blue lines above and below each eye; its maximum weight is about 1.8 kg (4 lb). Like the jolthead porgy, the whitebone porgy is one of a number of fish of the genus *Calamus* found in western Atlantic and Caribbean waters. Others include the sheepshead porgy (*C. penna*), grass porgy (*C. arctifrons*), and saucereye porgy (*C. calamus*). The Pacific porgy (*C. brachysomus*) occurs from Baja California to Peru, and sometimes along the coast of southern California.

SHEEPSHEAD
This large porgy is silvery to yellowish white, with an olive-brown back, a dark bar across its nape, and five or six dark, slightly diagonal bars on each side. It is found close inshore, often in the brackish zones of estuaries, and uses its strong, flat teeth to crush molluscs and crabs and scrape barnacles from rocks and pilings. Its maximum weight is about 9.1 kg (20 lb). The red porgy (*Pagrus pagrus*) reaches a similar size and is found in relatively deep waters from New York to Argentina.

JOLTHEAD PORGY
The jolthead porgy gets its name from its habit of using its head to dislodge molluscs from rocks. Its body is a metallic, silvery yellow with bluish overtones; there is a blue line below each eye, and an orange patch at each corner of the mouth. The maximum weight of the jolthead porgy is about 3.6 kg (8 lb), and its flesh is good to eat but may cause ciguatera poisoning (*see page 164*).

SHEEPSHEAD
Archosargus probatocephalus

FISHING NOTES

Techniques
These species are taken by bottom fishing and wreck fishing.

Tackle
Use a 5.4 to 9.1 kg (12 to 20 lb) class boat rod with a multiplier reel, 5.4 to 9.1 kg (12 to 20 lb) mono line, a 2.4 m (8 ft) single-hook leader or a two-hook paternoster rig, and hook sizes from 6 to 2/0.

Bait
In general, porgy do not readily take artificial lures. Black and red seabream can be taken on mackerel feathers lowered to the bottom and retrieved in a jerky fashion, but, like porgy, they are best fished for with cut or whole natural baits. These include crab, shrimps, mussels, clams, worms, and sandeels, and strips of mackerel, cuttlefish, squid or octopus.

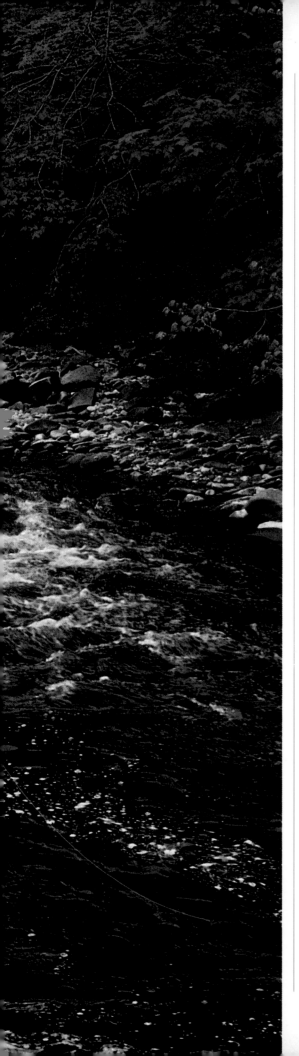

TECHNIQUES

THE BASIC TECHNIQUES of angling are easy to learn, but you could spend a lifetime and more mastering all the subtleties of any particular style. As a result, many experienced anglers tend to concentrate on one type of fishing, for example fly fishing, or on fishing for one particular species, such as bass or carp. While undoubtedly deriving great pleasure and satisfaction from their specialization, such anglers also deny themselves the variety and enjoyment offered by other kinds of fishing.

The predominant techniques used in a particular area depend as much, if not more, on the fish species sought after as on local custom and practice. For example, where the major freshwater quarry fish are predatory species, as is the case in much of North America, most fishing will be with artificial lures. But in parts of the world where non-predatory species provide the bulk of freshwater sport, as they do in Europe, the emphasis will be on fishing with hookbaits. This chapter covers the basic techniques of freshwater and saltwater angling, from pole fishing and legering to spinning and fly fishing, and from surfcasting and inshore boat fishing to big-game fishing. It also gives advice on setting up your tackle, and shows you how to tie the basic knots that join lines to reels, hooks and swivels to lines, and leaders to fly lines.

DEVELOPING SKILLS
Making the transition from hesitant beginner to skilled, confident, successful angler takes dedication and practice.

SETTING UP REELS

For a reel to work at its optimum efficiency, the line must be wound onto it properly and the spool must be neither underfilled nor overfilled. When loading a reel with line, it is also worth giving some thought to how you are going to use it. For example, many fixed-spool reel spools are deep with a big line capacity, but your style of fishing might require only a small proportion of the line to leave the reel. So instead of loading the spool with many hundreds of metres of high-quality and expensive mono, and actually using only, say, about a third of it, half-fill the spool with cheap nylon or even string and then attach a suitable length of "working line" on top.

FIXED-SPOOL & MULTIPLIER REELS

When loading these, it is important to wind the line on correctly and fill the spool to the correct level and line profile (the shape the wound line forms on the spool). Incorrect winding twists the line, which can reduce casting distance and cause line tangles. To load a fixed-spool reel, mount the spool of line in a spool holder and position it at right-angles to the front of the reel. The coils of line should leave the spool in the same direction as the bale arm of the reel rotates. When loading a multiplier, align the spool and reel so that the line runs straight from one to the other.

Spool

Overhand knot

REEL KNOT
Wet both knots to avoid damage and improve binding before pulling tight.

FIXED-SPOOL REEL
Position the reel and line spool as shown, so that coils of line unwind from the spool and wind onto the reel in the same direction, without twisting.

MULTIPLIER REEL
Position the line spool in front of the reel and in the same plane, so that the line runs straight off the spool onto the reel.

Filling a multiplier reel
In general, the spool of a multiplier should be filled with line to within around 2 mm (about $\frac{1}{16}$ in) of the flanges. However, some multipliers run better when slightly underfilled, but the only way to determine the optimum line level of a particular reel is by trial and error.

A level spread of line across the spool is vital if good casting distance is to be achieved, and to avoid problems such as rough running and vibration during casting. Although level wind mechanisms lay line evenly across the spool, they tend to feed the line on in a criss-cross fashion rather than in tight, closely packed turns. This can be a disadvantage in long-range fishing because it reduces the line capacity of the spool.

EVEN LOADING
An even spread of line will ensure that the reel runs smoothly. If the line profile is convex, concave, or irregular, it can throw the spool out of balance and cause wobbling or vibration during casting.

CORRECT LEVEL
When you find the line level that best suits your reel, mark it on the spool with a small dab of white enamel paint. This mark will show you how far to fill the spool when you load a new line.

Filling a fixed-spool reel
The line profile of a correctly filled fixed-spool reel is a smooth cone, tapering gently from the back of the spool to the front. The spool is full when the line at the front is around 2 mm (about $\frac{1}{16}$ in) below the lip. This ensures that the line will flow freely over the lip during casting, but will not fall off in coils and tangle.

CORRECT PROFILE

Poor line profile
Overfilling the spool will produce a convex line profile, and create terrible problems during casting because coils of line will fall off and tangle. Underfilling limits casting distance by increasing the angle (and thus the friction) between line and the lip of the spool.

CONVEX PROFILE

Profile correction
A poor line profile, such as this concave shape, can be corrected by winding on some of the line by hand in the opposite profile to that produced by the reel. Then, when the reel is about a third filled by this manner, wind on the rest of the line by turning the reel handle.

CONCAVE PROFILE

LOADING A FLY REEL

The best way to load a fly reel is to use a linewinder, but if you do not have one, you will need a second, similarly sized reel. Wind the fly line onto the second reel, join the backing line to it, wind the backing onto the reel until it is full, and cut it to length. Then take the first reel, tie the free end of the backing line to it, and wind on the backing and fly line.

1 When using a linewinder, first wind the fly line onto the empty reel.

2 Next, wind on backing until reel is full. Cut to length, then wind the backing from the reel onto one side of the linewinder, and the fly line onto the other.

1

2

3

3 Tie the end of the backing to the reel, wind it on, and join the fly line to it. Wind the fly line on top of the backing.

4 Slightly underfill the reel: when in use the line will not wind on as tightly as it does when you load it on at home.

4

JOINING BACKING TO FLY LINE

Backing is made of materials such as braided Terylene, braided monofilament, and solid monofilament, both round and flattened. Joining braided backing to a fly line is easy, because it is hollow and the fly line is pushed up inside it and held in position with a sleeve. Solid mono should be tied to the fly line, using a knot such as the needle knot shown here. The flattened type must first be tapered to make it thin enough to go through the needle hole.

Braided mono to fly line

1 Use a looped length of mono to pull the braided line through a 12 mm (½ in) length of braid sleeve.

2 Open up the hollow centre of the braid with a needle. Touch the braid ends lightly with a flame to prevent fraying.

3 Insert the fly line tip into the hollow braid. Work the fly line into the braid a little at a time.

4 With 5 cm (2 in) of fly line inside the braid, slide the sleeve up the line to just overlap the braid; glue it in place.

Solid mono to fly line

1 Push a needle into the end of the fly line and out through the side 6 mm (¼ in) from the tip. Heat needle until line starts to bend.

2 Remove needle when cool. Thread the mono through the fly line and five or six times around it. Bring end back and hold against line.

3 Unwind all the mono turns by winding the long loops in the direction shown, creating new, tight turns that trap the loose end.

4 Maintain grip on knot. Gently tighten by pulling alternately at points A and B. When knot is firm, pull mono tight.

LEADER TO FLY LINE

Some fly lines are fitted with braided loops at their tips to which leaders can be attached quickly and easily. You can also buy ready-made loops for fixing to lines, or you can make your own from short lengths of braided mono.

Forming a braid loop

1 Push a large-eyed needle 2.5 cm (1 in) into the braid. Thread the braid through the needle eye.

2 Pull needle through braid until loose end emerges. Use a matchstick to keep the loop from closing completely.

3 Adjust the loop to the required size and trim the loose end flush. Pull the loose end back inside the braid.

4 Secure the loop with a few drops of a waterproof superglue such as Permabond 102 or Minocon.

BASIC KNOTS

All anglers should learn how to tie secure knots. This is because there will usually be at least two knots in a fishing rig (one joining the line to the reel or pole, the other joining the hook or lure to the line) and every knot is a potential weak point. Before tightening a knot, wet it with water to reduce the friction that can damage the line, and when attaching a hook, lure, or fly to a line be careful not to impale a finger on the hook point. Trim all loose ends so that they do not snag in the rod rings.

KNOTS FOR JOINING LINE TO TACKLE

Blood knot

1 Pass the free end of the line through the eye of the hook.

2 Take the free end back and tuck it under the line.

3 Bring the end back over the line to form a loop.

4 Continue looping the end around the line, making about four turns.

5 Bring the end back and pass it between the eye and the first loop.

 6 Pull tight and trim off the end.

Spade end whip

1 Double the end of the line along the hook shank. Loop free end around both line and hook.

2 Make six turns with the free end and then pass it through the doubled line loop.

3 Carefully pull the knot tight and trim off the end.

Domhof knot (uni knot)

1 Pass the line through the eye of the hook and form a large loop alongside the hook shank.

2 Loop the free end of the line several times around the hook and the upper part of the loop, binding the two together. Then pass the end out through the loop and pull tight. Trim off the end.

Spool knot

This simple knot is the most effective way to tie the line to the reel spool.

Palomar knot

1 To join a swivel (or a lure or large hook) to a line, double the end of the line and pass it through the eye.

2 Tie a single overhand knot in the doubled line.

3 Pull the looped end over the swivel or hook.

4 Pull knot tight and trim off end.

KNOTS FOR FORMING LOOPS

Double overhand loop (surgeon's end loop)

1 Double the end of the line back against itself.

2 Tie an overhand knot in the doubled line.

3 Tuck the doubled end through the loop again.

4 Pull the knot tight and trim off the end.

Blood bight

1 Double the end of the line back against itself.

2 Turn the doubled end once around the line.

3 Pass the looped end back through the turn.

4 Pull the knot tight and trim off the end.

KNOTS FOR JOINING LINES

Water knot (surgeon's knot)

1 Place the ends of the two lines alongside each other, overlapping by about 15 cm (6 in).

2 Hold the two lines together and form them into a wide loop.

3 Keeping the two lines together, pass the ends through the loop four times.

4 Pull the lines to tighten the loop into a knot, and trim ends.

Blood knot

1 Overlap the ends of the two lines. Take one end and twist it four times around the other line. Then bring it back and pass it between the two lines.

2 Repeat with the other free end, taking care that the first stage does not unravel.

3 Wet the knot to lubricate it, then pull it tight and trim off the ends.

209

PLAYING & LANDING

Playing a hooked fish successfully requires sound knowledge of your tackle, which must be well balanced in all respects. Before you start, set the reel clutch to slip when the rod has reached its "fighting curve", and check the setting occasionally through the day because use and temperature changes can affect the setting. The techniques shown here can be adapted directly for boat and seashore fishing, but fly fishing employs a different style of line control. When playing a fish on a fly reel, either use your free hand to pay out line under tension and to recover it, allowing it to fall in loose coils, or release line from the reel against the check mechanism or finger pressure on the spool rim, and recover it by winding in.

REEL CONTROL

When using a fixed-spool reel, engage the anti-reverse and brake the spool with your finger, or, on reels that allow it, let the handle backwind against pressure on the pick-up carrier base. With a multiplier, control the spool with your thumb.

Control with anti-reverse "on"

Backwinding (anti-reverse "off")

Thumb pressure control

PLAYING

When a fish runs, apply firm pressure by keeping the rod well up, and if necessary increase drag by using one of the reel control methods. When the rod is in this position it is well placed to absorb any lunges the fish may make. Never allow the rod to point down the line, or a break is almost certain. Do not be afraid to let a fish run, because that is what tires it.

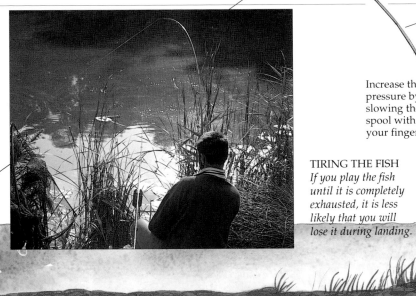

Keep the rod well up to exert maximum pressure on a running fish

Increase the pressure by slowing the spool with your finger

TIRING THE FISH
If you play the fish until it is completely exhausted, it is less likely that you will lose it during landing.

Using sidestrain

To turn a fish away from snags, lower the rod so that it is parallel to the surface and pointing in the direction of the run (but not down the line). In one firm movement, sweep the rod around hard in the opposite direction. This knocks the fish off balance, forcing it to turn towards the pull. Repeat until under control.

REPEATING SIDESTRAIN (*left*)
Sidestrain must be applied repeatedly because a hooked fish will make many runs.

Lay the rod hard over to turn the fish

Stop the spool with finger pressure

Fish is knocked off balance and turned from snags

GAINING LINE
Each time you pump the rod you wind in more line, bringing the fish progressively closer to the net.

Pumping
When the fish reaches the end of a run and is tiring, lower the rod tip while reeling in line to maintain tension. With the rod at about 30°, clamp the spool to prevent line being drawn off and raise the rod smoothly to about 70°. This is "pumping". Hold the rod in this position to see if the fish will run again, and if it does not, repeat.

Keep the rod bent under tension and do not allow slack line between rod and fish

Alternately lower and raise the rod

Take your finger off the spool as you lower the rod and recover line. Stop the spool with finger pressure again when you raise the rod to "pump"

Draw the fish nearer with each successive pump

LANDING

Beaching, tailing, lipping, netting, and even gaffing are all methods of landing fish, but not all are equally suitable. Tailing is an ideal method for Atlantic salmon but will end in disaster with sea trout. Lipping is suitable for the less "toothy" species. Beaching removes mucus from the scales, leaving a fish vulnerable to infection, so is not suitable if the fish is to be released. Gaffing is banned in many areas, because a mistimed stroke can allow a fish to escape but leave it badly injured and doomed to a painful death.

LIPPING A FISH
Grip the lower lip gently between your thumb and forefinger.

Lipping
A played-out fish can be lifted from the water to be unhooked, or held in the water for unhooking, by gripping its lower lip firmly but gently between thumb and forefinger. This is not suitable for fish with sharp teeth, such as pike. For these, gently slip the fingers of a gloved hand into one gill casing, clamp down with your thumb, and carefully lift the fish out or unhook it in the water.

NETTING FROM THE BANK
Keep the net low in the water so that you do not drag the fish against the rim. If the fish is heavy, lift the net out of the water by grasping the rim; lifting it by the handle could bend the rim.

Do not take the rod too far back or you will lose tension on the line

Stop the spool with finger pressure as you raise the rod to draw the fish in; release the spool if the fish makes a sudden lunge

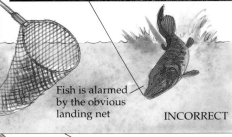

Fish is alarmed by the obvious landing net

INCORRECT

NETTING
Never attempt to net a lively fish by lunging wildly at it. When the fish is played out, it should be drawn over a fully submerged net with a single, smooth action of the rod.

Net rim is well submerged

A played-out fish will turn on its side

CORRECT

Draw the played-out fish to the net

BASIC CASTING

Over the years, the design and construction of both fixed-spool and multiplier reels have been greatly improved to provide trouble-free casting and fishing for everyone. However, to get the best from any reel, you must learn how to cast properly, and practise your casting until you have eliminated any faults in your technique. Skill is more important than strength, and when you acquire it, you will be able to place your baits where you want them with consistent accuracy. The basic technique shown here is that of casting a lure with a fixed-spool reel, but it can also be used for casting float and leger rigs and, with the appropriate reel and line control methods, with multiplier and closed-face reels. The techniques of fly casting and surfcasting are different, and details of these are given on pages 232–35 and 250–51 respectively.

REEL CONTROL

FIXED-SPOOL REEL

First open the bale arm. Then hook the line over the pad of the index finger of your rod hand, to take the weight of the terminal tackle and prevent it from stripping line from the reel. For extra support, press the line against the rod handle.

MULTIPLIER/BAITCASTER

With a multiplier, clamp the thumb of your rod hand hard on the spool to stop it turning, and put the reel into free-spool mode. With most baitcasters, clamping your thumb onto the spool depresses a bar that disengages it.

CLOSED-FACE/SPINCASTER

On these reels, the line passes through a hole or slot in the front casing and is guided onto the fixed spool by a steel pin. When you want to release the line at the end of a cast, you simply press a button on the reel to retract the pin.

THE OVERHEAD CAST

With the bale arm open, support the line on your index finger with the lure about 30 to 45 cm (12 to 18 in) below the rod tip. Hold the rod at the 2.00 position and in line with the spot at which you want the lure to land (A).

Lift the rod briskly but smoothly towards the 12.00 position by raising your forearm and cocking your wrist back (B). At the start of the lift, the inertia of the rod tip and the weight of the lure will cause the tip to droop.

Stop the rod at the 12.00 position (C). The tip will straighten, and then bend behind you as it is pulled back by the still-travelling lure. You will feel a pull on the rod tip as the lure reaches the limit of its travel.

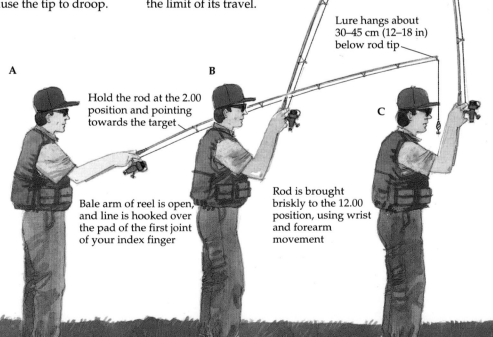

Rod tip flexes under its own inertia and the weight of the lure

Rod is stopped at the 12.00 position and, without pause, punched forward

Lure hangs about 30–45 cm (12–18 in) below rod tip

Hold the rod at the 2.00 position and pointing towards the target

Bale arm of reel is open, and line is hooked over the pad of the first joint of your index finger

Rod is brought briskly to the 12.00 position, using wrist and forearm movement

A   B   C

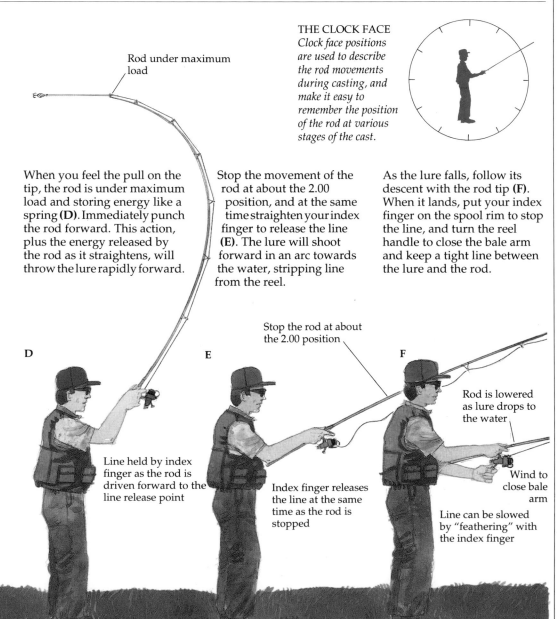

LURE FLIGHT

When casting, always pick a target spot in the swim and aim to land your lure (or other terminal tackle) in it. After releasing the line, follow the path of the lure with the rod tip so that the line flows freely through the tip ring. The lure should travel in a gentle arc towards the water.

COMMON CASTING FAULTS

The lure overshoots
• Too much power in the cast
• Line release not slowed by feathering the spool

The lure falls short
• Lure too light
• Line was released too early during the cast
• Rod held too high after line was released

The lure lands too hard
• Lure was released with the rod at too low an angle and failed to describe a gentle arc through the air

The cast is inaccurate
• The lure went off course because rod was allowed to move from side to side as the forward cast was made

Rod under maximum load

THE CLOCK FACE
Clock face positions are used to describe the rod movements during casting, and make it easy to remember the position of the rod at various stages of the cast.

When you feel the pull on the tip, the rod is under maximum load and storing energy like a spring **(D)**. Immediately punch the rod forward. This action, plus the energy released by the rod as it straightens, will throw the lure rapidly forward.

Stop the movement of the rod at about the 2.00 position, and at the same time straighten your index finger to release the line **(E)**. The lure will shoot forward in an arc towards the water, stripping line from the reel.

As the lure falls, follow its descent with the rod tip **(F)**. When it lands, put your index finger on the spool rim to stop the line, and turn the reel handle to close the bale arm and keep a tight line between the lure and the rod.

Stop the rod at about the 2.00 position

D

E

F

Rod is lowered as lure drops to the water

Line held by index finger as the rod is driven forward to the line release point

Index finger releases the line at the same time as the rod is stopped

Wind to close bale arm

Line can be slowed by "feathering" with the index finger

LINE CONTROL

FIXED-SPOOL REEL

To prevent the lure from overshooting the target, and to achieve a gentle landing, slow its flight by gently dabbing or touching the lip of the spool with the tip of your index finger. This "feathering" acts as a brake on the line.

MULTIPLIER/BAITCASTER

To slow down a bait fished on a multiplier or baitcaster, apply gentle thumb pressure to the revolving spool (but beware of friction burns). Overruns are rare with modern reels because they have magnetic braking systems.

CLOSED-FACE/SPINCASTER

Line control with these reels can be difficult, because the spool is shrouded and finger pressure on the lip is not possible. Slow the line by gently squeezing it between the index finger and thumb of your free hand as it emerges from the casing.

LURE FISHING – SPINNING

The relative ease of use of spinning tackle accounts for spinning being one of the most popular forms of fishing worldwide. When correctly loaded with a full spool of line, spinning reels allow long, effortless casts to be made and the angler often has to do no more than crank the handle to make the lure fish attractively. Obviously, the skilled practitioner will outfish the tyro, but spinning offers the beginner the best chance of comparatively easy success. Spinners are so termed because at least part of the lure revolves. Usually, there is a rotating blade that is separate from the body, as in standard spinners, spinnerbaits, and buzzbaits, but sometimes the whole lure rotates, as is the case in the Devon minnow and similar lures. Spinners attract fish by visual stimulus and by creating vibrations that act on the fish's lateral lines; if used correctly, they will appeal to any predatory fish.

ANTI-KINK DEVICES

The keel effect of an anti-kink vane or weight between the main line and trace helps to reduce line twist. An anti-kink weight should be fitted immediately above the swivel for maximum effect, but weights should not be used if they interfere with the action of a lure.

PLASTIC ANTI-KINK VANES

SPIRAL WEIGHT

HILLMAN WEIGHT

WYE WEIGHT

STANDARD SPINNERS

The most common type, the clevis, has a blade mounted on a shaft via a clevis (link). Another type, the sonic, has a blade mounted directly over the shaft. A standard spinner must be retrieved to make the blade rotate in stillwater, but in running water the current works the blade. Fish upstream in fast water, because fishing downstream makes the lure swim too shallow. In slow water, fish downstream because casting upstream allows the lure to sink too quickly.

CLEVIS TYPE

SONIC TYPE

Blade shapes and actions
The shape and thickness of a spinner blade affects the action of the lure. The high water resistance of a broad blade makes it ideal for stillwaters and slow streams, but in fast water it will rise to the surface. A thin blade has less resistance and can be fished in fast water without skating on the surface.

1 2
3 4
5 6
7 8

KEY TO BLADES
1 Indiana; 2 French;
3 Colorado; 4 Fluted;
5 In-line; 6 Willowleaf;
7 Ripple; 8 June Bug.

UPSTREAM SPINNING

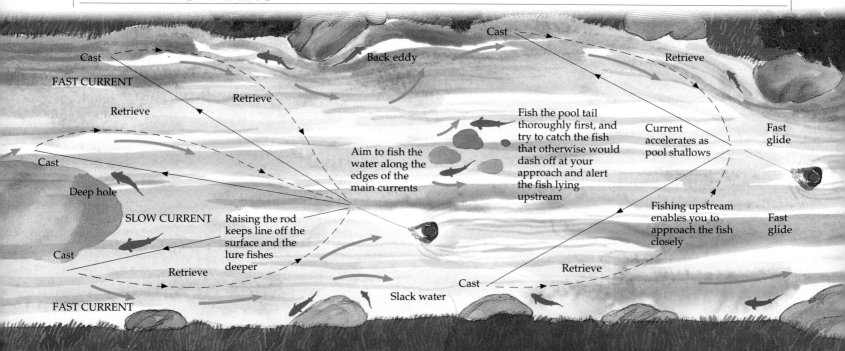

Cast

FAST CURRENT

Retrieve

Cast

Deep hole

SLOW CURRENT

Cast

Retrieve

FAST CURRENT

Back eddy

Retrieve

Aim to fish the water along the edges of the main currents

Raising the rod keeps line off the surface and the lure fishes deeper

Slack water

Cast

Fish the pool tail thoroughly first, and try to catch the fish that otherwise would dash off at your approach and alert the fish lying upstream

Cast

Retrieve

Retrieve

Current accelerates as pool shallows

Fishing upstream enables you to approach the fish closely

Cast

Fast glide

Fast glide

BUOYANT SPINNERS

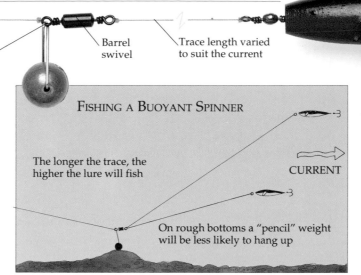

Main line / Weight is joined directly to swivel / Barrel swivel / Trace length varied to suit the current / Buoyant lure

In very cold water, when the fish are lethargic and lying deep, fish the lure slowly and close to the bottom. It is not possible to fish a heavy lure slowly enough without snagging, and the solution is to use a buoyant lure sunk by a suitable weight. By varying the trace length to suit the current, you can work the lure at the fish's eye level.

FISHING A BUOYANT SPINNER

The longer the trace, the higher the lure will fish

CURRENT

On rough bottoms a "pencil" weight will be less likely to hang up

COLDWATER SPINNING
A slow retrieve is vital in cold water, and a sunk buoyant lure fishes slowly without snagging.

SPINNERBAITS & BUZZBAITS

The most obvious difference between a spinnerbait and a buzzbait is in the blade. A spinnerbait has a fluttering blade – such as a broad, teardrop-shaped Colorado or Indiana, or a narrow, elliptical willowleaf – while the buzzbait has a single or double buzzblade rotating on a shaft. The buzzbait is designed solely for surface fishing, where its blade causes noisy, splashy disturbance. This makes it an excellent lure for weedy shallows or turbid water; vary the retrieve until successful. Twin-bladed lures, which create even more disturbance, are ideal for slow retrieves. Spinnerbaits are more versatile and can be fished at all speeds and from the surface to the bottom, or even jigged vertically around cover. Tipping the hooks of Indiana and willowleaf spinners with worms, minnows, or strips of pork rind can improve their success rate.

SUMMER SPINNING
In hot, sunny weather, when fish seek the shade of weedbeds and brush, buzzbaits are excellent lures for drawing them from their cover.

DOWNSTREAM SPINNING

Cast / Lure's path / Trailing branches

AREA 1 / AREA 2 / AREA 3

Heavy lure / Medium lure / Light lure

Retrieve / Retrieve / Retrieve

By using light lures it will be possible to fish downstream beneath trailing branches before snagging bottom

Cast at a shallower angle to avoid the lure fishing too quickly in fast water

SLOW CURRENT

Slack water

Cast squarer across current in slow water

Fast shallows

Cast / Cast

Search the river in a series of arcs as you wade downstream

Retrieve

Fast shallows

Lure's path

Lure's path

Cast / Cast

LURE FISHING – SPOONS

Spoons can be divided into the broad categories of trolling spoons and casting spoons. The trolling spoons are generally too thin to be cast far and their use is restricted to trolling from a moving boat. Casting spoons can be either of the weedless or non-weedless types, the former having hooks with nylon or metal weedguards that prevent them from snagging on weeds, submerged brush, or other aquatic debris.

A spoon's action depends on its shape, weight, and the speed of the retrieval. Deeply concave spoons wobble more than shallow ones, while light spoons have more action than heavy ones of similar size. Use light, thin spoons in shallow water or the top layers of a lake, and heavy, thick models in deep water. Each spoon has an optimum retrieve rate that imparts the most enticing action, and this can be found by trial and error.

SPOON-FISHING TACKLE

The most suitable tackle for spoon fishing is a light spinning rod and a fixed-spool reel, or a medium baitcasting rod and a multiplier reel, plus mono line with a short wire trace if necessary. There is no need for a sensitive rod, because bite indication is never a problem when fishing artificial lures. Always attach the spoon to the line or trace with a good swivel, because tying the line direct to the attachment hole of the spoon can interfere with its action, as can adding weight to the rig. In addition, line twist can be severe with some types of spoon. Fit a rounded snap swivel into the attachment hole and join the line to it.

ABU TOBY SPOONS

Additional split ring to reduce leverage

IMPROVED HOOKING
Abu Toby spoons are fine attractors, but do not always hook well, perhaps because the lever effect of such long spoons hinders the setting of the hooks. Two effective remedies to this problem are shown here.

Copper wire hook link pulls free on strike

Wire or mono hook link attached to split ring

TANDEM SWIVELS

Ball-bearing swivels

Split-ring connection

Swivels 45 cm (18 in) above lure

TANDEM SWIVELS
Two ball-bearing swivels joined by a split ring, about 45 cm (18 in) from the spoon, will virtually eliminate line twist.

CASTING PATTERNS

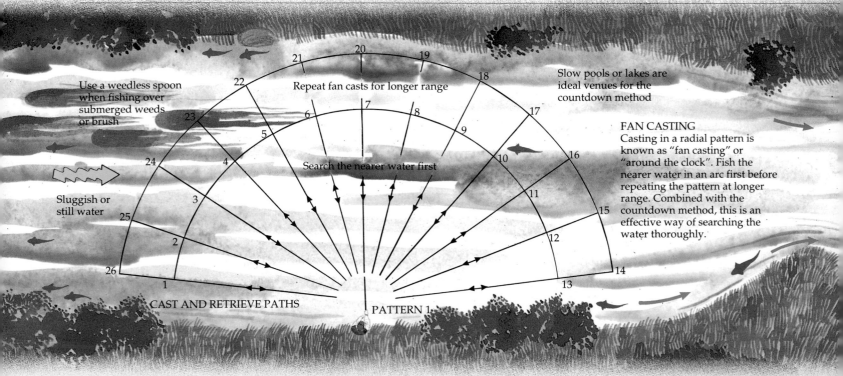

Use a weedless spoon when fishing over submerged weeds or brush

Sluggish or still water

Repeat fan casts for longer range

Search the nearer water first

CAST AND RETRIEVE PATHS

PATTERN 1

Slow pools or lakes are ideal venues for the countdown method

FAN CASTING
Casting in a radial pattern is known as "fan casting" or "around the clock". Fish the nearer water in an arc first before repeating the pattern at longer range. Combined with the countdown method, this is an effective way of searching the water thoroughly.

SPOON-FISHING TECHNIQUES

In lakes, the countdown method gives consistent fishing depth if the retrieve rate is constant, but rivers currents will affect the spoon's depth. Retrieve a spoon cast upstream quicker than one cast downstream because it will sink deeper, travelling with the flow. Use light spoons for upstream casting and for shallow or slowly retrieved downstream work. Heavy spoons are good when cast downstream in fast water or upstream in slow pools.

The countdown method

This helps you to find, and fish at, the feeding depth of your quarry. Cast the spoon out, allow it to sink, and count the number of seconds that pass until it hits bottom. Then retrieve steadily. If it reaches bottom on a count of, say, 10, and you get no strikes on the retrieve, on the next cast retrieve after a count of 8. Reduce the count by 2 on each subsequent cast until a fish strikes. Repeat the successful count to fish the taking zone.

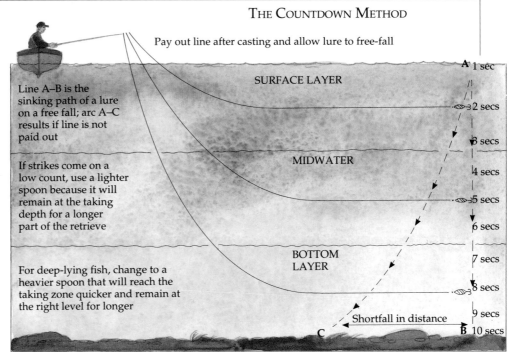

THE COUNTDOWN METHOD

Pay out line after casting and allow lure to free-fall

Line A–B is the sinking path of a lure on a free fall; arc A–C results if line is not paid out

If strikes come on a low count, use a lighter spoon because it will remain at the taking depth for a longer part of the retrieve

For deep-lying fish, change to a heavier spoon that will reach the taking zone quicker and remain at the right level for longer

SURFACE LAYER

MIDWATER

BOTTOM LAYER

Shortfall in distance

A 1 sec
2 secs
3 secs
4 secs
5 secs
6 secs
7 secs
8 secs
9 secs
C B 10 secs

LINE CONTROL

Cast

Between A and B, the lure sinks until current bellies line

A   B

Lowering the rod tip after casting across the river allows current to grip the line and prevents the lure from sinking deep

Path of lure

Faster surface current causes line to belly

CURRENT

Rod held low

Cast

C

Path of lure

A lure cast across the current runs deeper when the rod is held high, and the lure's path from C to D is more controlled

Rod held high

D

Line control

When fishing upstream, holding the rod tip high lifts the spoon in the water, while keeping it low allows the spoon to sink. This is most obvious with a short line. When casting across the flow, however, current drag on the line holds the spoon up while a high rod allows it to sink. This effect decreases the more downstream you cast, until the upstream rule applies.

Thick spoon cast upstream

Cast

Path of lure

Current eases as the river broadens

Path of lure

Downstream belly in line

Cast

DEEP-WATER CAST
In a deep stream with a strong current, use a thick spoon cast upstream. Reel in to keep the line just taut as you follow the spoon around with the rod tip held high.

ACCELERATION
Sometimes a belly in the line can be used to your advantage. Sudden acceleration of the spoon when the belly drags it can prompt a fish to strike at it.

Path of lure

SQUARE CAST
The squarer the cast the deeper the spoon will sink, provided the rod tip is held high and the line is off the surface.

Strong, deep current

Rod follows the spoon on its downstream path

Match weight of spoon to strength of current

A light spoon can be held fluttering over a likely lie

Back eddy

PATTERN 2

With the spoon downstream, lower the rod tip and retrieve

PATTERN 3

Lure retrieve path

Lure retrieve path

LURE FISHING – PLUGS

Within the ranks of what we term "plugs" are lures for fishing at all levels, from the surface to the bottom, and at all speeds. As with all artificial lure fishing, matching the lure to the quarry and the conditions is vital. In general, the smaller the quarry is, the smaller the lure should be: a 30 cm (12 in) lure might be none too large for a pike but it would not be effective for trout. Fishing cold or muddy water necessitates getting the lure down to eyeball level, and in such conditions the first choice of lure would be a vibrating plug or a deep diver, whereas in warmer water, where predatory fish are more alert, a quickly retrieved, shallow-diving crankbait or surface lure is called for.

THE OPEN LOOP

Open-looped knot

A split ring, link swivel, or tight knot can adversely affect a lure's action. Tying the lure to the line with an open-looped knot allows it to swing freely.

SURFACE LURE TECHNIQUES

Surface lures are at their most effective in shallow water, where fish lying near the bottom are not too far away to be attracted by them. The water should also be calm, because surface choppiness can affect their action. A propbait can be cast into small gaps in surface weed and then twitched back on a slack line or retrieved steadily, in which case the action of the propeller will cause more disturbance than is achieved by most surface plugs. To prevent the nose dipping below the surface and spoiling the action, tie the lure direct to the line or trace without a snap or swivel. Crawler-type lures with projecting arms or wide, scooped faceplates fish best over shallow water on a moderate retrieve: vary the retrieve until the best action is achieved. The popper or chugger surface lures have a concave face that makes a popping sound on a short, twitched retrieve, although when fished into small openings in weedbeds they are often taken when stationary. Stickbaits are the best surface lures for bringing fish up from the depths, and the basic method of retrieve for these is known as "walking the dog".

Minnow plugs
Drifting a floating minnow plug downstream allows you to fish at far greater range than you could cast such a light lure. For bankside lies, drift the lure down past the fish. When you stop the line, the lure will dive to about 30 cm (12 in), depending on the speed of the current, and you can then bring it back upstream through the lie. From midriver, fish the lure back in a series of arcs by swinging the rod from side to side during the retrieve.

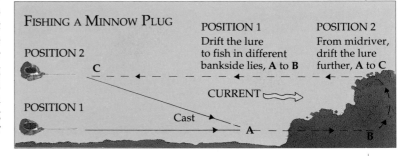

FISHING A MINNOW PLUG

POSITION 2

POSITION 1

C

POSITION 1

Cast

A

POSITION 1
Drift the lure to fish in different bankside lies, **A** to **B**

POSITION 2
From midriver, drift the lure further, **A** to **C**

CURRENT

B

PLUG FISHING METHODS

Stickbaits
Cast out a stickbait, jerk the rod tip vertically, then let the line go slack, and the lure will slip to one side. Repeat the action and the lure will dodge to the other side. This is known as "walking the dog". Fast jerks without letting the line go slack result in the lure moving to one side only. A fast, tip-actioned rod is best for this technique, and because stickbaits float it is an ideal method over submerged weeds or brush.

STICKBAITS
These are effective lures for most gamefish.

WALKING THE DOG

Cast

For a zigzag retrieve path alternate left and right jerks

Consecutive jerks make the lure veer off to one side

Jerk rod alternately left and right

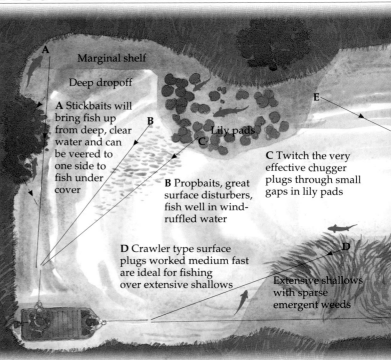

Marginal shelf

Deep dropoff

A Stickbaits will bring fish up from deep, clear water and can be veered to one side to fish under cover

Lily pads

B Propbaits, great surface disturbers, fish well in wind-ruffled water

C Twitch the very effective chugger plugs through small gaps in lily pads

D Crawler type surface plugs worked medium fast are ideal for fishing over extensive shallows

Extensive shallows with sparse emergent weeds

CRANKBAIT TECHNIQUES

Crankbaits, which are plugs with lips that cause them to dive to a greater or lesser degree, are a very useful group of lures. Some are sinking plugs, made in a variety of densities to fish at different depths, while others float at rest and dive when retrieved. Try out your crankbaits in deep, clear water to find their approximate maximum working depths, and use an indelible felt-tip pen to mark each lure with its depth. When fishing, choose the lure to suit the water. Fishing shallow water calls for a shallow-diving lure, while a sinking deep-diver is needed to fish deep holes. To attain maximum depth, make a long cast and keep the rod tip low on the retrieve. Raising the tip lifts the lure in the water, as does using too thick a line. Generally, in water temperatures above about 16°C (60°F), predators are more active and willing to hit a lure fished quickly, while in cold or dirty water they are lethargic and more likely to be tempted by a slowly moving crankbait. In cold water, bumping bottom is a good tactic, and the crankbait's tendency to fish nose-down means that the lip often bounces the lure clear of any potential snags.

DIVING LIPS
To tell whether a crankbait is a shallow or deep diver, look at the front of the lure. A small, steeply angled lip signifies a shallow diver, but a deep-running bait will have a long, fairly shallow-angled lip.

SHALLOW DIVER

DEEP DIVER

Floating divers

For prospecting the water layers with a floating diver, choose one that will dive to a depth of about 3.7 m (12 ft) on a fast retrieve. With this type of lure, it is possible to follow the bottom contours quite closely by varying the speed of retrieve and thus the depth of the lure. However, to fish the surface or deeper holes effectively, choose a lure designed specifically for those purposes. Fishing the lure on the shady side of a bottom feature such as a sunken tree, and parallel to it, keeps it in the likeliest water for the longest period.

THE VERSATILE FLOATING DIVER

To reach maximum depth, cast as far as possible and keep rod tip low on retrieve

On a slack line a lightly snagged lure may free itself

Stop winding and the lure will rise over obstructions

Stop winding to allow the lure to rise up to the surface

Wind slowly to ease the lure through emergent surface weeds

Winding slowly will make the lure swim on a level plane

Wind quickly to make the lure dive down steep gradients

F Vibrating plugs can be fished at all levels, in open water or along the edge of weeds, but snag easily

Shallow reef

H Jerkbaits are excellent for the larger fish, and should be worked with vertical jerks of the rod while winding the reel

E Thin-bodied minnow plugs run shallow even when fished on a long line, and can be drifted downwind for a long retrieve

Deep, open water

G A buoyant/diving crankbait allows a wide variety of water to be fished from weedy shallows to depths of 3.7 m (12 ft)

DEEP-DIVING PLUGS
This pike was taken on a deep-diving plug. These plugs, which have a lot of water resistance, should be used with multiplier reels.

Work the shaded side of cover

LEGERING

Legering is a versatile technique that allows the bait to be cast a long way and presented at or near the bottom to attract fish that feed there. Although it lacks the finesse of float fishing, it does allow the bait to be presented effectively in situations where a float rig would be working at its limits. These include fishing at long range, on fast rivers, under weed rafts, and in deep water or rough weather on big lakes and pits. Apart from when fishing with a bolt rig, legering generally involves using the minimum practicable amount of weight in a given set of circumstances, in order to produce the lowest level of resistance to a taking fish. The lowest possible resistance is achieved by freelining, a variant of legering in which the only weight on the line is that of the baited hook.

ROD RESTS
A legered bait does not need constant manipulation, so the rod can be left on rod rests until the bite indicator shows that it is time to strike.

BITE INDICATORS
Because there is no float on a leger rig, bites are detected either by touch (holding the line over a finger or between finger and thumb so that the tiniest pull on the line can be felt) or by using a bite indicator. The simplest indicator is the rod tip itself, but other methods are preferable when more sensitivity is required. Quivertips, springtips, and swingtips, fitted into the tip ring, show up taps that would be missed on a rod tip, while a bobbin clipped on the line between reel and butt ring allows some slack line to be taken before the strike is made. Monkey climbers are used either alone or in conjunction with electronic indicators that sound when there is a pull on the line.

SWINGTIP
A swingtip is sensitive, but limits casting distance. Add lead wire in strong winds or undertows.

QUIVERTIP
A quivertip will "soften" close-range bites and is sensitive enough to show bites developing.

MONKEY CLIMBER
This is connected to the line to indicate any pull on it. Add a light stick for night fishing.

TOUCH LEGERING
Point rod at the bait. Crook a finger over the line, or hold it between thumb and finger.

THE RUNNING LEGER

Main line of / suitable strength

Swivel

Loop of heavy nylon

Split shot clipped to nylon loop

Split shot leger stop fixed 30 cm (12 in) from hook

Hook link of breaking / strain to suit quarry

Hook size and bait to suit quarry

This is a simple but effective rig for close-range work. If split shot are used for weight and pinched on to the loop of nylon (the link), the rig will not snag since the shot will pull off when put under tension. If the shot on the link are butted up against one another, the rig can be made to roll along the bottom to make the bait run through the swim, which is often a highly effective method of fishing for chub and barbel. Conversely, if the shot is spaced apart, the rig will hold bottom firmly in fast water. The link on the running leger should be stopped about 30 cm (12 in) from the hook by a plastic leger stop or a BB shot. Use thick nylon for the link to ensure that it stands clear of the main line.

RUNNING LEGER IN ACTION

THE FIXED PATERNOSTER

Hook size and bait to suit quarry

15–90 cm (6 in–3 ft) hook link

Swimfeeder

Swivel

Main line of suitable strength

Snap link

This rig is excellent for fast-flowing waters, and especially effective on stillwaters when fishing over dense weeds, where running leger rigs are prone to snagging. Tie the main line and the hook link to one eye of a swivel, and to the other attach a 30 cm (12 in) mono link carrying the swimfeeder. A hook link of about 45 cm (18 in) will usually suffice, but for fishing on the drop increase it to 60 or 90 cm (2 or 3 ft), and when tentative bites are being experienced reduce it to about 15 cm (6 in). The swimfeeder link's breaking strain should be less than that of the main line so that it, and not the main line, will break if the swimfeeder should snag.

FIXED PATERNOSTER IN ACTION

THE SLIDING LINK LEGER

Bomb weight

15 cm (6 in) weight link

Running swivel

Plastic bead

Fixed swivel

Hook size and bait to suit quarry

30 cm (12 in) hook link

Main line of suitable strength

Sometimes it is desirable to allow the fish to take a little line before the strike is made. Predators, for example, often spend a while toying with a bait before taking it properly. In these circumstances, a sliding link is preferable to a fixed paternoster because it offers less resistance to the take. Thread a swivel and then a small bead onto the main line, and tie another swivel to the end of it. Attach the hook link to the other end of this swivel, and the weight link to the free-running swivel. Use lighter line for the weight link than for the main line so that the link can be broken if the weight snags. The bead prevents the swivels from tangling.

SLIDING LINK LEGER IN ACTION

THE BOLT RIG

Hook size and bait to suit quarry

Hook link to suit conditions

Swivel

Bead

Bomb weight

Backstop fixed to main line 15 cm (6 in) from swivel

Main line of suitable strength

This rig uses a heavy weight, which is free to slide along the line between a swivel and a backstop. It was first developed for carp that had grown wary of conventional rigs, which produced increasing tension as they moved off with the bait; deeply suspicious, they would reject it. A freelined bait might appear to be the logical answer, but the bolt rig works better. When a carp first picks up a bait fished on a bolt rig, it is not aware of the weight due to the short length of slack line. However, as soon as it begins to make off, the backstop on the line pulls up hard against the heavy leger weight. This startles the carp, causing it to bolt and hook itself.

BOLT RIG IN ACTION

221

FLOAT FISHING – RUNNING WATER

Floats attached bottom-end only, such as the waggler, come into their own on slow-flowing rivers, and a waggler really scores when the wind is blowing. Because it is attached bottom-end only, most of the line between the waggler and the rod is under water and thus impervious to the wind or surface movement. On fast-flowing waters, floats attached top and bottom (by a pair of float rubbers) are the order of the day. Loafers, sticks, and Avons all fall into this group.

CASTING A WAGGLER
For fishing at long range, let the float swing smartly behind you when you begin the cast and then push hard forward with the rod to achieve distance. A more relaxed version of this cast will achieve less distance, but with less risk of the hook rig catching in bankside vegetation.

SPLIT SHOT

Split shot do more than just add weight to the line. Positioned in particular ways on the line, shot can present a bait in various fashions, ensure that different types of bite register on the float, and prevent tangling of the rig in casting. Split shot are available in a variety of sizes from the biggest, termed SSG or swan shot, down to the so-called dust shot that is often used near to the hook to produce a slow descent of the bait through the water.

Shot size	Weight (grams)
SSG	1.89
AAA	0.81
BB	0.4
No. 1	0.28
No. 4	0.17
No. 6	0.105
No. 8	0.063
No. 10	0.034
No. 12	0.02
No. 13	0.012

PLUMBING THE DEPTH

When using a float, it is important to know the depth of the swim you are fishing, and you can find it by using a plummet. Fit the plummet onto the hook and gently lower it to the bottom, then reposition the float so that it just protrudes from the surface. The distance between the float and the hook will be the approximate depth of the water. Plumb various other points around the swim to build up a mental picture of the bottom.

THE PLUMMET
A plummet, a small weight, fits over or clamps onto the hook.

BASIC WAGGLER RIGS

STRAIGHT WAGGLER — Two AAA / One AAA and one BB / No. 8 / No. 8 / Three No. 6 / No. 8

INSERT WAGGLER — BB / AA

BODIED WAGGLER — AAA / Swan shot (SSG) / Two BB / No. 4 / No. 8

CURRENT

Two No. 6

No. 8

The straight waggler is used on medium-paced rivers. It is good at combating a downstream wind, and operates well at ranges of up to 27 m (30 yds). Putting the lower three shot close to the hook will send the bait down quicker, which can be effective for bottom feeders.

LOCKING SHOT
These lock a float attached bottom-end only to the required point on the line.

Float stem

Float adapter

Locking shot

The insert waggler float is ideal on wide, slow-flowing rivers when fish are feeding on the drop (the thin insert gives good bite indication). This rig can be used in quite deep swims, but because of the sensitivity of the float, it cannot be held back and must be allowed to drift freely.

Use a bodied waggler for fishing big, slow rivers at medium to long range. The buoyant bulb enables the rig to be heavily shotted for good casting distance. The shotting pattern can be modified for fish taking on the drop or to get the bait down quickly to bottom feeders.

BASIC STICK FLOAT RIGS

SHALLOW SUMMER RIG   MEDIUM-DEPTH RIG   DEEPWATER RIG

No. 10

Four No. 10, equally spaced

Nine No. 8, equally spaced

No. 10   No. 10

Seven No. 6

CURRENT

Three No. 8

No. 10

This shallow rig is effective during the warmer months of the year, when species such as bleak, dace, and chub will often be found taking food on the drop. Use a light stick float and space the shot evenly along the line at equal intervals. This rig is suitable for depths of up to about 1.5 m (5 ft).

DEPTH MARKER
Pinch a shot onto the line to mark the minimum depth you want to fish.

Float stem

10 mm (⅜ in) silicone rubber

No. 6 shot

This is a rig for medium depths and moderate currents. In depths of 1 to 1.8 m (3 to 6 ft), use a float with a wire stem or heavy cane base; use a light float in shallower water. In fast water, group some of the No. 8 shot just above the hook length. This rig is effective for chub and barbel.

This rig works well in depths of up to about 3 m (10 ft). Use a float with a heavy base to ensure that the bait gets down quickly to where the intended quarry is lying. This is a good rig to use for species such as barbel, roach, chub, and bream, when they are feeding on or near the bottom.

TROTTING A STICK FLOAT

Trotting a stick float involves letting it drift downstream with the current and holding back on it at intervals so that the bait swings upwards, enticing fish to take it. Set the float slightly overdepth, that is, so that the distance from the float to the hook is slightly greater than the depth of the water. Cast a little downstream of you, leave the bale arm open, and allow the float to "trot" along with the current. Press the tip of your forefinger lightly against the spool rim so that you can control the amount of line pulled from the reel as the float travels downstream. Holding back gently on the drifting float will make the bait trip along just off the bottom; holding back hard on it will swing the bait upwards.

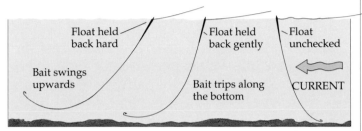

Float held back hard   Float held back gently   Float unchecked

Bait swings upwards   Bait trips along the bottom   CURRENT

TACKLE CONTROL
When you are trotting a float, you may find it easier to control your tackle if you are standing rather than sitting on the bank.

BACKSHOTTING

Use a No. 8 shot about 15 cm (6 in) from the top of the float

CURRENT

Backshotting
To minimize the effects of the wind on a stick float, sink the line for a short distance behind it by backshotting. In most situations, a single No. 8 shot pinched onto the line between the float and the rod, about 15 cm (6 in) from the float, will be sufficient.

FEEDING
To attract fish and get them feeding, use a catapult to throw small pieces of hookbait into the swim just before you cast. The loose bait will slowly sink or drift with the current, and fish that are feeding on it will not be unduly wary of your hookbait when it arrives.

FLOAT FISHING – STILLWATERS

For stillwater fishing, the float is usually attached bottom-end only. The line passes through a ring inserted into the base of the float, and the float is held in position on the line by split shot (known as locking shot) fixed either side of it. During the summer months, stillwater fish will often be found in the upper layers of the water and can be caught by fishing "on the drop" (fishing a bait that sinks slowly through the water). The setup in this situation involves positioning most of the shot around the float with just a few small dust shot down the line. When bites are not expected on the drop, use bulk shot halfway between the float and hook to get the bait down quickly through the upper layers. If bites are not forthcoming, try moving the bottom shot on the rig to anywhere from 10 to 45 cm (4 to 18 in) from the hook.

CASTING

For long-range work on large stillwaters, it is best to use an overhead cast. Wind the float to about a metre from the rod tip. Next, open the bale arm with your free hand (or, on a closed-face, reel, press the line release button) and as you do so press the line against the spool with the index or middle finger of your rod hand. With the line still trapped against the side of the spool, bring the rod back smartly over the shoulder of your rod arm. Punch the rod forward over your head, removing your finger from the spool to release the line. Allow the float to shoot out over the water, climbing as it does so. As the float describes an arc through the air, follow its path with the rod tip until the rod is horizontal. As the float nears the water, slow its flight and ensure a gentle touchdown by putting the index or middle finger of your rod hand on the side of the spool to slow the speed of the line as it leaves the reel.

Feathering
Slowing the speed of the line to make the float land gently on the water is known as "feathering" the cast. Feathering also reduces the risk of the terminal tackle becoming tangled. This is because when the line is slowed, the momentum of the terminal tackle pulls the whole rig out straight.

CONTROLLED LANDINGS
Feather the cast to make the float touch down gently on the water, and close the bale arm when it lands.

BASIC TECHNIQUES

The two basic stillwater techniques are the lift method and fishing on the drop. For the lift method, wind the line in so that only the tip of the float is above the water. If a fish takes the bait, the float will lift.

When fishing on the drop, first count the number of seconds it takes for the shot to cock the float (to pull it upright) after it has hit the water. On subsequent casts, if the float does not cock properly in the usual time, strike immediately: a fish has taken the bait.

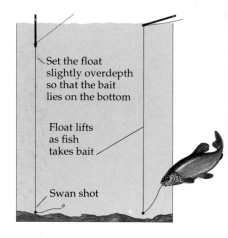

THE LIFT METHOD

Set the float slightly overdepth so that the bait lies on the bottom

Float lifts as fish takes bait

Swan shot

BASIC STILLWATER RIGS

BREAM RIG

Bodied waggler

AAA — AAA

BB

BB — AAA

No. 8

DRIFTBEATER RIG

Driftbeater or bodied waggler

Two AAA

Two AAA

}Two No. 4

No. 6

No. 8

LIGHT RIG

Stick float

BB — Two AAA

}Three No. 8

No. 8

No. 8

The ideal rig for catching bream. The bodied waggler's buoyancy allows it to carry plenty of weight, in the form of locking shot, to eliminate tangling and make distance casting easier. The bulk shotting near the hook takes the bait down quickly.

Driftbeaters fish well in rough, windy conditions and are best fished overdepth. Plenty of weight in the locking shot keeps the float steady, and progressively lighter shot pinched on down the rig allow the bait to be fished on the drop.

This rig is ideal for fishing at a range of about 14 m (15 yds), but can be used at distances up to 23 m (25 yds). It is at its best in light winds when there is minimal surface drift. Always feather the line when casting, to prevent tangling.

FISHING ON THE DROP

The float is being cocked by the bulk shot and the lightly shotted rig is beginning to descend

No. 4

No. 1

The float now lies deeper in the water as the midway shot on the rig begin to affect it

The float is cocked: any bites occurring now will be shown by the float going under

Any delay in the float assuming final cocked position means the bait has been taken on the drop

FISHING THE SLIDING FLOAT

Sliding floats come into their own when swims are significantly deeper than the length of the rod. Bodied wagglers, preferably loaded to some degree, are the best floats to use. This loading ensures that the float does not slide up the line during casting, while the buoyant body allows plenty of shot to be used along the rig to get the bait down to the bottom quickly. A stop knot is tied in above the float and its position is adjusted until the correct setting (which is the depth of the swim) has been found. The float runs freely up the line until it reaches the knot, which will not pass through the ring at the base of the float because of the bead.

THE SLIDING STOP KNOT
The sliding stop knot is easy to tie in fine mono. To ensure it does not catch on the rod rings during casting, either leave the ends about 10 mm (⅜ in) long or tie the knot in soft cotton.

Fine mono

Reel line

SLIDING FLOAT RIG

Bodied waggler (peacock quill or sarcandas reed stem)

Sliding stop knot

Bead

Three AAA

No. 8

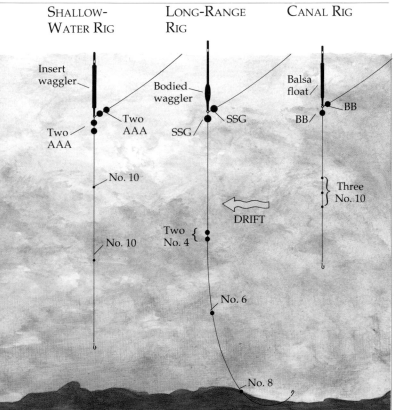

SHALLOW-WATER RIG

Insert waggler

Two AAA

Two AAA

No. 10

No. 10

LONG-RANGE RIG

Bodied waggler

SSG

SSG

Two No. 4

No. 6

DRIFT

No. 8

CANAL RIG

Balsa float

BB

BB

BB

Three No. 10

Insert waggler rigs such as this are best used with small shot spaced out between float and hook. They are not designed for use with heavy bulk shotting down the rig. In shallow swims, the shot on the rig need be no bigger than No. 10.

This rig is for use on big lakes and on gravel pits. The basic shotting pattern shown here could be altered for fishing on the drop, in which case slightly heavier shotting, such as a few well-spaced No. 8s, will give better bite registration.

The small balsa float ensures a quiet touchdown on casting, and most of the cocking weight is concentrated around the float. The rest of the shot are small and allow the bait to fall slowly and naturally through the water.

BANKSIDE VEGETATION
A sliding rig has only a short length of line beyond the float when casting. This is useful when bankside vegetation limits casting space.

SLIDING CONTROLLER FLOAT RIG

Bead   Swivel

Controller float

Line is greased to float

Sliding controller floats are excellent for presenting surface baits such as crust or air-injected lobworms for carp and chub, or floating casters for roach and rudd. The float acts basically as a casting weight, and when the bait is taken the controller is not pulled under the surface. Instead, the line runs freely through a ring attached to the top of the float. The line between the swivel and the hook should be well greased to reduce resistance to a taking fish. The sliding controller float can also act as a bite indicator: strike when it begins to slide across the surface.

225

POLE FISHING – STILLWATERS & CANALS

When fishing a stillwater, the first task is to use a plummet *(see page 222)* to find the shelf or dropoff where fish are likely to be. Start searching at about 5 m (16 ft) out, and shorten or lengthen the pole until it is found. On a canal, start by fishing just off the bank, and if you get no results, fish further out: if the canal is not too wide, fish the middle channel and then along the far bank. Most canals can be fished comfortably with a 10 m (33 ft) pole.

POLE TIPS

On waters where big fish are a distinct possibility, it is essential to use a pole with an elasticated tip. The tip elastic *(see page 228)* acts as a shock absorber and helps to prevent the hook being torn free. You can convert a flick tip to an elasticated tip by using one of the many conversion kits on the market. Alternatively, the components (tensioner, bung, elastic, PTFE bush, and line connector) can be bought individually.

ELASTICATED TIPS

FLICK TIPS

CASTING

Set up the top three sections, attach the line and terminal rig, and cast underhand or overhand to get the terminal rig out. Then add more sections to the pole (or extend it, if it is telescopic) until the required length is reached.

Always keep well away from overhead power lines when fishing with a pole, especially if it is made of carbon fibre, and do not use one during a thunderstorm.

UNDERHAND CAST
Hold the pole in one hand and the terminal rig in the other. Swing the pole up and out, and at the same time release the terminal rig.

OVERHAND CAST
This is similar to the underhand cast, but the pole is held and cast vertically, instead of from a nearly horizontal position.

BASIC STILLWATER RIGS

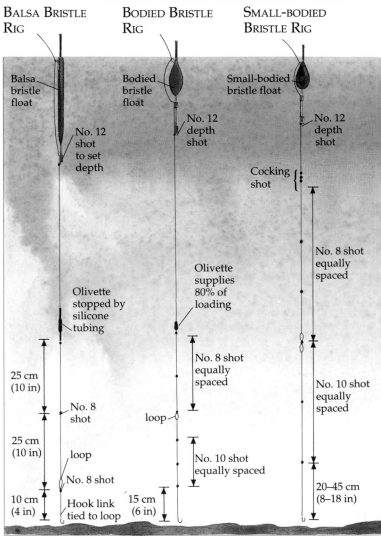

BALSA BRISTLE RIG

Balsa bristle float

No. 12 shot to set depth

Olivette stopped by silicone tubing

25 cm (10 in)

No. 8 shot

25 cm (10 in)

loop

No. 8 shot

10 cm (4 in)

Hook link tied to loop

BODIED BRISTLE RIG

Bodied bristle float

No. 12 depth shot

Olivette supplies 80% of loading

No. 8 shot equally spaced

loop

No. 10 shot equally spaced

15 cm (6 in)

SMALL-BODIED BRISTLE RIG

Small-bodied bristle float

No. 12 depth shot

Cocking shot

No. 8 shot equally spaced

No. 10 shot equally spaced

20–45 cm (8–18 in)

This float is designed for fishing baits near or on the bottom in a flat calm or slight ripple. It is a good float for detecting bites from roach and small bream, and when it is correctly shotted, only the bristle should show above the water. The shotting pattern gets the whole rig quickly down to mid-depth, after which the small shot sink the bait more slowly to the lake bed. This can produce bites on the drop as well as on the bottom.

The bodied bristle float has a cane stem and is used for fishing on the drop. It can be used in conditions from flat calm to choppy, and only the bristle should be visible above the surface, for bite detection. On this rig the shotting is evenly spaced to take the bait down at a steady rate. To get the bait down quickly to fish on the bottom, move the shot nearer the hook, and when fish are near the surface, place the shot directly under the float.

This is a good rig to use in deep water, and it is usually fished about 15 to 30 cm (6 to 12 in) overdepth. It is especially suitable for bottom-feeding species such as bream, because it gets the bait down quickly to them. The rig is set to depth with a No. 12 shot, and cocked by three closely grouped No. 8s. Below these are three equally spaced No. 10s, the lower of which is placed 20 to 45 cm (8 to 18 in) from the hook.

BASIC CANAL RIGS

DIBBER (FLAT-TOP) RIG | **MINI WAGGLER RIG** | **FLOAT LEGER RIG**

Dibber (flat-top) float

Mini waggler or grey canal float

Mini waggler or grey canal float

No. 12 depth shot

No. 4 locking shot

No. 4 locking shot

No. 8 shot equally spaced

No. 8 shot equally spaced

No. 8 shot equally spaced

Sliding knot

No. 10 shot 10 cm (4 in) from hook

No. 10 shot 30 cm (12 in) from hook

30 cm (12 in) hook link

AAA shot on 20 cm (8 in) link

The dibber rig can be used for fishing the far shelf of a canal in very choppy conditions, and it is also useful on a lake when an undertow is occurring. It is designed to take fish on the drop, and is a good rig for bream fishing. The shotting consists of a No. 12 depth shot, with eight No. 8 shot evenly spaced below it. A single No. 10 shot is positioned 10 cm (4 in) from the hook, and the top of the float should only just protrude above the surface, for bite detection.

This rig can be used on lakes and canals, and it is a good choice for bream, tench, or large roach. The float is attached bottom-end only, with locking shot pinched on at either side of the base ring, and the pole tip is usually sunk to keep the line under water. This prevents line drift, which can adversely affect bait presentation. Back shotting might also be required in a wind: pinch on a No. 8 shot about 20 cm (8 in) above the float to sink the line.

This version of the mini waggler rig is designed for use in rough conditions, when the bait needs to be firmly anchored on the bottom. A small bomb weight or an AAA shot is carried on a 20 cm (8 in) length of line attached to the main line by a sliding knot, which should be about 30 cm (12 in) from the hook. Reduce this distance if bites are not registering on the float but the bait is being sucked, and lengthen it if the undertow and wind increase.

HANDLING THE POLE

Take-apart poles are shipped (lengthened) by adding more sections, and unshipped (shortened) by removing sections. Telescopic poles and whips are shipped by pulling sections out, and unshipped by pushing them back in. Always keep pole sections free of dirt to prevent wear and ensure easy shipping and unshipping.

HOLDING A POLE
Fish from a sitting position. Hold the pole across one thigh or put the butt against your pelvis and hold it with one or both hands.

POLE RESTS
Pole rests keep the pole off the ground while you are changing the terminal tackle, unhooking fish, or groundbaiting.

UNSHIPPING
To land a fish caught on a long pole, unship the pole until it is short enough to allow the fish to be brought to the net or hand.

SWINGING TO HAND
When the pole has been unshipped to about two or three sections long, small or medium-sized fish can be swung to hand.

FISHING DISTANCE
A long pole allows you to place baits with great accuracy into distant swims, and to fish in areas that may be inaccessible with running tackle.

POLE FISHING – RUNNING WATER

Pole fishing on fast-flowing water requires small round-bodied floats, such as bung floats, that can be held back or allowed to run at the speed of the current. The bodied bristle float can be used on slow-flowing rivers. There are two basic styles of pole fishing for running water. The first involves using a long pole and a short line for holding back and slowing the bait's passage. The second style employs a long pole and long line – such as a 10 m (33 ft) pole and 9 m (30 ft) of line – for running the float and bait at the speed of the current and fishing the full length of the swim.

FEEDING METHODS

To attract fish to the swim when you are fishing on the bottom, throw in small balls of bread-based groundbait containing hookbait samples. When fishing on the drop, throw or catapult loose feed, such as maggots, into the water below the pole tip, or use a pole pot. This is clipped to the top section of the pole and filled with feed, then the pole is extended and swung out over the swim, and the pot is inverted to empty its contents into the water.

USING A CATAPULT
A good way to get groundbait or loose feed out to the vicinity of the hookbait is to use a catapult. When using one, either put the pole on the bank or on pole rests, or place it across your lap and hold it down with the forearm of the arm holding the catapult.

POLE ELASTIC

ELASTICS
Three sizes of elastic (No. 4, No. 5, and No. 6) on winders.

Elastic for use on elasticated pole tips *(see page 226)* is available in eight sizes (numbered 1 to 8), each of a different breaking strain. It is supplied on carriers or winders that can be used when empty for holding pre-assembled float rigs. Pole elastic is usually coated with a lubricant to ensure that it runs freely through the PTFE bung in the pole tip, and periodic applications of lubricant are advisable to keep a pole's elastic in good condition. Many anglers carry a number of additional pole top sections rigged up with elastics of various strengths for different species.

RIGS FOR RUNNING WATER

BODIED BRISTLE RIG

Bodied bristle float

No. 12 depth shot

No. 8 shot halfway between olivette and float

FLOW

Olivette

Loop

No. 8 shot equally spaced

Hook 5 cm (2 in) from bottom

CANE-STEMMED BODIED BRISTLE RIG

Cane-stemmed bodied bristle float

No. 12 depth shot

No. 8 shot equally spaced

Loop

No. 10 shot equally spaced

WIRE-STEMMED BUNG RIG 1

Wire-stemmed bung float

No. 12 depth shot

No. 8 shot

Olivette

No. 8 shot equally spaced

Loop

30 cm (12 in)

This rig is used for catching fish near the bottom in slow to medium-paced water between 1.5 and 2.1 m (5 and 7 ft) deep. The swim should be groundbaited and the float, attached top and bottom, run through at the speed of the current. The rig is weighted by an olivette with a single No. 8 shot above it and three No. 8s below it. The baited hook should fish just off bottom, and the bristle of the float should show above the water for bite indication.

A short version of this rig will catch surface and midwater feeders in the top 60 to 90 cm (2 to 3 ft) of medium-paced water, but it can be made longer to fish the full depth of the river, as shown here. It should be run through the swim at the speed of the current, with just the bristle of the float, which is attached top and bottom, showing above the surface. The shotting consists of eight equally spaced No. 8 shot above two equally spaced No. 10s.

With this versatile rig, you can fish a bait on the bottom below the pole tip, hold back in deep, fast water over groundbait, or run the bait through at the speed of the current. Position the bulk shot or an olivette at about 75 cm (30 in) from the hook, with three No. 8 shot spaced equally below it. Attach the float top and bottom, with the tip of the bristle showing above the water for bite indication. This rig gives excellent bait control, even in fast-flowing rivers.

WIRE-STEMMED BUNG RIG 2

HIGH-VISIBILITY BUNG RIG

FLOAT LEGER RIG

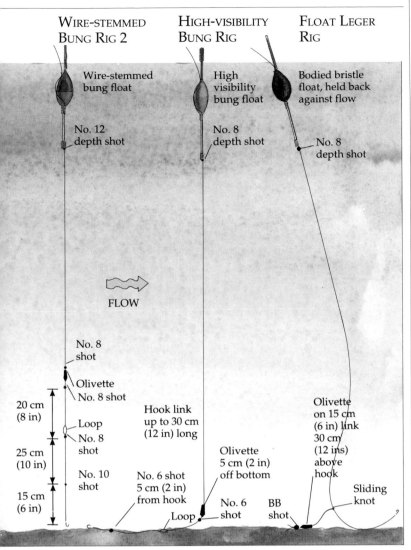

Wire-stemmed bung float

No. 12 depth shot

High visibility bung float

No. 8 depth shot

Bodied bristle float, held back against flow

No. 8 depth shot

FLOW

No. 8 shot

Olivette
No. 8 shot

20 cm (8 in)

Loop
No. 8 shot

25 cm (10 in)

No. 10 shot

15 cm (6 in)

Hook link up to 30 cm (12 in) long

Olivette 5 cm (2 in) off bottom

No. 6 shot 5 cm (2 in) from hook

Loop

No. 6 shot

BB shot

Olivette on 15 cm (6 in) link 30 cm (12 in) above hook

Sliding knot

Use this rig to present baits just off the bed for fish that feed in the bottom third of the water, and run it through at the speed of the current. Position bulk shot or an olivette 60 cm (2 ft) from the hook, or at one-third of the distance from the hook to the float. Fix a No. 8 shot just above the bulk shot or olivette, another just below it, with a No. 8 and a No. 10 spaced below that. Set the float so that the bristle just shows above the surface.

This rig is suitable for fishing close-in for small, bottom-feeding fish of up to 227 g (8 oz). Set the float so that the bristle is above the surface, and fish the rig through the margins, no more than about 1.8 to 3 m (6 to 10 ft) out and held back slightly. The simple shotting pattern consists of bulk shot or an olivette set 30 cm (12 in) from the hook, and a No. 6 shot just below it, and another No. 6 near the hook. The olivette takes the bait down quickly through the layers.

This rig can be used for presenting a static bait on the bottom. It will also allow you to make a bait move slowly along the bottom towards the bank, and to hold it back hard to inch the bait slowly through the swim. The float is well overshotted by a small bomb weight attached to the line 30 cm (12 in) from the hook by a short link of about 15 cm (6 in) of mono. Attach the float top and bottom, and set it so that only the bristle is protruding above the water.

POLE FISHING WEIGHTS

BARRELS

OLIVETTES

The weights most widely used in pole fishing are split shot and olivettes, plus small bomb weights for float leger rigs. Olivettes thread onto the line and are used in place of bulk shot; barrel leads can also be used, but they are more prone to tangling. Lead wire is better than split shot when using seed baits.

SPLIT SHOT

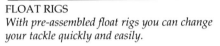

LEAD WIRE

FLOAT RIGS
With pre-assembled float rigs you can change your tackle quickly and easily.

OLIVETTE AND SPLIT SHOT SIZES

Olivette size (Paquita)	Weight (grams)	Olivette size (Torpille)	Weight (grams)	Shot size	Weight (grams)
12	3.0				
11	2.45	11	2.5		
10	2.1	10	2.0		
				SSG	1.89
9	1.85	9	1.5		
8	1.56	8	1.2		
7	1.36	7	1.0		
6	1.16				
5	0.82				
				AAA	0.81
		6	0.8		
4	0.67				
		5	0.6		
		4	0.5		
3	0.44				
		3	0.4	BB	0.4
2	0.37	2	0.3		
				No. 1	0.28
				No. 2	0.24
1	0.25				
		1	0.2	No. 3	0.20
				No. 4	0.17
0	0.17				
2/0	0.13	0	0.13	No. 5	0.13
3/0	0.105			No. 6	0.105
				No. 7	0.083
4/0	0.081				
				No. 8	0.063
				No. 9	0.049
				No. 10	0.034
				No. 11	0.026
				No. 12	0.020
				No. 13	0.012

TROLLING

Trolling is a method by which a bait, either natural or artificial, is pulled along through the water behind a moving boat. It is used on stillwaters and rivers for fish such as trout and walleye, and is also used on saltwater, for example in big-game fishing *(see page 258)*. The boat can be powered either by oars or by a motor, and the trailed bait, which can be fished at practically any depth, is intended to resemble a live fish to any predators it passes. Trolled spoons, plugs, and even flies can be made to fish deep by the addition of weights or by using lead-cored line, while natural baits are often fished below a sliding float, set overdepth, to give an early indication that a predator has taken hold.

READING A LAKE

Deep lakes can be divided into separate layers, the epilimnion, thermocline, and hypolimnion. During summer and autumn the epilimnion will be warmer than the hypolimnion, and the reverse is true in winter. The water temperatures within each of these two layers are fairly uniform, but there is a sharp change in temperature within the thermocline. Strong winds will cause the layers to tilt, resulting in the epilimnion becoming "thicker" on the lee shore. Fish that show a marked preference for cold water, such as lake trout, will move deeper as the summer progresses, and the best way to locate these deep-swimming fish is to use an echo sounder.

WIND

EPILIMNION

THERMOCLINE

HYPOLIMNION

TROLLING THE LAYERS

A wet fly can be trolled just under the surface by using a medium sinking fly line and a standard leader. To fish deeper, the same pattern can be trailed behind the boat on a lead-cored line, or alternatively a heavy tube fly can be employed. Small plugs, too, can be fished relatively deep on a lead-cored line, or on a small-diameter wire line that cuts easily through the water. To fish even deeper, it is necessary to move on to a heavy, vaned trolling weight attached well up the line above the lure. Alternatively, a downrigger can be used for really deep work, its great advantage being that the lure can be fished at a constant, preset depth.

BOATS
Trolling is best done from a motor-powered boat, but a rowing boat may also be used.

Trolling with multiple rods
A trio of anglers can fish together, with minimal risk of their lines tangling, by fishing at different depths and distances. The angler in the stern should fish his lure or bait shallow and closest to the boat, so that if a take occurs on one of the other rods he can get his bait in quickly and operate the motor.

TROLLING WITH MULTIPLE RODS

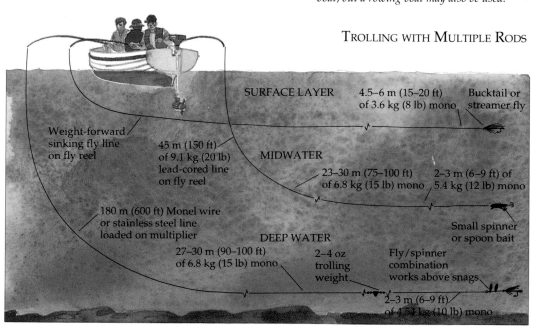

SURFACE LAYER — 4.5–6 m (15–20 ft) of 3.6 kg (8 lb) mono — Bucktail or streamer fly

Weight-forward sinking fly line on fly reel

45 m (150 ft) of 9.1 kg (20 lb) lead-cored line on fly reel

MIDWATER — 23–30 m (75–100 ft) of 6.8 kg (15 lb) mono — 2–3 m (6–9 ft) of 5.4 kg (12 lb) mono

180 m (600 ft) Monel wire or stainless steel line loaded on multiplier

DEEP WATER — Small spinner or spoon bait

27–30 m (90–100 ft) of 6.8 kg (15 lb) mono — 2–4 oz trolling weight — Fly/spinner combination works above snags

2–3 m (6–9 ft) of 4.54 kg (10 lb) mono

ROD LAYOUT

Each rod fishes a lure at different distances from the boat

15 m (50 ft)

9 m (30 ft)

21 m (70 ft)

USING A DOWNRIGGER

Monel cable to winch

Snap swivel

Swivel

Trolling weight

Line release leader

Quick-release clip holds reel line under tension

Reel line to rod

DOWNRIGGER TERMINAL TACKLE

Artificial lure or natural bait

Snap swivel

The downrigger not only fishes constantly at a preset depth, it also allows the fish to be played out on a line unencumbered by a heavy weight. This is because the large weight, around 1.4 kg (3 lb), that is needed to take the lure down to the required fishing depth, is attached to a separate, strong line, and connected to the reel line by a clip that releases the line when a predator strikes.

The downrigger is fished off the stern of the boat. The cable to which the weight is attached is normally run off a winch and marked at intervals with a waterproof marker pen so that the depth the lure is sent down to can be gauged. (Using an echo sounder makes this marking unnecessary.) After the rig has been sent down to the prescribed depth, the reel line is tightened right up to put a good bend in the rod. When a fish grabs hold of the lure, the clip releases the line and the rod tip springs back straight, indicating the take and often setting the hooks.

DOWNRIGGER IN ACTION

Rod is set up in rod holder

Rod tip springs up when a fish strikes

Cable to weight

Mono reel line

Trolling weight holds lure at chosen depth

Line is held by a quick-release clip

Bait or lure is chosen according to target species

Setting up
The leader to which the lure is attached can be anywhere between a metre and tens of metres in length. When lowering the lure and weight, the reel on the rod should have its clutch set but with the anti-reverse off or out of gear with the ratchet on. When the rig is in position and ready to begin working, the reel is set for action.

DOWNRIGGER WINCH
The cable that carries the trolling weight is run off a winch secured near the stern of the boat.

DEEPWATER FISHING
Using a downrigger enables you to fish at depths of 150 m (500 ft) or more.

BAITWALKING

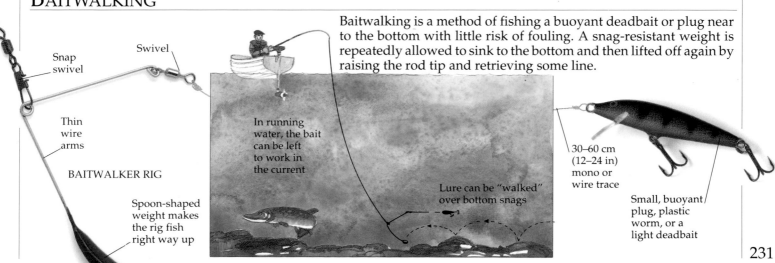

Snap swivel

Swivel

Thin wire arms

BAITWALKER RIG

Spoon-shaped weight makes the rig fish right way up

Baitwalking is a method of fishing a buoyant deadbait or plug near to the bottom with little risk of fouling. A snag-resistant weight is repeatedly allowed to sink to the bottom and then lifted off again by raising the rod tip and retrieving some line.

In running water, the bait can be left to work in the current

Lure can be "walked" over bottom snags

30–60 cm (12–24 in) mono or wire trace

Small, buoyant plug, plastic worm, or a light deadbait

THE OVERHEAD CAST

The overhead cast is an important part of all fly fishing. It is essential for anyone taking up fly fishing that they master it, and the better their technique, the more successful an angler they will be. The main elements of the basic overhead cast are the back cast and forward cast, plus the false cast, and these are described here together with suggestions on how to improve your technique and correct common casting faults. The way in which you hold the rod for casting is also important, but it depends largely on your personal preference and the distance you wish to cast. Try the grips shown here, then choose the one that most suits your casting requirements.

The momentum of the line bends the rod back

Stop the rod when it is at the 11.30 position

THE CLOCK FACE
These clock face positions are used to describe the rod movements during casting.

THE GRIP

Continental grip
In this grip, the forefinger points along the rod. This style is best for short, accurate casts with dry flies or nymphs on rivers and small stillwaters.

Continental grip

Standard grip
The style preferred by many all-round anglers who fish a variety of different methods and waters. Fine both for short, accurate work and for long-distance casting on large rivers and lakes. With the thumb running along the top of the handle, the strain on the wrist is not too great when a long line is aerialized.

Standard grip

Tournament grip
A strong but relaxed grip, ideal for long-distance work with weight-forward or shooting-head lines. Lacks the fine control needed for short, accurate casting.

Tournament grip

BACK CAST

A

B

C

Bring the rod sharply but smoothly upwards

Begin with the rod pointing down

Put your weight on your forward foot

BALANCED TACKLE
Good casting depends on balanced tackle. Fly size, line weight, and rod rating must match.

Back cast
A good back cast is the prerequisite for a good forward delivery, and neglecting this essential movement results in a poor casting technique. Before you begin, stand with the foot on your rod side forward, with the rod tip in the 4.00 position, about 6 m (20 ft) of line extended beyond the rod tip (**A**). Trap the line between your index finger and the rod handle.

To begin the back cast, bend your elbow to raise your forearm (**B**), accelerating the rod smoothly and progressively from the 4.00 position to the 11.30 position and lifting the line from the water (**C**). Stop the rod at this point and

pause briefly, allowing the line to extend fully behind you, before commencing the forward cast; momentum will flex the rod tip back a little to 11.00. This pause is vital, and practice will teach you how long it should be, but if it is too long the line will lose momentum and drop low behind you. If it is too brief it will result in a whiplash effect that can crack and thus weaken the fly line, or even cause the fly to snap off.

Keep your wrist straight during the back cast, because bending it allows the rod to drift too far back. This will make your forward cast more of a throwing action than a smooth, controlled delivery.

False casting

This enables you to get extra line in the air to increase your casting distance, and involves making repeated back and forward casts before allowing the line to land. The rod movements are the same as for an overhead cast, but instead of trapping the line with your rod hand index finger you hold it, between the butt ring and the reel, with your free hand. Pull line from the reel during each back cast and shoot it at the end of each forward cast. Work the rod between 1.00 and 1.30 and when sufficient line is aerialized, make a normal forward cast and release the line.

TIGHT LOOP

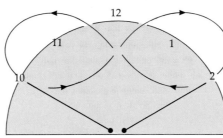

WIDE LOOP

Casting loops

The shape the line makes in the air is governed by the arc through which the rod tip is moved during false casting. A small arc will create a tight loop, a large arc a wide loop.

A tight loop, formed by moving the rod tip through an arc from 11.00 to 1.00 will enable you to cast farther than a large loop will, but a tight loop is not always desirable. For example, when casting a team of flies, the possibility of tangles is reduced by increasing the arc to 10.00 to 2.00 and thus casting a wider loop.

The bending rod acts like a spring, storing power that is released during the forward cast, throwing the line forwards

FORWARD CAST

D E F G

The line is released as the rod approaches 1.30 to 2.00

A brief pause allows the loose line to shoot

Follow through with the rod so the line does not fall short

The forward cast

With the rod flexed under compression and the line at full extension, accelerate the rod smoothly forward (**D**) to about the 2.00 position. Stop it there abruptly (**E**) and with a slight forward flick of your wrist. This wrist action is similar to the one you would use when lightly tapping a nail with a hammer, and when you do it you should aim your rod hand at an imaginary point about 1 m (3 ft) above the surface of the water.

Allow the rod to follow through as the line extends fully in front of you and falls gently to the water (**F**, **G**). The tapping motion and follow-through should be made in one continuous action.

Shooting line

There is an optimum length of line that any particular rod can aerialize, and to make a longer cast it is necessary to "shoot" line. This is achieved by pulling extra line from the reel, and allowing it to lie on the ground during the back cast.

When the rod reaches the 2.00 position (**E**) on the forward cast, lift the index finger of your rod hand to release the line. The momentum of the line extending in front of you will pull the loose line through the rings, adding extra distance to the cast. Aim high enough to allow all the extra line to straighten fully before it lands on the water.

COMMON CASTING FAULTS

The line drops too low behind
- Not enough power on the back cast.
- Rod tip dropping too low on back cast.
- Too long a pause on back cast.

The line will not shoot or straighten
- Line released too early.
- Failure to follow through.
- Insufficient power on forward punch.
- Slack line between false casts.

The line lands in a heap
- Too short a pause on back cast.
- Aiming too low.
- Aiming too high in a facing wind.

The flies snap off
- Too short a pause on back cast.
- Leader point too fine for the size and weight of the fly.

THE ROLL CAST

To make a roll cast, you lift the line off the water and roll it forward, without first making a back cast, by using a rapid forward punch that swings over and curves downwards. It is invaluable where there are obstructions behind you that prevent a normal overhead cast, and in many other situations, for example when you want to lift a sunk line and roll it onto the surface, prior to lifting it off for an overhead cast. The roll cast is a very versatile technique that should be part of every fly fisher's repertoire.

Making a roll cast
Begin by taking up a suitable stance, with one foot slightly in front of the other and the rod pointing down the line (**A**). Then begin a smooth, steady draw (**B**), raising your rod hand to just above shoulder height and lifting the rod to the 10.30 or 11.00 position (*see page 232*). This steady draw allows a loop of line to form between the rod top and the water. While the line is still moving, raise the rod slightly (**C**), then punch it rapidly forward and down (**D**). The rod is now flexed and under maximum compression, and the line follows its path, bellying out slightly behind you and coming off the water close to your feet. As you power the rod down through the 3.00 position, the belly of line will roll forward (**E**). Follow through smoothly (**F**) so that the line unfolds and straightens above the water.

STANCE

With any cast, the starting position is important if you are to achieve controlled turnover and make a smooth delivery, so take up position and stand with your best foot forward. For most right-handed anglers, this will mean the right foot, but it can pay to make the left foot the front foot, since this will open up the cast during the forward roll.

If necessary, take up any loose line with your free hand and hold on to it, as in the overhead cast, until late in the forward movement of the cast.

Start the cast when the large loop has formed

The rod is flexed by the weight of line on the water

Line loop is starting to form

Raise the rod in a semicircular path to the 11.00 position

Begin punching the rod briskly down and forward

Your rod hand attains maximum power

A

B

C

D

E

F

Rod moves line out to the side, clear of your body

Line is moving towards you

Line leaves the water close to you

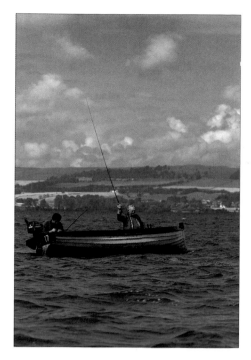

CASTING ON A RIVER (*right*)
When you are fishing on a river, the roll cast is useful if you want to change direction quickly or where obstructions prevent an overhead cast. Salmon anglers fishing large rivers with long rods find that the roll cast is also invaluable for lifting a sunk line to the surface before making an overhead cast.

CASTING FROM A BOAT (*left*)
Anglers fishing on the drift use the roll cast when short-lining with a team of three flies, or for lifting off a short line to cover fish that rise close to the boat. The roll cast, being one continuous movement, enables you to cover fish much faster than with an overhead cast, in which there is a delay while you make the back cast.

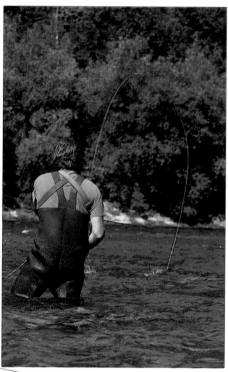

COMMON ROLL-CASTING FAULTS

Fly gets caught up behind
• When the rod is lifted too quickly, the bow from rod tip to water will not form properly, because the tension on the line is too great. The line will consequently lift and come through low, and then go behind you.
• If you hold your rod hand too low during the lift and roll, the line will come through too low and flat.

The line fails to roll out in front
• A lack of power during the forward movement, which should be a smooth but punchy action.
• The line is not straight or under tension before beginning the cast.
• Poor timing. If the lift and roll are hurried, the rod cannot build up power against the drag of the line as it comes off the water through the bow.

Line tangles on forward roll-down
• The rod has been brought up and over in the same vertical plane, causing the line to hang up. To remedy this, tilt the rod away from your body during the lift and roll.
• The line has not been kept tight by your line hand, causing a loss of power.
• A lack of power during the forward movement of the rod.

The belly of line travels forward in a rolling loop

The line loop is tightened by the full force of the rod

The line unfolds and straightens above the water

Follow through for a smooth line turnover

WET-FLY FISHING

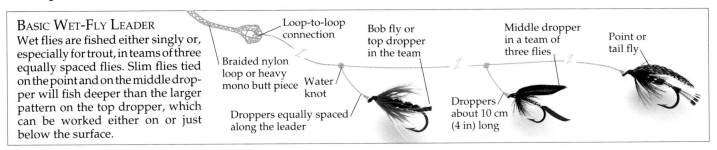

Wet-fly, because it encompasses so many different styles, is one of the most universal methods of catching gamefish, best suited to streamy water but also effective on slower, canal-like stretches and stillwaters if the fly is worked properly. Styles and tactics have evolved to suit different conditions, seasons, and species of fish. One thing never changes: whether using willowy rods and sparse Clyde-style fly dressings in northern England, or tip-actioned, single-handed wands and bucktail streamers in North America, devotees of wet-fly enjoy their sport in some of the most wild and beautiful areas of the world.

BASIC WET-FLY LEADER

Wet flies are fished either singly or, especially for trout, in teams of three equally spaced flies. Slim flies tied on the point and on the middle dropper will fish deeper than the larger pattern on the top dropper, which can be worked either on or just below the surface.

Loop-to-loop connection

Bob fly or top dropper in the team

Middle dropper in a team of three flies

Point or tail fly

Braided nylon loop or heavy mono butt piece

Water knot

Droppers equally spaced along the leader

Droppers about 10 cm (4 in) long

UPSTREAM FISHING

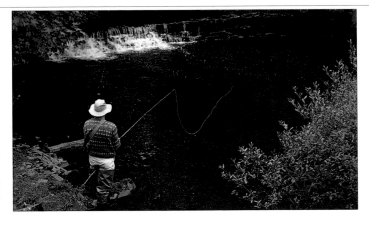

The upstream method uses the speed of the current to present a fly on smooth glides and steady streams, or on the flat pockets in broken water. Because you approach from downstream there is less chance of being detected by the fish, so takes can be very positive. If the fish can be seen and are on the move looking for food, allow enough lead with the cast for the fly to sink to the correct depth. For trout lying deep, use a leaded fly to get down to the holding depth. Watch for movement of the leader or the fish as the fly passes by.

APPROACHING UNSEEN
Stalking your quarry from behind, so that you are within its blind spot, allows you to approach much closer and to use a shorter cast than if you approached from another angle. A short line is less vulnerable to drag induced by the current, so it allows a faster response to a take.

Pay special attention to bankside lies

Guide the team through likely holding water

At the end of the drift, retrieve with a steady figure-of-eight or small twitches

CURRENT →

A fly retrieved across current at speed may sometimes bring a strike

Move upstream after covering all holding water from each fishing position

POSITION 2

Make a cast upstream and across and allow the flies to fish back down at the current's speed

POSITION 1

UPSTREAM FISHING

DOWNSTREAM FISHING

A wet fly fished downstream and across follows the path of the fly line in a sweeping curve, and as the fly swings through this arc, gamefish find its movement irresistible. Controlling the speed of the fly is the key to consistent success. As the fly line sweeps around, keep the rod in line with it, because this produces a more controlled swing and improves take detection. A square cast produces a fast sweep and is a good tactic when using a team of three wet flies for trout. A long cast downstream and across makes a shallower angle and a slower swing, which is more effective for salmon.

FISHING DOWNSTREAM AND ACROSS
When you are fishing downstream and across, search all the possible fish-holding water, especially the areas between the main current and slack water.

Line is released steadily as the rod is swung across the river in a series of arcs

Mending line

When a fish rises in a streamy run but comes short, the reason can often be poor presentation: if the fly is fishing too fast, the fish will miss it. "Mending" the fly line slows the fly as it swings across the fish, and is achieved by throwing an upstream bow into the line immediately after the cast. This gives a slower, more controlled swing over the path **A** to **D**. If a fish is holding at **B** or **C**, but the swing is still too quick, several mends might be needed before the fly passes over it.

Upstream belly is formed in the line

CURRENT

A

B

C

D

The rod must lead the fly across to position **D**

Deep wading

Even with upstream mending, the fly will fish too quickly over its path from position 1. Fishing from position 2 eases the problem because the angle is more acute, but the wading angler at 3 can cover the fish at the same speed but with a much shorter cast.

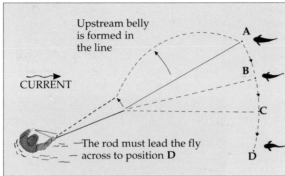

Position 3

CURRENT

Position 2

Position 1

Leading the fly

This is a method for fishing down water too deep to wade or where overgrown banks obstruct casting. Cast to **A**, then swing the rod across your body while releasing line to slow the fly. This makes the fly follow the path **A** to **B**. Repeating, by swinging the rod back to the start position and releasing more line, will drop the fly down to **C**. This can be repeated (to **D**, **E**, and beyond) until as long a line as practical has been fished. Takes will usually come on the swing across, so do not feed the line too quickly once the fly begins to move across.

Flies quarter the river in a series of sweeping arcs

Holding as much line as possible off the water allows the fly to sink deeper

Mend the line as necessary to slow the fly's drift

Make a cast downstream and across on a slack line

Take a pace or two downstream after each cast to slow the fly's drift

Work bucktails and streamers with the rod tip to imitate small baitfish

POSITION 1

POSITION 2

DRY-FLY FISHING

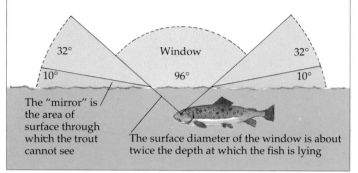

Dry-fly fishing becomes an obvious choice for the angler when trout are feeding on surface flies. Immortalized in the 19th century by experts such as Frederic M. Halford and Theodore Gordon, who placed great emphasis on exact imitation, dry-fly fishing has now become one of the most widely used methods for catching trout. It will also take many other species, including grayling, carp, and pike, and even salmon and sea trout can be caught on dry flies. The dry fly is fished on waters ranging from fast, rocky streams to large stillwaters, but the basic principle is always the same: to catch a fish on an artificial fly worked on or in the surface.

THE TROUT'S VISION

Because light bends when it enters water, a trout can only see objects on the surface that are (from its point of view) within an angle of about 48° each side of the vertical. This gives it a total "window" of vision of surface objects of about 96°, extended by a further 32° each side of the vertical for objects beyond the surface (including nearby anglers). Beyond the boundary of the window, light striking the surface at angles of less than 10° does not penetrate the water; all the trout sees is a reflection of its underwater surroundings.

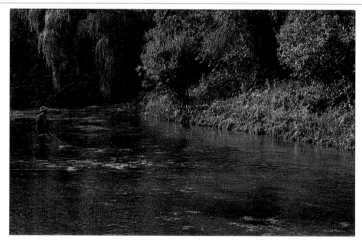

32°   Window   32°
10°   96°   10°

The "mirror" is the area of surface through which the trout cannot see

The surface diameter of the window is about twice the depth at which the fish is lying

UPSTREAM FISHING

In rivers, fish prefer to lie facing the current. By approaching them from downstream you increase your chances of remaining unobserved, and by casting just upstream of your target fish you can get your fly to drift gently downstream into its field of vision. Good watercraft is essential. Keep a low profile, learn how to identify likely lies, and cover the water carefully. Travel light for free mobility, and wear polarized sunglasses and a wide-brimmed hat or visor to cut out the reflected glare that makes it difficult to see into the water.

FISH FINDING
Back eddies and areas behind bridge buttresses are good places to look for feeding trout. Watch out for fish facing downstream into the reverse current of a back eddy: if you approach them from downstream they may spot you. Present the fly downstream of the target fish to avoid the line entering its window of vision.

Fish face downstream in a back eddy

CURRENT

Current divides

WINDOW
Try to place your fly just inside the trout's window, with as little leader as possible showing within it.

Fish lying tight into a steep bank will often only accept a fly hard into the bank

Cast a slack line to defeat drag caused by midstream current

Unless there are especially attractive features in midstream, fish are likely to be found near the banks

UPSTREAM FISHING

BLIND SPOT
A trout cannot see you when you are behind it, so upstream casting allows you to approach unseen.

STILLWATER FISHING

In stillwaters, trout tend to cruise the water, taking their food in a series of rises. By observing several successive rises you can anticipate the direction of travel of a fish, and cast your fly 1 to 3 m (3 to 10 ft) ahead of it so that there is time for the fly to settle before the fish reaches it. Let the fly drift naturally, and try to avoid drag: if drag occurs, your fly and leader will create a wake that will inevitably spook the fish. Use a fine, pale-coloured, double-strength or super-strong monofil for leaders when surface fishing, and avoid the darker sort that tend to scare the fish.

SURFACE FEEDING
Dry flies and emergers come into their own during light winds or flat calms, when fish feed on insects at the surface.

Dealing with a flat calm
Fish are easily spooked by a floating leader when dry flies are fished in a flat calm. Ensure that your leader sinks quickly by degreasing it with a mixture of fuller's earth and detergent or with a commercial degreaser. Keeping the line tight to the fly helps the leader to cut through the surface, as will a small nymph tied on a dropper above the dry fly or, as here, tied New Zealand style. The nymph sinks the leader but not the dry fly.

Dry fly or emerger pattern

Length and strength of leader between flies to suit conditions

Small, streamlined nymph

DOWNSTREAM FISHING

Fishing downstream is a good way to present a dry fly to fish in lies that are impossible to cover with upstream tactics. If a downstream trout is taking sedges, surface drag can be used to advantage by skating a fly across its nose to induce a take. This is achieved by making the line draw tight as the fly reaches the fish. The drifted fly can also be fished drag-free by feeding out line as it drifts downstream. The disadvantage with this method is that the fish is directly downstream of the angler, and this gives a poor hooking angle.

WADING
Unlike upstream dry-fly anglers, those fishing downstream usually wade. Wading gives you a better angle of presentation, better coverage of the water, and keeps your profile lower. When wading do not lift your feet too high: it can be dangerous in faster flows. Always wear a buoyancy aid.

The tightened line straightens and the fly begins to skate

SKATING THE FLY
To skate the fly across the stream in front of a feeding fish, tighten the line as the fly reaches it. The drag of the current will then pull the fly towards midstream.

Cast a slack line across and downstream

CURRENT

PROHIBITED!
Downstream fishing is not allowed on many streams because it is thought to give an unfair advantage to the angler. Check the local rules.

THE DRIFTED FLY
To drift a fly to a fish, pay out line so that the current carries it downstream without drag. The fish will see the fly before the line appears in its window of vision, so there is less chance of spooking the fish and more chance of a take.

DOWNSTREAM FISHING

Feed out loose line at a speed to match the current

NYMPH FISHING

Nymph fishing has progressed in many ways since the early 20th century, when G. E. M. Skues wrote his classic books on the subject. It no longer means just the subsurface fishing of an exact imitation of the trout's food, because today there are many different patterns, tied on hooks of various lengths, shapes, and sizes, that are classified as nymphs. For example, the use of fluorescents and bright synthetic fibres has led to a vast range of modern nymph dressings that arguably look more like lures than representations of the trout's food. In addition, there are now many tactics for fishing up to three patterns on a cast for both river and stillwater, so nymph fishing is no longer even restricted to using a single fly.

SIGHT INDICATORS

A sight indicator or bob is a visual aid, attached to the leader, that gives early warning of a taking fish. There are several different types available commercially, and most have a fluorescent finish that provides maximum visibility.

The Orvis Never-Miss foam ball can be slid to any position on the leader depending on water depth, and is reusable, unlike the self-adhesive Orvis Stay-On indicator. Moser's Butterfly Loop is an integral part of the leader system, being a length of braided nylon looped at each end for connection between the fly line and the leader butt. Visibility is enhanced by fluorescent wool incorporated into the braid.

Orvis Never-Miss

Orvis Stay-On

Moser's Butterfly Loop

RIVER NYMPHING

A nymph will often take trout that are on the move, either bulging below the surface or rooting about in the bottom weeds, and refusing to rise to a dry fly. This refusal to take a dry fly is often associated with preoccupied feeding on shrimps or ascending nymphs. It is essential to get the fly down to the feeding fish, so a weighted pattern is often required. Cast with enough lead to allow the fly time to sink to the required depth.

THE INDUCED TAKE
The clear waters of a chalkstream are ideal places to practise the induced take.

Inducing a take
Trout find flies that rise in front of their noses hard to resist. To induce a take in this way, you must be able to see the fish and make the fly rise at the right time. Allow a weighted fly to sink to the trout's holding depth, and then lift it, by raising the rod, as it nears the fish.

THE INDUCED TAKE

Dipping point · Sight bob · CURRENT · Nymph sinks in front of trout · Nymph rises as rod tip is raised

POSITION 1
When a fish in a lie refuses an upstream nymph drifted past it, the induced take comes into its own. Cast a weighted nymph beyond the fish. The leader is drawn down as the fly sinks, and when the fly drifts with the current towards the fish, raise your rod to lift it and induce a take.

CURRENT

Dipping point

Raise your rod tip when the fly is about 30 cm (12 in) from the fish

Watch the sight bob for any indication of a take

A high rod position means less line/water drag, and a faster strike

The cast is made upstream of a visible fish or its assumed position

Sight bob

To keep in touch with the nymph, retrieve line at the current's speed

Keep as much line as possible off the surface

UPSTREAM

STILLWATER NYMPHING

The larval and pupal stages of many aquatic insects are eaten by trout, as are water lice, tadpoles, snails, shrimps, daphnia, and corixids, to name just a few. Nymph fishers therefore tie flies to represent many such items of the trout's diet, creating either imitative or general patterns, and classify all of these flies as nymphs.

However, it is argued by some fly fishers that the only true nymphs are the nymphs of the Ephemeroptera (see page 100), and that all the other aquatic creatures represented with artificial flies are therefore misrepresentations. This is strictly true, but nymph fishing today is defined not by true imitations but by the methods used.

It is difficult to pinpoint exactly where nymph fishing ends and wet-fly and lure fishing begin, but most stillwater anglers who fish with an artificial fly that represents an aquatic lifelike presentation, consider themselves to be nymph fishers.

Stalking

This is a method for clear waters where the fish can be seen and a specific target selected, and is useful on small stillwaters for catching large, deep-cruising trout. Use a fly that has some weight and a good entry into the water, so that it gets down quickly to the cruising depth, and apply an induced take before the fish has passed by. On large waters, big fish can be ambushed in the margins.

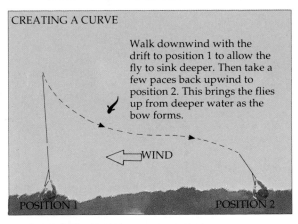

CREATING A CURVE

Walk downwind with the drift to position 1 to allow the fly to sink deeper. Then take a few paces back upwind to position 2. This brings the flies up from deeper water as the bow forms.

WIND

POSITION 1   POSITION 2

LINE COLOUR
Nymph fishermen find that pale-coloured fly lines are a great aid in detecting subtle takes.

CONCEALMENT
Study the cruising patterns of the fish when stalking, but stay hidden, keep a low profile, and wear sombre clothing.

Fishing a curve
Flies fished in a curve are always attractive to fish, in streams or in stillwaters. It is the change of speed and direction that deceives them. Wind puts a natural bow in the fly line, but it can pay to walk along the bank to create your own curve.

THE OPEN LOOP
Attach the fly to the leader with a universal or grinner knot, leaving a small loop when you tighten it. This will allow the fly to move freely and naturally.

Universal or grinner knot

Open loop allows fly to move more freely

STALKING FLIES
Walker's Mayfly Nymph is an excellent example of a leaded fly for stalking. Small, weighted bug or midge patterns can be effective with choosy fish on warm days, but these flies can be hard to see, so use a sight bob to make them easier to spot.

Walker's Mayfly nymph

Lead bug

POSITION 2
When wading a river, you can drift a nymph down with the current over water too deep to wade. Check the fly at intervals during the drift to make it rise in the water, simulating the movement of the induced take. Release more line after each check so that the nymph sinks again and drifts further down the pool.

POSITION 3
The dead-drift swing uses the acceleration of a fly through the arc created by the belly formed in the fly line as it drifts down with the current. Cast slightly upstream, and make the rod follow the line as it moves with the current. At the end of the drift the fly will speed up and lift as the belly straightens.

Rod follows the nymph around

Cast slightly upstream

Nymph swings around at the same speed as the current

Line speeds up and lifts the nymph in the water

Each time the line is checked, the nymph swings invitingly upwards

Drift   Check   Release   Drift   Check   Release

DOWNSTREAM

BOAT FLY FISHING

The technique of "fishing the drift" is an effective tactic for catching stillwater trout. This style of fishing involves working a team of three or four flies on a short line from a drifting boat, and is especially effective on breezy days and on wild waters. It has now largely been replaced by more modern, longer-line styles that use floating or sinking lines. With all these styles, the top dropper will take a lot of fish if it is worked properly. The secret is a steady lift at the end of the retrieve, holding the fly in the water's surface for as long as possible. Long leaders are now the norm, and the traditional flies have been replaced by newer patterns such as Raiders, Mini Muddlers, and emergers. However, a team of old favourites such as a Wickham's on the top dropper, a Silver Invicta on the middle dropper, and a Gold Ribbed Hare's Ear on the point is still an effective combination, particularly in high summer.

SAFE CASTING ANGLES

When two anglers share a boat, each must fish a restricted area to avoid interfering with the other's fishing and, more importantly, to avoid injuries that can arise from careless casting. If both are right-handed, angler A can fish safely in sector 3 and, with allowance for angler B's movements and safety, in sectors 1 and 2. Angler B can fish safely in sector 4. If one angler is left-handed, he or she should take position A and can then fish sectors 1, 2, and 3. If both are left-handed, the sector pattern is the reverse of that for two right-handed anglers.

Feeding fish working upwind

WIND

FISHING THE DRIFT

A 3 to 3.4 m (10 to 11 ft) rod gives good control when lifting the flies to the surface, and casts a wide enough loop to avoiding tangling them. Using long droppers improves presentation and allows for several fly changes before a dropper has to be replaced. Always keep in touch with the flies, and strike at the slightest sign of a rise to the team. Look for unusual movements downwind of the boat, and drift windlanes (flat tracts of water that run for considerable distances down the waves) because they usually hold fish.

LOCAL KNOWLEDGE
Lake fish populations are often localized, and without the assistance of a local fisherman or guide on waters that are unfamiliar to you, you could waste much time fishing unproductive areas. Here, a guide is controlling the drift of the boat, allowing the fisherman to retrieve his team of flies through the productive shallows around a rocky outcrop.

WIND

Bob fly or top dropper

The boat is allowed to drift sideways with the wind, and the flies are cast downwind of it

Feeding fish working upwind

In a strong breeze, use a large-sized or leaded pattern for the point fly so that it acts as a sea anchor to stabilize the team

The fly on the middle dropper takes fish attracted by the disturbance created by the top fly, or because it is an attractor in its own right

TOP DROPPER
Use a bushy fly in big waves and a sparser pattern in light winds. Highly visible flies such as Mini Muddlers not only catch many fish but also attract the trout onto the more sombre, imitative patterns on the other droppers.

In a strong breeze, the speed of the boat can be controlled by using a drift controller or drogue, which acts like a small underwater parachute to reduce the rate of drift

SUNK LINE FISHING

The tactic of lift and hold with a sunk, high-density (Hi-D) line can be very effective for fish lying deep. As the flies sink through the layers, use a steady retrieve to keep in touch with them and detect takes on the drop. Draw the flies to the surface as the boat drifts down on them, but stop the draw just as the top dropper comes into view or is about to break surface, and hold it there for as long as possible. Bright attractor patterns provoke the fish into taking as the flies are held before being lifted out, and nymphs fished behind a bright top dropper catch well when the trout are feeding on midges.

TIME FOR THE HI-D
A bright day early season, when the fish are lying deep, is just the time for the fast-sinking line and a flashy attractor on the top dropper.

FISHING THE HI-D

Fast-sinking, high-density lines are a necessity when you want to reach trout lying deep; WF #7 to #8 lines with 3 m (10 ft) rods are a popular choice. To find the holding depth of the fish, try the countdown method (*see page 216*). Once the holding depth has been found, vary the retrieve rate until you find the most productive taking speed.

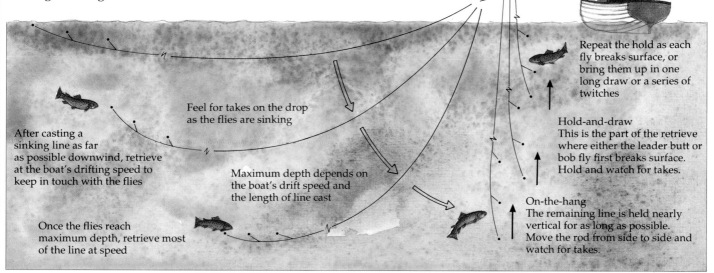

WIND

Boat drifts downwind

Repeat the hold as each fly breaks surface, or bring them up in one long draw or a series of twitches

Feel for takes on the drop as the flies are sinking

After casting a sinking line as far as possible downwind, retrieve at the boat's drifting speed to keep in touch with the flies

Maximum depth depends on the boat's drift speed and the length of line cast

Once the flies reach maximum depth, retrieve most of the line at speed

Hold-and-draw
This is the part of the retrieve where either the leader butt or bob fly first breaks surface. Hold and watch for takes.

On-the-hang
The remaining line is held nearly vertical for as long as possible. Move the rod from side to side and watch for takes.

DAPPING

Dapping, the technique of tripping a fly lightly over the surface of the water, has a reputation for producing large trout, salmon, and sea trout from large stillwaters. Long rods 4.6 to 5.2 m (15 to 17 ft) and a floss "blow line" that carries in the wind are essential. The filamentous strands of the blow line fray in use, but a knot tied every 45 cm (18 in) will prevent the line from disintegrating. Dapped natural flies are illegal on some waters.

WORKING THE FLY
The blow line is fed out to work the fly on the surface as far as possible downwind of the boat. The fly is worked by holding it just above the water and dropping it gently onto the surface at intervals, by allowing it to float, and by drawing it lightly across the surface. On windy days, a second fly adds stability.

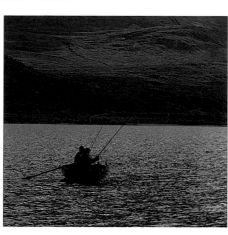

BOAT FISHING ETIQUETTE

When drifting along a shoreline, keep clear of bank anglers and do not drift too close to the shore. At the end of the drift, motor upwind well away from other boats, do not disturb the "hot spot" area where the fish are, and never cut into another boat's drift too soon. Only stand up if it is absolutely necessary, and always wear eye protection and a lifejacket.

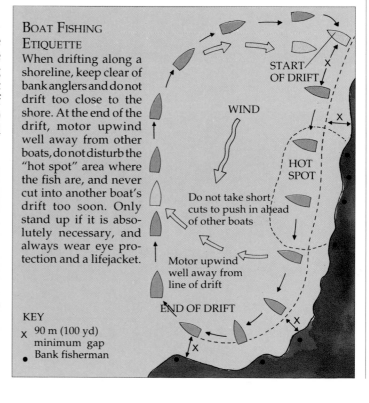

START OF DRIFT

WIND

HOT SPOT

Do not take short cuts to push in ahead of other boats

Motor upwind well away from line of drift

END OF DRIFT

KEY
x   90 m (100 yd) minimum gap
•   Bank fisherman

INSHORE FISHING

By using an outboard-powered dinghy or a small motor cruiser, you can fish waters that are beyond the reach of the shore angler but not far enough offshore to warrant being worked by larger boats. These include not only those close to the shore, but also the quiet bays, estuaries, and saltwater creeks that are often very productive because they are seldom fished.

SAFETY AT SEA

When you are in charge of a boat, of whatever size, it is essential that you are capable of handling it properly and that you and your companions know exactly what to do in an emergency. The boat must be seaworthy and of adequate size, with a reliable motor, a full tank of fuel, and basic emergency equipment including life-jackets, compass, flares, a first-aid kit, and, if possible, a radio. Before setting out, get an up-to-date weather forecast, and let someone know where you are going and when you expect to return.

UPTIDE FISHING

During fishing from an anchored boat in shallow water, the noise from the boat and the anglers can create a "scare area" into which most fish (apart from flatfish) are reluctant to stray. This area extends not only around the boat but also below it. In shallow water, if the fish cannot go deep enough to avoid the sound they may avoid the area of the boat altogether, and then it will not be possible to take them by drop-down fishing, in which the baits are simply lowered over the side.

Uptide fishing, in which the baits are cast uptide and well away from the boat, will overcome this problem. It works best in depths to around 12 m (40 ft), but it can be used much deeper. Wired sinkers are used to anchor the baits, and the length of line cast needs to be at least three times the depth of the water being fished.

Anchor rope

Boat anchored and facing into tide

TIDE FLOW

Traces are anchored by grip sinkers

Downtide belly in line helps the sinker to grip the bottom

TIDE FLOW

A
B
A
B

Tackle cast uptide to A drops back to grip bottom at B

Lines belly downtide

A
B
A
B

Casting and striking
Use a 2.7 to 3 m (9 to 10 ft) uptide rod with a fixed-spool reel or small multiplier, and cast uptide and away from the boat. After it hits bottom, the sinker will roll back a short way before taking hold. When you get a bite, wind in quickly until you feel the weight of the fish on the line, and then strike.

SELF-HOOKING TRACE

Reel line 5.4–8.2 kg (12–18 lb) mono

36.3 kg (80 lb) b.s. swivel

Bead

113–170 g (4–6 oz) fixed-nose grip sinker

18.1 kg (40 lb) mono link is longer than hook link

1/0–4/0 hook

36.3 kg (80 lb) b.s. swivel

90 cm (3 ft) of 18.1 kg (40 lb) mono

UPTIDE BREAKAWAY

BREAKAWAY

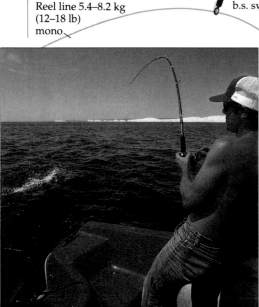

UPTIDE SHARK
Uptide fishing from a dinghy accounts for a small shark. Sharks are not the usual quarry of anglers fishing uptide, but the technique frequently takes dogfish, tope, and other small inshore sharks.

SELF-HOOKING TRACE
This trace is used for species such as cod and flatfish, which start eating the bait almost as soon as they pick it up. As they move off with the bait, they hook themselves by pulling against the grip of the sinker. The flowing trace (see opposite) is used for fish that run with the bait.

UPTIDE SINKERS *(above)*
Sinkers for uptiding can be of the breakaway type or have fixed wires on the flank or the nose (see pages 60–61). Those with long nose wires give the best grip; breakaways work best in shallow waters with medium tides.

DOWNTIDE FISHING

Not all boat-angling situations either suit or demand the technique of uptide fishing, nor do they require specialized rods. Downtide, drop-down bottom fishing in waters that are deeper than about 9 m (30 ft), particularly reef and general drift fishing, can be done perfectly well with standard boat tackle. Rods are generally around 2.1 m (7 ft) long, reels do not need to have good casting ability, and a wide variety of traces can be used.

The sinkers do not have to hold bottom securely, so need not be wired. They must, however, be able to maintain bottom contact, and so they must be matched to the strength of the tide and of the line – the lower each of these is, the less weight will be required. In addition, the weight of sinker being used should be changed as the strength of the tide increases or decreases.

Anchor rope

TIDE FLOW

Boat facing into tide

Bow rods use heavier sinkers to prevent fouling stern rods' tackle

Lighter sinkers drift further downtide

Length of line fished and sinker size should vary to suit tide

TIDE FLOW

Stern rods are usually the most productive

Anchor rope

Fish work uptide on scent trail from baits

Spacing the baits
In drop-down fishing, the baits all lie in line with the rod tips and therefore require careful spacing. If the rods at the front of the boat carry heavy sinkers and the stern rods the lightest that will hold, the current will drag them at different speeds and they will not tangle.

FLOWING TRACE
Fish such as bass, which run with a bait before eating it, will drop it if they feel any resistance from the sinker. The flowing trace allows unhindered feeding movement, so that the angler can wait until the fish has the bait inside its mouth before striking. When using a flowing trace, the reel is set on free spool to allow the line to be taken through the boom without moving the sinker.

FLOWING TRACE RIG

90 cm (3 ft) of 18.1–27 2 kg (40–60 lb) mono

Reel line 9.1–13.6 kg (20–30 lb) mono

Sliding boom

Bead

1/0–4/0 hook

36.3 kg (80 lb) b.s. swivel

170–340 g (6–12 oz) sinker to suit tide

DOWNTIDE SINKERS *(below)*
To maintain bottom contact without having to pay out an excessive line, you need a sinker that combines adequate weight with a simple, streamlined shape that offers little resistance to the current. The bomb meets these requirements and is the shape least likely to snag, making it the best choice for most downtide fishing.

SPREADER RIG

Wire paternoster

Reel line 9.1–13.6 kg (20–30 lb) mono

13–15 cm (5–6 in) arm

13–15 cm (5–6 in) arm

15–45 cm (6–18 in) snood depending on tide

15–45 cm (6–18 in) snood depending on tide

1–3/0 hook

1–3/0 hook

Bomb sinker to suit the tide

TORPEDO

BELL

FLAT BOMB

SPREADER RIG
This is a type of paternoster, a rig that presents baits on short lengths of mono, called snoods or droppers, above a sinker. The snoods are attached to the trace or to booms, and spaced so that they do not tangle with each other. This spreader rig has two wire booms, each carrying a short snood, allowing two baits to be fished at the bottom as a team. The snood lengths should be varied with changes in the tide: use snoods of 45 cm (18 in) in a fast-flowing tide, but shorten them to about 15 cm (6 in) at slack water to help minimize tangling. Flatfish, whiting, and codling are among the species that are highly susceptible to this type of bait presentation.

OFFSHORE FISHING

Fish tend to increase in numbers, size, and variety of species with greater water depth and distance from shore. But this does not mean that you will always have to sail a long way out to find large fish: they move to wherever their instincts tell them to be at any given time, which may be not far from the shore. For example, the biggest examples of cod, conger, and turbot are usually to be found well offshore at depth, but they could just as easily be within a few minutes' sailing time of port. One of the factors that determines the location of large fish is the availability of food, including sandeels and the mackerel that prey on them. These and other food items are found in large numbers over features such as offshore sandbanks and reefs, regardless of their distance from shore, so these features are often very productive fishing venues for the offshore angler.

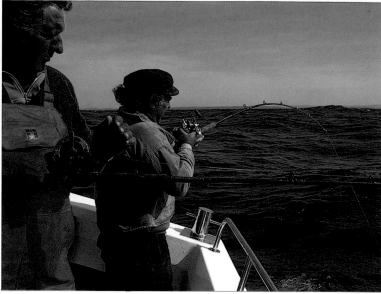

DRIFT FISHING
Fishing on the drift over rough ground is no place for light tackle, because fierce tides demand heavy sinkers to take the terminal tackle down to where the largest fish feed. In addition, big fish have to be bullied to prevent them from gaining the sanctuary that rough ground affords.

FISHING OVER SANDBANKS

Sandbanks are exciting places to fish, because they are one of the few types of offshore feature likely to concentrate clean-ground species of fish in the way that wrecks attract rough-ground species. Moreover, the fish likely to be feeding in good numbers around a large, steep bank include prized angling species such as bass, turbot, brill, and cod. The supporting cast can include numerous species of ray, plus plaice, dab, whiting, and even pollack.

Bank-fishing rigs
Bank-rig design depends on whether you are fishing at anchor or on the drift. For anchored-boat fishing, use a standard flowing trace (*see page 245*), made of 1.2 m (4 ft) of heavy mono and armed with a 4/0 Aberdeen hook. When drift fishing, increase the trace length to 3 to 6 m (10 to 20 ft) and attach the sinker via a long, tubular boom.

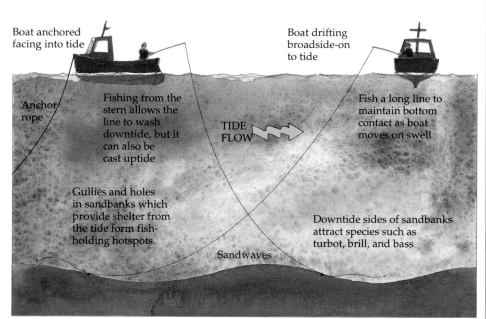

Boat anchored facing into tide

Boat drifting broadside-on to tide

Anchor rope

Fishing from the stern allows the line to wash downtide, but it can also be cast uptide

TIDE FLOW

Fish a long line to maintain bottom contact as boat moves on swell

Gullies and holes in sandbanks which provide shelter from the tide form fish-holding hotspots.

Downtide sides of sandbanks attract species such as turbot, brill, and bass

Sandwaves

BANK-FISHING SINKERS
Because a sandbank is a maze of ridges and gullies, end tackle often wanders from its intended path and this can lead to tangles. A studded watch weight is less prone to wandering and tangling than other types of sinker.

WATCH WEIGHT

Fishing on the drift
Drifting is by far the easiest way to fish a large bank, because it requires no prior knowledge of where the gullies and sandwaves are. If you start the drift well uptide of the lip of the bank, and pay out enough line to cope with variations in depth, your baits will cover every nook and cranny along the boat's line of travel. Bites show as a slow pulling-over of the rod tip (and of the rod itself, if unattended). Bass, turbot, and brill are typical bank species.

Fishing at anchor
When fishing from an anchored boat, you cannot cover as much ground with your baits as when fishing on the drift. As a result, you need to place your baits in the areas most likely to hold feeding fish, which are gullies and the downtide slopes of sandwaves. Free-swimming fish, such as bass, are usually found near the lip of the bank, skate and rays near the base, and flatfish over the middle section. The most reliable way to find these features is to use an echo sounder.

FISHING OFFSHORE REEFS

A reef attracts a rich variety of marine creatures, including fish, because it offers abundant cover, and the varying bottom topography provides a wide range of habitats. Because of the large number of species likely to be present, the reef angler is often faced with the question of which one to fish for, and having decided, may well find the baits being taken by other species anyway. For example, fishing specifically for conger does not rule out other species taking the bait, although the size of the baits and hooks will have a limiting effect. One of the most effective rigs for general reef fishing is baited mackerel feathers, and this fact is reflected in the alternative rigs shown here. Like feather rigs, they present the baits above the sinker so that they flutter enticingly and are clear of bottom snags. They avoid many of the common problems with shop-bought feathers, including short snoods and poor hooks.

FISHING ON THE DRIFT

TIDE FLOW

Boat drifts broadside-on to tide

Maintain bottom contact with as short a line as possible, to minimize snagging

The stronger the tide, the longer the line needed to maintain bottom contact

A near-vertical line is best, but only possible on a slack tide

Fishing on the drift
When drifting reefs or heavy ground, the type of tackle to use and the likelihood of losing it are determined to a large extent by the range of species present. For example, extensive areas of rock and kelp attract summer cod. These must be approached hard on the bottom with baits, small plastic squid, or pirks, and tackle losses will, unfortunately, be high. Over more varied heavy ground with pinnacles and rock faces, pollack will feed anywhere from the bottom to midwater. The need for bottom contact is therefore greatly reduced, unless the drift is slow enough to give bream, wrasse, and ling an opportunity of taking the baits.

DRIFT RIG

Reel line 13.6 kg (30 lb) mono

36.3 kg (80 lb) b.s. swivel

18.1 kg (40 lb) mono

30–45 cm (12–18 in) of 18.1 kg (40 lb) mono

4–2/0 hook

45 cm (18 in) of 27.2 kg (60 lb) mono

2/0–6/0 hook

Swivels locked with stops or superglue

DRIFT-FISHING RIG
The hooks should fish clear of the bottom, above a bomb sinker attached by a weak mono link so that the rig can be pulled free of the sinker if it snags. Hooks can also snag, so use Aberdeens if possible – they are made of lighter wire than standard hooks and may bend out of hangups.

30 cm (12 in) weak mono link

170–340 g (6–12 oz) sinker to suit tide

Fishing at anchor
There is less risk of hangups when fishing at anchor than when drift fishing because the terminal tackle is stationary. In addition, the static baits can be fished hard on the bottom, making them accessible to slow-feeding species – such as conger, ling, wrasse, and bream – that might not take a drifted bait. However, a grapnel anchor with a trip release should always be used, to avoid costly anchor loss if hangups do occur, and sinkers should be attached by weak links to minimize tackle losses.

FISHING AT ANCHOR

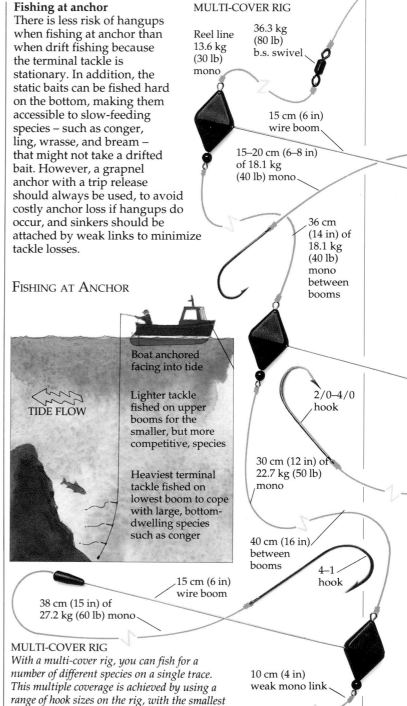

TIDE FLOW

Boat anchored facing into tide

Lighter tackle fished on upper booms for the smaller, but more competitive, species

Heaviest terminal tackle fished on lowest boom to cope with large, bottom-dwelling species such as conger

MULTI-COVER RIG

Reel line 13.6 kg (30 lb) mono

36.3 kg (80 lb) b.s. swivel

15 cm (6 in) wire boom

15–20 cm (6–8 in) of 18.1 kg (40 lb) mono

36 cm (14 in) of 18.1 kg (40 lb) mono between booms

2/0–4/0 hook

30 cm (12 in) of 22.7 kg (50 lb) mono

40 cm (16 in) between booms

4–1 hook

15 cm (6 in) wire boom

38 cm (15 in) of 27.2 kg (60 lb) mono

MULTI-COVER RIG
With a multi-cover rig, you can fish for a number of different species on a single trace. This multiple coverage is achieved by using a range of hook sizes on the rig, with the smallest at the top, and perhaps a different bait on each hook. The rig shown here has booms, but swivels or open blood loops can be used instead.

10 cm (4 in) weak mono link

Weight to suit tide

WRECK FISHING

Ships can be wrecked anywhere from the shore to mid-ocean, but the best angling wrecks will be in water deeper than 60 m (200 ft), and the greatest concentrations are usually found in the vicinity of major ports. Wrecks can end up on virtually any type of ground, and from an angling point of view it does not matter where they settle out. In time, algae begins to grow on a wreck, followed by encrusting animals such as barnacles; eventually, a complete food chain is established. For fish, a wreck on sandy ground is like an oasis in a desert, and in rocky areas it provides more food and even better cover, for both predators and prey, than the surrounding rocks. A broken-up wreck will offer more cover than one that is relatively intact, so it will attract larger numbers of fish. The more broken-up a wreck becomes, the better its angling potential will be.

FISHING AT ANCHOR

Working a wreck from an anchored boat is a very specialized affair that makes great demands on the skills of both skipper and anglers. The skipper must make allowances for wind and tide, both of which can vary greatly over very short periods of time, and make continual fine adjustments to keep the stern of the boat just uptide of the edge of the wreck. Anchoring is always done at the slacker periods of neap tides and requires good sea conditions. At best, anglers will get 2 to 2½ hours of anchored fishing before the new tide starts to swing the boat out of position and it is time to switch to fishing on the drift. However, as the boat starts to swing, baits missing target can land on the sandwaves that build around some wrecks and are caused by the tide. Clean-ground species, including large anglerfish and turbot, often frequent these sandwaves and sometimes feed tight up to the hulk.

Boat anchored facing into tide

Anchor chain

TIDE FLOW

To ensure that all rods are fishing over the wreck, all lines should be of similar diameters and all sinkers of equal weight

Water pressure on thick lines will push them too far downtide of the wreck

The long periods of slack water at neap tides are ideal for fishing at anchor

Wreck

Fishing into the hulk

When fishing into a hulk for fish such as large conger and ling, you need very heavy tackle and wire traces, and big baits placed right into the main wreckage, where they feed. Conger live in holes, and you need to drop the baits almost onto their heads to get them to show any interest. They take incredibly lightly and must be given time to do so, but they must be dragged quickly from their retreats the instant the hook is driven home, otherwise they will not be moved. Ling are quicker onto the baits than conger, so the best conger wrecks are those where the ling population has been thinned.

RUNNING LEGER FOR CONGER

The strong, simple running leger is the best rig to use for big-fish work over snaggy terrain. Provided you follow the basic design, you can vary the lengths and components to suit your personal preferences, but for conger fishing it is better to use wire rather than mono for the terminal trace.

RUNNING LEGER – CONGER RIG

Bead

22.7 kg (50 lb) b.s. swivel

1.2 m (4 ft) of 45.4 kg (100 lb) mono

Sliding boom

Reel line 22.7 kg (50 lb) mono

Crimp

10/0 hook or larger

Streamlined sinker to suit tide

22.7 kg (50 lb) b.s. swivel

30 or 45 cm (12 or 18 in) of 45.4 kg (100 lb) wire or 68 kg (150 lb) longliner's mono

FISHING ON THE DRIFT

Drift fishing over wrecks is far easier on both skipper and anglers than fishing at anchor. A buoy is dropped to mark the starting position, and after each drift over the wreck the boat is taken back uptide for another pass.

Fish on most wrecks divide into two main categories: those feeding at or near the bottom, such as conger, ling, and cod, and higher-level feeders, such as pollack and coalfish, which hunt prey fish all around the pressure wave caused by water forced up over the wreck by the tide. Conger, and more particularly ling, can be taken on a slow drift but are better approached at anchor. The rest are best fished for by drifting with rubber eels and pirks.

TACKLE LOSSES
Most wrecks offer excellent fishing, but tackle losses due to snagging can be high, even in calm weather and a placid sea.

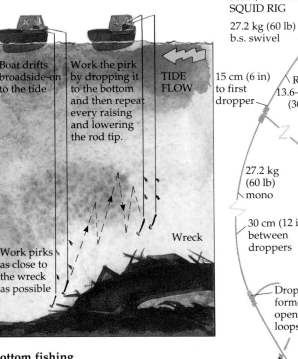

Boat drifts broadside-on to the tide

Work the pirk by dropping it to the bottom and then repeat every raising and lowering the rod tip.

TIDE FLOW

Work pirks as close to the wreck as possible

Wreck

Bottom fishing
Baited pirks, and small plastic squid rigged above a pirk, are excellent lures for cod and ling, and will occasionally take deep-feeding pollack. Both are fished right on the bottom, so tackle losses can be high, and it is essential to use pirks of the correct weight for the strength of tide. Plastic squid should be rigged on short, heavy mono standoff droppers, as close to the pirk as practicable.

Fishing the flying collar
This rig is effective for pollack and other species feeding above the wreck, but cod and ling might also grab at it in the initial stages of the retrieve. Flick the rig away from the boat to avoid tangles on the drop, and count the number of turns of the reel handle you make on the retrieve to get an idea of where fish might take. Set the drag light, or the hook will tear free as a taking fish kicks for bottom in one continuous, powerful run.

FISHING THE FLYING COLLAR

Flying collar rig lowered to wreck or seabed

TIDE FLOW

Wreck

Boat drifts broadside-on to the tide

When the rig touches bottom, wind in 50 to 60 turns of the reel handle; if no bites occur, lower the rig and repeat

FLYING COLLAR RIG

Boom (flying collar)

Bead

Swivel

170–227 g (6–8 oz) sinker

At least 3 m (10 ft) of 18.1 kg (40 lb) mono

10–20 cm (4–8 in) rubber eel

8/0 hook

PIRK/PLASTIC SQUID RIG

27.2 kg (60 lb) b.s. swivel

15 cm (6 in) to first dropper

Reel line 13.6–22.7 kg (30–50 lb) mono

27.2 kg (60 lb) mono

30 cm (12 in) between droppers

Droppers formed from open blood loops

30 cm (12 in) to pirk

Plastic squid (or rubber eels) on droppers

Pirk size and weight according to tide

249

SURFCASTING

Casting a bait from the beach into the surf is one of the most enjoyable styles of shore angling. It is also one of the most physical forms of angling, using more body movement than any other. However, in surf fishing it is not brute force that produces a good cast but correct technique. The first step is to master the basic casting action, which you can do quite quickly, but to develop good casting rhythm and movement you must practise until they become automatic; distance will come naturally once the rhythm is perfected. The off-the-ground cast is easy to learn, but it cannot be learned properly from books alone; a few lessons from a skilled surfcaster or a qualified casting coach will amply repay the time invested.

LOADING A SHOCK LEADER

MULTIPLIER REEL

FIXED-SPOOL REEL

To load a shock leader (see page 253) onto a multiplier, start with the knot near the right-hand flange. Lay it in open coils to the left and then to the right, stopping short of the knot. Open coils prevent the leader from biting into the main line, and if the knot is on the right it will not cut your thumb during the cast.

It is not necessary to load the leader manually onto a fixed-spool reel because the reel will cross-lay it automatically. However, starting with the knot at the rear of the spool and winding a minimum of six evenly spaced turns forward reduces the chance of the knot stripping bunches of line on the cast.

The grip
The reel-up position is more commonly used than the reel-down, and feels more natural. The reel-down position is favoured by many distance casters because the stronger hand supplies the power, leaving the weaker to control the spool.

REEL-UP POSITION

REEL-DOWN POSITION

THE OFF-THE-GROUND CAST

Look upwards at about 45°

Body unwinding powerfully

Left hand at shoulder level

A

B

Right hand extended

Pull rod through in a javelin-throwing movement

Body in coiled-spring position

Right knee bent and weight on right leg

Low rod tip

Shock leader and sinker laid out on beach

Sinker lifts from beach

The stance
Scrape a line in the sand or shingle to mark out the direction of the cast. Then stand with your right foot on the line and your left foot 15 cm (6 in) back, with both feet angled slightly forward. With the reel set ready to cast, swivel your waist and shoulders to position the sinker on the beach with the rod tip just off the ground.

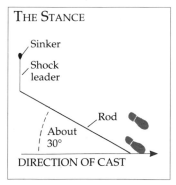
THE STANCE

Sinker

Shock leader

Rod

About 30°

DIRECTION OF CAST

The Cast
Set the reel for casting (see page 212), with the sinker hanging at 90 cm to 1.2 m (3 to 4 ft) from the tip ring. Brake the line with your thumb or finger, depending on the type of reel you are using. Then adopt the correct stance, taking your weight on your right leg (A). Your left hand should be next to your right shoulder, your left elbow raised, and your

right arm extended. Turn your head to face the cast direction, looking upwards at about 45° (B). Start to uncoil your body powerfully but smoothly to the left, simultaneously pulling the rod forward like a javelin along its own axis, not in a side sweep. Your left hand starts to rise while your right arm moves in close to your chest

COMMON CASTING FAULTS

Laying out the tackle on the beach before setting your feet in position reduces the "feel" through the muscles of your legs, back, and waist. Set your feet first, then swivel your waist and shoulders to lay out the sinker on the beach.

A second fault is to push the rod too soon in the initial stages of the cast (steps **A** to **C**). The rod should follow you rather than be pushed ahead of you. Concentrate on getting your head turned in the casting direction and "unwinding" your body like a spring, and the arm movement should then follow naturally.

SUITABLE TERRAIN
Off-the-ground casting is a technique for fairly clean, smooth beaches. It cannot be used on very rough ground, or when wading in the surf.

Rod tip moving forward towards release point

Left hand at its most forward and upward position

Right hand and shoulder punch forward

Punch/pull action accelerating

Release the line as soon as your right arm is fully extended

C

Right arm close to the body

Left hand pulls rod butt firmly down

D

Body weight transferring from right to left leg

Weight on left leg

E

Pull butt quickly but smoothly into the body

F

Left hand stops close to rib cage

as its elbow flexes. With your left arm now at its fullest extension, and your right hand at eye level, transfer your body weight to your left leg (**C**). The extra power that comes into the cast from the transfer of body weight translates into increased casting speed, which can be felt through the rod because the butt seems to tighten up in your hands.

As your left arm reaches maximum extension, start to punch your right hand upwards and at the same time pull the rod butt down sharply towards your ribcage with your left hand (**D**). This casting action should be one smooth, continuous movement, with no break between the initial "javelin throw" and the punch/pull sequence.

Continue the punch/pull sequence, accelerating the rod smoothly towards the release point (**E**). Your left hand should be pulling the rod butt towards your ribcage and your right arm should begin to straighten from the elbow. Your chest should be pointing in the direction of the cast with most of your body weight transferred to your left leg.

The powerful but smooth punch/pull action results in a fast, smooth turnover of the top tip. Release the line, when your right arm is at full extension and your left hand is tucked in against your ribcage (**F**). Stop the reel as soon as the sinker hits the water, to prevent the line from overruning under its own momentum and tangling.

SHORE FISHING 1

When fished at distance from a low vantage point, such as a beach, all traces present baits hard on the bottom regardless of where the sinker (weight) is positioned. Most traces are variations on the simple themes of the running leger and the paternoster, and the exact type of terminal rig to use at any particular time depends on local geography, sea conditions, and the way in which the target species is known to feed. To perform at their best, terminal rigs need to be as simple and free from self-snagging as possible. Use booms *(see page 60)* to keep sinkers and snoods (short lengths of line that carry the hooks) clear of each other and of the reel line.

LEADER KNOTS

Basic knot
A leader knot must be strong, reliable, and have a slim profile for safe passage through the rings. Tighten the half hitch with pliers before tying the knot in the reel line.

1 Tie a half hitch in leader; thread reel line through it.

2 Pull half hitch tight, then tie a knot in reel line.

Reel line

3 Tighten reel line knot, pull up to half hitch.

High-performance knot
Tie the reel line through a hole in the leader for a strong but very slim knot. This works best when the reel line is much thinner than the leader.

1 Flatten end of leader with pliers and make a hole with a hot needle.

2 Tie a knot in reel line.

Reel line

3 Tighten knot close to hole; trim and superglue.

BASIC TWO-HOOK PATERNOSTER

Split ring

30 cm (12 in) snood

Plastic boom

60 cm (24 in) between snoods

30 cm (12 in) snood

Grip sinker attached by oval split ring

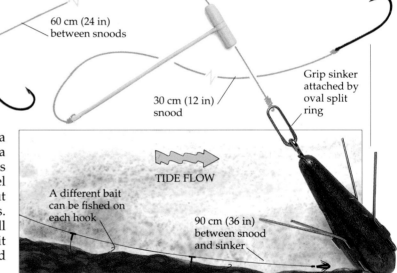

TIDE FLOW

A different bait can be fished on each hook

90 cm (36 in) between snood and sinker

Slow-moving fish, and those unlikely to run with or drop a bait at any hint of resistance, are best approached with a simple two-hook paternoster rig. In this one, each snood is tied to a loop dropper, formed by knotting a loop in the reel line and supported by plastic tubing to reduce tangles, but booms and swivels are effective alternatives to droppers. The wired grip sinker, besides anchoring the bait, will encourage fish to hook themselves as they pull the bait against its resistance. This is without equal as an all-round rig for a wide range of fish including flatfish and codling.

BASIC RUNNING LEGER

Split ring

Sliding boom

Bead

Swivel

90 cm (36 in) snood

Wired grip sinker

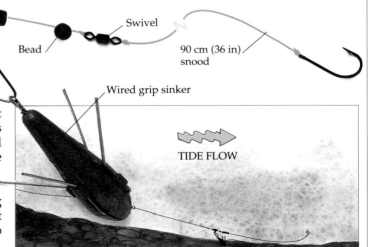

TIDE FLOW

Some fish, such as bass, like to run with a bait and might eject it should they sense something is wrong. Others, such as tope, make long runs before swallowing baits properly. All these fish must be allowed to take line freely before the strike is made, and the basic running leger rig allows them to do so. It is not a rig that lends itself to distance work, but it is excellent for medium-distance casting and for backing up the beach on a flooding tide. It is also a very good big-bait trace for fish such as conger, dogfish, and rays, although no fish will have any qualms about picking it up.

BASIC RUNNING PATERNOSTER

Split ring

Sliding boom

30 cm (12 in) mono shock leader

Bead

Swivel

30–60 cm (12–24 in) snood

The difference between this rig and the running leger is that the sinker is carried on a length of mono shock leader. (A shock leader is one that is made of heavier line than the reel line, to absorb the strain of casting a heavy sinker.) Having this shock leader between the sliding boom and the sinker makes for easier casting, because both sinker and bait hang at about the same point above the ground when you are standing in the casting position. It is a better rig than the running leger for slow or finicky fish that do not have to be allowed lots of line before the strike can be made.

TIDE FLOW

Wired grip sinker connected by split ring

ANCHORING THE BAIT

Uptide casting
Although tides appear to move up and down a beach, the direction of flow is often parallel to the shore. When such lateral currents are strong, bottom-holding and bite-detection problems can make the shore angler's life extremely difficult. The way to get around these problems is to use a wired grip sinker. These are available in a variety of sizes and wiring styles to offer differing degrees of hold to suit a wide range of conditions. When fishing a grip sinker uptide, cast well uptide of your rod rest and allow the sinker to fall freely. Before re-engaging the reel gearing, walk back to the rest, free-spooling line to create a bow. The force of the tide on the bow will help the grip wires to dig in well. A taking fish will dislodge the sinker, and the line will fall slack as the fish drops away downtide.

ROD POSITION
In heavy surf it is not only the strength of the tide that can cause difficulty in anchoring the bait: seaweed brought in by the breakers can foul the line and drag the sinker free. Holding the rod high, while feeling for bites, helps the line to clear the breakers.

CASTING A GRIP SINKER

Cast uptide of your fishing position, and allow line to pay off the reel as you walk back downtide

TIDE FLOW

Sinker will drop downtide until water pressure on the line drives the grip wires into the bottom

When a fish bites, line will fall slack as the fish drops away downtide

CASTING POSITION

Walk downtide after casting

FISHING POSITION

Avoiding snags
Typical snags that can cause tackle "hangups" include flotsam, weed, and heavy ground. When fishing heavy ground close in, and when there is heavy ground between you and cleaner, snagfree ground, sinker shape is important. All sinkers can snag, but the bomb-shaped type is less likely to than the rest. Where hangups are inevitable, attach the sinker by means of a sacrificial weak link.

WEIGHT LIFTER
Hangups can be a problem when shore fishing, because it is often difficult to lift the terminal tackle clear of any snags. A vaned device, known as a weight lifter, helps lift the sinker clear of snags when the tackle is retrieved rapidly with the rod held high.

Searching the bottom
There are times when using the rolling leger technique with a plain bomb sinker offers a distinct advantage over using an anchored bait, especially when fish are reluctant to move about or when they gather in isolated pockets, which are not always easy to locate. By casting the bomb well uptide and allowing it to roll slowly back down, you can search and cover large areas of ground with the bait or baits. However, if the tidal currents are strong, the bomb will travel too quickly to present the bait effectively, and it is prone to hangups on snaggy ground.

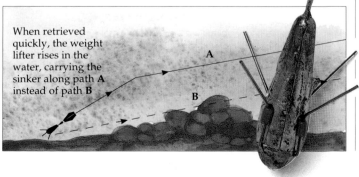

When retrieved quickly, the weight lifter rises in the water, carrying the sinker along path **A** instead of path **B**

A

B

SHORE FISHING 2

Not all shore fishing is done from the gradually shelving vantage point of a beach, nor do all coastal species of fish feed on or near to the bottom at all times. The sea is a three-dimensional world, with its unseen downward dimension assuming increasingly greater importance for anglers where deep water touches land. This could be beneath rock ledges, below harbour walls, or alongside piers and breakwaters. To get the best out of shore fishing in deep water, you must position your baits at the most appropriate depth. This could mean, for example, suspending a lugworm or a strip of fish beneath a float, or working a suitably heavy or weighted lure through the feeding zone. Spinning and float fishing have much to commend them as techniques for shore fishing, but it is important to use suitable tackle. The range of saltwater spinning and float tackle is increasing, but you may have to turn to the heavier end of the freshwater tackle stand to find what you need.

THINK FIRST
A dropnet, which can be lowered on a rope, is the only feasible means of landing fish from such a precarious position. Plan how to land your catch before starting to fish – not after.

FLOAT FISHING

Float fishing is regarded by many sea anglers as a sort of extension of freshwater fishing, and indeed, much of the tackle used is freshwater gear. Its use is limited, however, but not so much by the range of species that can be caught on it as by the conditions often prevailing where those fish live and feed. Fishing for mullet in quiet harbours, for example, presents no problems to standard freshwater tackle, but other situations call for a heavier approach. For instance, heavy tackle is needed when fishing baits just above kelp for wrasse, because these powerful fish will dive for cover the moment they take a bait. Fishing for pollack from rocky headlands, when they are feeding at some distance from the shore, also requires heavy tackle to get the baits out far enough and to control the situation at long range. Freshwater rods suitable for light float fishing include 3 to 4 m (10 to 13 ft) float and leger rods and 2.1 to 3 m (7 to 10 ft) spinning rods. Use a surfcaster for the really heavy work.

Sliding float fishing
Always use a sliding rather than a fixed float when fishing at depths greater than the length of the rod. With any float rig, you can wind in line only until the float reaches the top rod ring, and if the float is fixed for fishing at, say, 6 m (20 ft), you will still have 6 m (20 ft) of line paid out. This will make it difficult to retrieve the terminal tackle or to play or land a hooked fish. A sliding float rig is also preferable where casting room is limited, such as on a cramped rock ledge: with only the float and hook length hanging free, casting control and accuracy are much improved. A small sliding stop knot tied on the line above the float controls the depth at which the hook will fish, but winds easily through the rod rings.

SLIDING FLOAT RIG

Stop knot
Bead

Sliding float

Stop knot 5–7.5 cm (2–3 in) above split ring

28–42 g (1–1½ oz) drilled sinker

Bead

Split ring

60–90 cm (2–3 ft) mono

Hook size and bait to suit quarry

HEAVYWEIGHT FLOAT RIG

Partially inflated balloon

Bead

Stop knot

Split ring free to slide on line

Stop knot

57–85 g (2–3 oz) drilled sinker

Bead

Split ring

60–90 cm (2–3 ft) mono

Hook size and bait to suit quarry

Heavyweight float fishing
This rig is designed for situations where standard sea float tackle cannot cope. These include fishing in a fast current, where as much as 142 g (5 oz) of weight may be required to maintain depth, or when a big bait is to be drifted out to predators such as small sharks (*see page 256*). It is based on the sliding float principle, and uses a very large float, such as a balloon. This is tied to a swivel or split ring, running freely on the line below a bead and stop knot. Below the swivel or split ring are a drilled barrel sinker, a bead, and then a mono or wire hook length.

HARBOUR FISHING
This garfish was taken from the deep water off a harbour wall, an ideal venue for float fishing.

BOTTOM FISHING

Bottom fishing over heavy ground is always difficult, and losses of both tackle and fish will probably be high. These problems must be accepted as unavoidable if you are to have any reasonable hope of success, but there are ways of minimizing them. The most important of these is to keep your rigs as simple as possible. Basic single-hook terminal tackle is not only less likely to snag than a more complicated rig, but is also cheaper and therefore more expendable. Hangups usually occur either at the hook or the sinker, so these should be attached by weak links so that the rest of the rig can be pulled free of them if they snag (but do not use a weak link for the hook length if you are after sharp-toothed species). Alternatively, you can use a buoyant leger rig to float the bait clear of the bottom and thus of potential snags.

Supported-line fishing
This technique employs a balloon to support the line, so that the terminal tackle rises clear of snags when it is retrieved: it has no effect on bait presentation. Using a supported line, you can cast onto clean ground to the seaward side of snags and be reasonably sure that the tackle will make it back for another throw. You can use whichever bottom-fishing rig you prefer: simply slide a swivel or split ring, attached to a balloon, onto the reel line before attaching the terminal tackle.

Buoyant leger fishing
Using a buoyant leger rig, it is possible to float a bait at a fixed distance above the bottom. This offers improved bait presentation as well as reducing the risk of snagging. For example, it can help to prevent the bait from becoming "lost" between rocks and therefore inaccessible to fish, and reduces the risk of crab damage that can render a bait worthless within minutes of it touching bottom. The rig is simply a balsa float slipped onto the hook length of a leger rig, and the height to which the bait rises is determined by the position of a stop knot.

BUOYANT LEGER RIG

Reel line

Bomb sinker

Bead

Split ring or swivel 60 cm (2 ft) from stop knot

Fluorescent green balsa float 7.5 cm (3 in) long, 12 mm (½ in) thick

Stop knot 15–30 cm (6–12 in) from hook

Hook size and bait to suit quarry

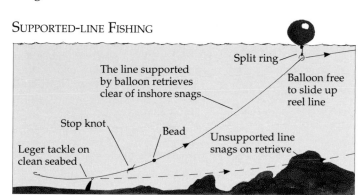

SUPPORTED-LINE FISHING

The line supported by balloon retrieves clear of inshore snags

Split ring

Balloon free to slide up reel line

Stop knot

Bead

Unsupported line snags on retrieve

Leger tackle on clean seabed

SPINNING

SHALLOW SPINNING RIG

90 cm (3 ft) trace

21 g (¾ oz) anti-kink weight

Small rubber sandeel

SHALLOW SPINNING RIG
Cast this rig with a gentle lobbing action. If you cast too vigorously, the uptrace sinker will travel ahead of the lure, causing tangles.

Spinning offers certain advantages over bait fishing, one being that with only a small box of lures and a light rod and reel to carry, you can easily cover long stretches of coastline in a day's fishing. Rocky shores provide some of the best saltwater spinning venues, because they usually attract a wide variety of the predatory species, such as mackerel, bass, and pollack, which strike readily at artificial lures. When spinning, search the water as thoroughly as possible by varying the lure depth and using a radial casting pattern *(see page 216)*. Suitable lures include plugs, spinners, wobbling spoons, and bar spoons, and you should carry a selection of different types so that you can use whichever is most suitable for the species you are seeking and for the prevailing conditions. Fish usually attack from below, so use dark-coloured lures when the sky is bright and switch to lures with light or reflective finishes when fishing in poor light conditions.

LANDA LUKKI TURBO SPOON
Use a heavy lure like this for deep spinning.

Lure weight
The greater the distance you can cast a lure, the more water you can cover with it. For this reason, and to fish deep in strong tides, a heavy lure (fished on tackle that can handle it) is often preferable to a light one. Ideally, the lure should be self-weighted, but this is not always possible, and you may need to add a streamlined anti-kink weight to the line *(see page 214)*. To minimize the risk of tangling, straighten the line by checking its flow from the reel just before the lure hits the water, or start winding in the moment it touches down.

SAFETY FIRST
Rocky shores usually have deep water close inshore. This makes them suitable venues for spinning, which generally works best in waters more than 1.8 m (6 ft) deep. However, deep water and spray-soaked rocks are a dangerous combination: wear suitable shoes with good grip and always fish with a companion.

SHARK FISHING

Sharks can be caught by a number of techniques, including drift fishing, bottom fishing from an anchored boat, shore fishing, and trolling with natural baits, either live or dead *(see page 258).* They can also be taken on fly tackle. The basic techniques shown here are suitable for sharks that feed in the middle and upper layers, such as blue shark, mako, and porbeagle, and for tope and other small sharks that feed near or at the bottom.

Because sharks have abrasive skins and very sharp, strong teeth, it is essential to use a wire trace at the end of the terminal tackle. One end of this trace is attached to the hook by a crimped loop, and crimped loop at the opposite end joins it to the main line (or to an intermediate length of heavy mono trace) via a swivel.

CRIMPING A WIRE TRACE

1 Slide the crimp onto the wire. Pass the wire through the hook or swivel eye, then tie a single loop knot and pull it tight with pliers.

2 Slide the crimp over the loose end of wire. Leave a short length of the loose end protruding beyond the crimp.

3 Loop the loose end, and tuck it back inside the crimp. This will prevent the sharp end of the wire from causing any damage.

4 Squeeze the crimp tightly closed with the pliers. Squeeze it at as many points as possible along its length.

DRIFT FISHING

Blue sharks and makos are mainly open-water species, feeding on pelagic shoal fish such as mackerel and pilchard, while porbeagle hunt closer to the shore over shallow-lying reefs. All can be caught from a drifting boat on 13.6 to 36.3 kg (30 to 80 lb) class boat rods, using baits suspended by floats (balloons) over a slick of rubby dubby. Sharks have a keen sense of smell and can lock onto very low concentrations of scents, so the slick will attract their attention. Moving their heads from side to side to detect the greatest concentration of scent, they will follow it to its source.

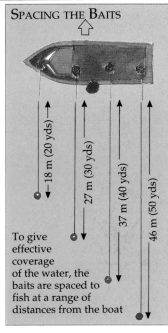

SPACING THE BAITS

18 m (20 yds)
27 m (30 yds)
37 m (40 yds)
46 m (50 yds)

To give effective coverage of the water, the baits are spaced to fish at a range of distances from the boat

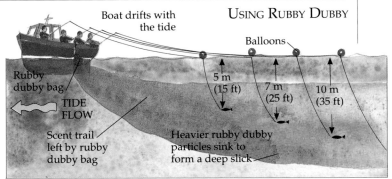

Boat drifts with the tide

USING RUBBY DUBBY

Balloons

Rubby dubby bag

TIDE FLOW

5 m (15 ft)
7 m (25 ft)
10 m (35 ft)

Scent trail left by rubby dubby bag

Heavier rubby dubby particles sink to form a deep slick

Bait depths
Until you discover at what depth the sharks are feeding, your baits should be set to fish at different depths, as well as at different distances from the boat. The bait fished furthest from the boat should also be the deepest, and that closest to the boat should be the shallowest.

Rubby dubby slick
As the boat drifts along, it leaves a widening slick of rubby dubby behind it. The heavier pieces of rubby dubby sink deeper than the lighter ones, so the slick deepens, as well as widens, the further it is from the boat. This ensures that all the baits are within the slick.

SHARK DRIFT RIG

Light line to balloon
Bead
Main line 13.6–36.3 kg (30–80 lb) mono

Stop knot   Swivel

BALLOONS *(left)*
Tie the balloon to a short length of thread. Tie the thread to a swivel on the line, or staple it to a short rubber tube, and jam the tube onto the line with a matchstick.

Crimp

3 m (10 ft) of 91 kg (200 lb) mono

22.7 kg (50 lb) b.s. swivel

Forged 14/0 hook

60–90 cm (2–3 ft) of 91 kg (200 lb) wire

Crimp

SHARK RIG
To avoid damage to the main line, the trace of a shark rig should be at least as long as the fish being sought — some say longer, because many sharks roll around when hooked and get wrapped up in the trace. A long wire trace is difficult to handle, so use a relatively short length of braided wire at the hook end and attach it to the main line via an intermediate trace of heavy commercial monofilament.

BOAT FISHING FOR TOPE

The tope is one of the many small and medium-sized shark species that hunt near or at the bottom, feeding on fish such as cod, whiting, and flatfish over clean or mixed ground close inshore. Tope seem to hunt either as loners, or in single-sex groups that gather over feeding grounds. They can be caught by bottom fishing from an anchored boat or from the shore, and the best bait is cut or whole fish.

When fishing from an anchored boat, you can use either uptide or downtide casting techniques *(see page 244)*. For uptide fishing, use a soft-tipped uptide rod around 3 m (10 ft) long, and a wired grip sinker that will hold bottom in the prevailing tide. Pay out enough line to allow a belly to form in it when the sinker has taken hold. For downtide work, use a 13.6 kg (30 lb) class boat rod and a suitable plain bomb sinker.

CATCH AND RELEASE
This tope has provided fine sport on suitable tackle and is being returned safely to the sea.

BOAT RIG FOR TOPE

Bead

36.3 kg (80 lb) b.s. swivels

Crimp

Sliding boom

Main line 8.2 kg (18 lb) mono uptide, 13.6 kg (30 lb) downtide

1.2 m (4 ft) of 22.7–27.2 kg (50–60 lb) mono

30 cm (12 in) of 27.2 kg (60 lb) wire

Crimp

8/0 to 10/0 hook

BOAT RIG FOR TOPE
This rig is just a variation of the very effective flowing trace (see page 245). Like the larger blue shark, a running tope can chafe and bite through light mono, so the trace must be longer than the fish. Use about 30 cm (12 in) of wire and 1.2 m (4 ft) of heavy monofilament.

Uptide or downtide sinker to suit tide

Anchor rope

UPTIDE FISHING
Use a soft-tipped rod to prevent sinker being pulled free by current.

TIDE FLOW

DOWNTIDE FISHING
The stronger the current, the further the sinker will carry before holding bottom.

Grip sinker

Bomb sinker

SHORE FISHING FOR TOPE

Stop knot   Bead   Balloon tied to swivel (or matchstick method)

BALLOON FLOAT RIG

Shore rigs
Use either a simple flowing trace rig, or one with a balloon float and weighted by a drilled barrel sinker. A long flowing trace prevents damage to the main line, and also allows the fish to pick up the bait and make a run before the hook is set. Casting a long trace with a big bait is difficult, but you should use one made up of at least 1.2 m (4 ft) of heavy monofilament and 30 cm (12 in) of wire.

Bead

Bead

Tope are often found within casting range of the shore. Rock ledges and headlands looking out onto sand can attract them, as do steep beaches of sand, shingle, or mixed ground. Use a good-quality shore rod that can cast weights of up to 170 g (6 oz). The reel should be loaded with about 275 m (300 yds) of 9.1 to 11.3 kg (20 to 25 lb) mono, because a tope can run a long way when hooked.

Main line 9.1–11.3 kg (20–25 lb) mono

113 g (4 oz) drilled sinker

1.2 m (4 ft) of 22.7 kg (50 lb) mono

30 cm (12 in) of 27.2 kg (60 lb) wire

Crimp

36.3 kg (80 lb) b.s. swivels

Crimp

6/0 to 8/0 hook

FISHING FOR DOGFISH

Smoothhounds and most of the small sharks collectively known as dogfish, including the smooth dogfish, are shallow-water species that feed mainly on crabs and molluscs. These sharks have flattened teeth that crush rather than cut, and are commonly caught by casting from the shore and by boat fishing over shallow offshore banks. When hooked they are capable of putting up a hard fight.

PENNEL-RIGGED HOOKS

4/0 hook

Rubber sleeve over hook shank holds hook in place on line

22.7 kg (50 lb) mono

4/0 hook

Line threaded through eye and rubber sleeve

Dogfish rigs
For sharks with crushing rather than cutting teeth, you need a heavy mono flowing trace about 1.2 m (4 ft) long. Use a single hook or a pennel rig, baited with peeler crab portions. The advantage of the pennel rig over a single hook is that you can present a bigger bunch of crab portions, with a hook at each end.

257

BIG-GAME FISHING

Big-game fishing is the pursuit, with rod-and-line tackle, of a wide range of large fish, including billfish, sailfish, wahoo, tarpon, the larger species of tuna, and large, active sharks, such as the mako and tiger. Most big-game fishing is done from charter boats, many of which provide tackle, bait, and instruction if required. The species sought depends partly on the preferences of the anglers and partly on what is available in the waters being fished, as do the techniques and tackle employed. Some big-game fishers prefer fly tackle, but the

majority use boat tackle in the 5.4 to 59 kg (12 to 130 lb) IGFA classes, and methods such as lure trolling, deadbait trolling, and even livebaiting. All have their advantages and drawbacks, all catch plenty of fish, and on its day, each one can outfish the others. It all depends on the circumstances and conditions prevailing at the time, and no technique is good enough to warrant the neglect of the others. An open mind is just as important for success in big-game fishing as it is in any other form of angling.

LURE TROLLING

There are a great many species of fish that will take a trolled lure, so it is difficult to predict what you are going to catch when trolling, but there is a hard core of species that will regularly respond to the technique. These include marlin, sailfish, tuna, and similar large pelagic feeders favouring deep, open water, often where the ocean floor is

quite literally miles below the surface. Middleweight gamefish such as wahoo, dolphinfish, and bonito will also hit a moving lure in open water. Whether these fish are truly big-game species is arguable, but large specimens occur, and at any size all of them are hard to subdue. Lure trolling is especially useful in open water where the fish are

not concentrated in any particular area, because it allows the coverage of a lot of ground. The lures work as a spread at the surface, and are chosen so that each has a slightly different action. Together they create noise and leave a trail of bubbles behind them, which draws large predatory fish up from below. These then attack the lures.

Lure-fishing pattern
Big-game boats typically fish four rods at a time: one from each side, held clear of the boat on outriggers up to 14 m (45 ft) long, and two from the stern. Between them they usually fish a combination of submerged lures and lures that skip the surface. Each rod fishes with a different length of line paid out, for example 37 m (120 ft) and 43 m (140 ft) for the outrigger lines, and 21 m (70 ft) and 27 m (90 ft) for the stern lines. This spread of lures is designed to create the impression of a small school of baitfish, but when a fish gives chase, it will not necessarily go for the outermost lures. The stern lines often produce the most strikes, perhaps because fish are attracted towards them by the wake of the boat.

LURE TROLLING

Reel line clipped to outrigger by release clip

Outrigger

Boat trolls at steady speed to suit the lures being fished

43 m (140 ft)

27 m (90 ft)

Stern line

Teaser

A "teaser" is designed for maximum flash and movement at the surface, and draws fish up to the other lures

21 m (70 ft)

37 m (120 ft)

LURE SELECTION
Although manufacturers often label their lures as being for particular species, such as marlin or tuna, the fact is that any lure can take any species in the right circumstances. Select a range of lures, including Kona Heads and plastic squid, that will give you a good choice of colours, sizes, and actions to suit the quarry you happen to be after and the prevailing conditions.

KONA HEAD LURES

BIG-GAME SPECIES
In addition to billfish and other very large species, many smaller fish – such as this barracuda – are often grouped under the general heading of big-game fish. Other such species include dolphinfish, albacore, king mackerel, and amberjack.

Bait Fishing

There is nothing more stimulating to the aggressive instincts of most predatory fish than the natural scent or movement of a prey fish. This makes natural baits generally more effective than artificial lures, but there are some drawbacks to using them. For example, wahoo are very adept at chopping baits off just astern of the hook, and some species take livebaits more readily than others: black marlin are more susceptible to a slowly trolled tuna or dolphinfish than to a lure, but sometimes the reverse is true of blue marlin. Livebaits also attract sharks, which are only rarely willing to strike at a lure. This can be a problem if other species are your quarry, and it does not diminish when dead or cut baits are used, because the sharks home in on the scent instead of the vibration. However, there is more chance of a dead or cut bait being grabbed by one of the highly prized species than by a shark if it is trolled rather than fished static.

Deadbait trolling

The appearance and smell of a deadbait make it potentially more attractive to predators than an artificial lure, but the presentation should allow it to "swim" in a natural manner or this advantage will be lost. With mullet, balao, and other small baitfish, rigging is fairly simple, but larger baits such as bonito and dolphinfish need to have their mouths stitched shut to reduce water resistance, and their pectoral and dorsal fins stitched erect to keep them upright. Large baits should be trolled at a much slower speed than small baits and lures.

Deadbait Rigs

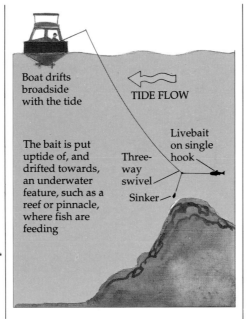

BALAO RIG

Mouth wrapped with soft wire

MULLET RIG

Small sinker

BALAO RIG
Pass the hook into the mouth and out through the body cavity, then close the mouth over it. To close the mouth, bind it with soft wire.

MULLET RIG
Cut a hole between the pelvic fins and remove the entrails. Push the hook shank through the hole into the mouth, and attach it to the line via a wire loop through the lips.

Boat drifts broadside with the tide

TIDE FLOW

Livebait on single hook

The bait is put uptide of, and drifted towards, an underwater feature, such as a reef or pinnacle, where fish are feeding

Three-way swivel

Sinker

Livebait drifting

This technique is used mainly to catch amberjack and other species when they are feeding over small targets such as pinnacles and reefs. The main drawback with the technique is interference from other species, particularly sharks, although when amberjack are present in large numbers they usually monopolize the feeding. Small baitfish, such as grunts, are hooked through the nostrils or lips, sent down with a heavy sinker uptide of the holding area, and drifted along the bottom towards the target.

Livebait trolling

Livebaits must be treated with care if they are to remain alive, and trolled slowly to prevent them from drowning. Use only those fish that have suffered minimal hook damage during catching, and rig them in the least injurious way possible. The best approach for large baits such as bonito and dolphinfish is to use the bridle rig, which involves tying the bait to the hook instead of impaling it on it, and thus minimizes bleeding. Small baits can also be rigged this way, but are are more effective when put onto a wide-gape livebait hook via their nostrils.

FISHING VENUES
Mid-ocean islands, such as the Azores, offer deepwater fishing for species such as marlin within a short sailing time from harbour.

Trolling and Drifting

SLOW TROLLING

FAST TROLLING

DRIFTING
This is a good way to present natural baits over localized fish-holding areas such as reefs, pinnacles, and wrecks.

DRIFTING

TIDE FLOW

FAST TROLLING
This allows you to fish for the faster-swimming species, such as wahoo and bluefin tuna. Use lures with shallowly angled faces.

SLOW TROLLING
For trolling at about 5 to 8 knots, use long, lightweight, softhead or rubber lures with steeply angled faces.

LIVEBAIT TROLLING
When trolling livebaits, two rods only are fished to prevent crossover tangles. Four deadbaits can be worked over the surface by slow trolling.

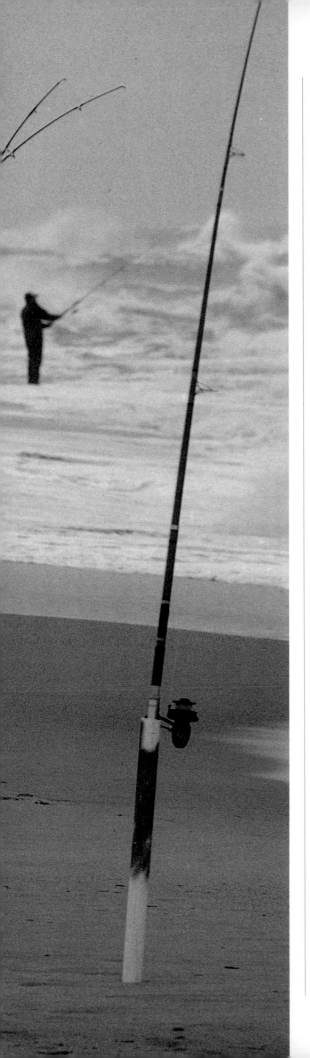

THE WATER

THE OBSERVANT ANGLER WHO LEARNS how to "read" the water, whether it be a small pond or a stretch of ocean, will be able to deduce what fish might be present, whereabouts in the water they are likely to be, what they are feeding on, and where and how to present the lure or bait to catch them. Acquiring and using this knowledge does not guarantee a catch, but it makes one much more likely than guesswork or relying on luck will.

If you fish a particular water regularly, spend time studying it at different times of the day and watching the movements and feeding habits of the fish. This will help you to locate and catch fish on that water, and also provide you with knowledge of fish and their habitat that you can put to good use on other waters.

Binoculars and polarized sunglasses are a great help when you are studying the activities of fish. Binoculars enable you to watch for small, distant clues to fish movements, such as slight surface disturbances. They are especially useful at sea, for spotting changes in water colour that might indicate fish-holding areas, for instance, or shoals of baitfish rising to the surface to escape attacking predators.

In this chapter, you will find the signs to look out for on a variety of different waters, including streams, stillwaters, and the open sea.

LOOKING FOR CLUES
Time spent studying the water to find out where the fish are likely to be is never wasted.

STREAMS & RIVERS 1

Streams and rivers can be divided into two basic types: chalk (or limestone) streams, fed by springs and containing high levels of calcium carbonate and other mineral nutrients; and rainfed (or freestone) streams, fed mainly by surface runoff and generally low in minerals. They can be further subdivided into three zones: the rushing upland stream; the moderately paced middle reaches; and the wide, deep, lower reaches.

CHARACTERISTICS OF STREAMS

Streams generally originate up in the hills or mountains, where rainfall is at its highest. Their tumbling upper reaches tend to be rich in oxygen but cold and rock-strewn, offering little in the way of either comfortable habitats or food for fish. As these young waterways begin to flow through less rugged countryside and are joined by tributaries, they grow in size and slow in pace, allowing vegetation to gain a foothold. Aquatic weeds begin to establish themselves, while earthy, rather than rocky, banks play host to trees, bushes, and plants. When the river becomes old, winding slowly across a wide flood plain, the types of aquatic weed and the species of fish present change, with those able to tolerate lower oxygen levels in the water and greater turbidity (muddiness) becoming dominant.

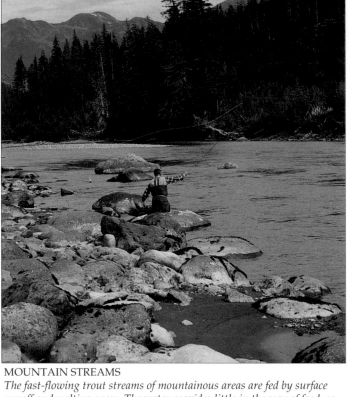

MOUNTAIN STREAMS
The fast-flowing trout streams of mountainous areas are fed by surface runoff and melting snow. The water provides little in the way of food, so the fish they contain tend to be small.

Types of stream
Some streams have as their source a bubbling spring, created by rainwater that has percolated through a porous rock, such as chalk, until it has reached a material that it is less able to permeate, such as clay. Because the water cannot filter through the clay, it emerges as a spring at the base of the chalk. Other streams result from water seeping out of bogland, which is able to retain water and continue releasing it long into dry spells.

Rivers that begin their lives in rain-soaked hills are much more at the mercy of the weather than those that are springfed. Long dry spells can see a rainfed river reduced to the merest trickle, making life very difficult for the fish that inhabit it; in drought years, some rivers dry up completely. At the other extreme, sudden heavy rain can transform them into boiling torrents, sometimes in a matter of hours.

Snowfed rivers tend to be at their best in summer. During the spring months, snow on the mountains melts, creating a rise in the levels of the rivers that drain them. Sometimes, the thaw can be rapid, turning these streams and rivers into torrents. This meltwater is freezing cold, and not much good for fishing in. It is better to wait until towards the end of the snow melt, when air and water temperatures are rising, the flow has eased, and water levels are on the decline. A winter of low snowfall followed by a dry spring and summer will see the flow of snowfed rivers drastically reduced.

Streams and rivers emerging from reservoirs and managed lakes tend to enjoy steadier levels of flow, because it is possible to vary the amount of water passing through or over the exit sluice gates or weir. In times of low rainfall, compensation water can be released to keep up river flows, and because a stillwater acts as the source, the river may well never become too muddy, even after very wet weather.

The zones of a river
The species of fish present in a river vary from one zone to another. In the upper reaches, where the water is flowing at its fastest and clearest, and carrying the greatest amount of dissolved oxygen (caused by its being "broken up" by the mass of stones and boulders which make up the riverbed), trout and grayling will be found. Food is normally in limited supply, being restricted to the larvae of a few species of insect and shrimps (plus whatever terrestrials fall in), so the fish tend to remain small.

Further downstream, where the river becomes deeper and the flow steadier, weedbeds provide cover for fish and attract the animal life on which they feed. This, combined with the less turbulent flow, results in more species being present, including barbel, chub, dace, and roach. Trout and grayling may also be found, if the water is clean.

In the latter part of most rivers' lives, flow is slow, particularly in summer. The riverbed usually consists of soft mud and silt, and weed growth may be profuse. The mud and silt are often in suspension, which results in reduced visibility and an unsuitable environment for the species found further upstream. Instead, bottom-loving fish, more tolerant of water with lower dissolved oxygen levels, are present. These include bream and tench.

CHALKSTREAMS
The gin-clear water of a chalkstream has a high mineral content, enabling it to support abundant vegetation and thriving fish populations.

VEGETATION

Vegetation in and along streams and rivers provides many benefits to both anglers and fish. Trees and other plants growing at the water's edge can help to bind and stabilize the bank, protecting it from erosion, and aquatic weeds can help to filter pollution from the water as well as hold up water levels during times of low rainfall. Weedbeds of all kinds also provide protective cover for fish and a home for the many different species of invertebrate on which they feed, and provide predators, such as pike, with concealment while they lie in wait for their prey. Overhanging trees also give cover, and terrestrials such as beetles and caterpillars often fall from their branches into the water, as do berries (elderberries, for instance, are taken by roach and chub).

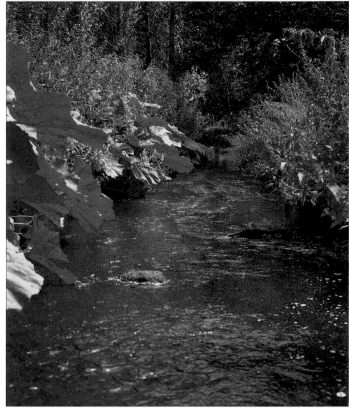

WEEDBEDS
Lush beds of weed are home to large populations of aquatic invertebrates, which attract feeding fish. Weeds protruding above the surface are easy to spot, but submerged weedbeds may not be so obvious: look for the slack water they create.

BANKSIDE VEGETATION
Fish like to lie beneath undercut banks and overhanging bankside trees and plants, which offer them shade from the sun, cover from predators such as herons (and anglers), and a source of insects and other foods.

SURFACE INDICATIONS

An ability to read the water can greatly improve an angler's success rate. Surface flow is rarely uniform, and patches of disturbance or areas of slack can provide clues as to what is happening under the water.

Underwater obstructions
Swirls and whorls in an otherwise uniform stretch of fast-flowing river reveal the presence of an underwater obstruction, such as a large boulder or an outcrop of rock. It is likely that an area of slacker water will exist behind it, and possibly on either side as the flow is deflected. Many fish, including trout and salmon, like to lie up and rest in such areas of slack water. In winter, a similar surface disturbance, or even a small patch of slack water, may betray the existence of a bed of true bulrush that has died back but is still big enough to obstruct the flow and create an area of sheltered water immediately behind it.

Fallen, sunken trees, often carried down the river on a flood before coming to rest, also create areas of slack water behind them and are much loved by roach, particularly where a sandbank is built up by the deflected flow.

Water flow
Where bends occur on rivers, the main flow is deflected by the outer bank and a visible "crease" develops between it and

WATER FLOW
By studying the flow patterns of a stream you can learn a lot about its underwater features. For example, rocks and weeds create ripples and patches of slack water, while deep holes, containing slack water that offers fish respite from the current, appear to be slightly darker than the surrounding areas of water.

the slacker inside water. When the stream or river is running at normal level, species such as chub tend to lie right on the crease. They swim slowly or just hold a position in the slacker water, but are always ready to move out into the main flow to inspect items brought down by the main current.

As river levels rise after rain, or temperatures plummet, the fish will move progressively into the slacker water. At such times, slack water and gentle eddies can be full of fish, because they offer a comfortable environment in which to escape the raging current.

Where a river or stream consists of a series of pools and rapids or glides, fish are often to be found right at the necks or tails of the pools. At spawning time, migratory fish frequently rest in these spots while making their way upstream to their spawning grounds.

263

STREAMS & RIVERS 2

UPLAND STREAMS & RIVERS

The bed of an upland stream usually consists of rocks, boulders, and stones, over and between which races fast, and generally shallow, water. In the highest reaches, trout are the only gamefish likely to be present, and these never grow to any size on their thin diet of insect larvae, freshwater shrimps, and the occasional worm.

These little trout, often still carrying their parr markings, spend their lives hiding in slacks behind stones and boulders, ever ready to dart out into the current to grab a passing morsel. In these small pockets of slack water they also grub about in the bed for the few invertebrates present.

Lower down, where the water is less turbulent, the trout are often joined by grayling and salmon. The salmon will be both immature parrs (this is where they were born) and adults that have returned to spawn in the headwaters from which they originated.

In this lower part of an upland stream, the water gradually deepens and there will be depressions in the bed gouged out by floodwater. It is in these depressions or holes and behind boulders and rocks that the trout and grayling are found. The returning salmon also rest behind rocks during their upstream journey, before seeking patches of smooth gravel on which to spawn.

LOWLAND STREAMS & RIVERS

Lowland streams contrast strongly with their upland counterparts. As the speed of the current slows, deposition of suspended material begins, resulting in a riverbed that changes downstream from rocks and boulders, through beds of gravel and sand, to silt banks. Each attracts its own varieties of fauna and flora and, as a rule, invertebrate life is plentiful. Because of this abundant food supply there are many varieties of fish present, including predators such as pike and perch.

Slacks and eddies

The calmer water behind submerged rocks and boulders provides comfortable living quarters for many fish. These underwater obstacles may not be visible in normal conditions, so a visit to a river during a dry spell, when the water level is low and the rocks are exposed, is well worth while. Draw a map or make a mental note of the positions of the rocks and the adjacent lies, so that you know where to find them when the stream returns to its normal height.

Other areas likely to hold fish include the slack water around and behind bridge supports, the eddies that often form where a river meets a smaller or slower flowing stream, and deep holes. These holes are scoured into the riverbed by the force of the flow during high water conditions. When the flow returns to normal, they often act as natural larders, collecting many invertebrate food items brought down on the current. Bottom-feeding fish such as barbel find such holes highly appealing.

LOWLAND RIVERS
Many lowland rivers are fast flowing, although not as fast as upland streams, and submerged rocks can cause considerable surface turbulence. Stretches that contain submerged rocks are usually best fished from the bank rather than from a boat, especially if you are unfamiliar with them.

BRIDGES
A bridge supported on piers built on the riverbed creates a variety of water conditions. Water channelled between the pier bases speeds up, while areas of slack water form behind the piers, and if the bridge is low it will provide the fish with plenty of shade on sunny days. Barbel and bream are among the species that are attracted to this shaded water.

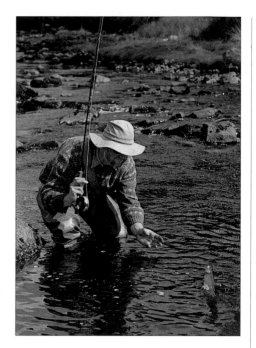

UPLAND STREAMS
(left)
The lower parts of an upland stream are good places to fish for trout, salmon, and grayling. Too fast, shallow, and rocky for boat fishing, they can be fished from the bank or by wading. Wading is especially effective when the river is wide or one bank is inaccessible because of vegetation.

UPLAND TROUT
(right)
The little trout in the high reaches of upland streams often retain their parr markings throughout their lives.

Confluences and islands

At the confluence of two streams of similar size and pace, a "crease", a small area of slack water between the two, is created. Fish like to lie in this slack, as it requires them to expend little energy yet allows them to move quickly into the stream on either side of them to intercept food drifting down with the current.

When two streams flowing at different speeds or of disparate size join up, the secondary (lesser) stream in both cases tends to be "held up". This results in the final length of the secondary stream running more slowly and even a little deeper. Fish are attracted to this steadier water, particularly during times of high water when the speed of the major stream increases to the point where it becomes uncomfortable for them.

Islands also hold great attraction for fish. This is because they deflect the flow, creating numerous areas of slack water,

and are often thickly covered with trees and undergrowth. Much of this vegetation overhangs the river, producing cover and a canopy from which terrestrial creatures often fall.

Weirpools and millpools

These turbulent spots, with their oxygen-rich water, are a great attraction to many species. Trout (if the river is clean) are found up in the fastest, white water of a pool, while lower down the pool species such as chub, barbel, and grayling will be in evidence. Species such as perch, bream, and roach, which have a preference for calmer water, lie in the steadier flow at the tail of the pool, and in the slacks and eddies created to the sides. Pike are not far away, either, often tucked in close to the bank and using the marginal weed for camouflage.

In some weirpools, the actual weir sill is quite deeply undercut, and a light leger

rig cast into the white water will be caught by the undertow and pulled underneath. Bites tend to be very positive, and sometimes the fish responsible for them can be very surprising. For as well as the expected chub and barbel, fish such as perch and bream will, remarkably, also take up residence below an undercut sill.

Dams

Dams are built across rivers to create reservoirs for drinking water or for driving hydroelectric turbines. A dam can help to maintain the flow of the river that runs out of the reservoir, keeping the levels topped up in times of low rainfall, but the effect on the fish in the river depends on how the water is released. Water released from spillways at the top of the dam is relatively warm, but water released from the base of the dam is often extremely cold. At hydroelectric dams in regions where the summers are hot, cold water released via the turbines often provides an ideal habitat for trout, but elsewhere a sudden introduction of cold water into a river normally fed from the spillways can have a severe dampening effect on sport, which only picks up again after the effects of the artificial flood have passed through.

Where water is constantly being released from the lake via the spillways in times of normal rainfall, it sometimes falls with such force that deep holes are formed below the dam. Fish are attracted to these and will only move out during times of heavy flow, finding refuge downstream and often behind the structures built to prevent bank erosion.

WEIRPOOLS
Weirs are built across rivers to raise the upstream water level or to control the downstream flow. The water tumbling over a weir mixes with air as it falls, and so becomes well oxygenated. In hot weather, when oxygen levels in the rest of the river are low, the dissolved oxygen in a weirpool makes it very attractive to fish.

265

STILLWATERS 1

The term "stillwaters" covers a broad spectrum of waters. At one end of this spectrum is the tiny, springfed farm pond, either a natural feature or created in a shady corner of a field to provide a source of cool drinking water for livestock on hot summer days. At the other end are enormous natural and man-made expanses of water, some of which (such as the Great Lakes of North America) are much bigger than many of the world's smaller countries.

CHARACTERISTICS OF STILLWATERS

Each type of stillwater presents the angler with a unique set of problems that must be solved if success is to be achieved. Different types also have many features in common, however, and the knowledge and experience gained when fishing one can be used to advantage on others. For example, while lakes may vary enormously in size and topography, all of them will usually have features such as bays, promontories (points), and shallow margins. In addition, the weeds found in the bays and shallows of big lakes and reservoirs are very often the same varieties seen in little ponds and medium-sized lakes, and in many cases the invertebrate life living among the weeds, and the species of fish in close proximity to them, are also the same. Your chances of angling success on any stillwater will be greatly increased if you learn what goes on beneath the surface.

Types of stillwater

The vast majority of stillwaters are natural features, fed by springs, streams, or rivers, and usually with one or more rivers draining them. A great many ponds and lakes are artificial, however, having been formed by the damming of a stream or river or by excavation. Most of those formed by damming are shallow where the watercourse enters and are at their deepest at the dam end.

Many of the small artificial stillwaters were created to form ornamental lakes, but most large waters were dammed to provide reservoirs of drinking or irrigation water, or for hydroelectric schemes. These waters vary greatly in size, from relatively small reservoirs that you could walk around in a couple of hours or less, to massive and deep expanses of water with shorelines measured in thousands of kilometres.

Another important group of stillwaters are those created by the flooding of worked-out pits and quarries, such as the gravel and clay pits resulting from the extraction of materials for use in the construction industry. The bottoms of flooded clay and gravel pits are often highly irregular, and the water can be very deep with few shallow areas. The water is also usually very clear, and weed growth is often profuse in less deep areas. The invertebrate life can be prolific, but often there are very few suitable spawning sites for fish. This situation leads to a food-rich environment containing a low population of fish, and because these fish have little competition, their growth rates are usually rapid.

GRAVEL PITS *(above)*
A flooded gravel pit can acquire a fish population naturally by the introduction of fish eggs by birds, but many pits are artificially stocked.

PONDS *(left)*
Small ponds often hold surprisingly large fish, especially when managed as fisheries, but overstocking can result in stunted fish.

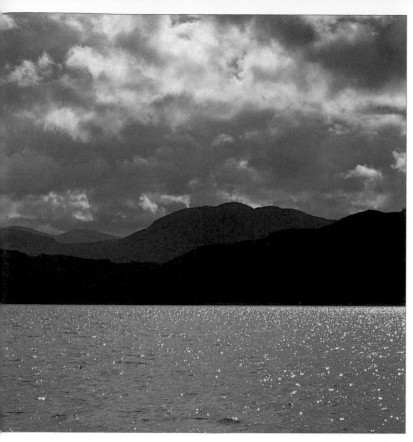

*The shores and
shallow margins of
large waters are in
most respects similar
to the edges of small
waters, and are fished
in much the same
way. But if you are
going to fish offshore
on a really large
water, it pays to
obtain a chart of it so
that you can locate
likely fish-holding
areas such as bars,
underwater plateaux,
shallows, and
deepwater dropoffs. A
sonar will help you to
search the bottom and,
together with a water
temperature probe, to
detect the colder layers
that may hold species
such as arctic char and
lake trout.*

Water colour
As stillwaters begin to warm up each
spring, minute plant organisms known as
phytoplankton begin to multiply. The
extent to which their population expands
depends on a number of factors,
including the depth and temperature of
the water, the amount of weed growth,
and the quantity of nitrates and
phosphates present in solution (washed
in from farmland treated with fertilizer).
In hot summers, shallow, fertilizer-
polluted stillwaters turn green as the
phytoplankton population explodes.

Phytoplankton are eaten by
zooplankton, which is the animal
constituent of plankton and includes fish
larvae and simple animal organisms such
as daphnia (water fleas). Great clouds of
orange-red daphnia can often be seen in
the warmer shallows of clear stillwaters,
rising and falling through the water
layers and drifting with the wind.

If zooplankton occur in sufficient
numbers, they help to keep a water clear
of phytoplankton, and this encourages
the growth of weeds, which need clear
water and sunlight to thrive. As well as
helping stillwaters to remain clear,
zooplankton are an important food item
for many species of freshwater fish, and
they are particularly loved by reservoir
rainbow trout.

Shallow waters usually warm up more
quickly than deeper ones, encouraging
the rapid growth of weeds and
phytoplankton. Exceptions to this include
springfed pools, with their constant
supply of cold water, and small pools
surrounded by thick tree growth, which
reduces the amount of sunlight that can
reach the water.

WATER COLOUR
*Many small stillwaters are turned
green in summer by the presence of
huge numbers of phytoplankton. A
large population of zooplankton,
which eat phytoplankton, plus a
good growth of aquatic weeds, which
consume nutrients that would
otherwise be taken up by
phytoplankton, can help to keep the
water clear.*

UNDERWATER FEATURES

When fishing stillwaters, try to locate
underwater features that attract fish.
Inflowing streams, for example, prove
attractive to fish because their water
often contains food, and may be cooler
and contain more oxygen than the
stillwater, particularly during long
spells of warm weather.

Fish also gather around rocks and
fallen or submerged trees, and feed on
the algae, snails, and other invertebrates
that take up residence on them. Shoals
of baitfish feel secure alongside or even
among submerged branches, and
predators lie in wait for them, close by
and well camouflaged in the same
branches. Another place to look for
predatory fish is near the dropoff line
between the marginal shallows and
deep water, where they lie in wait for
baitfish shoals patrolling the dropoff in
search of food.

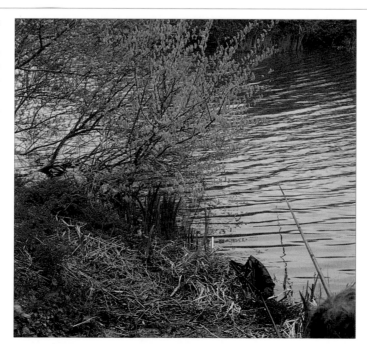

SUBMERGED TREES
*Trees that have fallen
into the water, for
instance when a
riverbank is eroded
and collapses, become
gathering places for
fish that find cover
and food among the
trunks and branches.
Submerged trees are
often also found in
flooded pits and in
lakes formed by
damming, and may be
in deep water a long
way from the shore.*

STILLWATERS 2
VEGETATION

Vegetation in stillwaters is usually restricted to the margins and shallows, and takes the form of weeds, rushes, beds of sedge, and water lilies. Weeds, rushes, and sedge provide many benefits, from helping to keep the water clear (by taking in nutrients to the detriment of phytoplankton), to giving sanctuary to various species of fish and the creatures on which they feed. Floating plants can also help to keep water clear of excessive phytoplankton. On ponds and small lakes where the surface is almost covered by such plants, the amount of sunlight entering the water is greatly reduced. Phytoplankton, being plants, cannot survive without any sunlight, so the water stays clear.

Reedbeds
Beds of reed line the margins of many stillwaters, and are as common on recently created waters as on well-established lakes. Their stems play host to a wide variety of animal life, including many invertebrates such as snails and the larvae of damselflies and dragonflies. Normally too dense for fish to swim in and out of, they are nonetheless attractive to some species. Pike and perch, for example, lurk alongside reed stems waiting for passing prey, beautifully camouflaged by their markings.

REEDBEDS (above)
Reeds are tall grasses that can reach a height of about 3 m (10 ft). When there is no wind, any movement of reed stems may be caused by fish.

WATER LILIES
(right)
Most species of water lily normally grow in depths of no more than about 1.8 m (6 ft). The presence of these plants in an area of water thus gives a rough indication of its maximum depth.

Water lilies
Fish love to lie under the broad leaves of water lilies on hot days, and can often be heard making distinctive kissing sounds as they suck small animals from the undersides of the pads.

Although the pads themselves are often tightly packed on the surface, sometimes even riding up over one another, the stems below the water never seem to form an impenetrable barrier. Predatory fish lie in ambush among them, and slim fish such as rudd and roach can swim between lily stems with ease.

Bigger, more rounded species such as carp can make their way through, but they tend to set the stems and pads rocking as they go – a phenomenon well worth looking out for when wandering the banks of a stillwater in search of fish.

Bankside plants

Trees, bushes, and other plants overhanging the banks of stillwaters provide cover for fish and are also a source of food, because terrestrial creatures such as spiders, beetles, and caterpillars frequently fall from their branches and leaves into the water. Fish also find a plentiful supply of food where the roots of marginal plants extend into the water, creating a habitat for insect larvae and snails.

OVERHANGING
PLANTS
The water beneath overhanging vegetation is a good place to fish for the many species, including trout, that feed on terrestrials. Trees and bushes offer concealment for you as well as cover for the fish, but can make casting difficult, so fishing from a boat is often a better option than bank fishing.

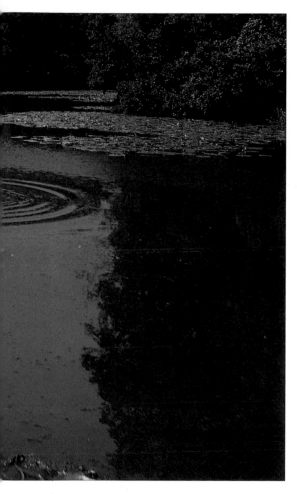

FISHING A SMALL POND *(above)*
On this small pond, good places to seek out fish include the lily beds (where a fish snatching a food item from beneath a pad has created ripples) and the water below the overhanging trees that line the banks.

Brush piles

Fishery managers responsible for lakes and reservoirs with virtually featureless beds often create artificial fish-holding areas. One common way of doing this is by anchoring large piles of tree branches or cut trees to the bottom.

These brush piles, whose positions are usually marked by buoys or indicated by signs on the shore, offer fish the same sort of cover and feeding opportunities that they get from submerged or sunken trees *(see page 267)*.

SURFACE INDICATIONS

In the flowing water of streams and rivers, underwater obstructions and other features create surface disturbances that can indicate areas likely to hold fish *(see pages 262–65)*. Surface indications of this type seldom occur on stillwaters, but the fish often betray their presence by creating their own surface disturbances.

Bubbles and ripples

Bottom-feeding fish such as tench and carp send up clouds of silt while searching the bed for food. And, as their noses disturb the silt, pockets of gas that are released from it bubble up to the surface. Patches of bubbles indicate one or more fish foraging in one particular area, and lines of bubbles reveal the presence of fish working along the bottom. Trout and other fish that feed at the surface create ripples that reveal their position, and big fish foraging in shallow water for food often set up bow-waves that can ripple the surface.

Wind lanes and scumlanes

On big waters in windy weather, lines of calm water may appear on the otherwise wind-ruffled surface. These "wind lanes" are often caused by obstructions on the bank, such as trees, that deflect the wind, creating a long, narrow slick of calm water. In strong winds, foam spray caused by breaking waves collects in the smooth water, creating "scumlanes".

During the summer months, hatching insects are blown into wind lanes and become trapped, unable to escape because of the greater surface tension of the unbroken strip of smooth water. Many species of fish, but particularly trout, will take advantage of this harvest and can be seen working their way upwind along the lanes.

SCUMLANES
In addition to the scumlanes formed by foam blown into wind lanes, there are those made up of pollen, leaves, twigs, and other pieces of debris that collect against a shore when the wind blows from the same direction for several days. These scumlanes attract fish because they often include items of food such as insects and daphnia.

269

SHORELINES

Unlike offshore waters, which can usually be read only by studying charts and by echo sounding, it is normally possible to make a direct survey of all the fishable stretches of a shore. Select the lowest spring tide available in daylight and walk the shoreline, making notes about landmarks and other features of the lower, middle, and upper shore, and perhaps using a camera or camcorder to record the scene for later reference.

TYPES OF SHORELINE

Shores vary in many ways, the most obvious being in the type of substrate (seabed material), which may be sand, shingle, rocks, or a mixture of these. Different species of fish often prefer different substrates, but the amount of shelter, the gradient of the shore, the presence of freshwater inflows, and food availability also play a part in determining the numbers and species of fish found along a shore. For the angler, the important thing is to understand what motivates fish movements.

Shingle beaches
Shingle beaches tend to give the impression of being devoid of life, but this is far from true. The shingle, which may be stacked high by wave action, is often just the visible part of a complex, multi-substrate mix, sometimes including clays and old peat beds, at or beyond the low water mark. Cod, bass, rays, conger, and even flatfish are regularly caught from shingle beaches.

Watch for signs of submerged banks causing variations in the wave pattern beyond the low-water mark. At low water, aim to drop baits on their seaward sides; as they deepen on the flood, drop the baits into the gullies in front. It is also worth putting baits close to boulders, groynes, and anything else that breaks the normal pattern of the shingle.

Sandy shores
The size of the sand particles on a sandy shore influences the types of fish-food organisms, and thus the species of fish, that will be present. Fine particles with high amounts of organic matter are good for lugworms, cockles, and shrimps, and therefore for the fish that feed on them. They also become stirred up and colour the water with the least bit of wave action, and the low light levels in the coloured water tempt species such as cod, which normally feed along the shore only at night, to feed during daylight.

Coarser sands, which settle out very quickly, are often associated with surf beaches, where bass, flounders, and small turbot are taken when a surf is running. A gentle gradient assists the wind in bringing good surf conditions, because friction between the seabed and the water slows the bottom of a wave, causing the top to overtake it and turn. This happens more readily in shallow water than in deep, and a line of breaking waves can be a sign of banks and gullies beyond the low-water line.

Any undulation on an otherwise featureless beach will be of interest to fish. They travel along channels, and are attracted to banks, which enhance wave movements, evicting concealed food items from the bed. Fish also gather at scour holes at the ends of breakwaters, picking up food items that have been washed into them.

SHINGLE BEACHES
On a shingle beach, the most productive water is usually out beyond the low-water mark, where the pebbles give way to grit and fine sand.

Cliffs
The main attractions of cliff-lined shores are almost-permanent water, very often with good depth, and the presence of a wide range of features including kelp jungles for wrasse, broken rock for conger, pinnacles for pollack, and clean ground for rays, tope, and flatfish.

However, cliffs must be fished with care. Every year, anglers are plucked from low ledges by large swells, and spray and rain make rocks dangerously slippery. Good climbing boots, a safety rope, a minimum of tackle, and reliable company are essential, as is a safe retreat route for when the tide floods in.

SANDY SHORES
In temperate waters, sandy shores attract species such as bass and flatfish. These are also found over sand in warmer waters, along with rays (such as this eagle ray), bonefish, and many species of shark, some of them large and dangerous.

SURF BEACHES (left)
The typical surf beach is a broad expanse of sand, facing the open ocean, where waves whipped up by the wind come crashing ashore. Fishing a gently shelving surf beach requires fairly long casting, but a steep beach should be fished with short- to medium-distance casts. When wading a surf beach, beware of the undertow, which can pull your feet from under you.

ROCKY BEACHES (below)
Some of the most productive shores are those with rocky, bouldery ground. Deepwater rock ledges with rough and clean ground within casting range also fish well.

PIER FISHING (above)
Long casting is usually unnecessary when fishing from piers, because many species, including bass, pollack, mullet, and conger, feed close to the underwater structure.

WEEDBEDS (above)
Despite the frustrations of snagged tackle, fishing weedbeds can be very productive because many species of fish are attracted to them by the cover and food they find there. Here, an angler is landing a large mullet that was hooked in a dense mat of weed.

Rocks, gullies, and kelp beds

Variations in shoreline geography, unless pronounced, are less important on rocky shores than on sand. This is because the numerous nooks and crannies offer fish a wide range of sheltered spots and feeding areas. As on sandy shores, however, the larger features such as gullies and holes still provide shelter from the tide, areas into which food might settle, and ambush points for picking off victims passing overhead. Shell-crunching wrasse and night-stalking conger take maximum advantage of the available cover, while pollack, bass, and cod often move in to hunt over patchy, broken ground.

Beds of kelp, a common type of seaweed, tend to show only along the extreme lower shore at the lowest tides. Some anglers curse them because tackle snags in them, but they provide good cover for baitfish, and large kelp "jungles" hold lots of big fish.

Piers, jetties, and sea walls

Man-made structures frequently offer deep water at their bases and the chance for anglers to hit different or even deeper water by casting from them. Casting can, however, place the bait beyond fish that have been attracted to a structure because of the food that is available there. An

open-framed pier standing on sand offers fish and their food a degree of shelter in an otherwise featureless world. Food collects in the scour holes, crabs thrive around the supports, and food is dumped in from facilities on the pier.

Most stone piers and harbour arms are built on deposited rock, which attracts a wide range of food types and fish. The bases of walls built on natural rock butting onto sand are usually rich in crabs, prawns, and small fish using the weed fringes for cover. Mullet browse microscopic organisms on the stonework, and predators such as bass may move in on the tide to feed after dusk.

271

ESTUARIES

Estuaries are dynamic environments, changing uniformly as the predictable freshwater inflow makes its effect felt, and changing unpredictably when heavy rains, often a long way inland, result in larger than normal amounts of freshwater flowing down the river. Even fish able to tolerate some degree of freshwater need time to acclimatize during sudden spates, which force them to move downstream or out into the sea to a point where they can find the salinity (saltiness) that they are accustomed to.

ESTUARINE FLOUNDER
In temperate waters, most estuaries are home to large numbers of flounder.

TYPES OF ESTUARY

In a typical estuary, the river creates a plume of freshwater that extends into the saltwater of the sea. An area of brackish water is created where the two meet and mix. The size of this brackish zone at any one time depends on the size of the estuary, the tide, and the amount of freshwater that is entering from the river.

Estuaries vary greatly in size and topography. Some rivers enter the sea through narrow, rocky channels, others carve their way through wide expanses of mudflats or marshland, and others create huge deltas. They also differ in the quality of the freshwater flowing downstream into the sea, but despite all their differences the same basic rules governing species diversity and distribution apply.

Estuarine species
The main factor limiting the species of inshore marine fish that enter a particular part of an estuary is salinity. Fish that can tolerate low salinity, such as mullet, move readily into the brackish water of an estuary, or even into the freshwater zone, in search of food. Other species, such as cod, cannot cope with low salinity and are found only in those parts of an estuary where the level of salinity is relatively high.

Migratory fish, such as salmon and sea trout, travel down estuaries to mature at sea, and return as adults to run upstream to spawn. As they run through estuaries, they adjust their body chemistry to cope with the changes in salinity.

Upper reaches
The species in the upper reaches of an estuary are invariably limited, often to immature flounder, an occasional bass, and mullet where the flow is slack. Channel geography and food availability are the main factors determining where fish are likely to be found. Look for them where bends in channels create slow spots, obstacles create still eddies, and shallow bays onto which a rising tide spills offer quiet areas. Dips and holes within these quiet areas have the added attraction of being gathering points for food carried along by the flow.

Lower reaches
The lower reaches of an estuary often contain the same sort of fish-holding areas as the upper reaches. In addition, larger estuaries may have extensive banks of deposited silt that attract fish because they are rich in food items such as worms, molluscs, and crabs. In small estuaries with fast-flowing, channelled outlets, bars of deposited silt often form where the easing of the flow allows suspended material to fall. Such bars have all the attractive qualities of large banks, but on a very localized scale, making fish very much easier to locate. Wind throws up a tell-tale surf over a bar, and this rough water also churns food out of hiding. This is carried to the downtide edge of the bar, where fish gather to feed.

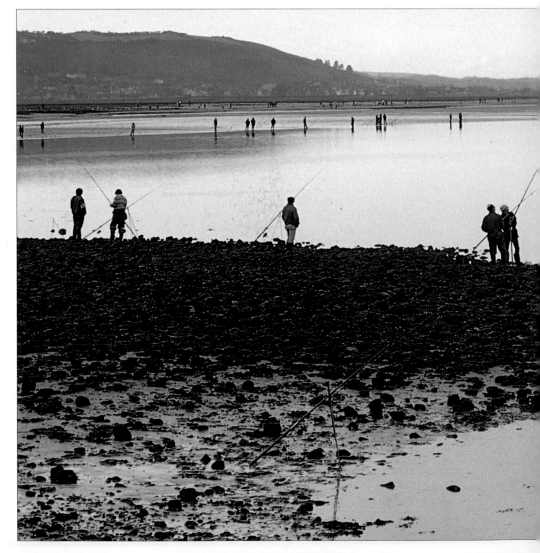

Creeks, lagoons, and stream outfalls

Large estuaries can form a number of special geographical features at or near their mouths, of which creeks are perhaps the most common. Mullet and flounder enter these muddy openings on the tide, and sole will push into them if they are adjacent to the open shore.

Lagoons formed by deposited silt trapping large expanses of water can quickly become food-rich because water movement is greatly reduced, allowing the contained area to warm more than adjacent areas. Access for fish may well be restricted, but once they are inside, the attractions of the relatively warm water and abundant food supply ensure continued patronage and, very often, good rates of growth. Mullet and flounder are typical of the species found in lagoons.

Stream outfalls, whether dissecting beaches or discharging over rocks, are themselves usually too small to contain fish. Their importance comes from the very localized changes in salinity that they create, which fish such as bass and flounder are seemingly unable to resist. For anglers, the water around any discharge of freshwater into the sea, however small, is worth investigating.

Mangrove creeks

Coastal creeks lined with mangrove trees are common in the subtropics and tropics in areas of organic enrichment, particularly where shallow banks and flats have been formed by the deposition of organic debris from rivers.

The trees grow on these banks and flats, supported by cagelike root structures that hold their trunks above the water. When submerged at high tide, these root structures offer an ideal sanctuary for small fish and are important nursery areas for a number of estuarine and coastal species.

Wherever small fish gather, they attract larger predators, and barracuda, tarpon, crevalle jack, guitarfish, and stringray are typical of the many predatory species found in mangrove creeks. Look for them in the deep holes scoured out on bends, in the areas of slack water downtide of sharp bends, and lying in ambush among the roots of the mangroves.

MANGROVE CREEKS *(above)*
Tarpon love to explore mangrove creeks and, like this one, are not deterred by shallow water. Channels and creeks in mangrove swamps contain many good places for fish to lie up in. For example, a twisting creek scours deep holes on its bends into which food will settle, and which provide fish with respite from the strong flow. The downtide corner of a sharp bend also provides shelter from the flow, and is a convenient point for a big fish to lie in wait for a passing meal.

ESTUARY MUD *(left)*
Most broad estuaries have large expanses of mud. This mud can support very large populations of the marine creatures, such as molluscs and worms, that many fish species feed on.

OFFSHORE TEMPERATE WATERS

To the uninitiated, the sea appears to be a vast and featureless expanse of water, offering no clues as to where within it the fish might be. But, beneath the surface, it contains many features that attract a rich diversity of life, including fish that gather at them for cover and to feed. The location of many features, such as wrecks and outcrops of rock, can be read directly from charts and checked from a boat by echo sounding. At times, fish can also be found by reading surface indications, usually in shallow water or close to the shore. These indications include swirls and eddies created by rocks, and the activities of seabirds.

TAKING SOUNDINGS
An echo sounder provides you with a profile of the seabed beneath your boat, enabling you to locate features that might hold fish. This monochrome echo sounder trace shows the outline of a large wreck lying in deep water.

TYPES OF WATER

The nature of any stretch of sea plays an important part in determining the numbers and species of fish that are present. For example, a featureless seabed of sand results in low fish diversity and angling productivity, while rocks and wrecks are good places to fish because they attract large numbers of many different species. Deep water has better temperature stability than shallow water, so its fish population remains more stable throughout the year. If it is too deep or too turbid (coloured by silt), however, there may be insufficient light penetration for weed growth, which provides fish with cover. Inflowing freshwater reduces salinity (*see page 272*), and pollution by sewage attracts species that feed on it, such as mackerel, but deters those that need the high levels of dissolved oxygen found in unpolluted water.

Banks and gullies
On otherwise featureless ground, such as sand or mud, banks and gullies are the best places to look for fish. Banks are usually found near islands and headlands, where fierce tidal currents carry sand and silt in suspension. Where the tidal flow eases, material settles out into huge, ever-changing mounds, crisscrossed by gullies and sand waves. Baitfish, especially sandeels, swarm over such areas, attracting bass, turbot, brill, and other predators.

Gullies cut into banks by tidal action provide predatory flatfish with excellent ambush points, and bass hunt sandeels taking refuge there from the tidal flow. Away from banks, gullies accumulate creatures such as crabs, worms, and small fish, which are carried across the shallows by the tide until they drop into the deeper water of the gullies. This abundant food supply attracts many species including flatfish, bass, cod, ray, and shark.

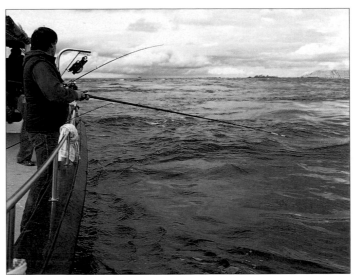

BOAT FISHING
(above)
Fishing from an anchored or drifting boat over a good fish-holding area, such as a gully, wreck, or reef, is usually very productive.

SANDBANKS *(left)*
The presence of a sandbank, a good place to fish, is often indicated by surface "boils" where the tidal flow is forced up over the bank.

Dropoffs

Large dropoffs, where the depth of the water increases sharply, are invariably areas of intermediate ground linking either fairly featureless areas or more productive ground. Unless they have attractive features of their own, such as fish-holding weedbeds, most of those that link featureless areas hold few fish and thus have little value to the angler. Dropoff edges linking productive areas, however, attract many species of fish.

Predatory flatfish gather along downtide slopes, breaking from cover to intercept sandeels passing overhead, and rays gather there to shelter from the current. Tope and other sharks hunt dropoffs between reefs and banks, picking off fish carried away from the edges by the tide, and reef conger may take refuge in convenient lairs.

Dropoffs should be fished from a drifting boat, starting well uptide of the area where fish are expected to be and going well beyond it.

Islands

The value of islands as concentrators of fish depends on a combination of layout and size. Groups of islands are more useful than single islands because they have a far greater effect on the surrounding waters. By deflecting, channelling, increasing, or suppressing the tidal flow, they create a broad range of habitats likely to draw in good numbers of many different fish species.

Areas of disturbed tidal flow aid the formation of banks and sand waves. Fast water attracts sandeels and mackerel, which in turn draw in tope, bass, pollack, and even porbeagle. Wrasse and conger feed in the quieter corners of bays and coves, and slack areas along the edges of strong flows allow sedentary species such as skates and rays to choose the degree of flow that suits them best.

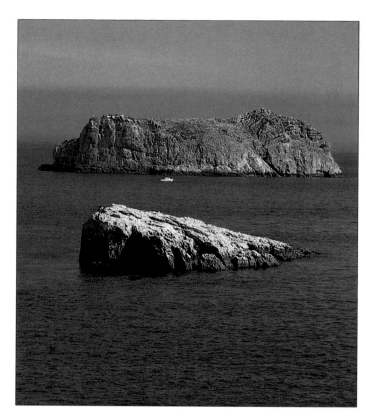

ISLANDS
Islands tend to attract large numbers of fish because their interaction with the tidal flow creates a variety of different habitats. For example, where two islands are close together, the water rushing between them can scour out a deep hole in the seabed. Big skate often take up residence in such holes, feeding on the large numbers of food items that get swept into them by the tide. Skate will also congregate in the deep water on the downtide sides of islands.

Pinnacles and ledges

Submerged rock pinnacles are often found on deepwater reefs, and their peaks, reaching up towards the surface, may attract species that normally favour shallower water. The pinnacle base will be much the same as any other reef, attracting a wide variety of organisms, small fish, and their predators.

The peaks of submerged pinnacles can present a hazard to boats, and ledges are usually more hospitable places to fish, particularly on the drift. A lack of features can bring a certain uniformity of fish food items, and of the fish themselves, but small reef species are common, and larger predators will be nearby.

Wrecks and reefs

Wrecks are, in effect, man-made reefs, and they attract and hold the same kinds of fish as natural reefs. What these fish are depends on the depth. Shallow wrecks and reefs could have a good number of bass, plus wrasse, conger, and small pollack, which give way to cod, coalfish, ling, better pollack, and bigger conger as the depth increases.

On a wreck or a reef, the fish usually concentrate where cover and food availability are greatest, but some lie just off or along one side. It can take several drifts or some very skilful anchoring to present the bait where feeding fish are holed up.

SURFACE INDICATIONS

Away from the shore, areas likely to hold fish can be located by looking for surface indications, some man-made, others natural. Cardinal buoys and isolated danger marks indicate hazards to shipping, and many of these hazards, such as rocks, attract fish. Port and starboard navigation buoys mark channel edges, and sometimes areas of deep-lying, rocky ground – good places to fish – are dotted with crab pot markers.

Man-made markers are generally more reliable than natural surface indications. For instance, the edge of a steep bank is often betrayed by lines of white water, but these will not lie above the lip. The deeper the water, the further

CRAB POT MARKERS
Ground that supports a large population of crabs also attracts good numbers of fish. Crab pot markers are a reliable indication of such ground.

downtide they appear, and in rough weather they may merge with existing waves. Swirls, erupting boils, overfalls, and eddies all denote seabed obstructions, such as reefs and wrecks, that are deflecting water upwards in the tidal flow. These signs may also appear at varying distances downtide of the obstructions that cause them.

Diving gannets are good indicators of mackerel near the surface; more general seabird activity may indicate that predators are driving small fish to the surface. The predators will usually be mackerel but could be something more highly prized, such as bass.

275

Offshore Tropical Waters

Tropical coastal waters support large numbers of many different species of fish, occupying every available niche from the seabed to the surface, and the upper layers of the water remain rich in fish well beyond the continental shelf. This makes tropical waters much more productive for anglers than their temperate counterparts. In addition to wreck, reef, and bank fishing *(see page 274)*, tropical waters offer bottom and midwater fishing from small boats and the shore, fly fishing, inshore trolling, poling the flats, and big-game fishing in the deep, blue water beyond the edge of the shelf.

Types of Water

The upper layers of tropical waters contain more fish than those of cooler seas, and some tropical species are unrestricted in their ability to roam the open ocean in search of food. Most species, however, must stay close to the areas that provide them with suitable food; upwellings, coastal shallows, and the sunlit reaches close to the surface are just such places. Over fishable seabed, much the same rules apply as in temperate waters, with wrecks, pinnacles, banks, gullies, and other features having concentrations of food and fish. In addition, large inshore gamefish like to patrol specific contours along the upper continental slope or the outer edges of fringing reefs.

Gullies, dropoffs, and banks

Tropical gullies, like those elsewhere, act as out-of-the-tide resting places and areas into which food carried on the tide can settle. Large predators, such as tarpon, love to hunt in shallow gullies, and the downtide edges of gullies, banks, and dropoffs make excellent ambush points for the slower bottom-living species.

Baitfish feeding over banks always draw predators, and the depth of the water determines just which predators these might be. There are almost invariably stingray and shark, and possibly amberjack, dolphinfish, crevalle jack, and striped marlin. Large sand-loving species, including jack, bass, and roosterfish, move into very shallow water, venturing almost onto the beaches.

Coral flats

Bonefish, small shark, barracuda, and stingray are the principal coral flat species. Stingray happily lie in wait for food, but the more free-swimming species both browse and hunt and so are easily spooked by an approaching boat. For this reason, angers use light, shallow-drafted skiffs that are poled within casting distance of the fish.

FEEDING TARPON
(above)
Tarpon often gather to feed at the surface, where they can be caught by casting to them from a drifting or anchored boat.

REEF FISHING *(left)*
Boats have gathered to fish just outside the reef to the right of this small island.

CORAL FLATS
(below)
Coral flats, extensive areas of coral sand in very shallow water, are prime areas for bonefish and stingray.

Coral reefs

Small to medium-sized fish such as porgies, snappers, and groupers congregate in large numbers over the offshore coral reefs. Their distribution over a reef depends to some degree on its depth, and the biggest groupers are often found on the deepest parts.

Sunken coral heads are important features of the shallow parts of reefs. These huge, mushroom-shaped growths of coral are home to a wide variety of small marine creatures and the fish that feed on them. These fish in turn attract predators, including small sharks.

Gullies sculpted into reefs or between sections of reef present slow-moving predators with good ambush points, while faster-swimming species hunt along the gullies and around the reef slopes. Barracuda patrol the upper edges of the dropoffs, while hammerhead and possibly larger reef shark species are the main predators further down. Where gullies are particularly deep, otherwise offshore species will move into them, even where they are close inshore.

Huge pinnacles lunging skywards from deep water are where the very largest groupers and other reef creatures are to be found. Like the deeper gullies, areas of pinnacle rock and pinnacle coral (where the water is shallow enough for coral to grow) provide some of the best hunting and ambush points on the reef. Efficient predators grow fat on the easy pickings, and this is where the best fishing is likely to be found.

Deep water and dropoffs

The blue water of the deep sea is about as featureless as the ocean gets, but variations in the uniformity of the sea are created by upwellings of cold, nutrient-rich water. This water contains multitudes of tiny organisms, which attract baitfish shoals; small predators congregate to hunt the baitfish, and are themselves taken by large gamefish. Upwellings are thus good places to fish, and their locations are often revealed by flocks of seabirds that gather to feed on the baitfish.

Fishing dropoffs, which are easily located by means of charts and an echo sounder, is a different matter. Baitfish concentrate more predictably, for example in midwater at the outer edges of deep reefs or deep rock pinnacles. The upper edges of drops are patrolled by sharks, particularly hammerhead, and barracuda hunt along the shallowest edges of a reef. Close to the surface and along shallow edges, the higher water temperatures suit fast-swimming game species such as wahoo and sailfish.

All these fish respond to lures and slowly trolled livebaits. Where the water is at its deepest, a spread of lures and additional teasers will tempt fish such as marlin and sailfish up from depth. Other fish may not strike at surface lures and will require baits set perhaps 10 to 12 m (about 30 to 40 ft) down on downriggers.

Floating weed rafts

Floating weed rafts are a regular phenomenon in areas touched by major oceanic currents. The North Atlantic Drift, for example, brings attendant circulating clumps of algae known as sargassum. These can combine to form quite large rafts, which make a very important contribution to the biology of an area. They are also extremely valuable from an angling point of view, acting as a surface signpost on an otherwise featureless sea.

Dolphinfish and some smaller species have a habit of taking refuge beneath floating objects. These need not be weed rafts – they could be boxes, oildrums, tree roots, or other flotsam – but sargassum is the most abundant. Alongside any sizable floating object is a good place to stop a boat and start chumming with handfuls of cut fish. Very soon, the dolphinfish shoals will gather off the stern where some truly exciting light-tackle sport is virtually assured.

Dolphinfish may well be gamefish in their own right, but they are also a source of food for larger predators such as marlin. Trolling Kona Heads along the outer edges of long sargassum rafts, as opposed to more aimless quartering of areas likely to be patrolled by marlin, can thus be very productive.

TROLLING (above)
The best way to fish for fast-swimming big game species, such as marlin, wahoo, tuna, and sailfish, is by trolling with lures or natural baits.

TEASERS (left)
Trolling a string of brightly coloured teasers in addition to lures or baits will tempt marlin, tuna, and sailfish up from the depths.

CONSERVATION

The origins of all vertebrates, including ourselves, can be traced back to the primitive fish that evolved in the waters and swamps of the late Cambrian period, which ended over 500 million years ago. Some of the descendants of these early fish left the water to colonize the land, while others remained aquatic and evolved into the 22,000 or more species of fish alive today. These fish, like most living creatures, live in harmony with their environment, their numbers rising or falling according to the availability of food.

Some, however, are theatened with extinction. This may be a slow, natural process, caused for instance by changes in weather patterns to which a species cannot adapt, but many immediate and avoidable threats are posed by human activities.

POLLUTION

One of the most visible and widespread threats to fish, particularly freshwater species, is pollution of the water in which they live. This pollution takes many forms, including the discharge of inadequately treated sewage into rivers, lakes, and seas; the poisoning of waters by industrial waste products, agricultural chemicals, and oil spills; acidification of lakes and streams by acid rain; and contamination of the groundwaters that feed springs. Anglers, by the very nature of their sport, are often the first to become aware of changes in water quality caused by pollution. If you suspect that a stretch of water is becoming polluted, report it immediately to the relevant authorities and to local conservation groups.

Another threat to fish comes not from the quality of the water but from its quantity. Increasing demands for water, brought about by population growth, industrialization, and irrigation, have seriously depleted many rivers and lakes.

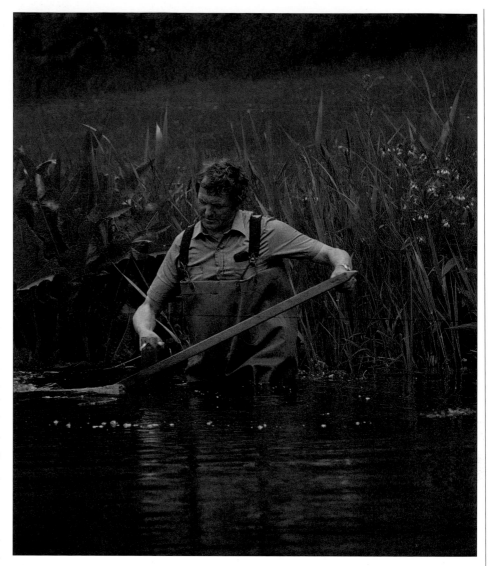

Eutrophication

The process of eutrophication is something of a paradox, in that it is the enrichment of water by the inflow of nutrients, which might appear beneficial but is actually a serious problem. The nutrients involved are nitrates and phosphates. Nitrates enter rivers, lakes, and the sea when rain washes nitrate-based fertilizers from farmland soil; phosphates also come from fertilizers, but their main sources are industrial and domestic effluents (phosphates are widely used in detergents).

When these nutrients enter water in excessive amounts, they promote the rapid growth of algae. These algae cover the surface of the water, preventing sunlight from reaching submerged plants. This sets up a chain reaction in which the submerged plants die, the bacteria that decompose the remains use up oxygen dissolved in the water, and this reduction in available oxygen causes the death of more plants and subsequently of the animal life inhabiting the water, including the fish.

WEED CUTTING
Good fishery management often involves some degree of intervention, such as cutting away excess weed growth, in order to keep the water in prime condition.

Acidification

Over the past few decades, thousands of lakes and many rivers in the Northern Hemisphere have become devoid of fish because of the effects of acid rain. Scandinavia and Canada are two of the worst-affected areas. This rain is created when sulphur dioxide, nitrogen dioxide, and nitrogen oxide – released into the air when fossil fuels are burned – react with moisture in the air to form sulphuric and nitric acids.

Acid rain makes the water in rivers and lakes acidic, and also frees large amounts of aluminium from the soil. The acidity of the water kills fish eggs and fry, and the aluminium affects the gills of fish, making them clog up with mucus. The combination of acidity and aluminium also kills off most plant life and the small creatures that fish feed on.

Many of the chemicals used in modern intensive farming can prove very harmful if washed into streams, lakes, or the sea. These chemicals include fertilizers, which promote excessive algae growth, and herbicides and pesticides that can damage aquatic plant, insect, and animal life.

FISH STOCKS

One of the most serious threats to many species of fish is that of overfishing. This is a particular problem for marine species that are fished for commercially, because of the huge numbers that are caught and the difficulty of enforcing size limits and catch quotas.

Freshwater fish are generally easier to protect from serious overfishing. For example, in most developed countries, freshwater fishing is largely for sport and is successfully regulated by licenses, permits, closed seasons, minimum size limits, and, in some cases, catch limits. In addition, most freshwater fish are relatively easy to breed for stocking depleted waters and for maintaining population levels.

Sea anglers can contribute to the maintenance of fish stocks by imposing personal minimum size limits and releasing, unharmed, any fish they do not intend to eat.

Catch-and-release fishing
Releasing fish after capture is an excellent way to help maintain fish stocks, and on some fisheries it is mandatory. However, fish must always be handled carefully if they are not to die from injury caused by rough treatment.

Use barbless hooks, or flatten barbs with pliers to make hooks easier to remove. If possible, leave the fish in the water and hold it gently while you unhook it, so that you cause as little damage as possible to its scales and its protective coating of slime. If the fish has swallowed the hook, carefully cut the leader as close to the hook as possible and leave the hook in place rather than try to remove it; the fish's digestive juices will soon break it down.

After unhooking, support the fish in the water with both hands and turn it to face into the current, if there is one. If it is exhausted, continue supporting it until it has recovered its strength and is ready to swim away.

SHARK CONSERVATION
Releasing sharks after capture, as this angler is doing, will help to ensure their survival. Many shark species have declined alarmingly in numbers, partly because of angling but also because so many are being taken for their fins. Shark finning is a particularly nasty form of commercial fishing: the sharks' fins are cut off, and the still-alive but fatally maimed fish are dumped back into the sea to die.

SPECIES UNDER THREAT
Several hundred species of fish have been classified by international and national agencies as actually or potentially in danger of extinction. Those listed here are some of the threatened, endangered, or vulnerable species that anglers might encounter. They should not be fished for in the areas named (in most cases it is illegal to do so), and if one is caught by accident it should be carefully unhooked and released.

Acipenseridae

Shortnose sturgeon (*Acipenser brevirostrum*)	USA, Canada
Lake sturgeon (*Acipenser fulvescens*)	USA, Canada
Adriatic sturgeon (*Acipenser naccarii*)	Italy
Atlantic sturgeon (*Acipenser oxyrhynchus*)	USA, Canada
Common sturgeon (*Acipenser sturio*)	Europe
Pallid sturgeon (*Scaphirhynchus albus*)	USA

Clupeidae

Allis shad (*Alosa alosa*)	Europe

Lamnidae

Great white shark (*Carcharodon carcharias*)	South Africa

Percichthyidae

Eastern freshwater cod (*Maccullochella ikei*)	Australia
Trout cod (*Maccullochella macquariensis*)	Australia
Clarence River cod (*Maccullochella sp.*)	Australia
Mary River cod (*Maccullochella sp.*)	Australia

Retropinnidae

Australian grayling (*Prototroctes maraena*)	Australia

Salmonidae

Atlantic whitefish (*Coregonus canadensis*)	Canada
Kiyi (*Coregonus kiyi*)	USA, Canada
Whitefish (*Coregonus lavaretus, C. albula, and C. oxyrhynchus*)	Europe
Blackfin cisco (*Coregonus nigripinnis*)	USA, Canada
Shortnose cisco (*Coregonus reighardi*)	USA, Canada
Shortjaw cisco (*Coregonus zenithicus*)	USA, Canada
Huchen (*Hucho hucho*)	Eastern Europe
Apache trout (*Oncorhynchus apache*)	USA
Gila trout (*Oncorhynchus gilae*)	USA
Adriatic trout (*Salmothymus obtusirastris*)	Balkans

GLOSSARY

A

Adipose fin A small, fatty fin between the dorsal fin and the tail fin.

AFTMA The American Fishing Tackle Manufacturers Association. Its activities include setting technical standards for fishing tackle, and its fly tackle specifications have become the world standard.

Alevin A recently hatched salmon or trout (*see also* **Grilse, Kelt, Parr, Smolt**).

Algae Any of a number of groups of simple plants that contain chlorophyll but lack true roots, stems, and leaves. They live in water or moist ground, and include diatoms, seaweeds, and spirogyra.

Amphidromous fish Fish that regularly migrate between freshwater and saltwater for reasons other than spawning, for example to feed or to overwinter (*see also* **Anadromous fish, Catadromous fish, Potamodromous fish**).

Anadromous fish Fish that spend most of their lives in the sea but ascend rivers to spawn (*see also* **Amphidromous fish, Catadromous fish, Potamodromous fish**).

Anal fin The fin behind the anus of a fish.

Aorta The main artery carrying blood from the heart.

Articular The rear bone of the lower jaw of a fish. It is hinged to the upper jaw and the quadrate (*see also* **Dentary, Maxillary, Premaxillary, Quadrate**).

B

Bag limit The maximum permissible number or weight of fish that can be taken from a particular water: always check local regulations before fishing.

Baitfish Any small fish, such as minnows and sandeels, that are preyed on by larger species and commonly used as angling bait.

Baiting needle A long needle used for mounting dead fish and other large baits onto terminal tackle.

Banks The right bank of a river is on your right when you are facing downstream, and the left bank is on your left.

Basin A depression in the Earth's surface; the drainage basin of a river system; a very large depression in the Earth's surface, containing an ocean and the rivers that drain into it, for example the Pacific Basin (*see also* **Drainage basin**).

Benthic A term describing anything living at or near the bottom of a lake or the sea.

Biomass The total mass of all the living organisms in a given area or (aquatic biomass) in a given body of water.

Bowfishing Fishing with a bow and arrow. It is permitted on many American waters, and the quarry is usually "trash" fish (such as carp) that are competing with more highly prized species such as bass. The arrow is tied to the end of the line, and the reel is mounted on the bow.

Brackish water Water that is slightly salty (*see also* **Salinity**).

Breaking strain The maximum load or weight that a line, swivel, or other piece of tackle can sustain without breaking.

B.s. The abbreviation for breaking strain.

Bulk shot A number of split shot grouped together on a line to concentrate weight at a particular point.

Butt pad A leather or rubber pad, strapped around the waist, into which the butt of a rod is placed so that greater leverage can be exerted when fighting large, powerful fish. It is also known as a rod socket (*see also* **Fighting chair**).

C

Caeca See **Pyloric caeca**

Catadromous fish Freshwater fish that move to the lower river or sea to spawn (*see also* **Amphidromous fish, Anadromous fish, Potamodromous fish**).

Caudal peduncle The relatively slender part of a fish's body between the last dorsal and anal fins and the base of the tail fin (the caudal fin). It is also known as the "wrist" of the fish.

Cleithrum A bone at the rear of the skull of a fish. It is the main bone supporting the pectoral fin (*see also* **Pectoral fin, Supracleithrum**).

Coarse fish Any freshwater fish of angling interest other than trout, salmon, char, grayling, and whitefish (*see also* **Gamefish, Panfish**).

D

Deadbait Dead fish or other creatures used as bait for predators (*see also* **Livebait**).

Dead drift A fly-fishing technique in which the fly (dry or wet) is allowed to drift freely along in the current.

Demersal fish Fish that live in deep water or on the sea floor (*see also* **Pelagic fish**).

Dentary The front bone of the lower jaw of a fish (*see also* **Articular, Maxillary, Premaxillary, Quadrate**).

Deoxygenation Reduction in the dissolved oxygen content of a water, caused by hot weather or the introduction of pollutants such as sewage. Excessive deoxygenation is fatal to fish.

Detritus Accumulated silt and organic debris on the bed of a river or stillwater.

Disturbance pattern A wet- or dry-fly pattern that creates a fish-attracting disturbance when retrieved or worked across the current (*see also* **Wake fly**).

Dorsal fin The fin on the back of a fish, sometimes divided into two or three partly or entirely separate sections.

Drainage A drainage basin or a drainage system; the process of draining.

Drainage basin The catchment area of a river system (*see also* **Basin**).

Drainage system A river and its tributaries.

Drogue A cone-shaped bag, usually made of canvas, which can be trailed behind a drifting boat to slow it.

E

Eddy A patch of water that is less disturbed than the surrounding water, found for instance on the edge of a current or where two streams converge (*see also* **Pool, Riffle, Run, Scour, Slack**).

Electrofishing Passing an electric current through the water to stun the fish, so that they can be collected unharmed for tagging or scientific examination or for relocation to another water.

Euryhaline fish Fish, such as most species of salmon and trout, that can live in both freshwater and saltwater.

F

Fighting chair A swivel chair bolted to the deck of a boat, from which a big-game angler can fight marlin and other large, powerful fish that can take a long time to subdue. The angler is strapped in by a harness, and either the harness or the chair is equipped with a butt pad or rod socket (*see also* **Butt pad**).

Filter feeder A fish that feeds by filtering plankton from the water.

Fingerling A small, immature fish, such as a juvenile trout.

Fish ladder A series of interconnected pools created up the side of a river obstruction, such as a weir, to allow salmon and other fish to pass upstream.

Foul-hook To hook a fish anywhere but in the mouth.

Fresh-run fish A migratory fish, such as a salmon, that has just left the sea and is travelling up a river to spawn.

Freshwater The water of rivers and most stillwaters, containing little or no dissolved salts (*see also* **pH, Salinity**).

Fry Very young fish, especially those that have only recently hatched.

G

Gall bladder A small pouch, on or near the liver of a fish, which stores bile. Bile is a fluid produced by the liver, and aids the absorption of food by the gut.

Gamefish Any fish valued for its sporting qualities (*see also* **Coarse fish, Panfish**).

Gill arch The structure behind the gill covers of a bony fish (or within the gill slits of a cartilaginous fish) that supports the gill filaments and gill rakers.

Gill filaments The parts of a fish's gills that absorb oxygen from the water.

Gill rakers Toothlike projections on the gill arches. They can be used to trap food items, such as plankton, carried in the water flowing through the gills.

Gonads The reproductive organs that are responsible for the production of sperm or eggs (*see also* **Testes, Ovaries**).

Grain A unit of weight, used for instance in the classification of fly lines. 1 gram = 15.4 grains, 1 oz = 437.6 grains.

Greenheart A tropical American tree, *Ocotea rodiae*; its wood was once used for making fishing rods.

Grilse A young Atlantic salmon making its first spawning run, usually after one and a half to two years in the sea (*see also* **Alevin, Kelt, Parr, Smolt**).

H

Handline A simple tackle rig often used by youngsters fishing from piers and harbour walls. It consists of a sinker and a hook attached to a line that is wound on a wooden or plastic frame.

Hatch The simultaneous surfacing of large numbers of insect nymphs of the same species. At the surface, the adult insects (or duns) emerge from the nymphal cases and usually rest for a while before flying off (*see also* **Rise**).

I

Ice fishing A specialized form of angling, developed in North America, for fishing through holes cut in the ice of frozen-over waters. The species sought include crappies, walleye, northern pike, pickerel, and perch, and the principal techniques are jigging and tilt (or tip-up) fishing. Jigging involves working a natural bait with a short stick, which has a specially shaped handle around which the line is wound. In tilt fishing, the bait is fished static from a rig incorporating an arm or flag that tilts up to signal a bite.

Ichthyology The scientific study of fish and their habits.

IGFA The International Game Fish Association, based in Fort Lauderdale, Florida. It maintains lists of record fish and also sets technical standards for fishing tackle.

Introperculum In bony fish, the front lower bone of the gill cover (*see also* **Operculum, Preoperculum, Suboperculum**).

Invertebrate A creature that has no backbone, for instance an insect or a worm (*see also* **Vertebrate**).

J

Jig A small artificial lure with a metal head, often dressed with feathers.

Jigging Fishing by jerking a jig or other bait up and down in the water; an ice-fishing technique (*see also* **Ice fishing**).

K

Keeper ring A small ring just above the handle of a fly rod, to which the fly can be hooked when not in use.

Kelt A salmon or trout that has spawned (*see also* **Alevin, Grilse, Parr, Smolt**).

Krill Tiny, shrimplike crustaceans, of the family Euphausiidae, that form an essential part of the marine food chain.

L

Lacustrine A term that describes anything of, relating to, or living in lakes.

Ladder See **Fish ladder**

Left bank See **Banks**

Lie A quiet or sheltered spot in the water where a fish can rest, hide from predators, or wait for food to come by.

Limnology The scientific study of lakes and ponds and the plant and animal organisms that live in them.

Livebait Any natural bait, such as a worm, maggot, or small fish, that is used live (*see also* **Deadbait**).

Loch-style fishing Stillwater flyfishing with teams of wet flies cast a short distance downwind from a drifting boat.

Low-water fly A sparsely dressed fly on a small hook, used mostly for salmon fishing in shallow water.

M

Mark An area of the sea that offers good fishing, usually one that can be located by taking the bearings of shore features.

Marrow spoon A long, slender spoon that can be passed down the gullet of a dead fish to remove its stomach contents. It is used mainly by trout anglers to find out what the fish are actually feeding on at a given time.

Maxillary The rear bone of the upper jaw of a fish (*see also* **Articular, Dentary, Premaxillary, Quadrate**).

Milt The semen of a male fish; a term for the semen-filled testes and sperm ducts of a male fish, also known as soft roe (*see also* **Ova, Roe, Testes**).

N

Neap tides The tides that occur midway between spring tides. They have smaller rises and falls than those at other times of the month (*see also* **Spring tides**).

Nictitating membrane A thin membrane that can be drawn across the eyeball to protect and clean it. Found on many fish species, including some sharks.

O

Oesophagus The gullet of a fish.

Operculum In bony fish, the uppermost and largest of the gill cover bones (*see also* **Introperculum, Preoperculum, Suboperculum**).

Osmosis The process by which a fish takes in or excretes water through its skin in order to maintain the correct balance of salts and fluids within its body tissues.

Otoliths Oval, stonelike structures within the ears of a fish or other vertebrate, which help it to maintain its balance; they are also known as ear stones.

Ova The eggs of a fish or other creature. The mass of eggs within the ovarian membranes of a female fish is termed hard roe (*see also* **Milt, Roe, Ovaries**).

Ovaries The reproductive glands (gonads) of a female fish, which are responsible for the production of eggs (*see also* **Testes**).

Oviducts The ducts between the ovaries and vent in most female fish, along which the ripe eggs pass during spawning.

Oviparous fish Fish that lay eggs from which the young later hatch. All skates, some sharks and rays, and most bony fish are oviparous (*see also* **Ovoviviparous fish, Viviparous fish**).

Ovoviviparous fish Fish whose eggs are fertilized and hatched within the female's body. The eggs are enclosed in separate membranes and the embryos within them receive no nourishment from the mother. Most sharks and rays are ovoviviparous (*see also* **Oviparous fish, Viviparous fish**).

P

Panfish Any small American freshwater food fish, such as a sunfish or perch, that is fished for by anglers but is too small to be considered a true gamefish (*see also* **Coarse fish, Gamefish**).

Parabolic-action rod Another term for a through-action rod.

Parr Young salmon and trout up to two years old, distinguishable from smolts by the dark bars (parr marks) on their sides (*see also* **Alevin, Grilse, Kelt, Smolt**).

Pectoral fins The pair of fins just behind the head of a fish.

Pelagic fish Fish that live at the surface, in the upper waters, of the open ocean (*see also* **Demersal fish**).

Pelvic fins The pair of fins on the lower body of a fish; also called ventral fins.

pH The pH number of a liquid, such as water, indicates its acidity or alkalinity. Pure water has a pH of 7; water with a pH of less than 7 is acidic, and water with a pH of more than 7 is alkaline. Acid rain typically has a pH of less than 5.

Pharyngeal teeth Teeth at the back of the throat, found in many fish species such as the members of the carp family. These teeth crush food as it is swallowed (*see also* **Vomerine teeth**).

Pisciculture The breeding and rearing of fish, for example in hatcheries and fish farms.

Pool A relatively wide, rounded area of a river, usually found just downstream of fast, narrow run (*see also* **Eddy, Riffle, Run, Scour, Slack**).

Potamodromous fish Fish that migrate regularly within large freshwater systems (*see also* **Amphidromous fish, Anadromous fish, Catadromous fish**).

Predatory fish Any fish that prey on other living creatures, particularly other fish.

Premaxillary The front bone of the upper jaw of a fish (*see also* **Articular, Dentary, Maxillary, Quadrate**).

Preoperculum In bony fish, the bone at the rear of the cheek, just in front of the gill cover (*see also* **Introperculum, Operculum, Suboperculum**).

Pyloric caeca Fleshy, fingerlike tubes at the junction between the stomach and intestine of a fish. They produce enzymes that play a part in the digestive process.

Q

Quadrate The bone that joins the upper jaw of a fish to its skull (*see also* **Articular, Dentary, Maxillary, Premaxillary**).

R

Rays The soft or spiny supporting elements of fish fins.

Redd A hollow scooped in the sand or gravel of a riverbed by breeding trout or salmon as a spawning area.

Reversed-taper handle A rod handle that tapers towards the butt end.

Riffle A small rapid in a river or stream (*see also* **Eddy, Pool, Run, Scour, Slack**).

Right bank See **Banks**

Riparian A term that describes anything of, inhabiting, or situated on a riverbank; often used in connection with ownership and fishing rights.

Rip-rap Broken rock, deposited loosely on a riverbed or on the banks to help prevent erosion. It is also used to form breakwaters and embankments.

Rise The action of a fish coming to the surface to take an insect; the taking to the air of a large hatch of mayflies or other insects on which trout feed (*see also* **Hatch**).

Rod socket See **Butt pad**

Roe A collective term for fish milt and ova (*see also* **Milt, Ova**).

Run A fast-flowing stretch of river; the movement of fish inshore or upstream for spawning; the flight of a hooked fish trying to escape; a small stream or brook. (See also **Eddy, Pool, Riffle, Scour, Slack**.)

S

Salinity The level of dissolved salts in the water. Freshwater normally contains less than 0.2% salts, brackish water contains up to 3% salts, and saltwater (such as seawater) more than 3%. Normal seawater contains 3.433% salts – 2.3% sodium chloride (common salt), 0.5% magnesium chloride, 0.4% sodium sulphate, 0.1% calcium chloride, 0.07% potassium chloride, and 0.063% other salts.

Saltwater Water containing a high level of dissolved salts (*see also* **Salinity**).

Scour Erosion caused by flowing water; a shallow, fast-flowing, gravel-bottomed stretch of river (*see also* **Eddy, Pool, Riffle, Run, Slack**).

Seminal vesicle A small gland that adds nutrient fluid to the milt of a male fish during spawning (*see also* **Milt**).

Sink-and-draw A method of fishing in which the lure, fly, or bait is made to rise and fall alternately during the retrieve by raising and lowering the rod tip.

Sink-tip A floating fly line with a sinking tip, used to fish flies just below the surface.

Slack Tidal water where there is little surface movement during the interval between the ebbing and flowing tides; a stretch of river with very little current, for instance above a weir (*see also* **Eddy, Pool, Riffle, Run, Scour**).

Slip A narrow strip of feather. Slips are widely used in fly tying.

Smolt A young salmon or sea trout, silver in colour, on its first journey to the sea (*see also* **Alevin, Grilse, Kelt, Parr**).

Spring tides The tides that occur around the time of full and new moons. They have larger rises and falls than those at other times of the month (*see also* **Neap tides**).

Strike To tighten the line to set the hook when a fish bites, usually by raising the rod tip or lifting the rod.

Suboperculum In bony fish, the rear lower bone of the gill cover (*see also* **Introperculum, Operculum, Preoperculum**).

Supracleithrum A bone at the upper rear of the skull of a fish. It is one of the bones that support the pectoral fin (*see also* **Cleithrum, Pectoral fin**).

Surface film The apparent elasticlike film on the surface of water, which is created by surface tension.

Surface tension The natural tendency of the surface of water (and other liquids) to behave like an elastic sheet. It is caused by forces acting between the water molecules: the molecules at the surface are much more strongly attracted to each other, and to the molecules below them, than they are to the molecules of air above them.

Swim The stretch of a river, or the part of a pond or lake, that is being fished in at a particular time.

T

Take The action of a fish in picking up or grabbing a bait or lure.

Taper The narrowing in diameter, from butt to tip, of a rod, and the narrowing of the end section of a fly line. The rate of taper determines the action of the rod or line.

Terminal tackle The tackle, including the hook or lure, attached to the end of the reel line (main line).

Testes (singular: testis) The reproductive glands (gonads) of a male fish, which are responsible for the production of sperm (*see also* **Ovaries**).

Tilt fishing A technique used in ice fishing; is also known as tip-up fishing (*see also* **Ice fishing**).

Tippet The thin end section of a fly leader, to which the fly is tied.

Tube fly An artificial fly consisting of a metal or plastic tube, dressed with feathers, hair, or other materials and threaded onto the line. The hook, usually a treble, is then attached to the end of the line.

V

Vas deferens The duct that carries sperm from the testis of a spawning male fish (*see also* **Milt, Testes**).

Vent The anus of a fish. It is also the orifice through which a spawning female fish lays her eggs (or, in the case of a viviparous fish, gives birth) and through which a male fish discharges his milt during spawning (*see also* **Viviparous fish, Milt**).

Ventral fins See **Pelvic fins**

Vertebra An individual segment of the backbone of a fish.

Vertebrate A creature that has a backbone, for instance a fish or a mammal (*see also* **Invertebrate**).

Viviparous fish Fish whose ripe eggs are fertilized and hatched within the female's body; they give birth to live young. Unlike those of ovoviviparous fish, the developing embryos receive nourishment from the mother. Some sharks and some bony fish, such as surfperch, are viviparous (*see also* **Oviparous fish, Ovoviviparous fish**).

Vomerine teeth Teeth on the vomer, a bone at the front of the roof of the mouth of bony fish (*see also* **Pharyngeal teeth**).

W

Wake fly A dry fly that creates a splashy, fish-attracting wake when pulled across or through the surface of the water (*see also* **Disturbance pattern**).

Wobbling A freshwater spinning technique using a lure, or a small, dead fish mounted on treble hooks, for bait. The bait is cast a long way out, and retrieved in an erratic fashion by making side-to-side movements of the rod tip and at the same time varying the speed of the retrieve.

Wrist See **Caudal peduncle**

Y

Yolk sac The membrane-covered food pouch found on the belly of a newly hatched fish. It nourishes the growing fish until it is able to feed itself.

INDEX

INDEX OF SCIENTIFIC NAMES

ACKNOWLEDGMENTS

This book was the work of a dedicated team of authors, photographers, and illustrators, plus a huge network of specialists and suppliers, to whom we would like to express our gratitude.

First, thanks to Martin at Photo Summit, whose coffee and excellent prints helped to get the book started; to John Wilson for his time, hospitality, and advice; to Mike Millman for his help and his willingness to try the impossible at short notice; to Ron Worsfold for the loan of his pole rigs; and to the late and much-missed Trevor Housby for his advice and encouragement.

Of all our suppliers, special mention must be made of Don Neish and Peter Morley at Don's of Edmonton, for supplying tackle at ludicrously short notice. Other individuals and companies whose contributions were especially valuable were Simon Bond (Shimano); Alan Bramley and Fiona Hemus (Partridge of Redditch); Bob Brownsdon (Shakespeare); Peter Drennan and daughter Sally (Drennan International); Sue and Chris Harris (Harris Angling Company); Chris Leibbrandt (Ryobi Masterline); David McGinlay (Daiwa); and John Rawle (Cox & Rawle).

We would also like to thank Richard Banbury (Orvis); Breakaway Tackle; Browning; Paul Burgess (Airflo); Jeremy Buxton (Asset Optics); Pat Byrne (D.A.M.); Alan Caulfield (Penn); Darren Cox (DCD); Roy Eskins (HUFFishing); Brendan Fitzgerald (House of Hardy); Michael McManus (Carroll McManus); Nick Page (Nican Enterprises); Graeme Pullen (Blue Water Tackle); Andrew Reade (Keenets); Nicholas Stafford-Deitsch (Edington Sporting Co.); Mike Stratton (Thomas Turner & Sons); B.W. Wright (Nomad); Val and Chris (Vanguard Tackle, Boston); Bruce Vaughan and Dennis Moss (Wychwood Tackle); Clive Young (Young's of Harrow); and Nick Young (Leeda).

Finally, special thanks to Barbara, Hilary, and Jane for their support in difficult times; to the unflappable Janet at Ace; to Steve, Andy, Tim, Nick, Sara, and Gary at the studio; to Krystyna and Derek at Dorling Kindersley for their patience; and to Peter Kindersley, whose confidence allowed it to happen.

Revised edition
Special thanks go to John Bailey for his help in updating the book, to Steve Gorton, Stuart Dexter, and Henry Gilbey for photography, and especially to Dan Gapen Sr. of The Gapen Company, Jan Porter of Shimano (UK) Ltd, and all at Sportfish and Farlow's of Pall Mall for providing a wonderful selection of lures, rods, and reels.

CREDITS

Illustrators
Colin Newman *pages 124-203*
Ian Heard *pages 210-219, 226-259*
Lyn Cawley *pages 82-87, 92-93, 208-209*
Alan Suttie
   pages 15, 52, 206, 223-225, 259
Maurice Pledger *pages 220-221*

Photographers
Key: *t top, c centre, b bottom, l left, r right*

2 Peter Gathercole
3 Steve Gorton
6 Trevor Housby
7 *t* Mansell Collection, *c* Tim Heywood, *b* Mike Millman
8 *t* Trevor Housby, *c*, *b* Peter Gathercole
9 *t*, *c* Mike Millman, *b* John Wilson
10 John Wilson
12-49 Steve Gorton and
   John Bailey (*12-25, 32-45*)
   Stuart Dexter (*26-27*)
   Henry Gilbey (*28-31, 46-49*)
50-53 Steve Gorton and Andy Crawford
54-57 Peter Gathercole
58-79 Steve Gorton and Andy Crawford
80 John Wilson
82-87 Steve Gorton
88-91 Steve Gorton and Andy Crawford
92-93 Steve Gorton; worms, sandeel by Mike Millman
94-95 Mike Millman
96-97 Steve Gorton
98-121 Peter Gathercole, with additional photos 100 *t*, 102 *b* by Heather Angel
122 Oxford Scientific Films/Richard Davis
123 Oxford Scientific Films/Rudolf Ingo Riepl
204 Peter Gathercole
206-209 Steve Gorton
210 *t* Andy Crawford, *c* John Wilson, *b* Mike Millman
211 *t* and *b* John Wilson, *c* Peter Gathercole
212 Jim Tyree
213 Jim Tyree, *b* John Wilson
214 Steve Gorton
215 *t* Steve Gorton, *tl* and *c* John Wilson
216-218 Steve Gorton
219 *t* Steve Gorton, *b* John Wilson
220-221 Steve Gorton
222 *t* and *b* Steve Gorton, *c* Jim Tyree
223 *c* and *br* Jim Tyree, *bl* Steve Gorton
224 *t* Steve Gorton, *b* Jim Tyree
225 *t* Steve Gorton, *c* Jim Tyree
226-227 Jim Tyree
227 *b* Rodney Coldron
228 Jim Tyree, Andy Crawford
229 Mike Millman, Andy Crawford
230 John Wilson
231 *t* and *b* Steve Gorton, *cl* and *cr* John Wilson
232 *c* Steve Gorton, *b* Peter Gathercole
235 *tl* and *tr* Peter Gathercole
236 *c* Steve Gorton, *t* and *b* Peter Gathercole
237 Peter Gathercole
238-243 Peter Gathercole
244 John Darling
246 Mike Millman
249 Mike Millman
250-251 Jim Tyree
251 *tr* John Darling
252-253 Steve Gorton
253 *c* John Darling
254-255 Mike Millman
257 John Darling
258-259 Trevor Housby
261 Heather Angel
262 *t* Peter Gathercole, *b* John Wilson
263 John Wilson

264 *t* John Darling, *c* Jim Tyree, *b* John Wilson
265 *tr* Peter Gathercole, *b* Rodney Coldron
266 *t* Peter Gathercole, *c* Jim Tyree, *b* John Wilson
267 *c* John Wilson, *b* Mike Millman
268-269 John Wilson
270 *c* Jim Tyree, *b* Mike Millman
271-273 Mike Millman
274 *t* and *b* Phill Williams, *c* Mike Millman
275 *t* Mike Millman, *b* Phill Williams
276 Mike Millman
277 *c* John Wilson, *b* Mike Millman
278 Peter Gathercole
279 *t* Oxford Scientific Films, *b* Mike Millman

Manufacturers and Suppliers
The tackle was supplied by the manufacturers named in the main body of the book, except the Abu tackle, which was supplied by Don's of Edmonton. The floats, pages 62-63, were supplied by Drennan, and the Milo pole floats by Keenets. The lures, pages 88-91, were provided by Harris Angling Company. The flies were tied by Peter Gathercole. Other suppliers who have provided equipment for this book include:

Airflo, Fly Fishing Technology Ltd., Powys;
Asset Optics, Oxfordshire;
Blue Water Tackle, Hampshire;
Breakaway Tackle, Suffolk;
Browning, Bedfordshire;
Carroll McManus Ltd., East Sussex;
Cox & Rawle, Essex;
Daiwa Sports Ltd., Strathclyde;
D.A.M. (UK) Ltd., Worcestershire;
DCD, Warwickshire;
Don's of Edmonton, London;
Drennan International Ltd., Oxford;
Edington Sporting Co., Wiltshire;
Farlow's of Pall Mall, London;
The Gapen Company, Minnesota;
Harris Angling Company, Norfolk;
House of Hardy, London;
HUFFishing, Bedfordshire;
Keenets (UK) Ltd., Wiltshire;
Leeda Group, Worcestershire;
Nican Enterprises, Hampshire;
Nomad UK, Lancashire;
Orvis, Hampshire;
Partridge of Redditch, Worcestershire;
Penn UK, Strathclyde;
Ryobi Masterline Ltd., Gloucestershire;
Shakespeare Company (UK) Ltd., Worcestershire;
Shimano Europe, Swansea;
Shimano (UK) Ltd, Evesham;
Sportfish, Pall Mall, London;
Thomas Turner & Sons, Berkshire;
Vanguard Tackle, Lincolnshire;
Wychwood Tackle, Oxfordshire;
Young's of Harrow, Middlesex.